CRITIQUES OF CONTEMPORARY RHETORIC

Second Edition

Wadsworth Series in Communication Studies

Critiques of Contemporary Rhetoric

SECOND EDITION

KARLYN KOHRS CAMPBELL
University of Minnesota

THOMAS R. BURKHOLDER
Southwest Texas State University

Wadsworth Publishing Company
I(T)P® An International Thomson Publishing Company

Belmont • Albany • Bonn • Boston • Cincinnati • Detroit • London • Madrid • Melbourne •
Mexico City • New York • Paris • San Francisco • Singapore • Tokyo • Toronto • Washington

Communication Studies Editor:
  Todd Robert Armstrong
Editorial Assistant: *Michael Gillespie*
Production Services Coordinator:
  Debby Kramer
Production: *Scratchgravel Publishing
  Services*
Designer: *Anne Draus, Scratchgravel
  Publishing Services*

Print Buyer: *Barbara Britton*
Permissions Editor: *Robert Kauser*
Copy Editors: *Anne Draus, Meg Korones*
Cover Designer: *Jeanne Calabrese*
Compositor: *Scratchgravel Publishing
  Services*
Printer: *Quebecor Printing Book Group/
  Fairfield*
Cover Printer: *Color Dot*

Printed in the United States of America
  2 3 4 5 6 7 8 9 10

For more information, contact Wadsworth Publishing Company:

Wadsworth Publishing Company
10 Davis Drive
Belmont, California 94002, USA

International Thomson Publishing Europe
Berkshire House 168-173
High Holborn
London, WC1V 7AA, England

Thomas Nelson Australia
102 Dodds Street
South Melbourne 3205
Victoria, Australia

Nelson Canada
1120 Birchmount Road
Scarborough, Ontario
Canada M1K 5G4

International Thomson Editores
Campos Eliseos 385, Piso 7
Col. Polanco
11560 México D.F. México

International Thomson Publishing GmbH
Königswinterer Strasse 418
53227 Bonn, Germany

International Thomson Publishing Asia
221 Henderson Road
#05-10 Henderson Building
Singapore 0315

International Thomson Publishing Japan
Hirakawacho Kyowa Building, 3F
2-2-1 Hirakawacho
Chiyoda-ku, Tokyo 102, Japan

Library of Congress Cataloging-in-Publication Data
Campbell, Karlyn Kohrs.
    Critiques of contemporary rhetoric / Karlyn Kohrs Campbell, Thomas
R. Burkholder. — 2nd ed.
       p. cm.
    Includes bibliographical references (p.) and index.
    ISBN 0-534-19500-8
    1. English language—Rhetoric.   2. Speeches, addresses, etc.-
-History and criticism—Theory, etc.   3. Rhetoric—Political
aspects.   4. Speeches, addresses, etc.   5. Criticism—Authorship.
6. College readers.   I. Burkholder, Thomas R.   II. Title.
PE1479.C7C36 1996
801'.95—dc20   95-49493

 This book is printed on acid-free recycled paper.

CONTENTS

I

THE ART OF RHETORICAL CRITICISM

CHAPTER FIVE
Evaluation: The Final Stage of Criticism 109

II

THE PRACTICE OF RHETORICAL CRITICISM

PREFACE

The first edition of *Critiques* appeared in 1972 in the midst of public discourse that called into question much of what had been common sense. The civil rights movement had begun to sensitize us to the racism that pervaded our society; the second wave of feminism challenged the sexism that was equally pervasive. The anti-war movement confronted the lies that we were being told about what was occurring in Vietnam. The need to encourage students to analyze that discourse was vital, and *Critiques* was an early effort to explore the assumptions underlying rhetorical criticism, to describe phases in the critical process, and to provide models that students might imitate in looking at the public discourse of protestors against and defenders of the status quo—scientists, Black Panthers, women's liberationists, educators, and political leaders.

Much has changed since 1972. The revolution now has a conservative tinge, and the voices of those supporting efforts to promote equality of opportunity have become more defensive. But the need for critical analysis of public discourse persists. The critiques in this book reflect the continuities and the changes. We return to the rhetoric of the Vietnam War in order to understand how argument and character fused in the discourse of Robert Kennedy as well as that of Richard Nixon. We listen to the voice of one Chinese leader, Zhao Ziyang, who sympathized with the protestors in Tiananmen Square. We hear the voice of a triumphant revolutionary, Nelson Mandela, as he speaks to the diverse audiences that compose the U.S. public. We heed the voice of a judge, Miles Lord, who confronted the issue of corporate responsibility in a dramatic extension of his role. We also return to consider the words of the most effective voice of conservatism in recent time, President Ronald Reagan, as he addressed the final Republican National Convention before he left office. We believe that the issues explored in contemporary public discourse cry out for critics who struggle with and help us to understand the symbolic power and appeal of disparate voices.

The critical perspective of this book has not changed, but it has expanded. From the outset, *Critiques* has been a book committed to diverse approaches to analysis and to inventive critical practices. Accordingly, we have not treated criticism as an assortment of formulas to be used to analyze texts. Instead, we present criticism in the same way that we teach our students—that is, as a critical process that begins with close analysis of the text, is followed by extended historical–contextual research, and culminates in the invention of a critical approach suited to the discourse being analyzed. Alternative critical perspectives are presented as three broad streams that emphasize different facets of the rhetorical process: argument, appeal, and language. Virtually all critical approaches incorporate these three dimensions despite differences of emphasis. We recognize that the lack of neatly cataloged types of criticism is frightening to beginners, but we believe the alternative to be worse—fledgling critics who follow formulas and do not learn to invent a framework adapted to the discourse they are analyzing.

In this second edition we have greatly expanded the material on the critical process, and we have illustrated each step in that process with an example that is carried through from descriptive analysis to a fully developed critique. We hope that kind of model will help students to understand more clearly how to proceed. However, we recognize that all texts are different—each is an example of the incredible symbolic inventiveness of human beings—so these models can only be used as general guides.

The model critical essays reflect a diversity of critical approaches just as the discourses analyzed reflect varied issues and points of view. In this edition, there are no texts for beginning students to analyze; all texts are accompanied by critiques. We believe that students are best served by selecting discourse for analysis that is of special significance for them.

In 1972, Karlyn Kohrs Campbell wrote that the preceding decade had produced a renaissance of interest in rhetoric. In the decades since then, that interest has only increased. We have come to recognize even more clearly what a powerful role public discourse plays in the welfare of the nation and in the well-being of each of us. The senatorial debate on the Persian Gulf War was a reminder of the life-threatening significance of foreign policy decisions. The Contract with America was created by Republicans to be a powerful rhetorical appeal in the 1994 election. The presidential candidates who look forward to the next election appeal to the electorate on such issues as welfare reform, affirmative action, Medicare and Medicaid reform, deficit reduction, environmental regulation, and the ongoing conflict in the Balkans, among others. Television coverage links us directly to the speeches of foreign leaders, to congressional hearings, and to those who battle in courts of law. Rhetorical criticism has become a form of consumer protection that equips us to weigh vital words and to make judgments about arguments, appeals, and advocates. The great rhetorical theorist and critic Kenneth Burke thought of criticism as a kind of equipment for living. It is equipment we believe is vital to the lives of citizens in a democracy.

There are many people who have contributed to this book. First and foremost, we thank our students who have improved our skills as teachers of criticism and as critics. We are proud that some of them are contributors to this volume. We also thank those who have helped us in our research. In particular, we appreciate the help of Margaret Vaverek and Pam Spooner of the Albert B. Alkek Library at Southwest Texas State University. All of this book is more accurate because of the efforts of Nate Dick and Wendy Atkins-Sayre, our research assistants. Finally, we have benefited greatly from the insightful and probing comments of our reviewers: Bill Balthrop, University of North Carolina, Chapel Hill; Dana Cloud, University of Texas, Austin; Steve Depoe, University of Cincinnati; Roseanne Mandziuk, Southwest Texas State University; Sally Perkins, California State University at Sacramento; and David Williams, Northeast Missouri State University. We thank them for all their help in making this a better book.

Karlyn Kohrs Campbell
Thomas R. Burkholder

CRITIQUES OF CONTEMPORARY RHETORIC

Second Edition

I

The Art of
Rhetorical Criticism

CHAPTER ONE

Rhetoric, Language, and Criticism

This book is about criticism of the persuasion that surrounds us—speeches at political conventions; editorials in newspapers; opinion essays in magazines; debates in Congress, state legislatures, and political campaigns; and all the efforts of protesters and reformers. Although much is to be gained from the study of speakers long dead, this book focuses attention on responding intelligently to rhetoric that we encounter daily. Criticism is not a matter of "being critical" or of attacking that rhetoric. Rather, rhetorical criticism is the *process* of analysis, interpretation, and evaluation of persuasive uses of language.

Aspiring critics struggle with temptations in their criticism of rhetoric. Contemporary speakers and writers treat issues that deeply involve many people and directly affect their lives: gun control, sexual harassment, abortion, AIDS, crime and punishment, to name only a few. Because of their personal involvement, one important motive for critics is to expose and debunk rhetors who advocate positions and policies with which they disagree and to strengthen and support the arguments of rhetors who reflect their points of view. That motive is not dishonorable because criticism is always partly persuasion.

Criticism is never wholly impartial and objective. In all cases, it is to some extent evaluative, judgmental, and subjective. That is, critics ask their own audiences to see a discourse as they see it, to understand and judge it as they do. Some critics yield to the temptation to make criticism simply and wholly persuasion, a subtle and dangerous persuasion that masks advocacy behind the appearance of objectivity and technical analysis. We have even coined a name for such critics: "spin doctors," those whose commentary on presidential debates, for example, is designed to serve partisan ends. The ethical problem reflected in the tension between the essential persuasiveness of rhetorical criticism itself and the temptation to become a subtle but powerful advocate for persuaders with whom the critic agrees is central to the evaluation of contemporary rhetoric. To help solve that problem, in this chapter we discuss the nature of rhetorical discourse and introduce the fundamental concepts of rhetorical criticism. In later chapters, we explain and illustrate the critical process in detail.

THE NATURE OF RHETORIC

Although the study of the principles and practice of rhetoric is perhaps the most ancient academic discipline, the term *rhetoric* is ambiguous and difficult to define because it is used in at least three ways: It often refers to public statements that are abstract, empty, bombastic, "full of sound and fury, signifying nothing"; such statements are labeled "mere rhetoric." It frequently refers to written or oral discourses that intentionally or unintentionally alter attitudes and mobilize action—that is, "persuasion." Finally, it sometimes refers to academic disciplines that study the techniques, principles, and practices of persons who deliberate, argue, and advocate in order to alter attitudes and behavior. As we use the term in this book, *rhetoric* refers to persuasive discourses, written and oral, encountered face-to-face or through the electronic or print media, that seek to affect attitudes and actions.

At times the term can and should be used in a much broader sense, because rhetoric can refer to any use of symbols to influence others. That includes functions other than persuasion, such as interpersonal identification, confrontation, self-identification, alienation, and negotiation. Rhetoric also includes forms other than written and oral discourse, such as gestural and visual communication, the use of space, and certain dimensions of music, dance, motion pictures, television programs, and painting. In this book, however, the term *rhetoric* is used in the narrower sense, not because the broader usage is in any way illegitimate, but because we intend this book to be an introduction to the practice of rhetorical criticism. Beginning rhetorical critics will find that practice more rewarding when they study works that are fully formed, that are carefully planned, that display rhetorical characteristics most clearly, and that do not require specialized expertise. For example, rhetorical criticism of popular music requires musical knowledge. Analysis of any programming for television, including advertising, requires some familiarity with camera, editing, and other production techniques; analysis of particular television forms—such as sitcoms, news, soaps, westerns, drama, and so on—requires familiarity with those forms and their history. Likewise, studies of film require expertise about technological aspects of cinema as well as familiarity with the earlier filmic, literary, and rhetorical works out of which films emerge and to which they refer. In recommended readings included in later chapters, we list examples that are models of criticism of these forms of rhetoric, but because they require specialized knowledge and critical approaches adapted to their particular characteristics, in this book we focus our attention on rhetoric that achieves its ends primarily through words.

Such rhetoric has five typical characteristics. First, it is *propositional* or in *prose*. That is, it is artistic discourse, formed from complete thoughts, with the sentence as its basic unit. Rhetoric is humanly designed, created, and fashioned, in contrast to random comments and casual conversation, which often consist of sentence fragments joined by association. Rhetorical discourse is planned and structured in such a consistent and coherent fashion as to announce and justify certain conclusions. Hence, rhetoric is artistically formed and created, based on principles developed through practice and codified in theory.

Second, rhetoric addresses problems; it is *problem solving*. What constitutes a problem may be described loosely as the difference between what is desired and what exists, or as the gap between personal or societal goals or values and existing structures, procedures, or conditions. This characteristic focuses attention on the evaluative and subjective dimension inherent in rhetoric.

The substance of rhetoric is not facts but a translation, elaboration, and evaluation of data. For instance, some students are satisfied to receive a C grade; their goal is simply to get the "ticket," a college degree. Other students are dismayed by receiving a C; their goal is to enter graduate or professional school, and an average grade may prevent them from reaching it. Although the facts may be the same, individuals can interpret and weigh them differently.

Rhetorical discourse concerns the values that individuals and societies should adopt, the implications of those values, and the means or policies individuals and societies should enact to express or attain those values. In this sense rhetoric is properly termed *advisory* or *hortatory* because, directly or indirectly, it always gives advice, takes a position, interprets, evaluates, and judges. Rhetoric does not simply transmit information; it is always a translation and interpretation of the meaning of the facts. It evaluates the facts and asks the listener or reader to see or feel about them as the rhetor does.

Third, rhetoric is *public,* addressed to others. Although some very important rhetoric is intrapersonal deliberation or self-persuasive argument, for the most part rhetoric is public because it deals with circumstances and conditions that require concerted action. No single individual can alter them. That is, although individuals seek to convince themselves of the rightness of their actions or motives through internal dialogue, rhetoric deals primarily with problems that individuals cannot solve alone, problems that require others who share the same attitudes and way of looking at things and who are willing to commit themselves to similar cooperative action.

Thus, public persuasion needs to be artistically adapted to others. Family members and close friends may be able to read between the lines in face-to-face conversations, but to mobilize others in support of a cause, a rhetor needs to spell out clearly and in detail the proposals and justifications for them. In effect, the rhetor's language must be socialized, modified and adapted to the experiences of those who are addressed, and justified with reasons they would find cogent. In addition, because rhetorical discourse is *addressed,* it usually concerns social and political questions: What does it mean to be a citizen? Who should be admitted to citizenship? How are conflicts between groups with differing interests to be resolved? What should a society be and do? In short, rhetoric deals with issues that require shared attitudes and cooperative action for their resolution.

Fourth, rhetoric is usually *practical* or *pragmatic.* That is, most public discourse seeks to alter symbolic behaviors, attitudes, and actions. Rhetoric is not simply an expression of feelings or a sharing of information for its own sake. Instead it is designed to communicate feelings and information for a purpose, to evoke a concrete and relevant response from audiences to an issue or set of circumstances. In some cases, public discourse expresses feelings, but even then, that expression may be related to channeling or forestalling some kinds of actions. For instance, in 1992, former Los Angeles Mayor Tom Bradley tried to express the anger and frustration many of his fellow African Americans felt after the verdict in the first trial exonerating the police officers who had savagely beaten Rodney King. His speech was designed, at least in part, to try to prevent frustration and anger from erupting in rioting. As that example illustrates, however, sometimes even the best efforts of a highly credible rhetor will fail. Rhetoric, then, is characterized by its instrumentality—that is, by its intent to influence further behavior.

Finally, in what may seem a contradiction, rhetorical discourse is frequently *poetic.* As used here, the term *poetic* refers to discourse that displays ritualistic, aesthetic, dramatic, and emotive qualities. For Greco-Roman theorists rhetorical and poetic qualities were two elements of a unified art of composition. Even today, we refer to great speakers as "eloquent" and to great rhetoric as "eloquence." Such references indicate that the poetic qualities of rhetorical discourse are often an important basis for evaluation. We expect rhetoric to be part of public rituals and to celebrate and reinforce cultural values. We expect rhetorical discourses to be pleasing to the ear, and we treasure those that move us deeply, such as Martin Luther King, Jr.'s "I Have a Dream," John F. Kennedy's *"Ich bin ein Berliner,"* and Barbara Jordan's keynote address to the 1976 Democratic National Convention. We expect rhetoric to build to a climax, to heighten conflict, to move us by speaking to our experiences and feelings, and to leave us with a sense of closure. Although the poetic dimension in rhetorical discourse is usually less prominent than in those works we term "literature," rhetoric that ignores the poetic in its language and movement is usually modest at best, and incomplete and ineffective at worst. The degree to which a rhetorical discourse manifests poetic qualities such as vivid description, figurative language, and narrative will directly affect the size of the potential audiences, now and in the future, and the nature and intensity of the response evoked. In other words, although poetic qualities are more typical of literary works, they are also an essential part of rhetoric. Conversely, even highly poetic works have a rhetorical dimension.

Rhetoric, then, refers to written and oral discourses that are persuasive. Rhetorical discourses typically are artistically adapted to audiences and are propositional or in prose, problem-solving, public, practical, and poetic. Such discourses are shaped and crafted works dealing evaluatively with information and issues that require shared attitudes and cooperation in order to be resolved. Rhetorical discourses seek concrete changes in language, attitude, and action. Finally, their power to move audiences arises from poetic qualities of language and structure.

Because rhetorical criticism seeks to illuminate and explain the workings of rhetorical acts, critics work from frameworks or systems of assumptions about how symbols appeal and how their use can affect the beliefs, attitudes, and values of others. Throughout this book we refer to these as critical perspectives, approaches, or systems, and each of them is rooted in a theory or theoretical position that elaborates and explains the processes of appeal and influence. In the next section we describe three major theoretical outlooks based on humans as rational beings, as creatures with basic needs, drives, and desires, and as symbol users and abusers.

THE BASES OF RHETORIC

One of the most puzzling and interesting aspects of rhetorical theory is the search for explanations of how and why people are capable of and vulnerable to persuasion. How and why is it that we can influence others and be influenced by them? Unless we assume that each of us is totally isolated from all others, a stance called solipsism, we must assume that everyone can influence and be influenced to some degree. Based on this assumption, there are three interrelated and overlapping explanations for human persuasibility.

The first and most familiar explanation locates the source of influence in argument and claims that humans are open to persuasion because they are beings capable of conceptualizing options and of exploring competing justifications as well as the implications and consequences of different courses of action. Through persuasive discourse humans can discover available choices and examine them for coherence and consistency; through deliberation humans can come to select one choice rather than others on the basis of the reasons underlying them. This rationalistic explanation emphasizes the importance of choice and deliberation in any theory of human influence and stresses the lack of empirically verifiable answers to the questions central to rhetoric. Thus, rhetoric treats issues about which honest and informed people may disagree.

Such issues are apparent in the three types of propositions we normally encounter. Some of those issues are not open to disagreement and thus are not to be resolved through rhetorical action. For example, a statement such as "A given number of abortions are performed in the United States each year" is a *proposition of fact.* That abortions are performed is undeniable, and their "given number" can be determined simply by counting. In other words, the choice and deliberation characteristic of rhetorical action are unnecessary, even useless, in resolving issues of fact. In contrast, rhetorical action is essential for resolving many other issues. For instance, statements such as "Abortion is justified" or "Abortion is unjustified" are both *propositions of value* because they require decisions about worth or merit. In this case, disagreement is quite clearly possible. To resolve the issue we must consider values in our deliberation. Rhetors on both sides provide reasons or develop arguments to influence those who must decide, the audience or audiences. Finally, statements such as "U.S. laws should allow abortion" or "U.S. laws should prohibit abortion" are *propositions of policy* because they involve decisions about a course of action. Again, disagreement is clearly possible, so rhetors on both sides provide reasons or develop arguments to influence decision makers. Frequently, those arguments advocating or opposing a course of action incorporate earlier decisions about issues of value, which are necessarily prior to issues of policy.

The second explanation for human persuasibility locates the source of influence in the human psyche and claims that humans are persuadable because they have certain psychophysiological characteristics, including basic needs, that can be aroused and channeled through discourse. As animals, humans have basic survival needs, including food and water, shelter, and sex; as social beings, we require group membership and a sense of belonging; as individuals, we need to develop unique identities and to feel that we are valued by others. Within each human culture or society, certain group values, such as courage and honesty, emerge and become the bases on which individuals attain esteem and status within the group.

Not only can rhetors activate basic drives, such as arousing fears about our safety and security, but they can channel these drives in directions consistent with cultural values. For example, although condominiums and apartment complexes provide shelter, most Americans still hope to own a single-family dwelling. A psychophysiological explanation of influence emphasizes the importance of "attention" and "motivation" in rhetoric. It asks critics to heed rhetors' appeals to personal needs, hopes, and fears and to socially developed values as important elements in the process by which they seek to motivate audiences. Although it may smack of manipulation, this explanation focuses attention on how discourse can be used to arouse intense emotional reactions, to induce audience participation, and to create roles for audience members that invite them to behave as the rhetor desires. Note, however, that such appeals can also be made through arguments and supported by evidence, so the rationalistic and psychophysiological explanations are related and can overlap.

The third explanation for human persuasibility locates the source of influence in language and claims that humans are persuadable because they are symbol-making, symbol-using, and symbol-misusing animals. That is, we humans are rhetorical because we swim in a sea of language that we use to detect, identify, and interpret stimuli surrounding us in order to assign them meanings that, in turn, affect future behavior. Hence, persuasion is a result of the interaction between humans and their language; people are capable of persuasion because of their ability to respond linguistically and semantically.

When used symbolically, a stimulus, such as a word, represents the user's concept of an object, event, person, condition, or relationship, and that concept indicates an attitude or meaning that another person can perceive, identify, and interpret. In turn, the stimulus and its attendant concept can influence the other person's attitude toward the object, event, condition, person, or relationship. Those who prefer this explanation believe that individuals create and develop their own sense of identity, their concepts of others, and their images of the world in symbolic interactions. In addition, they hold that human motivation is importantly different from that of other animals because the interaction between humans and language transforms physical, biological, and social needs and drives into cultural norms and values.

As people engage in the rhetorical process, they are an inseparable compound of animality and what Kenneth Burke calls "symbolicity." The process of becoming human, of being socialized and acculturated, is essentially a symbolic one; that is, our basic drives are linguistically transformed into socially and culturally acceptable motives that can never be divorced from their symbolic origins. Through language and in interaction with others, we humans transform basic needs—say, for food—into socially accepted forms—the kinds of foods typical of areas or ethnic groups, such as lutefisk or menudo—and choose culturally acceptable means for their satisfaction.

This explanation of human persuasibility focuses attention on the significant role of language in rhetorical transactions. It suggests that rhetors' language provides important clues to their attitudes and values, and it encourages critics to be concerned with how speakers or writers use particular terms to describe or classify.

As should be obvious, these three explanations for human persuasibility are interrelated and inseparable. We are all psychophysiological creatures with basic individual and social needs. These are invariably modified through language, however, and argumentation and deliberation are key elements in that process. In other words, rhetorical critics are concerned with argumentation, with appeals to psychophysiological processes, and with the language and symbolic strategies of a rhetorical discourse. The resources of language, however, need special treatment.

THE RHETORICAL DIMENSIONS OF LANGUAGE

In its ordinary sense, *language* refers to verbal symbol systems such as Swahili or Hmong. However, language includes a wide variety of both verbal and nonverbal symbol systems, constituted not only of words but also of space, movement, sound, pitch, time, color, and so on. In their most developed forms these symbol systems are called dance, music, sculpture, architecture, painting, poetry, and so forth. Through the use of many different symbol systems, humans can order sensations and assign them meaning so they become identifiable experiences and perceptions that can be remembered. Instead of being bombarded with a "blooming, buzzing confusion" of myriad unfamiliar stimuli, humans use language to make order of this chaos and to deal with a structured world of recognizable objects, events, and conditions. Because verbal symbol systems are of greatest concern here, the analysis that follows centers primarily on the characteristics of verbal language.

An important dimension of language is *naming,* the process by which individuals notice, recognize, and label certain elements or qualities in themselves and in the world around them. Names permit people to recognize and select relevant or significant events and phenomena from the multitudes of surrounding stimuli. The vocabulary of an individual or group is a rough index of what is and has been important to that person or group, an assumption reflected in the "verbal ability" sections of many college or graduate entrance examinations.

Naming becomes a process of ordering the world and of focusing an individual's attention. A name is not a label for one thing but rather for a group or category of relatively similar objects or events with certain similar qualities or characteristics. Nouns, verbs, adjectives, and adverbs are labels for categories of objects, actions, events, feelings, qualities, and characteristics found or noticed under many different conditions at many different times by many different persons. Even conjunctions and prepositions label certain kinds of recurring relationships. As labels referring to categories, names permit people to ignore the differences among individual objects and events and to lump the objects or events together into manageable units to which they can respond in relatively similar ways. For example, if we identify an object as a "chair," we respond to it as, and predict that it will be, a manufactured object with arms or a back, intended for the category of actions labeled "sitting," and we ignore the unique characteristics of a particular chair. If this process is to work, however, a set of criteria must be agreed upon to determine whether a particular object, person, or event may be included in a particular category—that is, whether it may be labeled with a particular name. Such sets of criteria are called *definitions.*

A definition specifies the indispensable attributes or characteristics that something must have to be labeled in a particular way by a particular linguistic community. For example, to decide whether a creature should be called a "heifer," we need to know whether it is bovine, female, and has ever calved. (If it has calved, it is called a cow.) In relation to this particular name category, we need not be concerned with characteristics of size, color, breed, or the presence or lack of horns. These "accidental" characteristics simply distinguish one breed of heifer from other heifers and do not determine whether the creature falls into the larger category.

A definition of the shared and requisite characteristics that place something in a category for which there is a label is usually called *denotative.* For all terms there are specifiable, commonly understood bases for application or definitions. But people do not learn meanings from dictionaries where such definitions are collected. They learn them in particular, real situations, by having experiences with the use of labels and with members of the categories to which they refer. In the specific contexts in which meanings are learned, individuals have feelings about the situations, categories, and labels. These are *connotative* meanings. Thus, names are not simply factual or descriptive; they are also labels for the experiences of individuals with, and for their feelings about, the acts, events, objects, persons, conditions, and relationships to which the labels refer. As a result, names are also evaluative labels that stand for experiences and feelings; hence, meanings include subjective, emotional elements.

At a minimum, names are evaluative because they indicate interest and relevance. For example, if you knew the meaning of the word *heifer,* this knowledge indicates some past experience in which that term had some importance. If you grew up in a farming community, as we did, you learned the word because it represented particular problems, financial values, and special functions. If you heard the biblical story of Samson and his riddle, you may have learned the meaning of the word *heifer* to understand the metaphorical use of it (Judges 14:18). If your only contact with the word has been in reading this discussion, you may remember it and associate it with this book or with rhetoric.

The evaluative capacity of symbols is great. When we speak of "loaded" or "emotional" language, we refer to words that produce intense feelings; people who hear or read them have vivid, passionate reactions because of their experiences with the terms. No matter how limited the degree of emotionality, no term understood by or meaningful to a person is simply neutral or factual. It is always bound up with that person's experiences and will always contain evaluative associations resulting from those experiences. In other words, we usually attach both denotative and connotative meanings to most terms.

The words used to label acts, persons, objects, events, qualities, and relationships indicate an attitudinal bias in an individual's perception of the world, based on that person's experiences. In addition, the words that a person uses influence the attitudinal biases of others because the situations in which the words are used become new or additional experiences for both the user and the audience. By labeling or relabeling a particular phenomenon, rhetors place it in a category and thereby associate it, for readers or listeners, with other members of that category. Rhetors may also attempt to change the associations of a label by providing the audience with new experiences designed to alter their feelings about the category and hence their evaluation of it. These possibilities are greatly increased with abstract terms such as *truth, honesty,* and *socialism,* words for which there are no referents to which we can point. These terms can be defined only in relation to and by other words; they are what Kenneth Burke calls "dialectical terms" (see the discussion of dramatistic criticism in Chapter Four). Much rhetoric is directed toward changing labels, illustrated by fervent debates over whether *colored, Negro, Black, Afro-American,* or *African American* should be the preferred label for one ethnic group—a first step in altering attitudes and behavior.

Critics must carefully examine rhetors' attempts to structure or restructure the perceptions and attitudes of their audiences through their use of language. For instance, why do you suppose that Phyllis Stewart Schlafly entitled a speech opposing a comparable worth proposal "Shall I Compare Thee to a Plumber's Pay?" One reason that persuasion is possible is that language has the capacity to name, categorize, define, debunk, and evaluate. Among the most important rhetorical strategies are the techniques that rhetors use to change the connotations and the verbal behavior of their audiences.

This concept of language is closely related to the defining characteristics of rhetorical discourse. Rhetoric, in a narrow sense, may be thought of as an explicit, highly articulated version of the suasive dimension of language itself. As an art of prose, rhetoric is discourse that makes complete statements, draws conclusions, points out implications, and suggests evaluations. Just as language is never neutral or impersonal, so rhetoric, no matter how expository or informative it may seem, is always designed to gain acceptance for certain ways of evaluating and labeling things. Similarly, as the naming process includes feelings and attitudes toward what is named, so rhetoric, because it is concerned with problems, seeks to label and evaluate in ways that make present conditions unsatisfactory, even intolerable, for audiences.

Rhetorical processes are rooted in the essential qualities of language and in the capacities of humans as symbol users. Unless the language of a writer or speaker pleases and moves other people, unless it arouses feelings and associations, such language will be meaningless and irrelevant; it will remain outside experience, outside the associations that give significance to concepts and terms.

RHETORIC AS CONFLICT AND PROCESS

Numerous attempts have been made to describe the process of communication, and various models have been developed to diagram the stages, elements, and factors in a communicative transaction. However, many models of communication and rhetoric are rather static and linear. Although they have useful functions, our concern here is to locate and explore the conflicting forces and tensions inherent in most persuasive situations. These tensions and conflicts are not fixed and static; they are the core of the rhetorical *process*.

Rhetoric arises out of conflict within an individual, between individuals, or between groups. The basic conflict involves the perception of a problem, a gap between existing conditions and desired change or between current policies and practices and proposed goals. Often the conflict involves values: the psychological and financial rewards of sexism and racism versus the benefits and costs of equality of opportunity, technological development and employment versus preservation of the environment, nuclear weapons versus human survival, or desire for peace versus fear of humiliation or defeat. Such conflicts become public controversies when individuals come to believe that others do not feel or recognize the conflict as they do. In rhetorical processes, rhetors risk rejection by their audiences, attacks from others, and changes in their attitudes and perceptions compelled by these encounters.

In broad terms, rhetors invite discussion, choice, and action. Although they seek agreement, that is rarely an adequate description of what they do. In fact, much contemporary public rhetoric, rather than being conciliatory, provokes argument and dissent. It seeks to stimulate disagreement and to polarize individuals into conflicting groups. Critics must recognize that rhetors *select* their audiences and may seek different responses from different groups. In all cases, rhetors sift out from their potential readers or listeners those persons they wish to target, those they believe can be influenced to join them in achieving their purposes.

Critics are faced with difficult evaluations because conflict is a frequent and perhaps desirable outcome of persuasive discourse. Good rhetoric must stir up public discussion and controversy; it must speak to basic human conflicts if it is to fulfill its functions as rhetoric. The speeches and critiques that appear later in this book are a reflection of that belief.

Some conflict arises in rhetorical situations because the intent of the speaker may be different from the purposes of audiences. Regardless of the rhetor's purpose or message, members of the audience may seek confirmation of prior beliefs and attitudes. For instance, during the U.S. Senate hearings to confirm the nomination of Clarence Thomas to the Supreme Court, many listeners expected that Anita Hill, the woman who accused Thomas of sexual harassment, would be an avowed feminist, and that is what they concluded from what Hill said, even though she disavowed that label before and after the hearings. Likewise, after the first trial that acquitted the police officers who had beaten Rodney King, many people were outraged. They had seen part or all of the videotape of the beating, and they expected the verdict to confirm their judgment of what had occurred. When jurors or the defense attorneys attempted to justify the verdict, outraged listeners expected such defenses to be based on racist attitudes, and such was the message that they "heard" even when jurors attempted to explain how details of the videotape led them to doubt that the police officers had been guilty of using excessive force as legally defined. Critics also must beware: They are active participants in the rhetorical process and have personal beliefs they seek to confirm, regardless of the purpose of the rhetor whose discourse they are examining.

In this view, rhetors initiate a continuous process that arises out of conflict, and as a result they are open to risks of attack and rejection, especially when their purposes differ from those of their audiences. The process places great emphasis on change, which both rhetors and audiences resist; accordingly, a variety of responses from different audiences may lead to confrontation and polarization. The medium of this process is language, which allows rhetors to label and relabel, structure and restructure their own reality and that of their audiences to induce changes in thought, attitude, and action. The discourses in this book are part of cultural dialogues that continue. The issues remain unresolved; the policy questions are not settled. Rhetors are unlikely to induce major changes through single discourses. At best, rhetors stir up an internal dialogue in audiences, causing them to rethink and reconsider, leaving them open to future persuasive messages from other rhetors on that issue. The discipline of rhetoric is devoted to the study of these processes.

RHETORIC AS AN ACADEMIC DISCIPLINE

The discipline of rhetoric is the study of symbolic attempts by humans to make order of their world, to discover who they are, and to interact with others in ways that make their lives more satisfying. In this sense, rhetoric includes the study of the persuasive dimension of all language. Specifically, it examines those discourses that are distinctively suasive. As a theoretical discipline it explores three interrelated questions: (1) How and why are people capable of and subject to influence, and what is the nature of human motivation? This question explores the intrapersonal, cultural, and social dimensions of rhetoric, the relationship between people and their language. (2) What is the relationship between rhetoric and reality? This question focuses on the symbolic relationships between people and the world around them, and its permutations are most obvious in disputes over how to interpret the facts we have. (3) What is the relationship between rhetoric and cultural history, and relatedly, what are the ethical or valuative standards to be used to judge persuasive discourse? This question concerns relationships among individuals, groups, and cultures. All rhetorical theorizing attempts to answer one or more of these questions.

RHETORICAL CRITICISM

As we said at the beginning of this chapter, rhetorical criticism involves the description, analysis, interpretation, and evaluation of persuasive uses of language. These functions generate the phases or stages of the critical *process:* (1) descriptive analysis of the rhetorical act in terms that permit identification of the means by which it works to influence, (2) historical–contextual analysis of the relationships between a discourse and its context in order to identify the forces that contribute to or work against its purposes, (3) development of a critical perspective, approach, or system that guides the finished critique, and (4) evaluation or judgment of discourses based on explicit criteria so that the grounds for evaluation are apparent to readers. Well-done, thorough criticism increases the capacity of readers to appreciate rhetorical discourses and enables general audiences to make informed and deliberate judgments based on persuasive appeals. Ultimately, good criticism and good critics aspire to add to our understanding of how humans use symbols to influence one another. Such criticism improves the quality of persuasive discourse in society and tests and modifies both the theories of rhetoric and the critical systems derived from them. In that sense, criticism is perhaps the most important means through which knowledge is created in the study of rhetoric.

In the next four chapters in Part I, we consider each stage or phase of the critical process in greater detail: Chapter Two explains the first stage, descriptive analysis. Chapter Three is a discussion of historical-contextual analysis. Chapter Four explains how a critical perspective or system is selected or invented to guide the analysis. At the end of each of those chapters, we illustrate that phase of the critical process by applying it to a rhetorical act entitled "Whites Say I Must Be on Easy Street" by Nell Irvin Painter, a professor of history at Princeton University. Chapter Five explains how standards or criteria for evaluation are developed.

Part II illustrates the complete critical process. The first essay is our finished critique of Painter's essay. It illustrates how the stages of the critical process come together to form the finished critique. Following our critique of Painter's essay are six other rhetorical acts and critiques of them. On one hand, these rhetorical acts and the approaches or perspectives taken in the critiques are diverse; they illustrate the varied forms both rhetoric and rhetorical criticism can take. On the other hand, each of the critiques illustrates the principles of good criticism and how the four stages of the critical process culminate in an enlightening analysis of the persuasion that surrounds us. In that sense, they are excellent models for your own critical efforts.

CHAPTER TWO

Descriptive Analysis:
The First Stage of Criticism

In its final form, rhetorical criticism is the result of a four-stage process: (1) Critics analyze a discourse or a group of discourses in order to identify distinctive characteristics. (2) They attempt to understand the discourse in relation to its milieu or context. (3) They select or create a critical perspective, approach, or system to guide the critique. (4) They make evaluative judgments of its quality, of its effects, or sometimes of both, based on explicit criteria that make the grounds for evaluation apparent to readers. These stages or phases are not distinguishable in a written criticism. Rather, critics must complete these tasks in *preparing* to write a piece of criticism. In the completed critique, *each phase of the process is integrated into a unified essay.* There is no guarantee that performing these steps will produce a "great" criticism, but an insightful and creative criticism can be composed only by going through the four stages. In this chapter we explain and illustrate the first stage of the critical process: descriptive analysis.

The critical approach used in this book rests on our strong personal commitment to organic criticism that responds to the special qualities of the rhetorical act under examination, in contrast to formulaic or prescriptive criticism. The *prescriptive* approach to criticism applies a formula or set of prescriptions to all discourses. For example, in the past the critical system or formula often called neo-Aristotelianism was used prescriptively to analyze discourses in terms of the classical canons or standards of invention, disposition, style, and delivery, and the classical modes of proof: *logos* or rational argument and proof, *pathos* or audience adaptation and/or creating a state of mind or feeling, and *ethos* or the means by which rhetors make themselves seem worthy of belief. Further, critics following that formula often evaluated discourse in terms of its effectiveness in achieving the rhetor's purpose with the immediate audience. What made such criticism formulaic was that *all* rhetorical acts were required to meet the same rationalistic criteria.

Critics of contemporary rhetoric need to consider what critical perspective best illuminates the rhetoric to which they are responding. For some discourses traditional precepts constitute an ideal and workable critical system; for many others, especially in the contemporary U.S. milieu, they are inappropriate. Traditional, rationalistic theory, in keeping with its classical origins, is committed to the values of reason, order, and law. These values are sometimes challenged in rhetorical acts arguing that power holders use such values to rationalize injustice and oppression (see Robert L. Scott and Donald K. Smith, "The Rhetoric of Confrontation"). Contemporary critics must examine and develop critical systems to describe and evaluate such rhetoric in ways that do not *inevitably* force them to censure its purposes and strategies. Ultimately, the danger is not in any particular critical formula or system itself, but rather in viewing any *single* critical system as monolithic—that is, as appropriate in every case.

An *organic* approach to criticism asks critics to consider a rhetorical act on its own terms, not to approach it with prejudgments and prior assumptions. The first stage of criticism is an evidence-gathering endeavor that, if done carefully and thoroughly, puts the critic in possession of the act, giving the critic a detailed understanding of how the rhetorical act works to achieve its ends. An organic approach to criticism focuses on the specific goals of particular persuaders in specific contexts; it views rhetorical acts as patterns of justification and interaction that grow out of particular conditions. In adopting such an approach, critics apply critical categories that respond to qualities in the discourse; they are eclectic, experiential pluralists, selecting and adapting a critical framework in order to reveal and respond to the peculiarities of that rhetorical event.

Conflict between formulaic and organic approaches to criticism need not be irreconcilable. Good criticism is often the result of selecting and applying elements from one or more perspectives that seem best suited to illuminating the discourse under consideration. Several critical perspectives are described in later chapters. In one sense, these, too, are formulas or prescriptions that represent options for critics. But for many, if not most discourses, critics must "invent" a critical approach adapted to the particular work or genre they are evaluating.[1]

An essential premise of the organic approach is that the critical process should begin with a careful and exhaustive examination of the discourse itself, which we call descriptive analysis. Critics should come to know the discourse on its own terms, and they should do so encumbered by as few presuppositions as possible. Of course, the context in which the discourse was produced is of extreme importance to completion of the critical process. And critics will virtually always know something, perhaps a great deal, about the circumstances and events leading up to and surrounding the discourse. But that knowledge of context should be put aside for the moment, and further investigation of context should be delayed until examination of the discourse itself is completed. We believe that to do otherwise and begin the critical process with an in-depth examination of the context is potentially risky for at least two reasons. First, it risks elevating historical–contextual issues to a position of importance above the discourse itself. Such an emphasis on historical issues is essential in rhetorical *historiography,* an equally important, but different, scholarly activity. In rhetorical *criticism* the discourse itself should be of prime importance. Second, it risks creating a counterproductive bias in the critical process. By carefully examining the context first, critics may form preconceptions regarding what the rhetor could have, or should have, said. Those perceptions could then easily distort the analysis and evaluation of the discourse.

Through descriptive analysis, critics attempt to discover what characteristics, if any, make a discourse or group of discourses distinctive. At the completion of this stage, critics should be familiar with the nuances of the rhetoric and aware of the rhetor's selections of language, structure, arguments, and evidence. Critics will then have excellent grounds for ascertaining a rhetor's purpose and the responses that rhetor seeks from the audience or audiences. They will also have extracted information to determine the role the speaker or writer has chosen to play, the ways the audiences are perceived and selected, and the choice of persuasive strategies.

Descriptive analysis should be entirely intrinsic; that is, critics should make descriptive statements solely on the basis of the *content*

---

[1]Sometimes critics find in the work of earlier critics and theorists a critical system that can be used "as is," without modification, to guide their analysis and evaluation of a particular discourse. More often, however, the critical approach must be "invented" by adapting an existing system to the discourse, or by combining and adapting elements from more than one existing critical system.

of the discourse itself. They should use extrinsic materials and sources only under very limited circumstances. One such circumstance is to determine the authenticity of the text. The other is to identify references to persons, places, events, and the like in the discourse with which they are unfamiliar; such identification may be necessary in order to understand how the references function in the discourse. Otherwise, the single source needed to complete this first phase of the critical process is the discourse itself.

ELEMENTS OF DESCRIPTIVE ANALYSIS

Descriptive analysis seeks answers to two fundamental questions: (1) What is the apparent purpose of the discourse, or what aim or goal does the rhetor seem to seek? (2) How does the discourse work to achieve that purpose, or what strategies does the rhetor employ to achieve the goal? Rhetorical strategies are many and diverse. Thus, we suggest descriptive analysis of discourse in terms of the following seven elements: *purpose, persona, audience, tone, structure, supporting materials,* and *other strategies.* Keep in mind that, with the possible exception of purpose, each of the other six elements should be considered for its strategic function in the discourse. Be aware that the elements frequently overlap and are interrelated. How they are manifested and how they function may vary considerably from one discourse to another. We have resisted the temptation to include "arguments" in the list of elements of descriptive analysis. To do so, we fear, would risk biasing this phase of the critical process in favor of rationalistic criticism. Moreover, because all the components that compose "arguments" in a traditional sense are present in the seven elements, we believe that careful descriptive analysis is a necessary first phase of criticism, even when critics eventually choose to employ a rationalistic perspective.

Purpose

Purpose refers to the *argumentative conclusions,* particularly the major conclusion or thesis, of the discourse and the *responses desired* by the source from those who receive the message. Analysis of purpose usually requires careful analysis of the structure through which major ideas are developed and their relationships emerge. In many discourses the conclusion, or thesis, is explicitly stated. In others, the purpose is implicit and must be inferred from the content. Implicit purpose is closely allied to the tone of the discourse. In an analytical description of the implicit purpose, critics attempt to determine the kinds of responses that the rhetor seeks from the audiences or from different parts of the audience. Such purposes may include the traditional goals of acceptance and understanding or such "radical" goals as feeling ashamed or experiencing confrontation, polarization, and alienation. Implicit purposes are related to the rhetor's perceptions of the audience or audiences addressed.

Persona

Persona refers to a role or roles that a rhetor takes on for strategic purposes, much as an actor assumes a role or character in a play. Persona is revealed in the language of the discourse. For example, when addressing the people of the United States, the president may take on the role of commander-in-chief of the armed forces, the role of a moral or spiritual leader, the role of prophet, the role of teacher or authority on United States history, and so on. More than one persona may be adopted within a single discourse. Persona influences an audience by creating or contributing to a rhetor's *ethos* or credibility.

At this stage, critics are concerned with the relationship between the discourse and the identities rhetors create for themselves through the discourse or the roles they assume in its development. What is the function of the discourse for its author? How does it serve to create an identity for the speaker or writer? To what degree does the discourse serve as self-expression or self-persuasion? If the discourse were the only piece of evidence available from which to determine the character of the author, what inferences could be made about that person? A discourse reveals the attitudes and beliefs of its author. The rhetor's views of humanity, truth, and society may reveal the philosophic position or perspective from which that person speaks. Moreover, rhetors may take on particular identities or roles to strategically enhance their persuasive influence.

Audience

The actual or *empirical* audience is composed of all those who receive the rhetor's message. For speeches, the empirical audience includes those who are present when the speech is delivered as well as those who read a transcript of the speech or watch or hear a video or sound recording of the speech at some later time. Listeners who are present when a speech is delivered are sometimes called the *immediate* audience, whereas those who read or hear it later are called the *mediated* audience; however, live television and radio broadcasts of speeches to distant audiences have blurred that distinction. Usually, sources external to the discourse itself must be consulted to draw final conclusions regarding the nature and size of the empirical audience. That task is best left for the second phase of the critical process (see Chapter Three).

In this first phase of the critical process, conclusions regarding audience should be based on evidence found in the discourse itself. Those conclusions may be tentative, because subsequent research using sources external to the discourse may reveal new information regarding audience. Nevertheless, identifying the audience suggested by the text is essential for understanding how a discourse is intended to work.

Speakers or writers construct their discourse for particular individuals or groups. In descriptive analysis, critics concentrate on the ways that discourses select or *target* an audience or audiences. They locate statements that indicate that the rhetor is aware of more than one audience. They decide who will compose the target audiences and what part of the potential empirical audience would likely be alienated by the discourse. They also attempt to identify the sorts of people for whom the appeals are constructed and examine the supporting materials. At this stage, critics may also wish to consider what groups, if any, are excluded from the rhetor's audiences (see Philip Wander, "The Third Persona").

Rhetors also seek to reach audiences composed of "agents of change"—that is, persons with the capacity to do whatever it is that the rhetor desires. Expensive cars can be purchased only by individuals with substantial income; hence, advertisements for Rolls-Royces appear in *Architectural Digest* rather than in *Reader's Digest*. Political candidates target voters, especially registered voters, because voters are the people who can elect them. Advertisers generally target women between the ages of 25 and 44 because they know that these are the people who make the majority of decisions about consumer products.

In some cases, rhetors face audiences who lack confidence that they can be effective. Voters may not go to the polls because they believe that a single vote cannot make much or any difference. Members of ethnic minorities may not register and vote because they believe their votes will be overwhelmed by those of an ethnically different majority. Today rhetors commonly use the term *empowerment* to describe a process by which individuals or groups come to believe that they *can* be effective, that their actions *can* make a difference.

Empowering an audience is just one form of a larger process of *creating one's audience*—that is, of symbolically transforming those addressed into the people the rhetor wants them to be. Sometimes that means creating a role for the audience that is attractive and praiseworthy, a role the audience wants to assume but that also entails the response the rhetor desires. For example, in a speech in 1969 announcing and defending the policy of Vietnamization (withdrawing U.S. ground troops from Vietnam but maintaining air support, matériel, and advisers), President Richard Nixon referred to the target audience as "the great silent majority of Americans." He made that role attractive by describing such people as patriotic and law abiding, but the role also entailed silent acquiescence to the policy he was announcing. In other words, rhetors sometimes invite members of the audience to assume a particular role or to think of themselves in a particular way. If the audience accepts that invitation, they become ideal listeners, those most likely to agree with the rhetor.

We have called the role that the rhetor assumes the persona. If we think of the rhetor's role as the *first* persona, then the auditor implied by, or the role that members of the audience are invited to play in, a rhetorical act can be considered the *second* persona. Edwin Black argues, "The critic can see in the auditor implied by a discourse a model of what the rhetor would have his [*sic*] real auditor become" (113). Because identity is shaped by the network of interconnected beliefs that an individual holds, the second persona has ethical significance. Accordingly, Black argues that identifying the second persona enables a critic to make a moral judgment of the model of humanity or character implied in a rhetorical work. (See also the discussion of criteria for evaluation in Chapter Five.)

Descriptive analysis of audience includes identification of the target audience, of the agents of change who can do what the rhetor seeks, and of the efforts by the rhetor to create the audience in the image desired either by developing a role consistent with the rhetor's purpose or by empowering the audience to make them effective agents of change. Critics must be able to provide evidence from the text of the discourse itself to support descriptive statements regarding audience.

Tone

Tone refers to those elements of discourse, primarily language elements, that suggest the rhetor's attitude toward the audiences and the subject matter. Because tone reveals the rhetor's attitude, it also often reveals the connotative meaning the rhetor intends to convey. Thus, tone can influence listeners or readers to see issues in a similar way through that shared connotative meaning.

Statements about tone are inferences drawn from stylistic qualities. Critics may describe tone in an infinite number of ways—as personal, direct, ironic, satirical, sympathetic, angry, bitter, intense, scholarly, dogmatic, distant, condescending, tough, realistic, sweet, euphemistic, incisive, elegant, and so on. Each such label should reflect, as accurately as possible, the language used in the rhetorical act as well as whether the language is abstract or concrete, socially acceptable or unacceptable, technical or colloquial; it should reflect sentence length and complexity. Critics should also be prepared to support each characterization with evidence from the discourse that shows most clearly the general attitudes of the rhetor toward the audiences and the subject.

Structure

Structure refers to the form of the discourse, the method by which it unfolds, and the nature of its movement. Critics should describe how and why the discourse develops, how it creates expectations in an audience, whether it promotes a sense of inevitability, and how the speaker or writer constructs a context for materials that follow. There are many kinds of structure, and rhetorical acts often develop in more than one way. The names for the kinds of structure reflect organizing principles that guide development of the discourse—for example: narrative–dramatic; historical–chronological; logical or pragmatic, such as problem–solution, cause–effect, or effect–cause; topical, or analysis by a number of facets or perspectives; and taxonomical, or division of a process into its relevant parts. These forms are not mutually exclusive; the discourses in this book all use combinations of them.

The structure of the discourse is important because it represents the rhetor's choice of the most significant perspective on the subject, issue, or section of reality examined. A *historical–chronological* structure emphasizes development through time. A *narrative–dramatic* form reflects an organic view of reality and assumes that vicarious sharing of integrally related experiences is essential to the understanding of a concept or situation. A *problem–solution* form emphasizes either the need to discover a concrete policy in order to resolve a troublesome situation or the identification of reasons, origins, and antecedents. A *cause–effect* form stresses the prediction of consequences. A *topical* form selects certain facets of the subject for attention and suggests that others are relatively unimportant. A *taxonomical* form focuses on the interrelationships either between the parts of an institution, such as the branches of the federal government, and how the parts work together or between the parts and the whole. Each structural form represents a choice of perspective that emphasizes certain elements of the subject over others. Writers or speakers use a given structure to develop the discourse in order to support their points of view and lead most directly to their desired goals. Moreover, structure can function to influence audiences by inviting them to see the same relationships between ideas that are seen by the rhetor.

With the exception of addresses using a narrative or historical structure based on a kind of plot line, outlining the major ideas and arguments of the discourse is a helpful critical technique for determining structural form. An outline may also serve as a basis for testing the coherence and validity of the rhetor's arguments. Because critics are concerned with ideas and conclusions rather than topics, a full-sentence outline is best. At this stage of analysis the chronological order in which ideas appear in the discourse is not important. The critic reorders concepts so that reasons and conclusions appear in logical relationships. At times, critics may need to experiment with alternate ways of understanding structure to discover which most accurately and completely reflect the patterns of development.

Supporting Materials

The supporting materials or evidence in a discourse are the explanations, illustrations, statistics, analogies, and quotations or testimony from laypersons or experts used to clarify ideas, to verify statements, and to make concepts vivid and memorable. In descriptive analysis critics are not concerned with testing the validity, reliability, and credibility of support materials because such processes require the use of extrinsic sources. At this stage they are concerned solely with describing the supporting materials and analyzing their functions in the discourse.

Types of supporting material are many and varied. Each form serves different functions. For instance, to the degree that an audience can identify with the persons or events, a detailed example is a vivid, personal, dramatic method of illustrating a principle, concept, or condition. Such instances may be real or hypothetical; they may be brief or extended. But their primary function is creating identification because one example has only limited demonstrative value. In most instances, a single case of anything is not adequate grounds for drawing a general conclusion; it may be an atypical situation, even a remarkable coincidence or accident. Illustrations, like dramas, "clothe ideas in living flesh," and their greatest strength is in their concrete impact on individuals. Extended examples also introduce narrative–dramatic form into a discourse.

Literal analogies, or comparisons, function primarily for the purposes of prediction; they connect what exists and is known with what is in the future and is unknown. Susan B. Anthony's comparison of white women's social, economic, and political condition under state and federal laws in the 19th century with that of slaves is a literal analogy. Figurative analogies are comparisons between things unlike in detail but similar in principle, such as the comparison of the denial of civil rights to the "Bank of Justice's" refusal to cash a citizen's check in Dr. Martin Luther King's "I Have a Dream" speech. Figurative analogies operate in the same way to connect the known, familiar, and simple with the unknown, unfamiliar, and complex.

Expert testimony or authoritative evidence provides criteria, standards, or principles to interpret data. Such evidence increases the understanding of an audience inexpert in the area being discussed. In addition, authoritative evidence demonstrates that experts share the rhetor's perspective or attitudes. Testimony from nonexperts generally serves the same functions as examples.

Statistical evidence demonstrates how frequently something occurs. Used in conjunction with examples, statistics provide evidence of the typicality of the examples and the size or scope of a problem. Statistical evidence is strengthened by cultural preference for the quantified and scientific, but because statistics are often perceived as dull and boring, audiences may have difficulty absorbing or retaining them.

In descriptive analysis, critics describe the supporting materials used in the discourse and their functions. They also consider how the supporting material is related to the tone, purpose, and structure of the discourse. Different structural forms require different kinds of supporting materials, and the rhetor may select a structure to avoid certain evidentiary requirements. The selection of a structural form to emphasize certain kinds of evidential questions is closely related to the descriptive analysis of strategies.

Other Strategies

The descriptive analysis of strategies determines how rhetors shape their material in terms of audience and purpose. Indeed, each of the elements of descriptive analysis serves strategic functions. Strategies may include the selection of purpose, persona, structure, arguments, and supporting materials. The tone expressed in the choice of language, the use of definitions, and repetition of key words and phrases may also be strategic. Critics might consider certain questions to determine the rhetor's strategies: What elements in the discourse create common grounds between the rhetor and the intended audiences? What attempts does the rhetor make to label or relabel, define or redefine, structure or restructure the experienced reality of the audiences? How does the speaker or writer attempt to provide new experiences for the readers or listeners? What changes in evaluation or association does the rhetor seek?

Examples of recurring strategies include, among many:

- refutation, or answering the arguments of opponents; inoculation, or providing a framework that makes the audience more resistant to opposing arguments

- *a fortiori* argument (literally, "to the stronger"), a strategy of arguing that if something is true in one particular and unlikely case, it is much more likely to be true in other cases

- labeling or relabeling, such as calling the Strategic Defense Initiative "Star Wars"

- repetition of a key phrase that becomes an ever more poignant refrain, such as Martin Luther King, Jr.'s "I have a dream"

- vivid depiction or description so that audiences experience events with immediacy

- allusions to culturally familiar materials, such as television programs, to prompt the audience to fill in details or to evoke powerful associations

- enthymemes, or arguments constructed so that listeners participate in forming conclusions by providing from their own experience and memory additional evidence or reasons intentionally omitted from the rhetoric.

SUMMARY

Descriptive analysis, the first stage in the critical process, is almost entirely intrinsic and organic. As textual analysis, it is intended to focus attention on the rhetorical act itself. At this basic stage in the critical process, critics gather the data that will provide the basis for subsequent analysis and interpretation. Therefore, care and thoroughness in this process are extremely important.

Descriptive analysis alone does not constitute rhetorical criticism; the remaining phases of the critical process must be accomplished before the critical act is completed. Nevertheless, we believe that descriptive analysis should be completed first, so that the discourse can be properly placed within its context and evaluated according to criteria selected or invented by the critic.

The following outline provides a useful review of the seven elements of descriptive analysis. However, the outline should not be considered either a prescriptive or an exhaustive checklist to be applied to all discourses, because how the seven elements are manifested can vary considerably from one discourse to another.

I. What is the act's *purpose*?

   A. What is the thesis—that is, the specific purpose, central idea, or major conclusion of the rhetorical act?

   B. How is the subject limited or narrowed? Frequently, a broad topic is reduced to an aspect more suited to limits of time, space, audience, or occasion.

   C. What audience response is desired? Desired response consists of the beliefs and actions sought from the audiences.

II. What role or *persona* does the rhetor (source) assume? Personas are roles adopted by rhetors in order to enhance the case made in the rhetorical act.

III. Who compose the target *audiences?* Rhetorical acts often suggest an ideal audience or audiences.

   A. What must you know, believe, or value to participate in this act?

   B. Who are the relevant agents of change?

   C. What roles, if any, are audience members invited to assume?

IV. What is the act's *tone*?

   A. What is the expressed attitude toward the subject?

   B. What is the expressed attitude toward the audience(s)?

      1. Are audience members addressed as subordinates (for example, expert to nonexpert)?

      2. Are audience members addressed as peers (for example, fellow students)?

      3. Are audience members addressed as superiors (for example, less powerful to more powerful or knowledgeable)?

V. How is the discourse *structured*?

   A. What does the introduction do? For example, introductions may gain auditors' or readers' attention, introduce the subject/issue or the perspective to be taken, narrow the subject, and create a relationship between rhetor and audience. Not all of these are done in every introduction.

B. What kind of organization is used to develop ideas? For instance, rhetorical acts may unfold using one (or a combination) of the following:

1. Chronological development—the development over time (starting with the earliest and working toward the latest event) or in sequence.

2. Topical development—an organization of material in terms of some of its parts or aspects.

3. Logical development—an organization examining processes that are necessarily related, such as the relationship between causes and effects or problems and solutions.

4. Narrative–dramatic development—an organization that is similar to a story, novel, or play, assuming that a vicarious sharing of integrally related experiences is essential to understanding a situation.

5. Taxonomical development—a focus on how the parts or elements of an institution or a process are interrelated and work together.

C. What does the conclusion do? For example, conclusions frequently summarize major ideas presented in the rhetorical act and reinforce the thesis or purpose.

D. What efforts are made to create relationships among ideas? Transitions, often internal summaries, call attention to relationships between ideas. They are reminders of what has gone before and preparations for what is to come. They enable the audience to follow the act's structural plan.

VI. What kinds of *supporting materials* are used?

A. Supporting material consists of evidence that describes, explains, enumerates, and proves. For instance, an act may include:

1. Examples—instances or specific cases that illustrate concretely and often in detail.

2. Statistics—numerical measures of size, scope, or frequency of occurrence.

3. Authority—quotation of an opinion or conclusion drawn by someone with expertise and experience in an area

relevant to the issue. Presumably, such a person has special abilities to interpret or translate information relevant to the issue addressed in the rhetorical act.

4. Analogies. Literal analogies, usually called comparisons, compare events, objects, persons, and so on that are obviously or literally (on the face of it) alike or in the same category. Figurative analogies are imaginative comparisons between things, events, and persons that are not obviously alike at all but that nevertheless are asserted to resemble each other in some way.

B. How is evidence adapted to audience members?

C. How is the selection of evidence adapted to the purpose?

D. What evidence is evoked from the audience?

VII. What *other strategies* are used? Strategies are reflected in the rhetor's selection of language, appeals, arguments, and evidence and adaptation of these to particular audiences, issue, and occasion.

A. What is the style of the rhetorical act? Terms and labels are often selected for their appropriateness and impact.

1. How does the language reflect the rhetor's role?

2. How does the language reflect the relationship between rhetor and audience?

3. How is the language adapted to the complexity of the subject?

B. How are appeals made to the needs, drives, desires, and cultural values of the audience?

C. What strategies are used to assist in proof?

D. What strategies are used to animate ideas?

E. What strategies are used to alter associations and attitudes?

F. Specific discursive and aesthetic techniques may include (but are not limited to):

1. Refutation—stating an opposing argument and showing its weakness.

2. Enthymemes—presenting an argument in such a way that audience members participate in its creation.

3. *A fortiori* argument—a special form of argumentative comparison that says, in effect, if it happens in that unlikely case, how much more likely it is to occur in this one.

4. Allusion—a reference to historical events, literature, mythology, or some other repository of cultural wisdom.

To explain descriptive analysis more fully, we shall illustrate its application. The rhetorical act we analyze descriptively was printed in a special "Hers" column of the *New York Times* on December 10, 1981. It was written not by a journalist or member of the *Times* staff, but by Nell Irvin Painter, then a professor of history at the University of North Carolina at Chapel Hill and now Edwards Professor of American History at Princeton University in New Jersey. We have chosen this essay because, as you will see, it works well to illustrate the various elements in rhetorical action and because, even though it was written in 1981, it treats a typical rhetorical issue of continuing importance, a question of public policy that rests on cultural values and requires the creation of social truths. The broad issue is what public policy should be to provide equality of opportunity in employment for women and members of minorities, legislation often referred to as "affirmative action." Paragraph numbers have been added so that we can make later references to precise areas of the text.

WHITES SAY I MUST BE ON EASY STREET [2]

Nell Irvin Painter

1   I've always thought affirmative action made a lot of sense, because discrimination against black people and women was prolonged and thorough. But I've been hearing talk in the last several years that lets me know that not everyone shares my views. The first time I noticed it was shortly after I had moved to Philadelphia, where I used to live. One evening I attended a lecture—I no longer remember the topic—but I recall that I arrived early and was doing what I did often that fall. I worked at polishing my dissertation. In those days I regularly carried chapters and a nicely sharpened pencil around with me. I sat with pencil and typescript, scratching out awkward phrases and trying out new ones.

2   Next to me sat a white man of about 35, whose absorption in my work increased steadily. He watched me intently—kindly—for several moments. "Is that your dissertation?" I said yes, it was. "Good luck in getting it accepted," he said. I said that it had already been accepted, thank you.

3   Still friendly, he wished me luck in finding a job. I appreciated his concern, but I already had a job. Where? At Penn, for I was then a beginning assistant professor at the University of Pennsylvania. "Aren't you lucky," said the man, a little less generously, "you got a job at a good university." I agreed. Jobs in history were, still are, hard to find.

4 While cognizant of the job squeeze, I never questioned the justice of my position. I should have a job, and a good one. I had worked hard as a graduate student and had written a decent dissertation. I knew foreign languages, had traveled widely and had taught and published. I thought I had been hired because I was a promising young historian. Unlike the man beside me, I didn't think my teaching at a first-rate university required an extraordinary explanation.

5 "I have a doctorate in history," he resumed, "but I couldn't get an academic job." With regret he added that he worked in school administration. I said I was sorry he hadn't been able to find the job he wanted. He said: "It must be great to be black and female, because of affirmative action. You count twice." I couldn't think of an appropriate response to that line of reasoning, for this was the first time I'd met it face to face. I wished the lecture would start. I was embarrassed. Did this man really mean to imply that I had my job at his expense? The edge of competition in his voice made me squirm.

6 He said that he had received his doctorate from Temple, and yet he had no teaching job, and where was my degree from? "Harvard," I said. It was his time not to reply. I waited a moment for his answer, then returned to my chapter.

7 Now I live in North Carolina, but I still hear contradictory talk about affirmative action. Last spring I was having lunch with some black Carolina undergraduates. One young woman surprised me by deploring affirmative action. I wondered why. "White students and professors think we only got into the University of North Carolina because we're black," she complained, "and they don't believe we're truly qualified." She said that she knew that she was qualified and fully deserved to be at Carolina. She fulfilled all the regular admissions requirements. It was the stigma of affirmative action that bothered her; without it other students wouldn't assume she was unqualified.

8 Another student said that the stigma of affirmative action extended to black faculty as well. She had heard white students doubting the abilities of black professors. Indeed, she herself tended to wait for black professors to disprove her assumption that they did not know their fields. She was convinced that without affirmative action, students would assume black faculty to be as good as white.

9   That's what I've been hearing from whites and blacks. White people tell me I must be on easy street because I'm black and female. (I do not believe I've ever heard that from a black person, although some blacks believe that black women have an easier time in the white world than black men. I don't think so.) White people tell me, "You're a twofer." On the other side of the color line, every black student knows that he or she is fully qualified—I once thought that way myself. It is just the other black people who need affirmative action to get in. No one, not blacks, not whites, benefits from affirmative action, or so it would seem.

10   Well, I have, but not in the early 1960s when I was an undergraduate in a large state university. Back then, there was no affirmative action. We applied for admission to the university like everyone else; we were accepted or rejected like everyone else. Graduate and undergraduate students together, we numbered about 200 in a student body of nearly 30,000. No preferential treatment there.

11   Yet we all knew what the rest of the university thought of us, professors especially. They thought we were stupid because we were black. Further, white women were considered frivolous students; they were only supposed to be in school to get husbands. (I doubt that we few black women even rated a stereotype. We were the ultimate outsiders.) Black students, the whole atmosphere said, would not attend graduate or professional school because their grades were poor. Women had no business in postgraduate education because they would waste their training by dropping out of careers when they married or became pregnant. No one said out loud that women and minorities were simply and naturally inferior to white men, but the assumptions were as clear as day: Whites are better than blacks; men are better than women.

12   I am one of the few people I know who will admit to having been helped by affirmative action. To do so is usually tantamount to admitting deficiency. To hear people talk, affirmative action exists only to employ and promote the otherwise unqualified, but I don't see it that way at all. I'm black and female, yet I was hired by two history departments that had no black members before the late '60s, never mind females. Affirmative action cleared the way.

13   Thirty-five years ago, John Hope Franklin, then a star student, now a giant in the field of American history, received a doctorate in history from Harvard. He went to teach in a black college. In those days, black men taught in black colleges. White women taught in white women's colleges. Black women taught in black women's colleges. None taught at the University of Pennsylvania or the University of North Carolina. It was the way things were.

14   Since then, the civil rights movement and the feminist movement have created a new climate that permitted affirmative action, which, in turn, opened areas previously reserved for white men. Skirts and dark skins appeared in new settings in the 1970s, but in significant numbers only after affirmative action mandated the changes and made them thinkable. Without affirmative action, it never would have occurred to any large, white research university to consider me for professional employment, despite my degree, languages, publications, charm, grace, *despite* my qualifications.

15   My Philadelphia white man and my Carolina black women would be surprised to discover the convergence of their views. I doubt that they know that their convictions are older than affirmative action. I wish I could take them back to the early '60s and let them see that they're reciting the same old white-male-superiority line, fixed up to fit conditions that include a policy called affirmative action. Actually, I will not have to take these people back in time at all, for the Reagan Administration's proposed dismantling of affirmative action fuses the future and the past. If they achieve their stated goals, we will have the same old discrimination, unneedful of new clothes.

DESCRIPTIVE ANALYSIS APPLIED

All audiences encounter rhetorical acts chronologically. That is, they begin reading or hearing with the introduction and continue through the conclusion. For ordinary observers, that encounter is usually a single reading or hearing. But critics engaging in descriptive analysis must achieve a much more thorough and complete understanding of the rhetorical act. Several close and careful readings are usually necessary. The analysis should be exhaustive; all the rhetorically significant aspects of the text should be identified and described. Further, all descriptive claims regarding the rhetorical act should be supported with evidence taken from the text itself.

Although audiences encounter rhetorical acts chronologically, talking about the results of descriptive analysis is usually best done topically, discussing each of the seven elements in turn. The following is our descriptive analysis of Painter's essay, presented topically.

Purpose

Painter introduces the topic at the beginning of the essay. She says: "I've always thought affirmative action made a lot of sense, because discrimination against black people and women was prolonged and thorough. But I've been hearing talk in the last several years that lets me know that not everyone shares my views" (1).[3] In addition to introducing the topic, affirmative action, this passage performs two other functions regarding Painter's purpose. First, it hints at her own position regarding affirmative action, "I've always thought affirmative action made a lot of sense," and provides an initial justification for her point of view, "because discrimination against black people and women was prolonged and thorough." Second, the passage acknowledges that the topic and Painter's position on it are controversial: "I've been hearing talk in the last several years that lets me know that not everyone shares my views."

The ultimate purpose of the essay is to justify Painter's position regarding affirmative action. The purpose becomes quite clear near the end of the essay. There, Painter says:

> Since then [the 1950s], the civil rights movement and the feminist movement have created a new climate that permitted affirmative action, which, in turn, opened areas previously reserved for white men. Skirts and dark skins appeared in new settings in the 1970s, but in significant numbers only after affirmative action mandated the changes and made them thinkable. (14)

The justification for her position, then, is that affirmative action is a desirable policy because it has opened employment opportunities previously denied to women and minorities.

Painter's case for affirmative action, however, is carefully limited: She justifies the policy as a means to ensure quality education and employment for *fully qualified* individuals. She says: "To hear people talk, affirmative action exists only to employ and promote the otherwise unqualified, but I don't see it that way at all." She goes on to credit affirmative action for her own educational and professional success. "I'm black and female," she says, "yet I was hired by two history departments that had no black members before the late '60s, never mind females. Affirmative action cleared the way" (12). Later, she clearly links the policy to qualified individuals through a personal example: "Without affirmative action, it never would have occurred to any large, white research university to consider me for professional employment, despite my degree, languages, publications, charm, grace, *despite* my qualifications" (14). In that way, her support for affirmative action is narrowed to the benefits of the policy for fully qualified individuals.

---

[3]Parenthetical citations are paragraph numbers.

Finally, at the end of the essay, Painter goes a step further to attack proposals for eliminating affirmative action: ". . . the Reagan Administration's proposed dismantling of affirmative action fuses the future and the past. If they achieve their stated goals, we will have the same old discrimination, unneedful of new clothes" (15).

In summary, Painter's purpose in this essay is to defend and justify her controversial position, to gain audience support for affirmative action as a policy to ensure quality education and employment for fully qualified individuals, and to attack proposals to eliminate or weaken affirmative action. That purpose, together with other evidence from the text, suggests the audiences Painter seeks.

Audience

One targeted subgroup within Painter's potential empirical audience is made up of women and minorities, those whom affirmative action legislation was designed to help, but who have grown skeptical about the effects of the legislation. The second targeted subgroup is made up of those white males and others who Painter feels may oppose affirmative action not because of rigid political ideology, but because they are unfamiliar with the benefits of the legislation.

Painter targets those audiences at the end of the essay when she says, "My Philadelphia white man and my Carolina black women would be surprised to discover the convergence of their views." That those are the individuals she wishes most to influence is apparent as she concludes, "I wish I could take them back to the early '60s and let them see that they're reciting the same old white-male-superiority line, fixed up to fit conditions that include a policy called affirmative action" (15). Those targeted individuals—women, minorities, and those who oppose affirmative action out of lack of information or ignorance rather than rigid ideology—compose the agents of action who can respond in the way the rhetor desires.

However, one subgroup in the potential empirical audience seems to be excluded from the target audience. Painter's attack on the proposal to eliminate or weaken affirmative action suggests that she does not expect to influence members of the Reagan administration and its strongly conservative supporters.

Persona

One means Painter uses to influence the target audiences is to assume a role or persona that enhances her credibility or ethos. That complex persona is revealed at various places throughout the essay.

At the beginning, Painter takes on the role of a careful, conscientious scholar. Relating an experience she had some years earlier, she explains:

> One evening I attended a lecture—I no longer remember the topic—but I recall that I arrived early and was doing what I did often that fall. I worked at polishing my dissertation. In those days I regularly carried chapters and a nicely sharpened pencil around with me. I sat with pencil and typescript, scratching out awkward phrases and trying out new ones. (1)

She was attending a lecture, presumably of a scholarly nature. Moreover, while waiting for the lecture to begin, she was working on her dissertation, "scratching out awkward phrases and trying out new ones." Those details portray her as a conscientious scholar.

Shortly, she adds that she is a historian and "a beginning assistant professor at the University of Pennsylvania" (3). She provides more details. "I had worked hard as a graduate student and had written a decent dissertation," Painter says. "I knew foreign languages, had traveled widely and had taught and published" (4). Although the audience must accept these facts based solely on Painter's own assertions, she nevertheless assumes the role of a well-qualified professor of history. Further, she reveals that she earned her doctorate in history from Harvard (6), perhaps the most highly regarded university in the United States. That fact enhances her credibility even further.

Later in the essay, Painter clearly assumes the role of professor as she provides her audience with a history lesson, much as she might in class. Explaining events both before and after the passage of affirmative action legislation, Painter says:

> In those days [before affirmative action], black men taught in black colleges. White women taught in white women's colleges. Black women taught in black women's colleges. None taught at the University of Pennsylvania or the University of North Carolina. It was the way things were.
>
> Since then, the civil rights movement and the feminist movement have created a new climate that permitted affirmative action, which, in turn, opened areas previously reserved for white men. (13–14)

More subtle, but equally important, evidence of Painter's persona exists. She says that she was "cognizant of the job squeeze" (4) and later that for one to admit being helped by affirmative action "is usually tantamount to admitting deficiency" (12). Her choice of the words *cognizant* and *tantamount*, not part of common usage, also helps her assume the persona of a well-educated individual.

Throughout the essay Painter also acknowledges that she is African American and female. In one sense, those facts serve to promote identification between Painter and one of the targeted subgroups. But they serve another strategic function as well. As an African American woman, by supporting affirmative action Painter takes on a somewhat unexpected role.

She first explains that opposition to affirmative action is significant, not only among whites but among African Americans as well. She explains, "That's what I've been hearing from whites and blacks. . . . No one, not blacks, not whites, benefits from affirmative action, or so it would seem" (9). Then she immediately places herself outside that opposition, against the trend: "Well, I have," she says (10). And later: "I am one of the few people I know who will admit to having been helped by affirmative action" (12). Because Painter has created the impression that many African Americans oppose affirmative action, her unflinching support for the policy makes her distinctive; she violates that expectation. Moreover, Painter reveals herself to be a courageous individual, unafraid to defend a controversial position.

Finally, at the end of the essay, Painter assumes something of the role of prophet, or at least one who can predict the future consequences of legislative action. Grounded in her role as historian and her knowledge of the history of affirmative action, she predicts: "If they [the Reagan administration] achieve their stated goals, we will have the same old discrimination, unneedful of new clothes" (15).

Taken together, these aspects of persona enhance Painter's ethos for members of her target audiences. Thus, the role or persona Painter assumes in the essay performs an important strategic function by lending credibility to the justification she offers for affirmative action.

Tone

Tone suggests the rhetor's attitude toward both the topic and the audiences. It can affect or influence audience members by inviting them to share that attitude. Painter adopts a personal tone. At the outset she says: "I've always thought affirmative action made a lot of sense" (1). Throughout the essay, the first-person, singular pronoun *I* continues to reveal her personal association with the topic. That tone reinforces her persona as one who is personally involved with the issue. Strategically, it also invites members of her audience, especially women and minorities, to identify personally with the issue as well. In this way, Painter strives to make the personal political for her readers and thus gain public support for affirmative action.

Although personal tone predominates in the essay and reveals Painter's attitude toward the topic, various passages reveal her attitude toward potential audience members. In relating her conversation with a white male that occurred some years earlier in Philadelphia, her tone starts off as matter-of-fact, even friendly. She says, "Next to me sat a white man of about 35, whose absorption in my work increased steadily" (2). But as her conversation with the man progresses, and he seems to imply that Painter has benefited unfairly from affirmative action, her tone shifts. She is surprised, a little embarrassed, and defensive: "I couldn't think of an appropriate response to that line of reasoning, for this was the first time I'd met it face to face. I wished the lecture would start. I was embarrassed. Did this man really mean to imply that I had my job at his expense? The edge of competition in his voice made me squirm" (5).

Later, as Painter relates a more recent conversation with several African American students who also express skepticism about affirmative action, her tone is again matter-of-fact: "Last spring I was having lunch with some black Carolina undergraduates. One young woman surprised me by deploring affirmative action. I wondered why" (7). And at the end of that section, she is disappointed, perhaps even sad, about the attitudes others hold regarding affirmative action. She says, "No one, not blacks, not whites, benefits from affirmative action, or so it would seem" (9).

When Painter announces her own support for affirmative action, her tone becomes assertive, almost defiant:

> I am one of the few people I know who will admit to having been helped by affirmative action. To do so is usually tantamount to admitting deficiency. To hear people talk, affirmative action exists only to employ and promote the otherwise unqualified, but I don't see it that way at all. I'm black and female, yet I was hired by two history departments that had no black members before the late '60s, never mind females. Affirmative action cleared the way. (12)

Here, tone reinforces her persona as a courageous individual. Members of her audience are invited to share that attitude.

Near the end of the essay, Painter is again saddened by the opposition to affirmative action she has discovered among members of her target audience. "My Philadelphia white man and my Carolina black women would be surprised to discover the convergence of their views," she says (15). But she is not angry with her target audiences. Rather, she seems to project a benevolent attitude when she says, "I wish I could take them back to the early '60s and let them see that they're reciting the same old white-male-superiority line, fixed up to fit conditions that include a policy called affirmative action" (15).

Structure

The introduction of Painter's essay is very long, consisting of the first eight paragraphs, for strategic reasons we shall explain shortly. As we said earlier, the first two sentences of the first paragraph introduce the topic and preview her purpose.

The remainder of the introduction, from the third sentence in the first paragraph through the end of paragraph 8, consists of two real, extended examples presented as a narrative. The detail of the narrative creates a little drama, as if it were a play with two acts. The setting in the first example, or the first act of the narrative, is a lecture hall; the scene opens with two people sitting side by side in chairs. The time is evening. One character has certain props, pages of typescript and a sharpened pencil, and she is editing her work.

The second paragraph introduces a second character, a slightly older white man who is intensely interested in what Painter is doing, so interested that he is willing to speak to a total stranger. She writes, "Next to me sat a white man of about 35, whose absorption in my work increased steadily. He watched me intently—kindly—for several moments. 'Is that your dissertation?' I said yes, it was. 'Good luck in getting it accepted,' he said. I said that it had already been accepted, thank you" (2).

Painter interprets his interest positively, as "kindly," and answers his opening question. She perceives his good wishes for getting her dissertation accepted as "friendly." The next paragraph begins, "Still friendly" (3). She thanks him, but she is proud to tell him that she doesn't need his good wishes; it has already been accepted.

The drama continues in the third paragraph. The next concern of someone who has completed a doctorate is finding a job, so the man wishes her well in that effort, but again she does not need his good wishes; she already has employment. As in other dramas, the tension escalates when she tells him that she is a beginning assistant professor at the University of Pennsylvania, a prestigious, Ivy League school. Painter says:

> Still friendly, he wished me luck in finding a job. I appreciated his concern, but I already had a job. Where? At Penn, for I was then a beginning assistant professor at the University of Pennsylvania. "Aren't you lucky," said the man, a little less generously, "you got a job at a good university." I agreed. Jobs in history were, still are, hard to find. (3)

For the third time, the word *luck* figures in their exchanges. The first two times the word was used phatically, as part of phrases that are so conventional as to be ritualistic, as, for example, when we say "How do you do?" when introduced to someone but do not expect the person addressed to tell us. This third time the meaning of *luck* has changed slightly. Here it suggests that luck, as accidental or undeserved good fortune, has played an important role. Painter responds to this slight shift, perceiving these words to have been said "a little less generously." However, she agrees that some luck was involved and explains, "Jobs in history were, still are, hard to find."

Dramatically, the next paragraph is an aside; as narrator, Painter steps outside the drama to address readers directly. As we explained earlier, what she tells us here, coupled with the data already provided in the story, is an integral part of her persona. We know that Painter is a historian with a doctorate who started her career as a faculty member at the University of Pennsylvania. In this paragraph, we learn more about her character. She is self-confident and self-assured. "I never questioned the justice of my position. I should have a job, and a good one," she says (4). She sees herself as deserving, and explains why. She asserts that she "worked hard" and wrote "a decent dissertation," but we have no evidence other than her assertion. She tells us she is well-qualified and provides some evidence related to academic criteria familiar to most readers: command of foreign languages, travel, teaching experience, and publications. In effect, she has provided a résumé that details her qualifications for us to judge. Based on those qualifications, she labels her being hired at Penn as "justice," as capable of an ordinary, not "extraordinary" or "lucky," explanation (4). At this moment, however, we do not really know which interpretation is correct. We know she has qualifications, but we don't really know how good they are.

The next paragraph takes us back to the first act of the drama. Painter writes: " 'I have a doctorate in history,' he resumed, 'but I couldn't get an academic job.' With regret he added that he worked in school administration. I said I was sorry he hadn't been able to find the job he wanted" (5). She responds with empathy, but he continues with a kind of attack, suggesting that, as an African American woman, she had an unfair advantage resulting from affirmative action: "He said: 'It must be great to be black and female, because of affirmative action. You count twice' " (5). In effect, he claims to have been the victim of what is usually called "reverse discrimination." "Did this man really mean to imply that I had my job at his expense?" Painter asks (5). She is shocked, speechless, embarrassed. His words suggest that he sees himself in a competition rigged in her favor. At that point, however, although we see things only from Painter's point of view, it is still possible that the man is right.

As the narrative continues, the man tells Painter that his degree is from Temple, a private university in metropolitan Philadelphia, and asks her where hers is from. When she tells him "Harvard," this portion of the narrative ends; the man has nothing more to say (6). This paragraph provides crucial details of the narrative. Although Temple University is a good school, its standing and that of its history department are significantly lower than that of Harvard and its history department. Throughout the narrative, Painter and the man have been compared, with the issue whether or not she should have been hired for the job in the history department at Penn. Within the narrative, Harvard functions as authority evidence, a kind of expert evidence that enables us to interpret data. The contrast between Temple and Harvard is a kind of shorthand that functions as an enthymeme: Because we already know something of the reputation Harvard has for quality, we are probably willing to complete the association in our minds and accept Painter's assertion that she wrote a "decent dissertation" and that she has the qualifications to be hired as a beginning assistant professor at Penn.

The first act of the narrative functions strategically. The story gains and holds our attention because characters emerge, because they act through dialogue, and because there is rising action, increasing tension and suspense. In effect, the story dramatizes the issue. If readers persist through the fourth sentence, they are likely to continue through the sixth paragraph, which ends the first act of the narrative. Moreover, the example also personalizes the opposing opinion in the voice of a resentful white male, someone with whom some readers are likely to identify and empathize. The narrative refutes that opinion, but it has been presented in a way that makes the reader understand why some might believe that affirmative action policies produce reverse discrimination. In other words, the narrative has gained and held attention, laid out the opposing view, and refuted it with a single example, the narrator.

Structurally, the second act of the narrative begins in paragraph 7 with a second real, extended example, but the expectations created in the first act of the narrative are fulfilled here. The movement between the first and second acts of the narrative is chronological: The first encounter happened in the past; the second occurs in the present. The setting also changes: The first encounter happened in Philadelphia; the second takes place in Chapel Hill, North Carolina. This second act of the narrative is also a matter of evidence and strategy. It is easy for issues of affirmative action to divide audiences of men and women, of African Americans and whites. The first act of the narrative illustrates the potential conflicts along ethnic and gender lines. Painter has identified herself as African American and female, and based on that example alone, it would be easy to misinterpret this rhetorical act as an attack on white men by a nonwhite woman. She tries to avoid that impression, although she may not be completely successful, by treating the white man quite sympathetically.

Painter attempts to broaden the argument and enlarge her audience. The characters in this second example are "black Carolina undergraduates," whose views of affirmative action are also negative. Painter says:

> One young woman surprised me by deploring affirmative action. I wondered why. "White students and professors think we only got into the University of North Carolina because we're black," she complained, "and they don't believe we're truly qualified." She said that she knew that she was qualified and fully deserved to be at Carolina. She fulfilled all the regular admissions requirements. It was the stigma of affirmative action that bothered her; without it other students wouldn't assume she was unqualified. (7)

Another student extends that problem to nonwhite faculty, arguing that "without affirmative action, students would assume black faculty to be as good as white" (8). Once again, the narrative sets out an argument that must be answered and disproved if the author is to achieve her purpose. The argument is cause–effect. The effect is a "stigma," a word for a blemish or a taint, that here refers to assumptions by whites that African American students aren't qualified and to assumptions by students that African American professors don't measure up to their white counterparts.

Paragraph 9 is an internal summary and a transition between the two examples, or the introduction, and the body of the essay. It pulls the two examples together, but it respects distinctions between the whites and African Americans and the men and women in the audiences she is addressing. Whites like the man in the first example assume she has an unfair advantage; she doesn't think nonwhites have ever expressed that view to her. She recognizes that some African Americans think women like her have it easier, but she disagrees. African American students like those in the second example all know that they are fully qualified; it is only others who need the help of affirmative action. In other words, as she sums it up, "No one, not blacks, not whites, benefits from affirmative action, or so it would seem" (9). And that is the central issue Painter addresses in the essay: Do qualified women and minorities—like her, like the Carolina undergraduate students—benefit from or need affirmative action as a means of entry into higher education, into good jobs?

The body of the essay, which begins with paragraph 10 and runs through paragraph 14, offers Painter's answer to that question. It is not presented in narrative form, but it provides other types of supporting material that we shall examine shortly. As we explained when discussing purpose, in this second part of the body, Painter attempts to explain the benefits of affirmative action. In one sense, the structure here is inductive. That is, Painter employs two specific examples to illustrate the general conclusion that affirmative action is beneficial. Those examples also will be discussed shortly.

The structure of the body is a form of logical organization, best characterized as problem–solution. Painter first explains the nature of the problem, overt discrimination against women and ethnic minorities. Before affirmative action, she says, "No one said out loud that women and minorities were simply and naturally inferior to white men, but the assumptions were as clear as day: Whites are better than blacks; men are better than women" (11). Affirmative action is the solution to that problem. Painter says; "Since then, the civil rights movement and the feminist movement have created a new climate that permitted affirmative action, which, in turn, opened areas previously reserved for white men" (14).

The conclusion of the essay is brief. It consists of paragraph 15. As we explained earlier, there Painter clearly identifies the subgroups in the empirical audience that make up her target audiences. Those subgroups are exemplified by what she calls "my Philadelphia white man and my Carolina black women" (15). In addition, the conclusion also includes Painter's attack on the Reagan administration's "proposed dismantling of affirmative action" (15), which grows naturally from her justification for that policy.

Supporting Material

Painter employs several types of supporting material, or evidence, to bolster her claims. The first to appear in the essay are the two real, extended examples, which we described earlier and which function as the two acts of the narrative. How those extended examples are intended to influence Painter's audience was explained in our discussion of structure.

Three other examples appear in the second part of the body of the essay. All three are used to demonstrate the need for affirmative action. The first is that of Painter's experiences as a student prior to affirmative action. She says:

Well, I have [been helped by affirmative action], but not in the early 1960s when I was an undergraduate in a large state university. Back then, there was no affirmative action. We applied for admission to the university like everyone else; we were accepted or rejected like everyone else. Graduate and undergraduate students together, we numbered about 200 in a student body of nearly 30,000. No preferential treatment there. (10)

The statistical supporting material, which appears at the end of this example, is designed to demonstrate what conditions were like for students prior to affirmative action. It appeals to the portion of her target audience exemplified by the female, African American students at the University of North Carolina.

Later, Painter applies her experience to other members of the target audience as well. Although these African American undergraduate and graduate students had met all regular admission requirements, she writes that

[W]e all knew what the rest of the university thought of us, professors especially. They thought we were stupid because we were black. Further, white women were considered frivolous students; they were only supposed to be in school to get husbands. . . . Black students, the whole atmosphere said, would not attend graduate or professional school because their grades were poor. Women had no business in postgraduate education because they would waste their training by dropping out of careers when they married or became pregnant. No one said out loud that women and minorities were simply and naturally inferior to white men, but the assumptions were as clear as day: Whites are better than blacks; men are better than women. (11)

This relatively long, extended example is part of the "history lesson" we mentioned when we discussed Painter's persona earlier. As such, its force or ability to influence her readers comes from Painter's qualifications as a historian. Not only did she personally experience conditions for students prior to affirmative action, but also her standing as a historian qualifies her to describe those conditions in a general sense.

Painter's own professional experiences and career provide a second, relatively brief, real example. She says, "I'm black and female, yet I was hired by two history departments that had no black members before the late '60s, never mind females. Affirmative action cleared the way" (12). Later she adds, "Without affirmative action, it never would have occurred to any large, white research university to consider me for professional employment, despite my degree, languages, publications, charm, grace, *despite* my qualifications" (14). This example also draws its persuasive force from Painter's persona, which established her "qualifications." That a person of her professional stature would not have been hired by major universities without affirmative action justifies that policy.

An additional example is that of the professional career of John Hope Franklin. Painter writes:

> Thirty-five years ago, John Hope Franklin, then a star student, now a giant in the field of American history, received a doctorate in history from Harvard. He went to teach in a black college. In those days, black men taught in black colleges. White women taught in white women's colleges. Black women taught in black women's colleges. None taught at the University of Pennsylvania or the University of North Carolina. It was the way things were. (13)

This example draws its force from Franklin's character and professional accomplishments. So in case readers are unfamiliar with him, Painter reveals that he was a "star student" who became "a giant in the field of American history." Significantly, Franklin's case precedes affirmative action and demonstrates that without that legislation, even the most highly qualified individuals suffered employment discrimination. Thus, the case of Franklin is an *a fortiori* example: If it is true in the case of "a giant in the field of American history," then it must certainly happen to most others as well. That is important strategically. Because Painter offers only these three examples of employment discrimination, her essay is open to the charge that these are isolated examples that do not reflect what usually takes place. Her careful development of her credibility as a historian is designed to erode that charge; she can be trusted to relate historical facts accurately without misinterpretation. And the *a fortiori* example is intended to refute the charge completely: If this happened to the highly qualified John Hope Franklin, then, without affirmative action, every qualified person who was not a white male faced such discrimination.

Other Strategies

Painter employs language strategically in several instances. One is her use of synecdoche, a figure of speech in which a part stands for the whole. Explaining the effects of affirmative action, she says, "Skirts and dark skins appeared in new settings in the 1970s" (14). She could as easily have said "women and African Americans" instead. But the phrase "skirts and dark skins" makes the passage more vivid.

Metaphor also adds vividness to the essay. At the end, Painter says, "If they [the Reagan administration] achieve their stated goals, we will have the same old discrimination, unneedful of new clothes" (15). "New clothes" is a metaphor for opposition to affirmative action and charges of reverse discrimination, which, according to Painter, only mask "the same old white-male-superiority line" (15). In her view, they are "convictions older than affirmative action" (15), which have simply been "fixed up to fit conditions that include a policy called affirmative action" (15). The metaphor helps to enliven the idea, and may even function as an allusion to "a wolf in sheep's clothing."

Irony is also employed in the essay. In passages already explained, it is certainly ironic that highly qualified individuals such as John Hope Franklin and Painter herself faced discriminatory attitudes and practices. At the end of the essay, the irony of what Painter sees as continuing racism and sexism is clear. She says, "My Philadelphia white man and my Carolina black women would be surprised to discover the convergence of their views. I doubt that they know that their convictions are older than affirmative action. I wish I could take them back to the early '60s and let them see that they're reciting the same old white-male-superiority line" (15). That members of her target audience, especially African American women, would adopt such a position is clearly ironic. That irony again contributes to the vividness of the essay, helps account for Painter's reactions to the people she encounters in the narrative, and perhaps also injects a tone of sadness.

Finally, the passage just quoted also includes a strategy of labeling. Painter says that the attitudes of the man in Philadelphia and the African American women in North Carolina are "the same old white-male-superiority line" (15) that existed before affirmative action. The label casts those attitudes in the most negative light possible. Moreover, the label reinforces the conclusions we drew earlier regarding target audiences. Members of the Reagan administration and their strongly conservative supporters would likely be alienated and angered by the label. In contrast, members of the target audiences would likely wish to avoid holding the attitudes that Painter labels so negatively. Thus, the label also provides a created audience strategy, inviting them to view themselves as individuals who shun "white-male-superiority" or who perhaps even feel guilty for holding those attitudes, and thus choose to end their opposition to affirmative action.

Descriptive analysis has put us in possession of this piece of rhetoric in a very detailed way; this analysis has identified and explained all the rhetorically significant aspects of Painter's essay. As a result of the analysis, critics are ready to move on to the second stage of the critical process and place the essay within its historical context. In Chapter Three, we explain historical–contextual analysis and illustrate that stage in the critical process by applying it to Painter's essay. Moreover, descriptive analysis has also provided the evidence needed to consider what critical perspective or system might be most appropriate when the critical process advances to the third stage, which we discuss in Chapter Four.

WORKS CITED

Black, Edwin. "The Second Persona." *Quarterly Journal of Speech* 56 (April 1970): 109–119.

Scott, Robert L., and Donald K. Smith. "The Rhetoric of Confrontation." *Quarterly Journal of Speech* 55 (February 1969): 1–8.

Wander, Philip. "The Third Persona: An Ideological Turn in Rhetorical Theory." *Central States Speech Journal* 35 (Winter 1984): 197–216.

RECOMMENDED READINGS

Several published essays illustrate the use of careful descriptive analysis. These include:

Black, Edwin. "Ideological Justifications." *Quarterly Journal of Speech* 70 (1984): 144–150. An editorial published in the *New York Times* is subjected to textual analysis.

Slagell, Amy R. "Anatomy of a Masterpiece: A Close Textual Analysis of Abraham Lincoln's Second Inaugural Address." *Communication Studies* 42 (1991): 155–171. A thorough explication of Lincoln's famous speech.

Stelzner, Hermann. " 'War Message,' December 8, 1941: An Approach to Language," *Quarterly Journal of Speech* 33 (November 1966): 419–437. Using historical data and close textual analysis, Stelzner brings to our attention the artistic choices Franklin Roosevelt made in what initially appears to be a relatively simple, straightforward report on the attack on Pearl Harbor.

CHAPTER THREE

Historical–Contextual Analysis: The Second Stage of Criticism

As we indicated in Chapter One, rhetorical acts do not come into existence or work to influence in isolation. Instead, they are a product of, and function within, a particular historical context. Rhetoric is *practical* because rhetors are motivated to speak or write by events and circumstances that they encounter. Their rhetoric is intended to resolve some problem or gap between personal or societal goals or values and existing structures, procedures, or conditions. Rhetoric is also *public* because it is addressed to a particular audience or audiences. The problems to be resolved through rhetorical action require the concerted effort of both the rhetor and the audiences. Thus, critics cannot adequately judge or evaluate rhetorical acts without understanding the historical context in which they occur. That understanding is the product of the second stage of rhetorical criticism. In this chapter, we discuss historical–contextual analysis and illustrate this stage of the process by illuminating the historical context of Nell Irvin Painter's essay.

Unlike the first stage, descriptive analysis, which is almost entirely intrinsic and organic, the second stage of criticism examines elements extrinsic to the discourse: the context and the occasion. Remember that any rhetorical act is a rhetor's effort to persuade audiences to view events and issues in a particular way. The "vision of reality" presented in the rhetorical act is the author's. Careful critics should consult sources outside the text to form their own conclusions about those events and issues. That is not to say that rhetors always distort issues, or that evaluating the "truth" of a rhetor's vision of reality is the sole function of criticism.[1] Nevertheless, criticism that accepts the rhetor's vision of reality, without comparing it to the views of others, is heavily biased in favor of the rhetor and may be seriously flawed for that reason.

In the second stage, critics consult external sources in search of information about the historical–cultural context, the rhetor, the audiences exposed to the act, and the persuasive forces, including other rhetoric, operating in that scene. Only when that task is completed can critics begin to determine why the rhetor made particular choices about tone, purpose, persona, structure, supporting materials, and strategies discovered and explained in the descriptive stage of the critical process. Indeed, as we pointed out in Chapter Two, sometimes tentative conclusions about a rhetorical act formed during the descriptive analysis stage must be modified as a result of new information discovered in the second stage of criticism.

THE RHETORICAL PROBLEM

The extrinsic elements that influence and sometimes limit the rhetor's choices constitute what we call the *rhetorical problem* faced by the rhetor.[2] In this second stage the critic does not try to recreate the rhetorical event but rather looks at it in a rhetorical way as an artistic, strategic attempt to respond to a particular set of circumstances. In order to understand and evaluate that attempt, the critic needs to understand the barriers, the limitations, and the sources of resistance that might prevent the act from achieving its ends. The rhetorical problem is an "umbrella concept" that covers all the obstacles that prevent the rhetorical act from accomplishing its intended purpose immediately and easily. These elements can include the historical–cultural context, the rhetors themselves, the audience or audiences, and other persuasive forces operating in the context. We must note that these elements usually are not independent of each other. Rather, they interact and influence one another to make up the rhetorical problem.

---

[1]Chapter Five suggests several criteria for evaluating rhetorical acts. The "truth criterion" is only one of them.

[2]The concept of "rhetorical problem" is borrowed from Karlyn Kohrs Campbell, *The Rhetorical Act,* 2d ed. (Belmont, CA: Wadsworth, 1995) 55–174.

Historical–Cultural Context

To interpret a rhetorical act, critics need information about the context in which the act occurred, including the particular events that motivated the rhetor to engage in rhetorical action and also the particular occasion, which may entail audience expectations about the function of an act and about what choices are appropriate to it. In other words, the act may be part of a particular genre or type of discourse, such as a eulogy for a person who has died, an apologia to defend oneself against accusations of misconduct, or a nomination acceptance address for some political office. Members of the audience may be so familiar with the type of occasion in general that they come to expect rhetorical acts that function in a particular way. Successful rhetors meet those general audience expectations and yet adapt their rhetoric to the specific occasion or issue. For example, the essay by Nell Irvin Painter, which we analyzed descriptively in Chapter Two, appeared in the "Hers" column that was then published regularly in the *New York Times* (and now appears in the *New York Times Magazine*). Readers of "Hers" expect the pieces to be editorial in nature and to address issues of particular interest to women, usually from a feminist perspective. Moreover, some event or occurrence motivated Painter to address the issue of affirmative action. Understanding the specific occasion or issue and discovering audience expectations are important parts of the second stage of criticism for Painter's essay and other rhetorical acts as well. However, the specific occasion or issue and the audience expectations for that particular occasion are only the narrow context for the rhetorical act. Critics should examine context in a broader sense as well.

Context also includes the cultural milieu and the climate of opinion in which a rhetorical act appears. Those factors develop over time and can exert a powerful influence over both the rhetor's motivation for engaging in rhetorical action and how members of the audience receive the rhetorical act. For that reason, critics must discover the place of the discourse in an ongoing dialogue about some issue. Because the rhetor's aim or purpose is to enlist the aid of the target audiences to influence that issue, a primary function of the second stage of criticism is to define or explain the issue. In so doing, critics seek answers to questions such as: What events preceded or followed the rhetorical act that focused public attention on the issue discussed or that made its claims more or less credible? Is the issue one that has been discussed over a period of years so there is resistance to additional rhetoric about it? Are there slogans that have polarized the audiences so it is hard to take a fresh position or to reach those on one or the other side? What are the social, political, and economic pressures on the rhetor and the members of the audience? What are the costs of responding to the rhetor's appeal? Is acceptance likely to produce ridicule or loss of status, position, votes, or other support? How is the issue related to deeply held cultural values—such as the commitments to free enterprise, equality of opportunity, conspicuous consumption as a sign of success, and so on? Answering questions such as these leads critics beyond the narrow context into the wider context for the rhetorical act.

Of course, the enlarged context can be virtually unending. The history of many issues that are the subject of contemporary rhetorical action can be traced for years, if not decades. For example, the issue Painter addresses, affirmative action, is a direct outgrowth of the civil rights movement of the 1950s and 1960s. The civil rights movement itself can be traced back to efforts to improve the quality of life for African Americans following the end of slavery in the United States in the 19th century. And those efforts, in turn, can be traced back decades further to the movement to abolish slavery. Those subjects are of great interest to rhetorical historians. But rhetorical critics must draw a line somewhere; recounting in detail the history of slavery in the United States, the abolition movement, emancipation, the civil rights movement, *and* affirmative action is unnecessary for understanding and evaluating Painter's essay.

Where, then, should critics draw the line? That is a matter of judgment. We believe the best way to make that judgment is to rely on the text. When critics complete the descriptive analysis in the first stage of the critical process, the rhetorical act itself should suggest what historical–cultural material is relevant. Whereas historians may examine rhetorical acts in order to illuminate historical events, critics examine historical events in order to illuminate rhetorical acts. At the end of the descriptive analysis phase, critics should have at least an initial idea of what historical information is needed in order to understand the rhetorical act in question. Of course, as we indicated earlier, critics must turn to sources external to the rhetorical act to gather the necessary historical–cultural information. As the second stage progresses, critics may modify their initial conclusions about what historical information is necessary. But beginning with the text keeps the rhetorical act itself at the center of the critical process. It also provides critics with a reliable starting point for judging where to draw the line with regard to historical–cultural analysis of the rhetorical problem.

Rhetor/Author

A rhetorical act does not blossom on its own. It is created and delivered by someone, and, thus, part of its meaning originates from the character of the rhetor or author. The association between act and rhetor/author is important because the character, credibility, or ethos of the rhetor can be a significant persuasive influence. In Chapter Two, we discussed the role or persona of the rhetor, which is created by the rhetorical act itself, and how that persona functions to enhance the rhetor's ethos. In the second stage, critics turn to external sources for similar information, independent of the rhetorical act. In some cases, the search requires discovering biographical information about the rhetor or data about the author. But again, critics must concentrate on understanding and evaluating the rhetorical act. Although biographical information is sometimes useful in fulfilling that goal, writing a full-blown biography of the rhetor is not the aim.

Instead, critics try to discover information about the history of the author or the rhetor's actual experience, knowledge, and prior rhetorical actions relevant to understanding the rhetorical act under consideration. Is the rhetor generally recognized as an expert on this subject? What statements made by the rhetor in the past limit his or her choices in this case? What associations or relationships—such as financial interests, constituency, ideology, ambitions, and the like—influence the rhetor's or author's choices? With what other issues and causes is the rhetor or author associated? Does the rhetorical act represent the rhetor's own thinking, or is it the product of speechwriters or an organization? Answering questions such as these can help reveal the relationship between the rhetor or source and the overall rhetorical problem.

For example, descriptive analysis of Painter's essay revealed that persona and ethos are particularly important elements in that rhetorical act. The persona Painter adopted grew out of her personal experiences, both as a student and as a university professor. Thus, biographical information about those aspects of Painter's life is important for understanding the rhetorical problem.

Audience

At this stage, critics are concerned with discovering as much information as possible about those actually exposed to the discourse, the empirical audience, as well as those specifically targeted by the rhetor. The medium (television, radio, print, live presentation, and so on) through which the audience members participated in the rhetorical situation is important in determining the characteristics of the actual audience or audiences. Whether or not that medium allowed the rhetor or source to reach the target audiences is important.

Whether a given audience was exposed to the entire discourse, excerpts, an edited version, or merely a commentary about it is also important. The attitudes and beliefs of the audience members—

discovered through demographic research on age, occupation, political affiliation, cultural experience and expectations, education, interests, economic status, and social class—affect their attitudes toward the rhetor and the issue and provide insights into the rhetor's choice of persuasive strategies. The audience members' degree of involvement with the issue and their feelings—apathy, ignorance, hostility, or the like—toward the issue, the rhetor or source, and the purpose of the discourse are also particularly relevant.

For example, because Painter's rhetorical act appeared in the *New York Times,* the empirical audience was limited initially to readers of that newspaper. Demographic information about those readers, if available, would help critics understand that empirical audience. Further, because our descriptive analysis of Painter's essay suggested particular target audiences, demographic information about readers of the *New York Times* should reveal whether the medium Painter selected allowed her to reach those target audiences. Moreover, because affirmative action has been an issue of public interest for some time, information should also be available to determine the beliefs and attitudes of audience members toward the issue, at least in a general sense.

Competing Persuasive Forces

Closely related to the historical–cultural context are competing persuaders and alternative policies and positions. Thorough critics determine what information about the issue was generally disseminated through influential media and consider whether and how the rhetor dealt with alternative policies and opponents. They also discover what groups are in conflict with the rhetor's position and what groups are associated with it. In addition, critics consider whether rhetors or sources attempt to associate with, or dissociate themselves and their position from, other groups or causes and try to discover possible reasons. The influence of competing persuaders on the audiences is of potentially great importance. Policies proposed by powerful groups are more likely to be accepted because they have the means to generate large amounts of supportive discourse and to disseminate their views widely. Policies such groups oppose have a smaller chance of success as do policies advocated by the less advantaged in the society.

Again, our descriptive analysis of Painter's essay suggested the primary competing persuaders: the Reagan administration and its conservative supporters. Examining their rhetorical attacks on the policy of affirmative action, and the influence of those attacks on members of the audience, is important for understanding the rhetorical problem Painter faced.

In summary, in the second stage of criticism, critics explicate the rhetorical problem faced by the author of the rhetorical act. In so doing, they turn to extrinsic sources to examine both the broad and narrow historical–cultural contexts, the source, the audiences, and the influence of competing persuaders. Although those elements are easy to enumerate individually, we must emphasize that they are often difficult to separate in practice. They are closely related, and the rhetorical problem is a product of their influence on one another. For example, public opinion about affirmative action is a significant aspect of the historical–cultural context for Painter's essay. But those opinions are also potentially significant characteristics of Painter's audiences and are at least partly the result of competing persuasive influences. Thus, critics must choose where and how to discuss those opinions in the second stage of criticism. Ultimately, the heading under which they are discussed is not as important as the discussion itself.

Supporting Materials

The second stage of criticism is also an appropriate time for critics to test the validity, adequacy, and credibility of the supporting evidence employed in the rhetorical act: How accurate are the citations? What sources are used? Are sources indicated? Are the supporting materials cited typical of the available data? During this stage of the critical process critics should consider all the tests applicable for the particular types of evidence.

Generally, all supporting material can be subjected to tests of relevance, verifiability, consistency, timeliness, and bias. In determining *relevance,* critics ask how well the supporting material is linked to the claim: Is the evidence actually relevant to the point being made? The *verifiability* of supporting material depends on whether the rhetor provides sources for the evidence. Ideally, rhetors provide enough information about their sources that critics or audience members can examine those sources to verify the authenticity of the evidence. *Consistency* is both internal and external. In determining internal consistency, critics ask whether the supporting evidence, as it appears in the rhetorical act, is consistent with itself. In other words, does the material contradict itself? External consistency can be determined only by comparing the evidence with prevalent research in the subject area and by examining the original source from which the rhetor took the supporting material. Thus, external consistency depends on verifiability. Critics ask whether the supporting material carries the same meaning in the original source that it appears to carry in the rhetorical act. In other words, is the supporting material taken out of context? *Timeliness* is especially important for issues that are "time-bound"—that is, for issues that change with time. Rhetors usually do not need to employ supporting material that is "hot off the press," but the supporting material must be recent enough to reflect the "current reality" of the issue being addressed. In determining *bias,* critics try to discover the motive the sources had for providing the supporting material. Sources closely associated with any issue may have a vested interest in how others view that issue; in short, they are rhetors themselves. Sometimes, that vested interest is so great that it produces a "disqualifying bias," which casts suspicion on supporting material taken from that source. However, the best sources of information on most subjects—authorities— are also those most closely associated with an issue. That association alone does not guarantee bias.

Aside from these general tests of supporting material, authority evidence and statistics can be subjected to additional tests. Because authority evidence draws its persuasive influence from the expertise and character of its originator, critics examine the credentials of that source. What are the source's qualifications? Is that person truly an "expert" on the issue being addressed? In examining statistical supporting material, critics try to discover the conditions under which the data were collected, the method of their collection, and the statistical manipulations to which they were subjected. Faulty statistical methods result in untrustworthy statistical data.

Supporting material that passes all these tests would be ideal, but in practice, few rhetorical acts include ideal supporting material. That is not necessarily a result of a rhetor's dishonesty. For example, speakers are seldom allowed adequate time to document fully the sources for all their supporting material. And even experienced, honest, and talented rhetors can be misled by their own sources; sometimes rhetors make honest mistakes.

Moreover, some rhetorical acts include very little supporting material. In Painter's essay, for example, our descriptive analysis revealed that, aside from examples drawn from her personal experience, Painter employed only one other example and a single piece of statistical evidence. Other rhetorical acts, such as eulogies and presidential inaugurals, may use even less supporting material or even use unconventional supporting material in unconventional ways. Thus, to expect all rhetorical acts to pass a rigid set of tests for supporting evidence would be unreasonable. Although we acknowledge the potential importance of careful analysis of supporting material, most public discourse does not conform to rigid standards of proof and logic. In such cases, other methods of examination and evaluation, which we discuss in Chapter Five, must be applied.

HISTORICAL–CONTEXTUAL ANALYSIS APPLIED

To illustrate historical–contextual analysis, we return to Nell Irvin Painter's essay, "Whites Say I Must Be on Easy Street." In this second stage of our criticism of Painter's work, we shall explain the rhetorical problem the rhetor faced. To do so, we turn to external sources to gather information about the historical–cultural context, the rhetor, the audiences, competing persuasive forces, and supporting material.

Historical–Cultural Context

The narrow context of Painter's essay, those events that immediately motivated her rhetorical action, is a matter of speculation. The text suggests that a series of encounters with peers and students, such as the two conversations she described in the introduction, may have provided the immediate motivation. But as we will explain shortly, Painter's interest in civil rights and affirmative action was not new. Further, her essay was published on December 10, 1981, near the end of Ronald Reagan's first year as president. Given Reagan's opposition to affirmative action, which we discuss later, his election and policies undoubtedly contributed to Painter's immediate motivation for rhetorical action.

In a broader sense, the issue Painter addresses—how the public should view the federal policy called affirmative action—has captured attention for years. According to Susan D. Clayton and Faye J. Crosby, "a glance at any newspaper reveals that affirmative action is currently one of the most controversial policies in the United States. The issues are complex, they stir strong feelings, and in the media everyone seems to have an opinion on the topic" (1). Yet despite the controversy, the issue remains unresolved. As James E. Jones, Jr., explains: "The modern debate over affirmative action has occupied us for over 20 years without achieving resolution of the underlying issues or contributing to clarification of what divides the nation" (346). Thus, the context in which Painter's essay occurred cannot be understood without first examining the origin and aims of affirmative action.

Authorities credit President Lyndon Johnson with initiating the policy. Title VII of the 1964 Civil Rights Act, which became law during Johnson's administration, contained what was probably the first legally significant reference to affirmative action. Clayton and Crosby say, "Section 706(g) [of Title VII] states that a court may order 'such affirmative action as may be appropriate' following a finding of intentional or nonaccidental discrimination. Title VII also specifies the means by which to enforce the new regulations, setting up the Equal Employment Opportunity Commission" (13).

The 1964 Civil Rights Act was intended to end the brutal effects of "intentional or nonaccidental discrimination," what most experts call "overt racism" when directed toward ethnic minorities. The aim was to promote equal opportunity through "race-neutral" policies. However, Johnson augmented the Civil Rights Act with two Executive Orders intended to go beyond ensuring equal opportunity. In September, 1965, he issued Executive Order 11246, which, according to Clayton and Crosby, "required any organization that had a contract with the federal government to take affirmative action to ensure the just treatment of employees, and potential employees, of all races, colors, religions, or national origin. . . . The order was amended to prohibit sex discrimination in 1967 with Executive Order 11375" (13–14). In 1972, these Executive Orders were amended again to apply to educational institutions (Washington and Harvey 9).

These changes were significant because they shifted the emphasis from promoting equal opportunity to redressing the effects of past discrimination. As Clayton and Crosby argue:

> Affirmative action refers to positive measures taken to remedy the effects of past discrimination against certain groups. Where a policy of equal opportunity requires merely that employers and institutions not discriminate on the basis of group membership, and in fact encourages them to ignore characteristics of group membership, affirmative action mandates a consideration of race, ethnicity, and gender. (2–3)

Because both ethnic minorities and women were victims of overt discrimination in the past, proponents of affirmative action argued that these new policies, which gave those groups special consideration, were necessary to attain genuine equality. In other words, because ethnic minorities and women were for so long relegated to low-wage, low-status, second-class positions in education and the workplace, racism and sexism had become "institutionalized" and thus could not be ameliorated through "equal opportunity" alone. Affirmative action was intended to combat institutionalized racism and sexism.

Institutionalized racism and sexism persist despite efforts to guarantee equal opportunity. Gertrude Ezorsky explains that "institutional racism can occur when employees are selected through personal connections or by qualifying for certain requirements or seniority standards. These procedures are intrinsically free of race prejudice, and they exist in areas where no blacks reside. Nevertheless, these institutional procedures perpetuate the effects of overt racism" (2). Studies indicate that "communicating job information to family, friends, neighbors, and acquaintances by word of mouth is probably the most widely used recruitment method," Ezorsky says. Thus, because they lack "ties to whites as family, friends, fellow students, neighbors, or club members, blacks tend to be isolated from the networks in which connections to desirable employment—where whites predominate— are forged" (15). Moreover, because of overt racism and sexism, ethnic minorities and women were frequently excluded from training programs that would prepare them for more desirable employment. Likewise, supposedly neutral policies, such as "last hired, first fired," perpetuate discrimination; because of overt racism and sexism in the past, ethnic minorities and women were often "last hired" and "first fired" (Ezorsky 10).

In higher education, the area of greatest interest for Painter, the history of both overt and institutionalized racism and sexism is similar. For decades, overt racism excluded ethnic minorities from the most desirable academic positions. According to Valora Washington and William Harvey, "before World War II, Hispanics and African Americans were virtually invisible in higher education." They go on to point out that even acquiring the necessary qualifications was no guarantee of employment in predominantly white institutions: "Even by 1936, there was a sizable group of African Americans with Ph.D.s, 80 percent of whom taught at three historically African-American institutions (Atlanta, Fisk, and Howard Universities)" (iii). The percentage of university faculty who are ethnic minorities has been consistently small for decades. Washington and Harvey conclude:

> By 1972—the year affirmative action in higher education was initiated—African Americans represented 2.9 percent of all faculty (including those at historically African-American universities). Other minority groups (including Hispanics, but not Asians) were 2.8 percent of the total faculty. There were only 1,500 faculty who could be identified as Mexican American or Chicano. (iii–iv)

In academia, as in employment generally, efforts to ensure equal opportunity were unable to overcome institutionalized racism. Traditional hiring processes, Washington and Harvey explain, "did not entail specific guidelines for posting announcements, advertising, interviewing, or extending offers. Personal connections, associations, and friendships constitute what is called the 'old boy system,' which was the mechanism through which vacant faculty positions were likely to be filled" (12). In addition, supposedly race-neutral employment policies were again subverted. For example, "an important race-neutral qualification standard in the academic marketplace is published research," Ezorsky says. "Publication requirements, however, worked against the recruitment of black professors because the majority taught heavy course loads in predominantly black colleges, which limited their time for research and writing" (22).

Affirmative action was intended to ameliorate the effects of institutionalized racism by filling the gaps in "race-neutral," equal opportunity programs. According to Ezorsky, "the primary importance of affirmative action lies in its effectiveness as a remedy for institutional racism, by which race-neutral policies and practices can lead to the exclusion of blacks" (2). On one level, the aim of affirmative action was to improve the economic conditions of ethnic minorities and women. But a larger aim was to help eliminate racism and sexism. As Clayton and Crosby explain: "On a deeper level, however, [affirmative action] also responds to a psychological and sociological condition, which is the perception that members of these groups are second-class citizens in the United States. It is hoped that affirmative action will eliminate the social barriers by eliminating the financial ones" (3–4).

Results have been mixed. On one hand, Clayton and Crosby believe that "both the decreased extent of gender discrimination and the increased sensitivity toward gender issues can be linked to our nation's policy of affirmative action" (11). On the other hand, the authors also argue that "women in America confront an unfair disadvantage in the marketplace. Being female serves both to restrict career choice and to handicap economic potential. Sex segregation is pervasive in the work force, with women largely excluded from the more prestigious and high-paying jobs" (9).

In academia, Washington and Harvey report that in 1972–1973, when affirmative action requirements were applied to colleges and universities, "African Americans comprised 2.9 percent of all college and university faculty." By 1976, after four years of affirmative action, "African Americans were 4.4 percent of all faculty" yet they remained "heavily concentrated in historically African-American institutions." But in 1979, seven years after affirmative action, and just two years before Painter's essay was published, "African Americans were still 4.4 percent of the full-time faculty in the nation" (p. 7). Apparently, the aim of diversifying college and university faculties remains elusive.

The mixed results of affirmative action are reflected in public attitudes toward the policy. Clayton and Crosby report the results of a recent survey:

> Among white respondents, 52 percent believed that affirmative action programs had helped blacks to get better job opportunities, and only 10 percent said they had hurt; the percentages among black respondents were slightly more neutral, with only 45 percent feeling

that affirmative action had helped but only 5 percent thinking it had hurt. Thus 38 percent of whites and 50 percent of blacks felt that affirmative action had made no difference. Asked if current government efforts to help blacks get better job opportunities had gone too far, 31 percent of whites and only 13 percent of blacks answered affirmatively. (21)

As these figures indicate, because the policy of affirmative action is intended to address the emotion-laden issues of racism and sexism, and because the results have been mixed, affirmative action continues to generate controversy. Although that controversy is an important aspect of the historical–cultural context for Painter's essay, we believe it is best examined in greater depth later, as a characteristic of Painter's audiences.

Rhetor/Author

Descriptive analysis demonstrated that persona is an important element in Painter's essay. That persona is based upon Painter's own experiences as an African American woman, both as a student and as a university professor. Thus, biographical information about Painter's academic career is important for understanding how persona functions in her essay.

Painter's academic credentials as a student are impressive. According to Nancy Elizabeth Fitch, Painter received her undergraduate degree in anthropology from the University of California at Berkeley in 1964, an M.A. from the University of California, Los Angeles, in 1967, and a Ph.D. in history from Harvard University in 1974. In addition, in 1962–1963, Painter studied at the University of Bordeaux in France, and in 1965–1966 at the University of Ghana (379).

Painter's career as a professor is equally impressive. Fitch reports that Painter taught at the University of Pennsylvania from 1974 through 1980. During that time she was also a resident associate of Afro-American studies at the W. E. B. Du Bois Institute at Harvard, 1977–1978. From 1980 through 1988, Painter taught at the University of North Carolina at Chapel Hill, and in 1989 she began teaching at Princeton University. In 1991 Painter was appointed Edwards Professor of American History at Princeton, the position she currently holds (379).

Fitch comments that "Painter herself has said that she is more researcher than teacher" (379). Her contributions as a scholar have earned her numerous awards. *Who's Who Among Black Americans* reports that Painter was awarded a John Simon Guggenheim Foundation fellowship in 1982–1983. In 1988–1989 she was a fellow of the

Center for Advanced Study in the Behavioral Sciences. She received a Peterson Fellowship from the American Antiquarian Society in 1991 and a fellowship from the National Endowment for the Humanities in 1992–1993. She is the author of over 30 publications and 18 reviews and review essays (1127). According to Fitch, "her books have been critically reviewed and include *Exodusters: Black Migration to Kansas after Reconstruction* (1977), *The Narrative of Hosea Hudson: His Life as a Negro Communist in the South* (1979), and *Standing at Armageddon* (1987)" (379). Moreover, Painter was National Director of the Association of Black Women Historians, 1982–1984; she was on the executive board of the Organization of American Historians, 1984–1987; and she was a member of the National Council of the American Studies Association, 1989–1992 (*Who's Who Among Black Americans* 1127).

Painter's experiences as an African American woman influenced her career from the beginning. "She became interested in history," Fitch explains, "because she found inadequate treatment of race and race relations in the United States in American textbooks and wanted to correct that situation." Fitch goes on to say that Painter "has been part of the recent discussion on multiculturalism on American campuses and has said that, if people remembered the past condition of college and university campuses, 'they would hesitate before assailing the attempt to forge a pedagogy appropriate for newly diversified student bodies and faculties'" (379).

Because of her background, it is not surprising that Painter was motivated to publish her essay, "Whites Say I Must Be on Easy Street," yet her personal experiences both contribute to her rhetorical problem and provide her with resources to overcome that problem and influence her audiences. On one hand, because Painter is an African American woman, readers would expect her to support affirmative action. That is, because she is a member of a group protected by the policy, readers might dismiss her essay as biased. In that way, her background contributes to her rhetorical problem. On the other hand, her background as a historian could enhance her credibility on historical issues related to affirmative action. And her personal experiences provide vivid examples to influence her readers.

Audience

As we indicated earlier, the policy of affirmative action continues to generate controversy. Because of the emotion-laden issues involved, racism and sexism, because resolving those issues addresses traditional values of fairness and equality, and because affirmative action potentially affects nearly everyone in the areas of education and employment, many individuals hold strong opinions about the policy.

Clayton and Crosby argue that "demographic characteristics can predict attitudes toward affirmative action. Not surprisingly, women, nonwhites, younger people, and Democrats show more support for affirmative action" (23). Presumably, then, men, whites, older people, and non-Democrats show less support for the policy. Because attitudes held by those groups of people influence how they might receive Painter's essay, the "ideal" audience, those disposed to be most receptive to her message, would be composed of young, nonwhite women who are Democrats. That ideal audience corresponds to the "target audience" revealed during our descriptive analysis of Painter's essay. Thus, the demographic characteristics of Painter's audience are important.

The initial empirical audience for Painter's essay was made up of readers of the *New York Times*. That is significant because the *Times* is a newspaper read by millions throughout the nation and around the globe; Painter's empirical audience was potentially very large. The *1986 Media Guide* calls the *Times* "the most important newspaper in the world" and notes its "history and standing, its immense influence on global opinion, and its responsibility in maintaining journalistic standards" (15). Thus, the *Times* and its readers play an important role in shaping public opinion. Although information about the political party affiliation of *Times* readers is not available, statistics for the other categories enumerated by Clayton and Crosby suggest that readers of the *Times* are demographically diverse.

For example, the *Simmons 1982 Study of Media and Markets* reports that readers of the *New York Times* are 54.7 percent male and 45.3 percent female (4). Ethnically, readership is 88.3 percent white, 9.3 percent African American, and 2.4 percent other ethnic groups; 3.2 percent are Spanish-speaking (28). Readers classified as "younger," ages 18–34, make up 32.7 percent of *Times* readers; somewhat older individuals, ages 35–54, constitute 36.9 percent of readers (8).

Given the "ideal" or "target" audience for Painter's essay, cross-referencing the relevant demographic characteristics for *Times* readers is revealing. Women classified as younger, ages 18–34, make up 15.3 percent of *Times* readers (*Simmons* 180). Ethnically, women readers are 11.1 percent nonwhite, and 2.9 percent are Spanish-speaking (*Simmons* 178). Although these percentages may seem relatively small, the number of people who make up Painter's empirical audience is potentially quite large because the circulation of the *New York Times* is so great. If Clayton and Crosby are correct about those individuals who "show more support for affirmative action," then Painter's target audience is also large, even though the percentage figures may seem small.

Nevertheless, we must point out that there are important exceptions to this generalization about Painter's audiences based upon demographics. Many individuals who are members of groups that theoretically benefit most from affirmative action oppose the policy. Some of those individuals are extremely influential people. In his confirmation hearings for a position on the U.S. Supreme Court, Clarence Thomas voiced opposition to the policy. As Clayton and Crosby also point out,

> Justice Thomas is not the only African American to oppose affirmative action: Thomas Sowell, Shelby Steele, and Glenn Loury are some of the more prominent black critics who have gained national attention as they have spoken and written against the policy. Stephen Carter, the William Nelson Cromwell Professor of Law at Yale University, has also questioned the wisdom of the policy, even as he characterizes himself as an "affirmative action baby." (1–2)

Apparently, membership in one of the so-called "protected classes" is no guarantee of support for affirmative action.

For example, Thomas Sowell, a senior fellow of the Hoover Institution at Stanford University, is harshly critical of numerical requirements for hiring ethnic minorities, often called "quotas," which have sometimes been enacted because of affirmative action. "Today's grand fallacy about race and ethnicity," Sowell says, "is that the statistical 'representation' of a group—in jobs, schools, etc.—shows and measures *discrimination*. This notion is at the center of such controversial policies as affirmative action hiring, preferential admissions to college, and school busing." He continues, "But despite the fact that far-reaching judicial rulings, political crusades, and bureaucratic empires owe their existence to that belief, it remains an unexamined assumption" (417). Sowell is blunt in his attack on advocates of affirmative action based on numerical goals or requirements. "'Representation' talk is cheap, easy, and misleading," he says. "Discrimination and opportunity are too serious to be discussed in gobbledygook" (419).

Glenn C. Loury, professor of political economy at the John F. Kennedy School of Government at Harvard University, is equally critical of affirmative action programs. Indeed, he believes that those programs can be harmful to the very groups of people they are designed to benefit. According to Loury,

> . . . The broad use of race preference to treat all instances of "under-representation" introduces uncertainty into the process by which individuals make inferences about their own abilities. A frequently encountered question today from a black man or woman promoted

to a position of unusual responsibility in a "mainstream" institution is: "Would I have been offered this position if I had not been a black?" Most people in such situations want to be reassured that their achievement has been earned, and is not based simply on the organizational requirement of racial diversity. As a result, the use of racial preference tends to undermine the ability of people to confidently assert, if only to themselves, that they are as good as their achievements would seem to suggest. (447)

In other words, Loury argues that affirmative action programs can hurt targeted groups by undermining their self-confidence and self-esteem, qualities essential for success in both education and employment.

In education, the area of greatest interest for Painter, Sowell argues that the effects of affirmative action can be even more significant. Under pressure to meet numerical requirements for admissions, Sowell says, colleges and universities tend to employ a double standard for screening applicants; admission requirements are lower for targeted ethnic groups than for other potential students. The result, he claims, is that "thousands of minority students who would normally qualify for good nonprestigious colleges where they could succeed, are instead enrolled in famous institutions where they fail" (422). The effect ripples through the academic population. According to Sowell,

When the top institutions reach further down to get minority students, then academic institutions at the next level are forced to reach still further down, so that they too will end up with a minority body count high enough to escape criticism and avoid trouble with the government and other donors. Each academic level, therefore, ends up with minority students underqualified for that level, though usually perfectly qualified for some other level. The end result is a systematic mismatching of minority students and the institutions they attend, even though the wide range of American colleges and universities is easily capable of accommodating those same students under their normal standards. (423)

Because Sowell and Loury are respected and potentially influential members of a group that supposedly benefits from affirmative action, their statements illustrate the rhetorical problem Painter faced with her target audiences.

Clayton and Crosby also observe that "ideology, more than personal circumstances, may ultimately underlie most people's positions on affirmative action," although they quickly add that "ideology is influenced by personal circumstances" (25). The assumption is that in general, individuals with liberal political ideology tend to support the policy of affirmative action, whereas conservatives tend to oppose it. Nevertheless, there are notable exceptions to this ideological generalization as well.

For example, Clayton and Crosby note that "the liberal Anti-Defamation League . . . has consistently filed briefs against affirmative action in court cases" (11). Apparently, some liberals fear that by "highlighting category differences," affirmative action will only increase conflict and undermine efforts to achieve equality (11). On the other end of the ideological spectrum, many ostensibly conservative leaders of the business community wholeheartedly support affirmative action. A 1984 survey of chief executive officers of large corporations revealed that 90 percent of their companies had implemented "numerical hiring objectives," similar to those frequently required by affirmative action, and 95 percent of those who had implemented such programs indicated that they would continue, regardless of government action (Clayton and Crosby 24). Those companies seem to believe "that affirmative action leads to a variety of benefits, including increased productivity, diversity of ideas, a more rational personnel policy, and improved community relations" (Clayton and Crosby 21). Thus, because of these noteworthy exceptions, conclusions about the influence of political ideology on attitudes toward affirmative action are far from certain.

This analysis reveals how the scope and diversity of Painter's audiences contribute to her rhetorical problem. Readers of the *New York Times,* those potentially exposed to the rhetorical act, were demographically and, presumably, ideologically diverse. The medium Painter selected allowed her to reach a large target audience but also required her to adapt her essay to diverse readers.

Competing Persuasive Forces

Although the policy of affirmative action has generated controversy for decades, for Painter, the major competing persuasive influences were members of the Reagan administration and its conservative supporters. Consistent with promises made during the 1980 presidential campaign, Ronald Reagan entered office committed to easing affirmative action requirements, if not eliminating the policy altogether.

According to Howard Ball and Kathanne Greene, "President Reagan's world view on civil rights is contrary to views held by his predecessors" (16). Reagan's position was apparently based on his firm belief that conditions that once may have justified policies such as affirmative action had changed. As Ball and Greene explain:

> For Reagan, the time has ended for extending special treatment to various groups in the larger society because an entire nation has changed its attitudes toward racial and gender discrimination. Wedded philosophically to an "ability conscious" society, rather than to a society based on color consciousness, the message from the highest White House levels is that harsh remedies, e.g., busing, set-asides, quotas, etc., for naked and unrestricted discrimination based on various neutral factors are no longer appropriate. (16–17)

In other words, Reagan believed that programs such as affirmative action were no longer necessary because overt racism no longer existed in the United States.

Proponents of affirmative action would argue that Reagan's belief was ill-founded in at least two ways. First, overt racism and sexism are far from dead in the United States. Ezorsky cites the following examples of overt racism, which she claims is common: increases in racial violence against African Americans, disparities in sentences imposed on murderers who kill whites compared to those who kill African Americans, housing discrimination, and lower funding and inferior education in predominantly African American schools (12–13). She concludes that "abundant evidence shows that overt racism is widespread today" (12). Clayton and Crosby go even further, suggesting that "resistance to affirmative action is sometimes a manifestation of hostility toward the beneficiary group" (24). Second, even if overt racism and sexism are not as virulent as they once were, Reagan's position seems to ignore the lingering institutionalized racism and sexism that affirmative action was intended to combat. Nevertheless, Reagan's beliefs and ideology influenced the policies of his administration.

According to Janet K. Boles,

> the [Reagan] Justice Department announced that it would no longer advocate affirmative action goals and timetables, even in cases where courts had found discrimination by employers. The enforcement of equal opportunity laws by both the Equal Employment Opportunity Commission (EEOC) and the Office of Federal Contract Compliance (OFCC) declined sharply under Reagan, and, as a matter of announced policy, class action suits were no longer filed. Under new regulations proposed by the administration, three-quarters of all federal contractors were exempted from filing affirmative

action plans; existing requirements that promoted jobs for women in construction were weakened as well. (69–70)

Furthermore, Jones explains that "under the Reagan administration the United States Department of Justice aggressively attacked affirmative action, appearing in the Supreme Court in opposition to existing programs and counseling cities and other local entities to revoke or modify their affirmative action requirements" (352). Charles M. Lamb added that "the philosophy on school desegregation of most Reagan political appointees at DOE [the Department of Education] is that assertive enforcement is unnecessary and cooperation is absolutely essential with school systems accused of discriminating" (85). These policy changes were consistent with Reagan's political ideology.

A long-standing objection to affirmative action is that the policy "reverses" discrimination by favoring women and nonwhites at the expense of white males. The Reagan position fueled that objection. As Boles says, "the Reagan administration was much more concerned with 'reverse discrimination' against white males in the work force" than with any continuing need for affirmative action (69–70). Indeed, Ball and Greene believe that Reagan saw affirmative action programs not as the remedy for, but as the cause of, racism in the 1980s: "In the president's [Reagan's] mind, the denial of equal opportunity in the 1980s results from 'the very laws designed to secure them.' The laws that have been developed, especially the affirmative action legislation and regulations of recent decades, must be set aside because they are morally reprehensible and legally unconstitutional" (15). Clearly, both in word and in deed, the Reagan administration constituted the major competing persuasive influence for Painter.

That influence shaped the attitudes and opinions of potential audience members and, thus, contributed to Painter's rhetorical problem. For example, Clayton and Crosby comment that "white male students have complained to us about not getting into law school because of affirmative action; the implication is that the slot a student 'deserved' was reallocated to a less-deserving member of a minority group" (23–24). Such resentment of affirmative action is not confined to academia. One survey indicated that "only 17 percent of whites and 7 percent of blacks felt that affirmative action programs often discriminated against whites, but 60 percent of whites and 42 percent of blacks felt that this sometimes happened" (Clayton and Crosby 21–22). These attitudes are undoubtedly due to the efforts of competing persuasive influences, and they help reveal the rhetorical problem Painter faced.

Supporting Material

Aside from examples drawn from her own personal experiences, Painter used just one important piece of supporting material, the example of John Hope Franklin. As Painter indicated in her essay, Franklin is a member of that generation of Americans who came of age before the civil rights movement. *Who's Who Among Black Americans* reports that he was born January 2, 1915, in Rentiesville, Oklahoma, the son of Buck Colbert Franklin and Mollie Parker Franklin. He attended Fisk University, a predominantly African American institution, receiving his A.B. in 1935. He received a masters degree in 1936 and a Ph.D. in 1941, both from predominantly white Harvard University (499).

From 1936 to 1937, Franklin was an instructor of history at Fisk. He was professor of history at St. Augustine's College, a predominantly African American institution, in Raleigh, North Carolina, from 1939 to 1943, professor of history at North Carolina College at Durham, a predominantly African American institution, from 1943 to 1947, and professor of history at Howard University, another predominantly African American institution in Washington, D.C., from 1947 to 1956. From 1956 through 1964, he was chair of the Department of History at Brooklyn College. During that time, he was also Pitt Professor of American History at Cambridge University, 1962–1963. From 1964 through 1982, he was professor of American History at the University of Chicago, and from 1982 to 1985, he was James B. Duke professor of history at Duke University. Currently, he is Professor Emeritus of History, Duke University (*Who's Who Among Black Americans* 499). Franklin's career as an educator was truly distinguished.

Despite the limitations placed on Franklin's career by the sort of overt racism we described earlier, he also became a renowned scholar. He was on the editorial board of *American Scholar,* 1972–1976, and he was chair of the board of trustees of Fisk University, 1968–1974. In 1969 Franklin was president of the Southern Historical Association, and in 1979 he was president of the American Historical Association. He is a member of Phi Beta Kappa and Phi Alpha Theta (*Who's Who Among Black Americans* 499). Franklin was a Guggenheim Fellow 1950–1951 and again 1973–1974. He is the author of *From Slavery to Freedom, a History of Negro Americans,* 1987; *The Militant South,* 1956; *Reconstruction After the Civil War,* 1961; *The Emancipation Proclamation,* 1963; *A Southern Odyssey,* 1976; *Racial Equality in America,* 1976; *George Washington Williams, a Biography,* 1985; *The Color Line: Legacy for the Twenty First Century,* 1991; as well as other works (*Who's Who Among Black Americans* 499).

Franklin's scholarly contributions in American history have received the highest recognition. He was awarded the Jefferson Medal in
1983, the Clarence Holte Literary Prize in 1986, the Cleanth Brooks
Medal, Fellowship of Southern Writers in 1989, the John Caldwell
Medal from the North Carolina Council on the Humanities in 1991,
the University of North Carolina Medal in 1992, and the Encyclopedia Britannica Gold Medal Award in 1990 (*Who's Who Among Black
Americans* 499). Painter's use of Franklin as an example clearly passes
all the relevant tests of evidence.

CONCLUSION

This brief analysis illustrates the complexity of the issues surrounding
the controversial policy of affirmative action. Honest individuals with
good intentions on both sides of the controversy deplore the overt
racism and sexism that the 1964 Civil Rights Act and the subsequent
Executive Orders were intended to overcome. Because fairness and
equality are celebrated as traditional U. S. values, the goal of equal opportunity in education and employment is applauded by virtually everyone. Policies enacted to help achieve that goal, however, continue
to provoke disagreement.

Advocates of policies such as affirmative action argue vehemently
that overt racism and sexism continue almost unabated. Moreover,
they argue that regardless of overtly racist and sexist actions, institutionalized racism and sexism continue to thwart equal opportunity
policies, making affirmative action necessary. Opponents of affirmative action argue just as vehemently that the policy creates a new form
of discrimination directed at groups not protected by affirmative action. Furthermore, they contend that the protected groups themselves
are harmed by the policy. Rhetors on both sides face a formidable rhetorical problem.

This analysis also illustrates how, in the second stage of the critical
process, critics try to describe the rhetorical problem. It reveals that
Painter addressed an issue, affirmative action, with a long and controversial history. Her empirical audience was large and diverse. Evidence
suggests that the medium of communication through which she
spoke, the *New York Times,* allowed her to reach relatively large target
audiences, but many within those targeted groups were probably
skeptical about Painter's purpose. Thus, she faced the problem of
adapting her rhetorical act to that large, diverse, and potentially reluctant audience. Painter's rhetorical problem was made more difficult by
the presence of powerful competing persuaders—Ronald Reagan, his

administration, and its conservative supporters. Their statements and actions fueled opposition to affirmative action. Research reveals that the persona Painter adopted in her essay was entirely consistent with her past accomplishments and experiences, as well as with her previous statements on the issues of civil rights and affirmative action. Finally, the primary example, other than her own experiences, that Painter employed, John Hope Franklin, was authentic and accurate.

The first stage of the critical process, descriptive analysis, revealed in detail how Painter's rhetorical act worked to achieve its purpose. The second stage, historical–contextual analysis, illuminated the rhetorical problem she faced. We are now prepared for the third stage of the critical process: selecting or inventing a critical perspective to guide our evaluation of Painter's essay.

WORKS CITED

Ball, Howard, and Kathanne Greene. "The Reagan Justice Department." *The Reagan Administration and Human Rights*. Ed. Tinsley E. Yarbrough. New York: Praeger, 1985. 1–28.

Boles, Janet K. "Women's Rights and the Gender Gap." *The Reagan Administration and Human Rights*. Ed. Tinsley E. Yarbrough. New York: Praeger, 1985. 55–81.

Clayton, Susan D., and Faye J. Crosby. *Justice, Gender, and Affirmative Action*. Ann Arbor: The University of Michigan Press, 1992.

Ezorsky, Gertrude. *Racism and Justice: The Case for Affirmative Action*. Ithaca, NY: Cornell University Press, 1991.

Fitch, Nancy Elizabeth. "Nell Irvin Painter." *African American Women: A Biographical Dictionary*. Ed. Dorothy C. Salem. New York: Garland Publishing, 1993. 379.

Jones, James E., Jr. "The Rise and Fall of Affirmative Action." *Race in America: The Struggle for Equality*. Ed. Herbert Hill and James E. Jones, Jr. Madison: The University of Wisconsin Press, 1993. 345–369.

Lamb, Charles M. "Education and Housing." *The Reagan Administration and Human Rights*. Ed. Tinsley E. Yarbrough. New York: Praeger, 1985. 82–106.

Loury, Glenn C. "Beyond Civil Rights." *Racial Preference and Racial Justice: The New Affirmative Action Controversy*. Ed. Russell Nieli. Washington, DC: The Ethics and Public Policy Center, 1991. 437–451.

Phelps, Shirelle, ed. *Who's Who Among Black Americans*. Detroit: Gale Research, 1994.

Simmons 1982 Study of Media and Markets. New York: Simmons Market Research Bureau, 1982.

Sowell, Thomas. "Are Quotas Good for Blacks?" *Racial Preference and Racial Justice: The New Affirmative Action Controversy.* Ed. Russell Nieli. Washington, DC: The Ethics and Public Policy Center, 1991. 417–428.

Wanniski, Jude, ed. *1986 Media Guide: A Critical Review of the Print Media.* Morristown, NJ: Polyconomics, 1986.

Washington, Valora, and William Harvey. *Affirmative Rhetoric, Negative Action: African-American and Hispanic Faculty at Predominantly White Universities.* Washington, DC: School of Education and Human Development, George Washington University, 1989.

RECOMMENDED READINGS

Lucas, Stephen E. "The Schism in Rhetorical Scholarship." *Quarterly Journal of Speech* 67 (1981): 1–20. An essay that explores conflicts between rhetorical history and rhetorical criticism and then illustrates their interrelationship through an analysis of Thomas Paine's *Common Sense.*

Nichols, Marie Hochmuth. "Lincoln's First Inaugural." *American Speeches.* Ed. W. M. Parrish and M. H. Nichols. New York: David McKay, 1954. This is the classic example of historical–contextual analysis. A critique of its narrow compass is found in Edwin Black, *Rhetorical Criticism: A Study in Method.* New York: Macmillan, 1965: 37–42.

Philipsen, Gerald. "Mayor Daley's Council Speech: A Cultural Analysis." *Quarterly Journal of Speech* 72 (1986): 247–260. This critical analysis dramatically illustrates the links between knowing the context and understanding the meaning of a rhetorical act.

CHAPTER FOUR

Selecting or Inventing
a Critical Perspective:
The Third Stage of Criticism

In the third stage of analysis critics select or "invent" a critical perspective or approach from which to interprete and evaluate a rhetorical act. They base their decisions on both their intrinsic descriptive analysis and their extrinsic analysis of the historical–cultural context. That is, information discovered and conclusions drawn in the first two stages guide critics to a perspective or approach suitable for completing the critical process. In this chapter we discuss the third stage in the critical process and illustrate it by inventing a critical approach to Nell Irvin Painter's essay.

In contrast to the first stage, which focuses on the discourse, and the second stage, which focuses on the context and scene, the third stage focuses on the critic, reflecting that person's interests and biases. In other words, on the basis of their conclusions in the first two stages and on their own knowledge and experience, critics make subjective decisions about the perspective best suited to a particular rhetorical act. Perhaps for that reason, George Bernard Shaw once wrote that "all criticism is autobiography," and other theorists have recognized that criticism is persuasive discourse. In this sense rhetorical criticism is entirely reflexive; all critical processes used to evaluate a discourse should also be used to evaluate the criticisms of that discourse.

Although our discussion of the first two stages of the process indicates strongly that critics must test their judgments both against the discourse and against research from other sources, "good" criticism is not objective and impersonal—it is evaluative. It makes clear and unmistakable judgments about the quality, worth, and consequences of rhetoric. Good criticism, however, is not purely and simply the subjective reaction of a critic to a rhetorical act. Better critical works can be distinguished from deficient ones in several ways. First, whether it makes positive or negative judgments, good criticism increases the reader's understanding and appreciation of the discourse it criticizes. It goes beyond what is obvious to an intelligent person at the first reading. Second, the analysis reflects accurately and fully the discourse being analyzed. Third, in such criticism the reader can clearly identify the bases for the critic's evaluation. In other words, good critics identify the perspectives and standards they use, and their criticism is coherent and consistent so the reader can recognize the grounds for critical judgments. Fourth, good criticism contributes to the ongoing dialogue about the role of persuasive discourse in a humane society. It addresses ethical and moral questions and gives readers a glimpse of an "ideal" rhetoric. Finally, in most cases good criticism contributes to a general understanding of how human beings use symbols to influence each other.

In light of their descriptive and historical–contextual analyses, critics should consider the following questions as a general guide in selecting or inventing a critical perspective through which to interpret and evaluate.

First, what distinctive characteristics of this rhetorical act should a critique emphasize and highlight? The purpose of criticism is to help readers become a more appreciative, insightful audience. Criticism should reveal the discourse, explore its peculiarities, expose its internal workings, and focus attention on artistic elements in the rhetoric.

Second, does the rhetoric itself suggest criteria for judging it? Critics should approach persuaders "on their own terms"—that is, take into account persuaders' purposes and the limits they have set for themselves. Frequently the authors of persuasive discourses suggest inherent standards for evaluation in statements of their beliefs about the proper analysis of an issue and the purposes of their discourses. Thorough descriptive analysis reveals such standards when they are present in a discourse.

Third, what critical system will allow the critic to focus on the criteria that seem most significant in responding to this discourse or genre? In some cases a critic will decide that certain judgments or evaluations of the discourse need to be made. A critic might deem the work highly unethical, significantly untrue, a unique approach to a complex ethical problem, a distinctively aesthetic work, or a major reinterpretation of an issue or value system. In each case a critic seeks a critical system that will allow intelligent and cogent explication and justification of those conclusions.

Fourth, what critical system would be most antagonistic in its judgment of the rhetoric, and which would be most sympathetic in its assessments? This question is designed to make critics self-aware and self-conscious, to force them to consider alternative conclusions that might be reached if different standards were applied. The contrasting criticisms of Richard Nixon's November 3, 1969, "Vietnamization" address by Karlyn Kohrs Campbell and Forbes Hill illustrate different critical approaches and differing evaluations of a highly influential and controversial presidential speech.[1] This question focuses the attention of critics on what the discourse is and is not to make them pause and question the fairness of their standards. It also makes them aware of both positive and negative grounds for rating the discourse.

No book could be long enough to describe all the different ways in which a critic might approach a rhetorical work. Ideally, criticism is a creative act in which a sensitive, knowledgeable interpreter responds to discourse that demands attention and explanation because of the power of its argument, of the power of its appeal, or the artistry of its language and construction.

Criticism views rhetoric as an art. Better still, it attends to the artistry of rhetoric. Its banner is George Campbell's definition of rhetoric: "That art or talent by which discourse is adapted to its end" (1). As we noted in Chapter One, there are three broad and overlapping understandings of rhetorical artistry. Rhetoric is seen as an art of argument and evidence, as an art of adaptation to audiences and their cultural norms, and as an art of symbols that exploits the resources of symbolic form. Those three general approaches to rhetorical action suggest three broad and overlapping approaches to rhetorical criticism.

RATIONALISTIC CRITICISM

For decades, rationalistic criticism dominated the scholarly analysis of public discourse in the field of speech communication. This kind of criticism emphasizes the role of rational argument and evidence in processes by which humans are influenced. A rationalistic approach

---

[1]See Karlyn Kohrs Campbell, "An Exercise in the Rhetoric of Mythical America," *Critiques of Contemporary Rhetoric* (Belmont, CA: Wadsworth, 1972) 50–58; and Forbes Hill, "Conventional Wisdom—Traditional Form—The President's Message of November 3, 1969," *Quarterly Journal of Speech* 58 (1972): 373–386. Also see their exchange in the "Forum," pp. 451–460. These critiques are discussed in the introduction to Campbell's second critique of Nixon's speech, which appears later in this volume.

assumes that rhetoric's function is to make truth effective, and that ethical rhetoric seeks judgments from audiences based on deliberation about available options because these are the "best" decisions a society can make.

Edwin Black sharply criticized this approach as traditionally applied, labeling it "neo-Aristotelian" (*Rhetorical Criticism*). As originally practiced, this critical approach usually categorized rhetorical acts into the classical genres explained by Aristotle: deliberative, forensic, and epideictic. Analysis typically involved a rather formulaic application of the classical norms or canons: invention, arrangement, style, delivery, and memory. The emphasis was on invention and arrangement and an analysis of the discourse in terms of the classical modes of proof—logos, pathos, and ethos—with the greatest attention given to logos, understood as logical argument supported with evidence. Critics focused their attention on the premises from which arguments were developed; the validity of the argumentative structure; and the credibility, relevance, and adequacy of the evidence provided. They assessed the rhetor's analysis of the issue and the rhetor's ability to respond to counterarguments and to adapt the materials of the discourse to the expectations, experiences, and interests of the audience. Finally, critics evaluated the effectiveness of the discourse in achieving the rhetor's purpose.[2] As we indicate in Chapter Five, however, many contemporary critics who employ rationalistic approaches apply the effectiveness criterion somewhat differently.

Given these assumptions, rationalistic criticism is best suited to works that extensively use supporting materials and have a deductive structure, asserting a claim or conclusion that is justified through a series of arguments. In many cases this type of criticism is particularly appropriate for discourse that supports policy proposals—in Aristotle's terms, deliberative rhetoric. The so-called stock issue analysis of policy debate is a form of rationalistic criticism that judges policy-related discourse in these terms: (1) whether a need for a change from the current policy has been established, based on demonstrated harm of significant scope that will persist while the policy continues; (2) whether an alternative policy would eradicate the problems identified; (3) whether that alternative policy would be practical to put into effect (have we the resources and expertise, for example); and (4) on balance, whether the policy would be beneficial.

The elements of rationalistic criticism are drawn primarily from Greco-Roman theory originating with Aristotle and developed by

---

[2]For a more complete explanation of neo-Aristotelian criticism as it is traditionally practiced, see Lester Thonssen and A. Craig Baird, *Speech Criticism: The Development of Standards for Rhetorical Appraisal* (New York: The Ronald Press, 1948).

Cicero and Quintilian. Key ingredients include the classical canons (norms or standards) and the three modes of proof; however, some of these are retained, albeit in a slightly different form, in the other critical approaches described later.

Invention

As used in rhetoric, *invention* refers to a rhetor's skill in choosing argumentative options and using creative lines of argument. In other words, it refers to a persuader's ability to identify available proofs and to select those best adapted to the issue under consideration, the specific occasion, and the particular audiences addressed or targeted. Of primary interest is the argumentative development or logos of the discourse—the means used to support and justify the claims being made. That is, a critic examines the choice of arguments and evidence in relation to what is available and in light of the special qualities and characteristics of the issue, occasion, and audiences. It is a question not just of what is the strongest argument or the most compelling evidence, but of what argument will be strongest and what evidence most compelling for these listeners or readers on this occasion. In other words, good invention requires adaptation; good reasons are both sound and cogent.

Evidence   Discussion of the logos of invention includes assessment of the evidence provided in a rhetorical act. Given the usual restrictions of time or space, rhetors must be highly selective in their use of evidence. Four basic types of evidence are available; each has strengths and weaknesses.

Examples, such as those used by Painter, are strong because they are vivid and can evoke identification, but they are weak as proof because, as single instances, they usually are too limited a sample from which to draw conclusions. Note that Painter overcomes much of that problem by using the example of John Hope Franklin, a paradigmatic or model case that is an ideal test. As we noted in Chapter Three, if a historian of Franklin's stature could not find employment in first-rate universities, then those of lesser talents and fewer qualifications would have faced even more insuperable barriers. Ordinarily, however, one or two instances would not be sufficient to meet normal standards of proof.

Statistics are the mirror image of examples. They are powerful measures of the frequency with which something occurs and, thus, strong proof of scope. They are difficult to absorb, however; most of us cannot process more than about three of them in a row. Note that the sheer fact of their use can be impressive, as illustrated in the massive amounts of them used in the infomercials of independent presidential candidate H. Ross Perot in 1992.

Literal analogies or *comparisons* serve two vital proof functions: prediction and evaluation. We compare two athletic teams to guess who will win a game—an example of evaluation for prediction. We also compare two situations to determine whether what was successful in one case could be successful in another. Analogies also help to make familiar what is alien. William Ouchi used analogies in his book *Theory Z* when he argued that the principles of Japanese quality management are similar to management principles in the most productive U.S. companies, such as IBM and Hewlett-Packard. If there are relevant differences in the two cases being compared, then the predictions will be faulty. It is often difficult to determine what differences are relevant and significant. How important is a home court advantage to a basketball team? How crucial is a player who is injured or ineligible? As we try to predict which team will come out on top, we struggle to determine which differences are relevant to and significant for the outcome of the game.

Authority evidence or evidence from experts is the means by which people who are less knowledgeable in an area can understand and interpret data from a specialized field. For example, the results of DNA comparisons are unintelligible to most of us; we need an expert to explain how such comparisons work and how the data may be interpreted. Only such an expert is able to determine whether the blood found at a murder scene has the same DNA as the blood of the alleged murderer, but juries and audiences generally will accept such a conclusion only if they find the expert who is testifying credible and comprehensible.

Stasis   Where there is a clash between two sides, as in a trial, critics taking a rationalistic approach sometimes have applied what the ancient Greeks called *stasis* and the Romans *status*. According to Cicero's report in *De Inventione,* Hermagoras of Temnos identified four possible loci or sites of dispute or clash (Bk. 1. 8, 16). First, is the issue a question of *fact*—that is, what really occurred? If there is agreement about what occurred, then other issues arise. What was the *weight* or *quantity* of the act—how serious was it? In criminal cases this question addresses whether the act was premeditated, done in the heat of passion, or occurred as a result of negligence. In addition, there are questions of *quality*; for example, are there mitigating circumstances that might lead to a more lenient judgment, up to and including justifications for the act such as acting in self-defense? Finally, there are issues of *proce-*

dure or jurisdiction such as double jeopardy, legal standing, the admissibility of evidence, or the right to bring suit on this issue to this court at this time (Cicero, *De Inventione* Bk. 2. 14–151).

As an illustration, consider the case of the Los Angeles police officers who faced criminal charges for beating Rodney King (mentioned in Chapter One). The police officers did not deny that they had struck King (fact); the existence of a videotape would have made such denial difficult. Instead, they contended they had committed no crime because they had followed approved police procedures for subduing a suspect (quantity). The prosecution countered that King was prone but moved in order to protect himself from their incessant blows, especially those to the head. They also argued that less injurious procedures for subduing suspects were available and in use by the department. In response, the defense argued that even if the number of blows appeared excessive, King was a large, strong man who behaved in ways that might reasonably be interpreted as evidence of being under the influence of illegal drugs (quality). Finally, after the officers were found not guilty of criminal charges, their attorneys argued that a trial on federal charges of having violated King's civil rights would constitute double jeopardy; hence, the charges should be dismissed (procedure).

Although the King case is an especially vivid instance of trials that reach audiences far outside the courtroom, the give and take of the courtroom focuses attention on the ability of advocates to identify the central issue and to respond to opposing arguments directly and effectively.

Pathos   Invention also involves elements that Aristotle identified as *pathos*—the rhetor's ability to adapt to the qualities and characteristics of audiences and to develop materials to put audience members in states of mind or feeling that make them more amenable or vulnerable to arguments and appeals developed in support of a position. In discussing pathos in his *Rhetoric,* Aristotle called attention to what we now call *demographics*—audience members' ages, socioeconomic statuses, relative power, and lineage/ethnicities or classes. He also emphasized what we call *psychodemographics*—the differences in attitudes among those who are young, in their prime, or older, those who are wealthy or poor, and those who are born into an aristocracy or into a lower class (1388^b31–1391^b7). In addition, he identified many emotional states, such as anger, pity, fear, and envy, that influence audience members' reactions to arguments and evidence (1378^a20–1388^b20). These are discussed in more detail under psychosocial criticism.

As traditionally practiced, rationalistic criticism viewed such adaptation as rather shoddy, even unethical. Yet arousing patriotic feelings clearly makes citizens far more willing to consider going to war, and arousing anger is a way to induce much of the public to accept rather weak evidence as compelling. Accordingly, rationalistic critics recognized the force of pathos and the importance of adaptation but preferred to argue, at least in theory, that the best rhetoric hewed to the straight and narrow road of rational appeals. In practice, critics adopting a rationalistic perspective viewed adaptation and emotional appeals as legitimate and appropriate only when they enhanced and supported rhetorical action that was primarily reasoned discourse.

Ethos   A third concern in invention is assessing source credibility or *ethos*—a term referring to the persuasive force of the character of the speaker. Aristotle saw such influence as arising only from characteristics of the discourse. He described ethos as prompted by evidence of the rhetor's good sense or social and practical wisdom, which he called *phronesis;* good will or concern for the long-term interests of the community, called *eunoia,* rather than personal, selfish interests; and good character or moral excellence, or *arete,* embodying the values cherished by the community of which the audience was a part (1377[b]15–1378[a]20).

Aristotle also believed that pathos was of greater importance in forensic or courtroom rhetoric: Adaptation to the jury was vital and jurors' state of mind was crucial to the way they viewed the arguments on both sides. By contrast, he believed that ethos was of greater significance in deliberative or legislative rhetoric, perhaps because our evaluation of the source of a policy is particularly important as we take a risky leap into the future (1377[b]29). Probably because the Greek city-states were small communities in which only adult male citizens were permitted to speak and vote, Aristotle made no reference to ethos arising apart from the rhetorical act. In a mass society in which we are unlikely to have personal knowledge of the rhetor, reputation becomes more important. Rhetors bring their personal histories and past records to any speaking situation, however, and they influence audience assessments of their credibility.

Critics should consider how the rhetor demonstrates personal involvement with the issue and expertise in the subject area, attempts to establish credibility, and demonstrates concern for the welfare of the audience. Recall the reaction in the 1992 presidential election campaign when George Bush's surprised response to supermarket scanners indicated how remote his life was from that of ordinary citizens. Critics also note whether the rhetor attempts to discredit the character and credibility of opponents and the means used in such attempts.

Arrangement

This canon calls for analysis of the development of arguments and evidence and of the selection, orderly disposition, and proportion of the parts of a discourse. The critic must determine how parts of the discourse perform their respective functions, describe the structural form, and judge the unity, coherence, and emphasis created by the method of development. The elements discussed in Chapter Two's section on structure are relevant here.

Style

The canon of style examines the language of rhetorical discourse to determine whether it is clear and simple, correct and precise, and appropriate to the issue, speaker, and audience. In other words, language is judged primarily in terms of qualities consistent with rational argument. In evaluating style critics sometimes describe how rhetors use language to make the discourse aesthetically pleasing to audiences, although they rarely judge the aesthetic worth of particular elements.

Delivery

For oral rhetorical discourses, this canon evaluates the influence of vocal and visual elements on the success of the act. In an age of mass media it is also important to consider how suitable a work is to the medium through which it is transmitted. Senator Edward Kennedy's dramatic delivery is very moving when experienced firsthand or via radio or audiotape; however, it is not well suited to the intimacy of the television screen. By contrast, President Ronald Reagan was able to use the medium of television particularly well in delivering speeches to the U.S. public.

Memory

In ancient theory, the canon of memory had two dimensions. One, of course, had to do with devices for remembering one's speech in eras before stone tablets and rolls of papyrus were superseded by index cards. Simonides of Ceos, for example, developed a mnemonic system based on the rooms of a house that both Cicero (*De Oratore*, Bk. 2. 351–354) and Quintilian praised. Such devices are still important and are still taught, especially for remembering names.

The second dimension of memory is far more important. It refers to the rhetor's command of the body of material, lines of arguments, types of evidence, illustrations, and the like that are available resources for use in a particular situation. Ancient teachers of rhetoric recommended that students memorize standard lines of argument. Today we would say that mastery of the canon of memory is apparent when someone is on top of a subject, able to respond quickly to questions or objections or to counter opposing arguments. In a sense, memory refers to knowledge of the subject and access to that knowledge on the spur of the moment—the kind of skill manifested by guests on William Buckley's *Firing Line* or *The NewsHour* with Jim Lehrer.

As presented, this is a highly abbreviated scheme for approaching a rhetorical work from a rationalistic perspective. In sum, rationalistic criticism emphasizes the role of logical argument and evidence in the process by which people are influenced. It also acknowledges the influence of the rhetor's character and credibility and of appeals to emotion. The rationalistic approach is often particularly useful in examining deliberative rhetoric, which advocates or opposes a policy or course of action.

PSYCHOSOCIAL CRITICISM

Theories and concepts related to research in psychology and sociology have led to the development of alternative approaches to criticism. Psychologically based critical perspectives have viewed persuasion as "that body of effects in receivers, relevant and instrumental to source-desired goals, brought about by a process in which messages have been a major determinant of those effects" (Fotheringham 7), or as the "conscious attempt to modify thought and action by manipulating the motives of men [*sic*] toward predetermined ends" (Brembeck and Howell 24). William N. Brigance even argued that "persuasion takes place not on an intellectual, but on a motor level" (21). After discussing the problems of defining persuasion and exploring exemplary cases of it, Daniel O'Keefe explained a core concept of persuasion: "a successful intentional effort at influencing another's mental state through communication in a circumstance in which the persuadee has some measure of freedom" (17). These statements strongly indicate a point of view that differs from the rationalistic; they suggest that the theoretical base for this critical system emphasizes the criterion of effects and the role that psychosocial factors play in influencing behavior. Consequently, psychologically based criticism analyzes audiences, the source or author, and the ways in which the rhetor uses the message to activate and channel the needs and motives of audiences. Such criticism is keyed to the rhetor's effectiveness in achieving goals. The critic's primary concern is to analyze and explain how and why these effects were produced.

Audience Adaptation and Pathos

Although Aristotle inveighed against warping the minds of the members of the audience, he emphasized that rhetors should adapt their materials to a particular target audience. Contemporary advertisers, who take a strongly psychosocial approach to persuasion, also emphasize audience analysis and adaptation. Like Aristotle, they are concerned with age, ethnicity, and class; but they are also interested in sex, marital status, educational level, religion, the region where one lives, and whether it is urban, suburban, or rural. In addition, their approach to psychodemographics attempts to categorize groups according to their lifestyles, values, and attitudes. These generate such audience categories as survivors, who are poor and old; sustainers, who are the struggling young; belongers, who are traditional conformists; achievers, or the people we sometimes call "workaholics," and so on. But the principle is still the same: The basic facts of one's life and one's attitudes and values, which predispose individuals to respond better to some arguments and appeals than to others, are key elements in rhetorical success.

In other words, psychosocial critics not only attempt to determine the target audiences but also analyze how persuaders adapt their rhetoric to the characteristics of the audiences they seek to reach and how they attempt to create predispositions conducive to acceptance of their messages. Some standard or formulaic means of adaptation have been developed through time.

Psychosocial Structure: Monroe's Motivated Sequence

Writing in the 17th century, the great English thinker and speaker Francis Bacon said, "The duty and office of Rhetoric is *to apply Reason to Imagination for* the better moving of the will" (*Advancement of Learning*, Bk. 2: 409). Bacon believed that both the appetites, what we would call basic drives, and reason, or the capacity to envision and plan for long-range goals, were good; but if they competed directly, reason would always lose. Hence, the special function of rhetoric was to body forth through illustration, through figurative language, description, example, and the like, long-range goals in ways that made them as vivid and appealing as the satisfaction of immediate desires. Bacon was talking about deferred gratification—for example, the ability to decline foods like French fries that are bad for your health even though their vivid smells make them highly appealing.

These concepts are illustrated in the five-step motivated sequence described by Alan Monroe in *Principles and Types of Speech:* attention, need, satisfaction, visualization, action. First, attract the attention of the audience to the issue or problem of concern. Second, arouse a need for change, often for a product or procedure. This might be done in ways related to the stock issue of need for a change (based on demonstrably significant harm that will persist while the policy continues) described earlier under rationalistic criticism. Third, as in stock issue analysis, show that a product or policy will eliminate the problem described in the need step. The fourth step most clearly reflects the influence of Bacon. At this stage the rhetor needs to describe vividly and depict memorably the satisfaction—what the situation will be if the plan is adopted or the product purchased. Many advertisements illustrate this step; for example, many diet aid or exercise machine ads include before and after photos, intended to help customers imagine a desired body shape that they can attain if they just follow a given diet or use a particular exercise device. Ads for athletic shoes show young, slim, muscular women who represent imaginatively the goal for which customers presumably strive. The final step is the closing, a call for action now to commit yourself to the cause or to buy the product, usually accompanied by some specific action such as signing on the dotted line. William Ouchi's book, *Theory Z,* mentioned earlier, follows this organizational format in promoting "quality management systems" as a way to improve U.S. business productivity. The book illustrates the power of the motivated sequence.[3]

The Rhetor's Ethos

Psychological criticism emphasizes the role of perceptions of the source in acceptance of the message. Traditionally, this was the study of ethos or credibility—the impact of the rhetor's character, intelligence, and sincerity as perceived by audience members. Some theorists suggest a variety of questions as a method of analysis: (1) How do rhetors associate themselves with what is virtuous and elevated? (2) How do rhetors bestow praise on themselves and their cause and blame on opponents and their cause? (3) How do rhetors create an im-

---

[3]We are indebted to Laurie Pryor, whose analysis revealed the use of the motivated sequence in this work.

pression of sincerity? (4) How do rhetors identify themselves with the experiences, values, and attitudes of their readers or listeners? (5) How do rhetors discount personal biases and interests? These questions, of course, assume that successful rhetors must do these things and that an understanding of them accounts for some part of persuasive success. Conversely, insofar as these things are not done or are done ineptly, that lack is presumed to be a clue to possible persuasive failure.

A second approach to analysis of rhetors' psychological impact assumes that audiences grant or withhold credibility and prestige to rhetors because of certain needs that they have. Thus, the ethos of the speaker might originate in a need or deficiency felt by the audience. In the process of granting a certain role to the rhetor the audience attempts to satisfy, conceal, or lessen this deficiency. Three general deficiencies usually result in three patterns of ethos.[4]

In the "hero" pattern, audience members feel deficient in their capacity to make intelligent choices about complex issues. They wish to escape from the pain and responsibility for such decisions. Consequently, they confer a heroic role on the rhetor and designate the rhetor as an authority endowed with decision-making power. Rhetors who seek such a role wish to enhance their power and position and emphasize their willingness to lead. In turn, they tend to argue authoritatively because of their special expertise or their knowledge of generally unavailable information. Powerful national leaders exploit such needs in their rhetoric.

In the "identification" pattern, members of the audience have an idealized image of themselves, what they would like to be but despair of reaching. However, they may reach this goal by granting prestige to a person they perceive as possessing qualities similar to their own idealized image. The ethos of many professional athletes may be of this type.

In the "agent" pattern, the specialization of a modern technological society requires people to delegate to others the power and responsibility for helping them achieve their goals. Consequently, they grant prestige to other persons who can function as agents or instruments. The prestige bestowed on physicians, who are essential agents in maintaining health, illustrates such ethos. Rhetors who seek this kind of prestige argue that they can do for the audience what the audience members cannot do themselves or that they have been instrumental in the achievement of goals (for example, as politicians who "run on their record"). The prestige that people grant or withhold from elected representatives is generally related to this pattern.

---

[4]The hero, agent, and identification patterns were described in an unpublished paper by Otis M. Walter.

The Psychological Power of Evidence

Evidence serves two interrelated functions. On the one hand, it is proof, offering data lending force to argument and appeal. On the other hand, evidence has power separate from its role as proof—power to convince on grounds that are not factual or logical. For instance, a single example merely proves that something happened once, but a particularly poignant, vivid story can so engage and upset us that its power goes far beyond the facts that it provides. Of particular significance are examples that create identification, causing listeners to imagine themselves in the situation described in the rhetoric.

Similarly, statistics are a good source of information about the frequency with which a particular phenomenon happens. For example, based on past data, one in four U.S. women will be raped during her lifetime and one in nine U.S. women will be diagnosed as having breast cancer. Such statistics have special force because they horrify us; their scope creates an impression because they dramatize the discrepancy between our values and our behavior, or they make a particular social or medical threat vivid for members of the audience. Because our culture venerates science and technology, we are prone to give a disproportionate weight to evidence that appears scientific or quantitative. Sometimes the sheer fact of using a lot of statistics is impressive, a phenomenon apparent in the long, statistics-filled political ads in the 1992 election campaign paid for and narrated by H. Ross Perot.

Some individuals with great talent or expertise in certain areas become sufficiently revered to be accepted as authorities on almost everything. A winning football coach is hired to sell us a particular chain of hardware stores; talented basketball players appear in ads for soft drinks; an Oscar-winning actor appears in ads for cameras. In these cases the appeal is based on celebrity, not expertise, which is in areas unrelated to these products.

Finally, analogies, especially figurative analogies, have great force. Literal analogies compare situations, processes, or entities that are alike in detail and are a basis for prediction. They are the grounds on which we try to figure out which horse will win a race, which team will win a championship, or which candidate will do the best job as mayor. Figurative analogies—comparisons of unlike entities that are alleged to be alike in principle—have no force whatsoever as proof. Nonetheless, they can be appealing and persuasive. Those who oppose legalized abortion compare their struggle to the struggle against slavery as a way to reassert the rightness of their cause and to legitimize extreme measures in its support. Those who deplore the tactics of such groups as Operation Rescue say that "just as nothing failed Christianity more than the Crusades, so nothing has failed pro-life efforts more than those who do harm or take life, as they now have [referring to the murder of Dr. David Gunn] in the name of life" (Kennedy 13). The appeal of figurative language is also apparent in the power of metaphors, such as "the cancer of communism," and slogans like "Pro-life" and "Pro-Choice," which appeal to us on grounds that are psychosocial, not rational.

The Psychological Power of Language

Psychosocial approaches to criticism do not analyze style as such but look at language as a means by which to induce intense reactions in audiences. Such reactions are called *signal responses* because responses are immediate and unthinking, rather like one's immediate reaction to a red or a green light. As noted in Chapter One, we learn language in situations, and we incorporate those experiences into meanings. As a result, some symbols have powerful connotations that attract or repel us. There are words that arouse us to instant fury, to deep sadness, or to intense feelings of patriotism, love, or awe. There are symbols, such as the U.S. flag, whose mistreatment arouses cries of fury at acts labeled desecrations. Criticism from this perspective takes account of language that is likely to arouse such powerful reactions from audiences. Republican presidential candidate and CNN *Crossfire* star Patrick Buchanan uses language in this way very skillfully.

Social Movements

Studies of social movements have added important dimensions to this general critical perspective. It is best described as psychosocial to emphasize the link between individuals and the society and culture in which they live. For example, the simple fact of unmet needs clearly does not necessarily energize groups or individuals to act. The question, then, is what must occur, what kind of a climate must exist, for individuals or groups to act, even to form organizations seeking social change?

One way of viewing social movements is especially suited to a psychosocial perspective. On the basis of the work of a variety of scholarly studies, political scientist Jo Freeman proposes a schema to describe the conditions that must exist (*Politics*). First, she argues, based on research by Ted Robert Gurr, that individuals must experience relative deprivation; that is, they must see themselves as deprived in relation to others who become a reference group or a basis for comparison. For example, as the contemporary women's movement came into being in the 1960s, many women compared themselves to men and saw that although they were men's equals in intelligence, talent, and education, they were deprived of entry into professions and good jobs on the basis of sex.

Mere perception of relative deprivation is not enough, however. For many years, for example, women were deprived relative to males, but no women's movement emerged. Freeman argues that there must also be a certain climate that erodes the power of the dominant ideology justifying such differences. In addition, those in the relatively deprived group must experience persistent aggravation that reminds them of their inferior status. In the case of women, in the 1960s evidence showed that the ideology justifying the notion that "woman's place is in the home" was eroding. In 1961 President Kennedy formed the Commission on the Status of Women, which issued a 1963 report that documented discrimination against women, providing detailed factual evidence of relative deprivation (*American Women*). In that year as well, Betty Friedan expressed the profound dissatisfaction of predominantly white, middle-class, college-educated suburban housewives with their roles (*Feminine Mystique*). In 1964 "sex" was added to Title VII of the Civil Rights Act—as a joke!—giving legal force to the erosion of the ideology that legitimated discrimination against women.

Aggravation also was increasing. As the divorce rate climbed, more and more women became single parents. For the most part they and their children received inadequate or no support from the fathers, and as women attempted to enter the labor market, they faced barriers that increased their resentment of their inferior status because of the intensity of their need for decent jobs. They also felt acutely the unfairness of being paid only 59 cents for work for which men earned $1.00.

In other words, from this perspective, what individuals perceive as unmet needs is affected by the social and political climate of the culture in which they live. Social movement studies based on these assumptions analyze the societal conditions that energize individuals, that create psychological needs that motivate individuals to action.[5]

---

[5]By contrast, resource mobilization theorists argue that social movements are conflicts of interest that are the normal, rational, institutionally rooted, political responses of aggrieved groups. In other words, grievances are necessary but not sufficient to explain the rise of social movements. More important are the actual and potential resources that an aggrieved group can mobilize in pursuit of its goals (Zald and McCarthy). On the other hand, political process theory argues that much of the success of social movements in affecting policy depends on the receptivity of the political system at the time that supporters of a new movement are psychologically and organizationally ready to challenge the status quo. In other words, the political climate and the attitudes of those in power during the period when the movement is best able to exert pressure become crucial (Costain).

All rhetorical action occurs in a social and political context that is relevant to its reception. As Aristotle pointed out, the commonplaces, or the assumptions from which arguments are generated in all fields (1391^{b}27), and the maxims or adages, which are commonsense truths, that often serve as premises for argument are social truths that are created by a culture (1394^{a}19–1395^{b}20). Similarly, dramatistic criticism, discussed next, points to the linguistic processes through which basic biological needs are symbolically transformed into culturally sanctioned methods for their satisfaction. In other words, psychological analysis is ever and always psychosocial analysis, given the close relationship between individuals and their culture and the symbol system in and through which they develop a sense of themselves.

Accordingly, the problems of analyzing intercultural rhetoric loom large. A rhetorical act produced by someone from another culture is likely to be misinterpreted because the critic does not share the social, political, and symbolic assumptions of the speaker. For example, it is hard for Americans to understand the symbolic force of Zhao Ziyang's speech to the protesting students in Tiananmen Square, analyzed by Lee Lin Lee later in this volume, because we do not share Zhao's cultural assumptions about discourse or know the personal history that gives special power to his words. Similarly, as Janice Watson argues in a critique that also appears later in this volume, African Americans heard a somewhat different speech than did other U.S. listeners when Nelson Mandela came to speak to the U.S. Congress in 1990.

The concerns of psychosocial criticism illustrate the assumptions underlying this perspective and, in some cases, place particular emphasis on the effects criterion. In particular, this perspective is concerned with audience adaptation, motivating structure, rhetor credibility, the psychological rather than the probative, force of evidence, and peripheral cues that influence audience judgments.

ELM: Linking Rational and Psychological Elements

Critics are interested in how attitude change occurs—that is, in the processes through which people come to hold certain beliefs and in estimating the likelihood that they will act on those beliefs. There are no simple answers to these questions, but one kind of answer is given by theorists Richard Petty and John Cacioppo (*Communication and Persuasion*). They call their theory the elaboration likelihood model (ELM) because their model of persuasion emphasizes self-persuasion: the likelihood that members of the audience will be stimulated to elaborate a message—to process or interpret it, to develop, clarify, or embellish it, and to consider its implications.

ELM is useful in understanding the areas of overlap between psychosocial and rationalistic perspectives on criticism because ELM emphasizes the links between argument and psychological processes. ELM postulates that persuasion occurs through two routes: a central route and a peripheral route. The central route is rationalistic and argumentative. It is directly related to mental processing prompted by the quality of the arguments and the evidence on which they rest. Based on research by Petty and Cacioppo and others, changes in attitude that occur via this route require more thought and work on the part of the viewer, listener, or reader. However, research studies also suggest that attitude changes resulting from this kind of processing last longer, are more resistant to counterpersuasion, and predict behavior better than changes produced via the peripheral route. In other words, a strong case can be made for the rationalistic view of the importance of argument and evidence.

As its name suggests, the peripheral route to attitude change is less direct. The peripheral route is associative, based on linkages that lack a logical connection. For example, someone you dislike advocates a position, and you reject it because of your dislike of the advocate. In other words, attitude changes produced peripherally result from associations. Some element in the persuasive context or situation, something external to the message—such as a cognitive, affective, or behavioral cue—comes to be linked to the message or position advocated. That link permits a member of the audience to make a relatively simple inference from the cue to the advocated position. Consistent with the above example, an audience member might conclude, "If Senator Jesse Helms [or Senator Edward Kennedy] favors it, it must be bad." Other examples might include deciding that whoever presents more arguments has the stronger case, that whoever quotes a beloved authority must be right, or whoever is the more humorous must be wrong.

According to this research, the most important variable affecting an audience member's desire and willingness to elaborate a persuasive message is its personal relevance—the expectation that the issue will have significant consequences for one's life. The greater the personal consequences, the greater the importance of forming an opinion based on the most accurate and complete information because the consequences of making a bad decision are greater. For example, young women are less likely to work at understanding messages about osteoporosis, a weakening of the bones related to hormonal changes that affects older women particularly; but women in their early fifties who are just beginning menopause are likely to pay close attention to messages about the pros and cons of hormone replacement therapy. In fact, they may even seek out such messages. When there are vital personal consequences, people are likely to be motivated to engage in the challenging, even difficult cognitive work of interpreting, elaborating, and evaluating the merits of a proposal.

Elaboration is also affected by one's worldview and training. For example, those who view the world legalistically find messages justified on legalistic grounds more persuasive. Those who see the world in religious terms are more likely to be persuaded by messages that are justified on religious grounds. And so on.

Audience members can be prompted to participate in elaborating messages by appeals to their self-concepts. In other words, audience members can be invited to play a role that increases the chances that they will participate in the message, as, for example, when a rhetor praises them for being the sort of open-minded individuals who are willing to consider all arguments fairly. Yet such appeals can also limit participation as, for example, when a rhetor praises audience members' stand on an issue and describes them as the sort of people whose beliefs cannot be undermined by the blandishments of opponents. These are examples of what we called creating the audience in Chapter Two.

For those highly motivated by self-interest to participate in elaborating a message, the quality of the argument is more important, but for those with low motivation, who see little personal significance for them, peripheral elements take on greater significance. For example, first impressions of rhetors and their nonverbal behavior, including delivery and voice, become more important for those with low motivation. In effect, they tend to look for simpler ways to evaluate the message and reach a conclusion. Or they can be influenced by the sheer number of arguments offered, a peripheral cue; they conclude that because a lot of reasons were given for it, it must be the best choice.

Elaboration is also affected by the time it takes to interpret a message. For instance, the strengths and weaknesses of radio and television advertising are partially explained by research comparing the impact of audio and video presentations of a message with print versions. The audio and video presentations give audiences less opportunity to process issue-relevant arguments because the amount and pace of exposure to the message are imposed on them; they cannot pause to think or turn back to an earlier statement. Accordingly, those exposed to audio and video ads are rushed and, hence, pushed to rely on peripheral cues, such as color, music, celebrity endorsement, and the like. However, choices made on that basis are less enduring and more vulnerable to counterpersuasion.

In sum, the accumulated evidence of research on persuasion is quite consistent with the ELM view that there is a tradeoff between participating in and processing messages—exploring and evaluating arguments and evidence—and the operation of associations or peripheral cues. In general, anything that reduces a person's ability and motivation to interpret issue-relevant arguments also increases the likelihood that simple associations—peripheral cues in the source (voice and dress), message (how many arguments), recipient (fearful), or context (a comfortable, pleasant room)—may have an effect. Note that what Aristotle called rhetorical deduction, the enthymeme, is actually an argument that invites and prompts audience participation or, in the language of Petty and Cacioppo, increases the likelihood of elaboration.

DRAMATISTIC CRITICISM

Theories of symbolic interaction, particularly those developed from the works of Kenneth Burke, led to the development of the third general approach to criticism. Dramatistic criticism analyzes language and thought as modes of action rather than as means of conveying information. In the simplest terms, a dramatistic approach to criticism will be particularly interested in the form of the message—that is, in the kind of symbolic act that occurred. Accordingly, dramatistic criticism shifts attention to style or language (symbols); to motives understood as meanings and to links between motives, meanings, and ideology or views of the world; and to structure as form with an appeal all its own.

Language and Symbols

As we indicated in Chapter One, language makes meaning out of experience by naming and categorizing. Burke describes language as a series of terministic screens through which humans see the world. Although each terminology reflects reality, inevitably it is selective, mirroring only parts of reality. Thus, each terminology also deflects reality, directing attention away from some elements of the world and directing attention toward other elements.

The most basic terms refer to items in the world or describe reality directly. These terms, which Burke calls *positive terms*, reflect the qualities of language discussed here and earlier; but it is possible to point to examples of colors, of trees and whippoorwills, of tofu and almonds. *Dialectical terms*, in contrast, can be defined only by and in relation to other words. One cannot point to democracy or socialism, to bureaucracy or administration, to honesty or beauty; one must define them with words. Often they are defined by comparisons or contrasts that focus attention on some aspect or facet—for example, contrasting capitalism and socialism to emphasize ownership of the means of production or feudalism and capitalism to call attention to the centrality of reciprocal obligations in one and the lack of them in the other. Finally, Burke identifies what he calls *ultimate terms* or god and devil terms—labels for fundamental, all-encompassing values such as life and death, liberty or death, ballots or bullets. Undergirding every system of thought or belief, he argues, are such ultimate values that will be embodied in language that repeatedly reflects those values (*Rhetoric of Motives* 183–189).

Identification and Consubstantiality

The importance of language is indicated by Burke's assertion that the key term of his new rhetoric is "identification," whereas the key term of prior rhetorical theory was "persuasion" (*Rhetoric of Motives* xiii–xv). As human beings we have experiences, some of which are shared. That body of shared experience Burke calls *consubstantiality* ([con = with] + [sub = under] + [stance = to stand]), meaning sharing ground, having a common basis (*Rhetoric of Motives* 20–23). But the sheer fact of common experience means little unless that commonality is recognized and acknowledged, a process that occurs through symbols, usually language. That symbolic process is identification, and Burke says simply, "A speaker persuades an audience by the use of stylistic identifications" (*Rhetoric of Motives* 46). He describes the shift in emphasis by saying, "Wherever there is persuasion, there is rhetoric. And wherever there is 'meaning,' there is persuasion" (*Rhetoric of Motives* 172). Stylistic identifications extend beyond language. In his words, "You can persuade a man [*sic*] only insofar as you can talk his language by speech, gesture, tonality, order, image, attitude, idea, *identifying* your ways with his" (*Rhetoric of Motives* 55). He also writes, "Only those voices from without are effective which can speak in the language of a voice within" (*Rhetoric of Motives* 39). In other words, a dramatistic approach to criticism focuses on language because it assumes that persuasion occurs primarily through it. Rhetoric, as Burke understands it, is "rooted in an essential function of language itself . . . the use of language as a symbolic means of inducing cooperation in beings that by nature respond to symbols" (*Rhetoric of Motives* 43).

The Pentad and Ratios

Burke provides a system for analyzing a rhetorical act in order to discern its meaning. He calls it a grammar of motives. Because it has five parts—act, scene, agent, agency, purpose—it is called the *pentad* (*Grammar of Motives* xv–xxi, passim). Each of these elements can be linked in a ratio to every other element, yielding 10 ratios. Both the pentad and the ratios can be misused, particularly if they are applied as a formula to determine who, what, when, where, and why. First and foremost, it is important to know that these terms are *not* means to describe or analyze reality, unlike the who, what, when, where, and why of a journalistic lead. Rather, they are terms for analyzing *talk* about human action. In other words, they are terms for asking how did X construe the scene, how did X label what occurred, what role did X assume, how were the means described or interpreted, and how was the purpose or meaning of the act understood?

For example, in 1991, in the first trial of the Los Angeles police officers who subdued Rodney King and were accused of using excessive force, the different perspectives of the prosecution and defense are illuminated by the pentad. The prosecution construed the scene as a racist police department and the act, 67 baton blows, 57 after King was on the ground, as excessive force energized by the attitudes of racist officers. The agencies, the stun gun and the batons, were treated as lethal force whose use was intended to injure or even maim, rather than subdue, King. In contrast, the defense construed the scene as one of rising urban crime that threatened to overwhelm the city. The police officers became a "thin blue line" that stood between the criminals and the rest of the citizenry. The defense attorneys minutely analyzed the blows on the videotape to argue that they complied in detail with the police department specifications for subduing a dangerous, even violent suspect. The defense attorneys even walked around the courtroom with a police baton to make that agency more familiar and less threatening to the jury. The purpose or meaning of the act was what was in contention, and they argued that what occurred was the appropriate and legitimate subduing of a large, potentially dangerous, resistant criminal who had attempted to escape arrest in a high-speed chase. Neither of these rhetorical acts is "reality"; all the pentad can reveal is how reality was construed in the talk of each side. That is, pentadic analysis enables us to recognize and compare the meanings or motives in these competing rhetorical acts. In other words, the pentad is a device, rather like the elements of descriptive analysis we explained in Chapter Two, that can be used to illuminate the meaning or motive in a rhetorical work.

The ratios or relationships between terms also illuminate how rhetoric influences. In the case of the trial of the Los Angeles police officers, note that the defense placed great emphasis on the scene, which was rising urban crime. They were arguing that the scene required or called forth certain kinds of acts—a scene–act ratio. In effect, a scene of increasing crime legitimated, even demanded, extraordinary efforts by police. Conversely, the prosecution argued from an agent–act ratio that racist police officers commit racist acts. The prosecution attempted to show a climate of racism in the police department and to introduce comments made on the police radios after the beating to indicate the attitudes of the officers involved.

Such analysis uses the elements of the pentad to parse grammatically or analyze a piece of rhetoric to discover its meaning or motive. Burke also indicates that the pentad can be used in ideological analysis by identifying which term receives the greatest emphasis. For example, if the scene is emphasized or made controlling, it reflects a materialist ideology that diminishes the possibilities of agents and, thus, their responsibility for what occurs (Burke, *Grammar of Motives* 127–161). David Ling analyzed Senator Edward Kennedy's speech following the accident at Chappaquiddick that resulted in the death of Mary Jo Kopechne to show how Kennedy emphasized the scene in order to reduce his own responsibility for what occurred ("Pentadic Analysis"). David Birdsell analyzed Ronald Reagan's speech on Lebanon and Grenada to show how Reagan emphasized the scene to reduce his own responsibility for the deaths of more than a hundred U.S. Marines in Beirut ("Ronald Reagan").

An emphasis on act reflects behaviorist or empiricist beliefs (Burke, *Grammar of Motives* 128, 227–262). Students often encounter this attitude in their professors who focus on actual performance on a paper or exam and explain that there are no A's for effort. Businesspeople focus realistically on the bottom line; professional athletes focus on winning. Olympic medals are given for a single performance. Empiricists and behaviorists focus on what people do. In a sense, critics are behaviorists who focus on what people do symbolically, on "deeds done in words."[6]

An emphasis on the agent reflects idealism or individualism (Burke, *Grammar of Motives* 128, 171–226). In effect, it assumes that agents can overcome any obstacle: "Just pull yourself up by the bootstraps!" "If they did it, why can't you?" Those who emphasize the agent give credit to individual effort and discount such advantages as wealthy parents, political connections, or opportunities to enter the family business or to attend top educational institutions. This ideological perspective heightens individual responsibility, and it is a familiar rhetorical pattern in the United States because it is highly consistent with an ideology of individual rights and with the capitalistic emphasis on entrepreneurship. It is vividly illustrated in Russell Conwell's popular 19th-century lecture, "Acres of Diamonds" (Carlson).

---

[6]See, for example, Karlyn Kohrs Campbell and Kathleen Hall Jamieson, *Deeds Done in Words: Presidential Rhetoric and the Genres of Governance* (Chicago: University of Chicago Press, 1990), in particular Chapter Nine on President Gerald R. Ford's speech pardoning Richard M. Nixon.

An emphasis on agency is also familiar and congenial to Americans, who tend to be pragmatists (Burke, *Grammar of Motives* 128, 275–286) and who believe that science and technology can find a solution to most problems. Rhetoric reflecting such an emphasis seeks to operationalize and systematize. For example, rhetoric emphasizing agency is likely to argue that a new form of management will solve business productivity problems.

Rhetoric emphasizing purpose is rare because rhetoric tends to be instrumental—a means to an end—rather than consummatory—an end in itself. The philosophical or ideological equivalent of such an emphasis is mysticism, in which action, such as contemplation, is done for its own sake (Burke, *Grammar of Motives* 128, 287–317). That perspective is reflected in assertions of art for art's sake, in the hedonistic pursuit of pleasure, in the miser's love of money, not for what it can buy but for the sheer joy of amassing it, touching it, and gazing at it. Some highly expressive rhetoric is consummatory, articulating feelings for the sake of doing so, in order to ventilate, to get it off one's chest, but such rhetorical action is relatively rare. Occasionally, expressive rhetoric can have an instrumental purpose, as is illustrated by Eliezer Ben Yisrael's "Letter to the World from Jerusalem."[7]

Structure as Form

Burke describes form as "the creation of an appetite in the mind of the auditor, and the adequate satisfying of that appetite" (*Counter-Statement* 31) and as "an arousing and fulfillment of desires. A work has form insofar as one part of it leads a reader to anticipate another part, to be gratified by the sequence" (*Counter-Statement* 124). One kind of form is rationalistic, a perfectly conducted argument, that advances step by step the premises forcing the conclusion, whether in a rhetorical work or a mystery story. Sometimes form is repetitive, whether in restatement of the same idea in different ways or in a refrain that takes on additional meaning with each repetition, as in Dr. Martin Luther King's "I Have a Dream." Some form is qualitative, where the introduction of one quality, such as tone, creates an expectation that another quality will follow or persist. Some form is conventional or formulaic. We are familiar with situation comedies and expect them to develop in certain ways, just as we expect certain

---

[7]Eliezer Ben Yisrael, "Letter to the World from Jerusalem," in Karlyn Kohrs Campbell, *Critiques of Contemporary Rhetoric* (Belmont, CA: Wadsworth, 1972) 188–191.

things in eulogies or presidential inaugural addresses. Here form is generic—the expectation that a culturally recognized pattern will be followed and completed—although we expect originality in that process as well. Minor forms include language patterns such as parallelism, beginning each point or phrase with a similar grammatical pattern; alliteration, the repetition of initial consonants, as in "nattering nabobs of negativism"; and antithesis, as in "Ask not what your country can do for you. . . ." What is distinctive about dramatism is that it recognizes that form or structure has an appeal all its own, that structure adds to and intensifies content, with the result that a climax construction persuades us of its claims by engaging us in the completion of its form.

Genres

Conventional forms are *genres,* the types of discourse that come to be defined socially or culturally. Genres identify situations that are culturally designated as occasions on which discourse is appropriate and specify, at least in general terms, the sorts of symbolic action that are expected to occur. From the time of George Washington, the people of the United States have felt that presidents should address the nation as they begin a term in office. By contrast, Asian cultures have defined a form of discourse in which a person in authority in a company or government takes responsibility, expresses regrets, and promises some form of penance for wrongdoing, a type of discourse that is not culturally recognized in the United States or Europe. Generic analysis need not be dramatistic, but the dramatistic recognition of the power and appeal of form underlies generic analysis whether that analysis emphasizes rationalistic or psychosocial qualities.

Briefly, then, dramatistic analysis emphasizes the role of language and symbols in rhetoric and focuses its attention on language to an extent not common in the other perspectives described in this chapter. Dramatistic criticism stresses the importance of language-based identification that calls into being recognition of commonalities among individuals and groups. It attends to social truths created through discourse and is particularly attuned to the aesthetic, ethical, and ideological dimensions of using symbols. It emphasizes form or structure in recognition of the appreciation symbol users have for patterns, whether minor forms or socially defined genres of discourse. Dramatistic analysis seeks to understand meaning and motive and treats symbol use as infused with values and filled with ethical implications.

SUMMARY

Sometimes critics simply select one or another of these broad critical approaches and employ it without modification. That is, after careful descriptive and historical–contextual analysis, a critic may decide that a rationalistic, a psychosocial, or a dramatistic approach is best suited for a particular discourse. It is then applied in a relatively straightforward fashion to complete the critical process. But, perhaps unfortunately, few rhetorical acts lend themselves easily to such analysis. The three approaches to understanding rhetorical action, which form the bases for the three broad critical approaches, often overlap. As a result, rhetorical acts seldom function in a manner that is easily and completely explained by any single approach. Thus critics often must invent a critical approach by adapting or modifying one or more of these broad perspectives to suit the particular rhetorical act. Of course, critics must also demonstrate that these invented approaches are coherent, internally consistent, and warranted by both the discourse itself and its context.

A CRITICAL PERSPECTIVE APPLIED

To illustrate this stage of the critical process, we return once again to Nell Irvin Painter's essay, "Whites Say I Must Be on Easy Street." On the basis of our conclusions about the text in the first stage, and those about context in the second stage, we invent our approach to Painter's essay by drawing from all three critical perspectives: rationalistic, psychosocial, and dramatistic.

In the second stage of the critical process illustrated in Chapter Three, we turned to primarily historical sources outside the rhetorical act to place Painter's essay in its historical–cultural context. In this third stage we again draw on extrinsic sources, this time other rhetorical critics and theorists, to explain and justify our critical perspective or approach. The conclusions we reached in the first two stages served to guide us to those rhetorical sources.

Rationalism

Descriptive analysis revealed that Painter's purpose is to defend and justify her controversial position in support of affirmative action, to gain audience support for affirmative action to ensure quality education and employment for qualified individuals, and to attack proposals to eliminate or weaken affirmative action. From a rationalistic perspective, then, her essay would be classified as deliberative rhetoric.

As we observed earlier, rationalistic criticism is based on classical theories of rhetoric that originated in ancient Greece, primarily with Aristotle. In his *Rhetoric* Aristotle categorized oratory, the form of rhetoric with which he was concerned, into three types: political, which we now call deliberative; forensic, his category for speeches delivered in law courts; and the ceremonial oratory of display, which we call epideictic. The system of classification was based on "the three classes of listeners to speeches" because, according to Aristotle, it is the hearer "that determines the speech's end and object." The distinguishing factor is the listeners' response to the discourse. Aristotle concludes, "The hearer must be either a judge, with a decision to make about things past or future, or an observer. A member of the assembly decides about future events, a juryman about past events: while those who merely decide on the orator's skill are observers. From this it follows that there are three divisions of oratory" (1358^b3–7).

In other words, political or deliberative rhetoric is characterized by audience members who function as judges of future events—that is, of proposed policies or courses of action. Before such audiences, Aristotle says, the rhetor aims "at establishing the expediency or the harmfulness of a proposed course of action: If he [*sic*] urges its acceptance, he does so on the ground that it will do good; if he urges its rejection, he does so on the ground that it will do harm" (1358^b20). Thus, in rationalistic terms, Painter's effort to gain audience support for affirmative action because it does good by helping to end racist and sexist practices in education and employment, and to promote audience opposition to the Reagan administration's effort to eliminate or weaken affirmative action because it would do harm, makes her essay deliberative rhetoric.

Although we believe this classification of Painter's essay as deliberative rhetoric is accurate and useful, we also believe that a straightforward, rationalistic approach to her essay would be inappropriate. Earlier we explained that rationalistic criticism is best suited to works that extensively use supporting materials and have deductive structure, asserting a claim or conclusion that is justified through a series of arguments. By those standards Painter's essay is seriously flawed. Descriptive analysis revealed scant supporting material; other than her personal experiences, Painter employed only a single example. Moreover, her essay is structured inductively, moving from her personal examples, and the example of John Hope Franklin, to the general conclusion that affirmative action is an expedient policy. Thus a strict rationalistic critique of Painter's essay would necessarily render a negative assessment. More important, rationalistic criticism, as generally practiced, would reveal little about how the essay works to influence its target audience.

Other aspects of Aristotelian rhetorical theory, however, are more useful. Descriptive analysis revealed the importance of persona and ethos in Painter's essay. Aristotle says that ethos, or a rhetor's character, "may almost be called the most effective means of persuasion he [*sic*] possesses" (1356ª13). That is especially true in deliberative situations like Painter's. According to Aristotle, "That the orator's own character should look right is particularly important in political speaking" (1377ᵇ29). Further, ethos takes on added importance in controversial deliberations where strong arguments exist on both sides. "Persuasion is achieved by the speaker's personal character when the speech is so spoken as to make us think him [*sic*] credible," says Aristotle. "We believe good men [and women] more fully and more readily than others: this is true generally whatever the question is, and absolutely true where exact certainty is impossible and opinions are divided" (1356ª2). Given the rhetorical situation Painter faced, including the intense controversy and division of opinion about the policy of affirmative action, Aristotle's theory provides insight into her use of persona to build ethos.

Aristotle also notes the strategic importance of depiction in deliberative rhetoric. "Now the style of oratory addressed to public assemblies," he says, "is really just like scene-painting" (1414ª7). Although Painter's target audience was not a formal assembly, her aim was clearly deliberative, and her readers were asked to judge the expediency of affirmative action policies much as a legislative body would. Moreover, the two extended examples in the introduction of the essay, as well as the detailed "history lesson" that follows, paint a vivid scene for the audience. Thus, although a strict rationalistic approach to Painter's essay seems unwarranted, the classical theories on which rationalism is based are useful for understanding her skillful use of ethos and the power of depiction in her examples.

Psychosocial Criticism

Bonnie J. Dow and Mari Boor Tonn suggest an alternative approach to deliberative rhetoric, such as Painter's, which is essentially psychosocial in nature. As we indicated earlier, psychologically based criticism analyzes target audiences, the speaker, and how the rhetor uses the message to activate and channel the needs and motives of the audience members. In their analysis of the political rhetoric of former Texas Governor Ann Richards, Dow and Tonn argue that, from a rationalistic perspective, deliberative rhetoric "is characterized as abstract, hierarchical, dominating, and oriented toward problem-solving." They note that such discourse is further characterized by "formal evidence, deductive structure, and linear modes of reasoning" (288). Their analysis of Richards's speeches reveals a distinctly different, yet equally powerful, form of deliberative rhetoric that they label the "feminine style." Dow and Tonn ground their explanation of feminine style in an analysis of rhetor and audience and proceed to analysis of the ways rhetors employ feminine style to activate and channel the needs and motives of their audiences.

Building on earlier work by Karlyn Kohrs Campbell (*Man Cannot Speak for Her*), Dow and Tonn explain that historically, in the process of craft learning, "women developed particular capacities for concrete and contingent reasoning, for reliance on personal experience, and for participatory interaction" (287). These experiences continue to characterize the lives of contemporary women. As Dow and Tonn argue:

> [W]hile the historical conditions of women have changed in many ways, their primary social roles have not. Women still learn the "crafts" of housewifery and motherhood. Few women still make soap or weave cloth; nonetheless the traditionally female crafts of emotional support, nurturance, empathy, and concrete reasoning are still familiar requirements of the female role. Moreover, current research indicates that these skills, as well as the way they are learned, may continue to foster development of specific communicative strategies for women. (287–288)

Because such experiences are so widespread, Dow and Tonn insist, those communicative strategies create expectations for participants. "Women are encouraged to exhibit communicative patterns that correspond to the tasks that women are expected to perform in the private sphere," they write, "just as men's communication reflects their primary roles in public life." As a result of those expectations, the authors conclude, "female communication is characterized as concrete, participatory, cooperative, and oriented toward relationship maintenance" (288). Although these characteristics of female communication are easily discerned in private, interpersonal settings, Dow and Tonn argue that feminine style is recognizable in public, rhetorical settings as well. "In a rhetorical situation," they explain, "these attributes produce discourse that displays a personal tone, uses personal experience, anecdotes and examples as evidence, exhibits inductive structure, emphasizes audience participation, and encourages identification between speaker and audience" (287). In sum, through acculturation into traditional social roles, women develop distinctive communication strategies that Dow and Tonn label "feminine style" and that are manifested in both interpersonal and rhetorical settings. Participants in those communicative settings are likewise acculturated to expect, and to respond to, those strategies.

In deliberative situations, where audiences judge courses of action, the implications of feminine style are significant in two ways. First, Dow and Tonn argue that in the case of an individual rhetorical act, "the strategy of using concrete examples and personal experience is empowering; it encourages audiences' reliance on their own instincts and perceptions of reality, even if these dispute dominant models" (291). Thus audience members who have been similarly acculturated are invited to identify with the personal experiences of the rhetor and are empowered to make their own decisions based on that identification. The audience response is essentially inductive, moving from personal experience and identification to broader conclusions about a policy or course of action. According to Dow and Tonn, "the use of a personal tone and of personal disclosure are interrelated characteristics of feminine style. The telling of personal experience presupposes a personal attitude toward the subject and a willingness for audience identification, a goal of feminine style" (292).

Second, and perhaps more important, feminine style helps create new and distinctive criteria for rendering what Dow and Tonn call "political judgment." Noting the self-disclosive, personal nature of feminine style, they argue that "reliance on such evidence . . . creates an implicit standard for political judgment that is based on the primacy of experiential knowledge and inductive reasoning" (289). This implication for feminine style goes beyond its power to move target audiences to accept or reject a given course of action. On the basis of their analysis of Richards's use of feminine style, Dow and Tonn argue, "We believe that this conclusion can be extended to include the potential for feminine style to function philosophically as well as strategically, by creating alternative grounds for testing the validity of claims for public knowledge" (291).

Our descriptive analysis of Painter's essay, completed in the first stage of the critical process, suggests that the critical approach outlined by Dow and Tonn is particularly well suited for explaining how the discourse works. Painter's aim is deliberative; she seeks a "political judgment" about the policy of affirmative action. But the "means of persuasion" she employs depart sharply from traditional, rationalistic expectations and instead conform closely to the characteristics of feminine style explained by Dow and Tonn. Further, our analysis of the context in which Painter's essay functioned, completed in the second stage, suggests that both the rhetor and the members of her target audience were influenced by the female acculturation process Dow and Tonn described. For these reasons, we believe this approach will be fruitful in evaluating Painter's rhetoric.

Nevertheless, we acknowledge that a critical perspective drawn from the rationalistic and psychosocial approaches is potentially problematic when applied to Painter's essay. As we indicated earlier, the psychosocial perspective emphasizes the criterion of effects and the role that psychophysiological factors play in influencing behavior. Also, we explained that such criticism is keyed to the rhetor's effectiveness in achieving goals, and that the critic's primary concern is to analyze and explain how and why these effects were produced. In the case of Painter's essay, evaluating effectiveness is probably impossible. No data exist even to determine the number of individuals who read the essay, let alone the number who responded as Painter desired. Further, Painter's discourse was one small segment of an ongoing debate over the policy of affirmative action. Linking any change in public support of, or opposition to, the policy to this single essay would be impossible. Thus, although both the rationalistic and psychosocial perspectives provide insight into how Painter's essay influences her target audiences, neither seems wholly appropriate for evaluating the discourse. The dramatistic perspective will help resolve that dilemma.

Dramatism

The power of ethos to move audiences and the power of feminine style to produce identification between rhetor and audience signal the overlap between elements of Aristotle's rationalism, Dow and Tonn's psychosocial approach, and dramatism.

For Aristotle, ethos is created by what a rhetor says. "This kind of persuasion, like the others," Aristotle explains, "should be achieved by what the speaker says, not by what people think of this character before he [sic] begins to speak" (*Rhetoric* 1356ª9). In this sense the persuasive force of ethos is not something a rhetor brings to a rhetorical situation; rather, it is created by the rhetorical act. Campbell explains how that creation takes place. Noting that the Greek word *ethos* is closely related to the word *ethnic,* she says that "ethos refers not to your idiosyncrasies as an individual but to the ways in which you mirror the characteristics idealized by your culture or group." Those characteristics and qualities are reflected in the discourse itself. "We judge the character of another by the choices that person makes about how he or she will live with other members of the community," she concludes (*The Rhetorical Act* 120). In other words, the persuasive power of ethos is derived from rhetorical acts that demonstrate that the rhetor possesses characteristics and qualities valued by the target audience. That is a matter of identification, because as Burke says, "you can persuade a man [sic] only insofar as you can talk his language by speech, gesture, tonality, order, image, attitude, idea, *identifying* your ways with his" (*Rhetoric of Motives* 55). Because Painter devotes so much of her essay to creating ethos and to establishing identification with the target audience, the dramatistic theory of identification can help explain the persuasive force of the essay.

Moreover, Painter's vivid depiction of events in her own life and in the lives of her students and of John Hope Franklin suggests that Burke's pentad is a useful tool for understanding her essay. That is, our descriptive analysis revealed that Painter creates a scene, prior to enactment of affirmative action, that is dominated by virulent racism and sexism, which denied qualified ethnic minorities and women access to education and desirable employment. Individual agents within that scene—John Hope Franklin, Painter herself as an undergraduate student, and so forth—regardless of their talents and qualifications, were largely powerless to act in ways that overcome racism and sexism. As Painter's drama progresses, a new agency, affirmative action, overcomes those scenic forces and makes access to quality education and employment possible for qualified individuals, regardless of race or sex. In other words, Painter holds events before and after affirmative action in stark opposition. In the time before affirmative action, fully qualified, talented agents are at the mercy of the scenic forces of racism and sexism, moved against their will into poor education and less desirable jobs. After affirmative action, the new agency overcomes those forces. *Agency* is the featured term in Painter's depiction.

Conversely, our historical–contextual analysis revealed quite a different depiction of events from opponents of affirmative action, such as Reagan and his allies. In their view scenic elements of racism and sexism may once have justified policies like affirmative action, but that agency is no longer needed because racism and sexism have been eliminated from the scene. Thus, in the new "ability-conscious" society, individual agents are responsible for their own success or failure. *Agent* is the featured term in their depiction.

Burke explains that pentadic analysis can reveal the philosophical assumptions that guide the rhetor and thus underlie the rhetorical act. He writes:

> Dramatistically, the different philosophic schools are to be distinguished by the fact that each school features a different one of the five [pentadic] terms, in developing a vocabulary designed to allow this one term full expression (as regards its resources and its temptations) with the other terms being comparatively slighted or being placed in the perspective of the featured term. (*Grammar of Motives* 127)

He goes on to enumerate the relationships between the terms and the philosophical schools, saying in part, "For the featuring of *agent*, the corresponding philosophic terminology is *idealism*. For the featuring of *agency,* the corresponding terminology is *pragmatism*" (*Grammar of Motives* 128). In this way pentadic analysis reveals the contrast between idealism and pragmatism in Painter's essay and suggests an approach for evaluating her rhetoric.

CONCLUSION

This discussion illustrates the third stage of the process in which critics select or invent a critical approach to guide analysis and evaluation. On the basis of our descriptive and historical–contextual analyses, the first two stages of the process, we invented an approach by drawing from the three broad critical perspectives: rationalistic, psychosocial, and dramatistic. Because those three perspectives overlap considerably, we believe our approach is coherent, internally consistent, and warranted by the discourse and its context.

We must emphasize that our decision to invent our critical approach in this fashion was the product of the first two stages. In other words, before we made our decision, we first came to know Painter's essay as fully as possible on its own terms through descriptive analysis. Then we examined the historical and cultural context of the essay. Only when these first two stages of the process were completed were we sufficiently well informed to decide what critical approach would be most useful in this case. Then, with our conclusions from the first two stages as a guide, we drew on the work of other rhetorical critics and theorists to explain and justify our critical approach.

Not all rhetorical acts require critics to invent a critical approach. Sometimes one or another of the perspectives we explained earlier can be selected and applied with little or no modification. Most contemporary discourse, however, is complex, and critics must approach it in creative ways. This chapter illustrates how that can be done. In Chapter Five we discuss the standards or criteria for evaluating rhetorical acts that are suggested by the rationalistic, psychosocial, and dramatistic perspectives. Immediately following Chapter Five, we illustrate the final stage of the critical process by combining our conclusions from the first three stages into a finished critique of Painter's essay.

WORKS CITED

American Women: Report of the President's Commission on the Status of Women. Washington, DC: U.S. Government Printing Office, 1963.

Aristotle. *Rhetoric.* Trans. W. Rhys Roberts. New York: The Modern Library, Random House, 1954.

Bacon, Francis. *The Advancement of Learning.* Vol. 3, *The Works of Francis Bacon.* Ed. James Spedding, R. L. Ellis, and D. D. Heath. 7 vols. London: Longman, 1879.

Birdsell, David S. "Ronald Reagan on Lebanon and Grenada: Flexibility and Interpretation in the Application of Kenneth Burke's Pentad." *Quarterly Journal of Speech* 73 (1987): 267–279.

Black, Edwin. *Rhetorical Criticism: A Study in Method.* New York: Macmillan, 1965.

Brembeck, Winston L., and William Smiley Howell. *Persuasion: Means of Social Control.* Englewood Cliffs, NJ: Prentice Hall, 1952.

Brigance, William Norwood. "Can We Re-Define the James–Winans Theory of Persuasion?" *Quarterly Journal of Speech* 21 (1935): 19–26.

Burke, Kenneth. *A Grammar of Motives.* Berkeley: University of California Press, 1969.

———. *A Rhetoric of Motives.* Berkeley: University of California Press, 1969.

———. *Counter-Statement.* Berkeley: University of California Press, 1968.

Campbell, George. *The Philosophy of Rhetoric.* Ed. Lloyd F. Bitzer. Carbondale: Southern Illinois University Press, 1988.

Campbell, Karlyn Kohrs. *Man Cannot Speak for Her: A Critical Study of Early Feminist Rhetoric.* Vol. I. New York: Greenwood Press, 1989.

———. *The Rhetorical Act.* 2d ed. Belmont, CA: Wadsworth, 1996.

Carlson, A. Cheree. "Narrative as the Philosopher's Stone: How Russell H. Conwell Changed Lead into Diamonds." *Western Journal of Speech Communication* 53 (1989): 342–355.

Cicero. *De Inventione.* Trans. H. H. Hubbel. Cambridge, MA: Harvard University Press, 1949.

———. *De Oratore.* Trans. E. W. Sutton. Cambridge, MA: Harvard University Press, 1959.

Costain, Anne N. *Inviting Women's Rebellion: A Political Process Interpretation of the Women's Movement.* Baltimore: Johns Hopkins University Press, 1992.

Dow, Bonnie J., and Mari Boor Tonn. "'Feminine Style' and Political Judgment in the Rhetoric of Ann Richards." *Quarterly Journal of Speech* 79 (1993): 286–302.

Fotheringham, Wallace. *Perspectives on Persuasion.* Boston: Allyn & Bacon, 1966.

Freeman, Jo. *The Politics of Women's Liberation: A Case Study of an Emerging Social Movement and Its Relation to the Policy Process.* New York: Longman, 1975.

Friedan, Betty. *The Feminine Mystique.* New York: W. W. Norton, 1963.

Gurr, Ted Robert. *Why Men Rebel.* Princeton, NJ: Princeton University Press, 1970.

Kennedy, Eugene. "Pro-life Advocates Have to Undo Harm Fringe Groups Cause," *Chicago Tribune* 22 March 1993: sec. 1, p. 13.

Ling, David A. "A Pentadic Analysis of Senator Edward Kennedy's Address to the People of Massachusetts, July 25, 1969." *Central States Speech Journal* 21 (1970): 81–86.

Monroe, Alan H. *Principles and Types of Speech.* 1st ed. New York: Scott, Foresman, 1935.

O'Keefe, Daniel J. *Persuasion: Theory and Research.* Newbury Park, CA: Sage Publications, 1990.

Ouchi, William G. *Theory Z: How American Business Can Meet the Japanese Challenge.* Reading, MA: Addison-Wesley, 1981.

Petty, Richard E., and John T. Cacioppo. *Communication and Persuasion: Central and Peripheral Routes to Attitude Change.* New York: Springer-Verlag, 1986.

Zald, Mayer N., and John D. McCarthy, eds. *Social Movements in an Organizational Society.* New Brunswick, NJ: Transaction Books, 1987.

RECOMMENDED READINGS

Black, Edwin. *Rhetorical Criticism: A Study in Method.* New York: Macmillan, 1965. 78–90. This is the text and critique of John. J. Chapman's address at Coatesville, Pennsylvania, on August 18, 1912. Black presents Chapman's speech as transforming our experiences of a lynching into a morality play in which we are implicated. He uses the text as an example of a case in which rationalistic criticism is inappropriate. This analysis illustrates the choice of a critical framework based on the characteristics of a text. That framework is generic, an invitation to see the speech as an example of the form of the morality play. The analysis also illustrates the importance of finding alternatives to rationalistic analysis for texts of this sort.

Campbell, Karlyn Kohrs. *Man Cannot Speak for Her: A Critical Study of Early Feminist Rhetoric.* Westport, CT: Greenwood Press, 1989. Chapter 7, 105–120. This analysis of Susan B. Anthony's defense of her right to vote as a forensic address explores the major types of arguments Anthony used. In Chapter 11, pp. 169–171, there is a brief treatment of Carrie Chapman Catt's 1917 "Address to the Congress of the United States," which was an affirmative case for a woman suffrage amendment to the U.S. Constitution. Both analyses illustrate rationalistic criticism.

Campbell, Karlyn Kohrs. "The Rhetoric of Radical Black Nationalism: A Case Study in Self-Conscious Criticism." *Central States Speech Journal* 22 (1971): 151–160. This essay contrasts the conclusions from a neo-Aristotelian and a dramatistic analysis of radical black nationalist rhetoric and illustrates how critical systems can be either antagonistic or sympathetic to a body of discourse.

Carlson, A. Cheree. "Narrative as the Philosopher's Stone: How Russell H. Conwell Changed Lead into Diamonds." *Western Journal of Speech Communication* 53 (1989): 342–355. This essay illustrates the appeal of narrative and the power of dramatistic analysis, but it also illuminates the psychosocial power of Conwell's appeals.

Dow, Bonnie J., and Mari Boor Tonn. "'Feminine Style' and Political Judgment in the Rhetoric of Ann Richards." *Quarterly Journal of Speech* 79 (1993): 286–302. This essay is a psychosocial approach to rhetorical analysis grounded in feminist theory. Through analyzing a body of discourse, these authors claim that, by the way she argues, Governor Richards is altering the bases for political judgment. The essay illustrates how critics can assess the impact of prior rhetoric on subsequent discourse, a different understanding of effects.

Hill, Forbes. "Conventional Wisdom—Traditional Form—The President's Message of November 3, 1969." *Quarterly Journal of Speech* 58 (1972): 373–386. The power of psychosocial appeals based on shared premises becomes clear in this analysis, which also illustrates the potential of an Aristotelian approach to criticism.

Zyskind, Harold. "A Rhetorical Analysis of the Gettysburg Address." *Journal of General Education* 4 (1950): 202–212. This essay illustrates how Aristotelian genres can be applied to illuminate how a speech works to achieve its ends.

Two additional essays, listed earlier, also serve to illustrate the approaches to criticism examined in this chapter. Gerald Philipsen's essay, "Mayor Daley's Council Speech: A Cultural Analysis," listed at the end of Chapter Three, illustrates the necessity of historical–contextual analysis in understanding a text, but it also indicates the psychosocial motives that led Daley to make this speech. A review of Amy Slagell's "Anatomy of a Masterpiece: A Close Textual Analysis of Abraham Lincoln's Second Inaugural Address," listed at the end of Chapter Two, should take note of Lincoln's powerful psychosocial appeals as well as his pleas for thoughtful deliberation about the consequences of action.

CHAPTER FIVE

Evaluation:
The Final Stage of Criticism

The aim of rhetorical criticism, as we said in Chapter One, is to evaluate discourse. Well-done, thorough criticism increases the capacity of readers to appreciate rhetorical discourse and enables general audiences to make informed and deliberate judgments based on persuasive appeals. Ultimately, good criticism and good critics aspire to add to our understanding of how humans use symbols to influence each other. Such criticism improves the quality of persuasive discourse in society and tests and modifies both theories of rhetoric and critical systems. Achieving that aim is the result of the critical process we discussed in Chapters Two, Three, and Four. Critics come to know the discourse on its own terms, place the discourse in its context, and select or invent an approach or system to complete the evaluation. The finished criticism is a product of information gathered and conclusions drawn in the first three stages of the process.

As the preceding chapters have demonstrated, however, the critical process is not as mechanical or formulaic as it may sound. Rhetorical action and, therefore, rhetorical criticism are arts rather than sciences. The three broad theories or explanations for rhetorical action, and the corresponding broad approaches to rhetorical criticism, are not separate, discrete formulas. In practice, they overlap so frequently that in most cases critics must invent a perspective or approach by drawing from two or more of them. Likewise, no single standard is adequate for judging or evaluating all discourse. Instead, critics must select the standard or combination of standards most appropriate for the discourse in question and the critical approach they employ.

Four basic standards or criteria are available for evaluation of rhetorical action. First, because such acts usually are instrumental, designed to attain some goal, they can be judged by an *effects criterion* that evaluates how successful they were in achieving their purpose. Second, because such acts usually address real-world problems and solutions, they can be judged by a *truth criterion* that assesses how accurately and fully they present problems and how carefully they assess the probable effects of solutions they propose. Third, because the definition of any problem involves values, these acts can be judged through an *ethical criterion* that weighs the impact of the values they espouse. Finally, because they are symbolic acts whose appeal rests in part on skillful use of symbols, they can be judged by an *artistic criterion* that assesses the role of language and form on their symbolic force. These four criteria vary in usefulness and in the ways they are applied in the three broad critical perspectives. Moreover, the four criteria may be applied individually or in combination. Strengths and weaknesses must be noted in each case. In this chapter we describe each criterion generally and then indicate how it might be applied in each of the critical approaches we have identified.

THE EFFECTS CRITERION

Because most rhetorical acts are instrumental—that is, intended to produce some observable result—the urge to judge their effectiveness is understandable. Political candidates seek votes. Leaders seek support for their policies and rejection of those of their opponents. Attorneys seek favorable verdicts. Product advertisers seek increased sales. Thus critics often are tempted to praise the successful messages of candidates, leaders, attorneys, advertisers, and the like and to condemn those that are unsuccessful. Such evaluation can be legitimate and useful, or it can be fraught with problems, depending on the discourse to be judged and the critical approach employed.

Rationalistic Criticism

Traditionally, critics who took a rationalistic or "neo-Aristotelian" approach applied the effects criterion in a straightforward manner, judging discourse on its short-term effectiveness in eliciting the desired response from the rhetor's immediate audience. In his landmark essay "The Literary Criticism of Oratory," published in 1925, Herbert A. Wichelns provided the foundation for rationalistic judgment in this traditional sense. The "point of view" of rhetorical criticism, Wichelns said, "is patently single. It is not concerned with permanence, nor yet with beauty. It is concerned with effect. It regards a speech as a communication to a specific audience and holds its business to be the analysis and appreciation of the orator's method of imparting his [*sic*] ideas to his hearers" (54). Wichelns's concern for judging immediate effectiveness was echoed by other critics. For example, in their widely used textbook, Lester Thonssen and A. Craig Baird asserted, "A rhetorical judgment is a composite of data and interpretation that is intended to reveal the *effect* of a given speech upon a particular group of listeners. The word *effect,* or *response,* is all-important. It suggests the central reason for rhetorical criticism" (9).

Following that dictum, traditional critics sought evidence of the effectiveness of a speech in secondary accounts of audience reaction, the results of elections or votes in Congress, reactions of eminent observers, and the like. As many subsequent scholars pointed out, however, traditional assessments of effectiveness were problematic.[1] Those shortcomings of judging effectiveness will be discussed later.

Most contemporary rationalistic critics employ the effects criterion in a different fashion, to judge discourse not in terms of its actual effects but in terms of how well a case was made that should have been persuasive in inducing the target audience to make sound judgments and to take the actions that such judgments imply (see Hill, "Conventional Wisdom"). Those critics carefully place the discourse in its historical context, isolate the target audience or audiences and the rhetor's purpose, and analyze the discourse in light of classical rhetorical theories. Judgment is based on how well the discourse is adapted to each target audience. But because this approach compares the discourse to guidelines suggested by classical theory, the contemporary effectiveness criterion typically overlaps with the artistic criterion. John M. Murphy's critique of a speech delivered by Robert F. Kennedy in Chicago in 1968, which appears in Part II of this volume, illustrates this contemporary use of the effectiveness criterion.

Obviously, because most rhetoric seeks to influence audiences in practical ways, considerations of how successful it was in doing so are always relevant. Because considerations of effects are so central to psychological approaches to criticism, that criterion and its shortcomings are discussed in more detail in the next section.

---

[1]For discussions of the difficulty of assessing effectiveness, see Edwin Black, *Rhetorical Criticism: A Study in Method* (New York: The Macmillan Company, 1965), especially Chapters II and III, and G. P. Mohrmann and Michael C. Leff, "Lincoln at Cooper Union: A Rationale for Neo-Classical Criticism," *Quarterly Journal of Speech* 60 (1974): 459–467.

Psychosocial Criticism

The effects criterion is an important standard for evaluating rhetoric in psychosocial criticism. At its simplest, it judges the success rhetors have in achieving their ends with their audiences—selling products, receiving votes, or raising money, for example. Because rhetoric is goal-directed communicative behavior, success or failure in eliciting desired responses is an important consideration in evaluating it. Under circumstances where some degree of control is possible, psychosocial assessment of effectiveness can be relatively accurate and useful.

A fast-food company such as McDonalds, for example, might test-market a new sandwich in a locality or region. The new product would be advertised heavily in the local or regional media, perhaps "at a special price" or "for a limited time only." At the end of a specified time period, sales figures for the new sandwich would provide reasonably reliable evidence of the effectiveness of the advertising campaign. Similarly, a political candidate might hire a consultant to conduct focus group interviews to discover the concerns and opinions of representative voters about key issues. Campaign advertising and the candidate's speeches would then be targeted to those concerns and opinions. As the campaign progressed, sophisticated polling techniques would measure voter reaction to the candidate's messages. The resulting data, again, would provide reasonably reliable evidence of effectiveness. The importance many persuaders place on such psychosocial measures of effectiveness was made clear during court proceedings prior to the 1994–1995 murder trial of former football star O. J. Simpson. Both prosecutors and defense attorneys hired special consultants, administered lengthy questionnaires, and conducted extensive interviews in an effort to find jurors sympathetic to their side and, ultimately, to tailor their cases to those jurors.

Most rhetorical critics, however, do not work in such controlled environments, nor do they have the resources to conduct such elaborate psychosocial analysis. For most critics, assessing effectiveness is problematic.

One major problem is the difficulty in determining just what is valid evidence of rhetorical effects. When a speaker addresses an immediate audience, clapping may be a polite social convention in honor of a visiting dignitary, a reaction to the occasion, such as the joy of graduation, rather than the speech, or a reflection of their feelings about the speaker, such as a beloved but rather muddled professor emeritus. Scales attempting to measure shifts of opinion are open to challenge because they tend to measure what individuals say has occurred. Responses to written rhetoric are often difficult to ascertain, although book sales may be an indicator. For example, several critics attempted to explain why Jonathan Schell's *The Fate of the Earth*,[2] a rather serious work on ecological questions, became a best-seller. Explaining effects is an important goal and function of criticism.

Equally daunting is the challenge of attempting to isolate the effects of a single rhetorical act from related persuasive efforts. Persuasive messages rarely appear in isolation; ordinarily they are part of an ongoing conversation about an issue of concern, and audience response is likely to be a result of all the persuasion. A related difficulty is the problem of assessing the long-range effects of a rhetorical work, which are even more difficult to determine. Some works have little immediate effect although their long-range effects may be considerable. For example, the immediate effects of Abraham Lincoln's address at Gettysburg were small, but Garry Wills has argued that the address reconceptualized Americans' understanding of the nature of their system of government in a way that was equivalent to the impact of the Declaration of Independence.[3] In order to avoid such difficulties, critics may choose to consider not the actual effects but the effects the discourse is capable of producing or could reasonably be expected to produce. However, such a move shifts the emphasis from effects, at least as ordinarily understood, to considerations of artistry and ethics, discussed later.

When applied in isolation, the effects criterion can also generate a major philosophical problem. Many persuasive messages are highly successful, but they have appalling social and ethical consequences. Tobacco and liquor advertising and the speeches of Adolf Hitler are illustrations. Growing cynicism about the U.S. criminal justice system is at least partly the result of the jury selection techniques we mentioned earlier. In isolation, the effects criterion implies that whatever works is good regardless of its societal impact—a destructive and inhumane position. When it is expanded to include a concern for long-range effects, the criterion is infused with ethical considerations. Thus, a simple assessment of immediate effects is, by itself, an inadequate basis for critical judgment; consequently, it is never applied alone in the critiques that appear later in this volume.

---

[2]Jonathan Schell, *The Fate of the Earth* (New York: Knopf, 1982). Brief analyses are found in Walter R. Fisher, "Narrative as a Human Communication Paradigm: The Case of Public Moral Argument," *Communication Monographs* 51 (March 1984): 1–22, especially pp. 11–12; and Robert C. Rowland, "Narrative: Mode of Discourse or Paradigm?" *Communication Monographs* 54 (September 1987): 264–275, especially pp. 267–268.

[3]Garry Wills, *Lincoln at Gettysburg: The Words That Remade America* (New York: Simon & Schuster, 1992).

Dramatistic Criticism

As we explained in Chapter Four, dramatism analyzes language and thought as modes of action rather than as means of conveying information. Dramatistic critics are less interested in the substance of the message and more interested in the form of the message—that is, in the kind of symbolic act that occurred. Accordingly, dramatism shifts attention to style or language (symbols); to motives understood as meanings; to links between motives, meanings, and ideology or views of the world; and to structure as form with an appeal all its own.

Questions of rhetorical effectiveness are not irrelevant to dramatistic critics. But whereas rationalistic or psychosocial critics might judge a rhetorical act solely on the basis of its immediate effectiveness, or on the basis of whether the discourse should have produced the desired response, dramatistic critics are more interested in judging the ethics and/or artistry of the means used to produce those effects. For example, in his critique of Hitler's *Mein Kampf,* Kenneth Burke acknowledged the power and effectiveness of the Nazi leader's rhetoric and went on to render an ethical judgment of the "kind of 'medicine' this medicine-man has concocted, that we may know, with greater accuracy, exactly what to guard against, if we are to forestall the concocting of similar medicine in America" (191). Burke's purpose in critiquing Hitler's book is typical of dramatism's concern for the long-term effects of rhetorical action. Assessment of long-term effects is primarily an ethical or artistic matter, as will be discussed later.

THE TRUTH CRITERION

In our culture, as in most, telling the truth is favored over its opposites—lies, distortion, willful misrepresentation, half-truths, and the like. From ancient times rhetoric and truth have been linked. In his explanation of why students should study the art of rhetoric, for instance, Aristotle said one important reason was "because things that are true and things that are just have a natural tendency to prevail over their opposites, so that if the decisions of the judges are not what they ought to be, the defeat must be due to the speakers themselves, and they must be blamed accordingly" (1355^a21–24). From that statement grows the assumption that good rhetoric, that which deserves the praise of critics, is rhetoric that upholds the truth. Its opposite deserves censure. In some instances, then, application of the truth criterion can produce valid and useful critical judgments. Unfortunately, assessing truthfulness is not always as simple as it might sound.

Rationalistic Criticism

Because it sees public discourse as a means by which truths may be realized in thought, attitude, and action, a rationalistic perspective invites critics to emphasize truth as well as effectiveness. The truth criterion is applied to test the accuracy and adequacy of the discourse as a picture or an explanation of reality insofar as it is known and understood. In other words, assessment of truth compares the intrinsic reality presented in the discourse with extrinsic reality to determine whether the evidence and claims are consistent with prevalent research in that area. Critics test the accuracy of evidence presented against other sources; they test the arguments presented against the pool of possible arguments.

For example, in Chapter Three, our historical–contextual analysis of Nell Irvin Painter's "Whites Say I Must Be on Easy Street" examined Painter's use of her own career and that of John Hope Franklin as examples. Our research revealed that the reality presented in the essay was consistent with information from extrinsic sources. With regard to those examples, then, the truth of Painter's essay would be judged positively. Although considerations of truth are an important part of criticism, applying this criterion is often challenging because most assessments of truth are not as simple as verifying the accuracy and authenticity of supporting materials.

In the realm of rhetorical action, truth is always relative. Aristotle recognized this when he called rhetoric "the counterpart of dialectic" (1354^a1). From a classical point of view, dialectic is a form of intellectual disputation, a question–answer format through which philosophers seek truth in an absolute sense. Rhetoric, however, establishes truth in a social sense: What is "true" is that which is accepted as true by the society. Different societies, and even different subgroups within a society, can hold different truths. The function of rhetoric is to gain acceptance of one truth over others. Or, as we said in Chapter One, the issues to be resolved through rhetorical action are those about which honest and informed people may disagree. Thus testing the truth of a rhetorical act can often be a matter of comparing one social truth with another, and critics should proceed with caution.

A larger philosophical question also arises. In analyzing the rhetoric of protest movements, critics often must ignore traditional notions of truth and consider "truths" held culturally or subculturally and reaffirmed by the interaction of the speaker and audience. These truths are symbolic. That is, they constitute definitions, redefinitions, and reinterpretations of the experiences of a particular group, and they are not verifiable in some absolute sense, particularly by someone from outside the group. Recognize, however, that a danger lurks here of simply redefining "truth" as group acceptance. What is true becomes what is believed to be true, despite the requirement that if such truths are to be made credible to those outside the group, there must be evidence that all can recognize as verifying that reality.

Finally, no rhetorical act is ever long enough to tell the whole truth. Of necessity, time and space limitations require the selection of evidence, arguments, and explanations. Inevitably, any piece of rhetoric analyzes an issue incompletely and presents only some of the relevant data. Moreover, on most issues, even highly informed experts disagree; in fact, much rhetoric arises out of such differences of opinion. The experiences and values of individuals influence what each perceives as true. Consequently, simple assessments of the truth are impossible. Even when applied strictly, the truth criterion compares one symbolic reality, the rhetor's, with other symbolic realities, the views of other experts, of the critic, and so on. Moreover, some discourses, particularly those of specialized experts, are accurate, virtually exhaustive, and thorough, but are effective only for a small group of others with similar levels of expertise and are largely unintelligible to the rest of us. If the truth criterion alone were applied, such works, however limited their audience, would have to be adjudged excellent. Hence, in isolation, the truth criterion has serious limitations.

Psychosocial Criticism

Laws prohibiting false and misleading advertising attest to the importance of the truth criterion for psychosocial criticism. Because this approach is primarily concerned with assessing effectiveness, the urge to praise "whatever sells" is great. The truth criterion tempers that urge.

Psychosocial critics begin with the same assumption as others: that telling the truth is favored over its opposites. The criterion is applied in much the same way as in rationalistic criticism: The intrinsic reality of the rhetorical act is compared with extrinsic reality. In other words, critics consider the claims made and the evidence provided in light of information available from other sources. For example, targeting consumers' concern for safety, the manufacturer of a luxury automobile presents media advertising touting the fact that the electrical contacts for the air bags in its cars are "plated in gold" to prevent malfunctions resulting from rust or corrosion. Apparently, consumers should buy this particular car, instead of another, because no expense has been spared, no detail overlooked, to ensure their safety. In fact, only a very limited number of firms manufacture electrical contacts for air bags and sell the parts to automobile manufacturers. All of the contacts are gold-plated. So, although the advertisement in question was not untrue per se, the central premise, that gold-plated electrical contacts, by themselves, make this car superior to others, is not true. As this example illustrates, psychosocial critics should employ the criteria of truth and ethics as well as the effects criterion.

Dramatistic Criticism

Dramatism employs the truth criterion in a slightly different fashion, again concerning itself with the long-term ethical and artistic implications of discourse. As we said in Chapter Four, dramatism views language as a series of terministic screens through which humans see the world. Although each terminology reflects reality, inevitably it is selective, mirroring only parts of reality. Thus each terminology also deflects reality, directing attention away from some elements of the world and directing attention toward other elements. In that sense, rhetorical action *creates* truth—the intrinsic reality of the rhetorical act. Further, because of the selecting and deflecting properties of language, dramatism acknowledges one of the major weaknesses of the truth criterion: that no rhetorical act is ever long enough to tell the whole truth.

From the dramatistic perspective, extrinsic reality is likewise symbolically created, so comparison of intrinsic and extrinsic reality only reveals competing views of reality or truth and does little to evaluate discourse. Instead, dramatistic critics examine the choices rhetors make as they create the intrinsic reality of the rhetorical act. Their concern is with the long-term ethical and artistic implications of the language used to select and deflect reality, which we discuss next.

THE ETHICAL CRITERION

Ethical considerations give attention to the long-term social and political implications of both the means and the ends of rhetoric. As we said earlier, the issues addressed through rhetorical action involve values. Both the desired response and the means used to elicit that response reveal the values embraced by the rhetor. The ethical criterion assesses the long-term implications of those values for the society.

Rationalistic Criticism

Ethical considerations also are linked to rationalistic assumptions. In one sense, the truth and ethical criteria overlap: A rhetorical act that violates the truth criterion may be judged unethical. In a larger sense, rationalistic criticism holds that reasoned, free, and open deliberation sustained by adequate and credible evidence is the best means to preserve underlying values. Those values assume that reason is the best tool for judgment and that debate reflecting all interests ensures that all options are considered and the best is selected. In this sense, discourse that deliberately polarizes audiences and seeks to stifle, rather than promote, legitimate dissent and debate about relevant issues becomes ethically questionable.[4]

As critics of this perspective on public discourse have pointed out, however, unless all interest groups have equal access to the marketplace of ideas, all points of view are not heard, and all options are not considered. For example, the 1992 presidential campaign featured a series of debates between the three major candidates, George Bush, Bill Clinton, and Ross Perot. But other candidates, such as André Marrou of the Libertarian party, were not invited to participate and were thus deprived of an audience.

Given socioeconomic differences among groups, a rationalistic system is likely to reinforce the privileges of those who have greater wealth and power. Those rhetors also have greater access to the marketplace and the ability to engineer consent from the less privileged and from those in government through advertising, through ownership of the communication media, and through paid lobbying and donations to political candidates. In an article discussing this issue during the time of civil rights and antiwar protests in the 1960s, Robert L. Scott and Donald K. Smith wrote, "A rhetorical theory suitable to our age must take into account the charge that civility and decorum serve as masks for the preservation of injustice, that they condemn the dispossessed to non-being, and that as transmitted in a technological society, they become the instrumentalities of power for those who 'have'" (8). The ethical criterion, as well as its limitations, will be discussed at greater length in relation to dramatistic forms of criticism.

Psychosocial Criticism

Because psychosocial criticism tends to praise rhetorical acts that are most effective, ethical considerations become particularly important. Effective means of analyzing target audiences, adapting persuasive messages to those audiences, and presenting those messages are stud-

---

[4]For an example of criticism that reveals such discourse, see Karlyn Kohrs Campbell, "An Exercise in the Rhetoric of Mythical America," *Critiques of Contemporary Rhetoric* (Belmont, CA: Wadsworth, 1972) 50–58.

ied and emulated by other rhetors. Ineffective means are quickly discarded. In that way prior rhetorical action can powerfully influence the form, if not the content, of later rhetorical action. Psychosocial critics employing the ethical criterion assess the implications of that influence for the society.

For example, our society cherishes the belief that free, full, and open debate about important issues is a cornerstone of democracy. Yet there is growing concern that 30-second political advertisements are creating an electorate that is unconcerned about, and perhaps even incapable of following and understanding, detailed discussions of the important issues in a political campaign. In other words, there is growing concern that the form of the discourse helps to create an expectation among voters that adequate debate and discussion of issues as important as selecting the best person to serve as governor, senator, or even president can be presented in 30 seconds. The long-term implications for the country are potentially staggering.

Dramatistic Criticism

As indicated earlier, there are two evaluative criteria of special importance in dramatistic criticism, although these criteria, like all the others, are relevant to all rhetoric. The first of these is ethical. Applying an ethical criterion involves assessing the social implications and the long-term effects of persuasive discourse. Obviously, societies and critics differ about which values should be encouraged and applauded and which discouraged and condemned. Ethical judgments ordinarily fall into two general areas: judgments about the consequences of discourse on the society and judgments about the impact of discourse on future rhetorical activity.

An ethical judgment about the impact of discourse on society requires assessing the values and the image of human beings and of society that are upheld as ideal. In a society based on democratic principles, the issues are closely related to protection of freedom of speech. Sometimes that is translated into advocacy of a "free and open marketplace of ideas" in which, at least in theory, all points of view would be presented for public discussion and deliberation. Such an ethic assumes that a marketplace that reflected all points of view and interests would be self-corrective, revealing the inadequacies of arguments and policies and correcting misinformation in open debate. It also assumes that the strongest arguments and evidence and the most accurate, careful interpretations would win the assent of a majority.

Note that this ethic is highly rationalistic in its assumptions, and those who hold differing views of influence offer cogent criticisms.

Most important, of course, is that citizens do not always choose what is best for the whole but often choose instead what is best for themselves. On any issue, those with the greatest stake will strongly argue for what is in their self-interest. In many cases those will be individuals and groups with greater economic resources, social status, and political influence than those in other interest groups. For example, as Americans contemplate health care reform, the views of physicians and insurance companies are disproportionately represented because of their substantial resources, high status, and substantial political clout, derived from their financial contributions to political candidates. In fact, dominant groups tend to be able to ensure that messages consistent with their interests will appear in mass media advertising, news, and entertainment, making it likely that even those groups disadvantaged by policies that enrich the dominant group will grant their assent. Accordingly, Congress may vote billions of dollars to bail out a major automobile company, for example, on the premise that "what's good for Chrysler is good for the nation." Analyses of the mass media by such thinkers as Stuart Hall and others have heightened awareness of how much the marketplace of ideas in a mass society is skewed toward the views of dominant groups.[5] In general, the first type of ethical assessment attempts to evaluate the long-term effects of messages and advocacy on society and on the human beings in that society.

The second area of ethical judgment is intrinsic. Edwin Black argues that "some techniques of argument can have an effect independent of the substance of the argument," that rhetoric works "to make certain techniques conventional, to shape an audience's expectations for discourses that they will later hear or read, to mold an audience's sensibilities to language" (56). In effect, rhetoric builds on prior rhetoric, and earlier rhetoric sets precedents for discourse that follows. As we have indicated, for instance, there is concern that television programming, punctuated into short segments divided by even shorter advertisements, has shortened the attention spans of audiences so that we are less and less willing to listen to more extended deliberations. Because most important issues are complex, this unwillingness or perhaps even inability to attend to such discourse and debate means that

---

[5]See, for example, Stuart Hall, "The Rediscovery of 'Ideology': Return of the Repressed in Media Studies," *Culture, Society and the Media,* ed. Michael Gurevitch, Tony Bennett, James Curran, and Janet Woollacott (London: Methuen, 1982) 56–90; "The Whites of Their Eyes: Racist Ideologies and the Media," *Silver Linings,* ed. George Bridges and Rosalind Brunt (London: Lawrence and Wighat, 1981) 28–52; and Glasgow University Media Group, *Bad News,* vol. 1 (London: Routledge & Kegan Paul, 1976) and *More Bad News,* vol. 2 (London: Routledge & Kegan Paul, 1980).

we are unlikely to hear a fully developed case for or against managed competition in health care, for a BTU tax as opposed to a gasoline tax in terms of fairness and protection of the environment, and so on. In other words, critics ask what would be the long-term effect if this kind of discourse becomes a norm that creates expectations and sets precedents for future rhetoric.

THE ARTISTIC CRITERION

Discussing the characteristics of rhetorical action in Chapter One, we noted that rhetorical discourse is frequently poetic—a characteristic that refers to the degree to which a discourse displays ritualistic, aesthetic, dramatic, and emotive qualities. That poetic quality of rhetoric suggests that artistry, as well as effectiveness, truth, and ethics, can be a useful measure of excellence. Critics using an artistic criterion judge how well a rhetorical act works to achieve its purpose, and thus this criterion is often used in conjunction with the effects criterion. Artistic judgments are, in essence, a matter of critics' tastes. But good criticism on artistic grounds goes beyond the critic's personal reaction to judge discourse against clearly defined standards of artistic excellence.

Rationalistic Criticism

Rationalistic forms of criticism treat artistic considerations as one would expect. Consistent with their emphasis on argument, discourses are expected to be unified, consistent, and coherent in structure and to be clear and precise in their use of language or style. Moreover, critics employing rationalistic approaches can render artistic judgments by carefully comparing a rhetorical act to classical guidelines or standards, usually drawn from the works of Aristotle or Cicero.

In this sense the artistic criterion is used in conjunction with or overlaps the effects criterion. Traditional critics might judge a rhetorical act positively because it achieved its purpose with the immediate audience, and then go on to render an artistic judgment in order to account for its effectiveness. Or more contemporary critics might conclude that a discourse should have been effective with target audiences because of its artistry. Murphy's critique of Robert Kennedy's speech, found in Part II of this book, and Forbes Hill's critique of Richard Nixon's Vietnamization speech, referred to in Chapter Four, are examples of the interaction between the effects and artistic criteria. In their critique of Abraham Lincoln's speech at Cooper Union in 1860, Michael C. Leff and Gerald P. Mohrmann draw on classical guidelines to argue that Lincoln's speech was an artistically excellent example of a familiar rhetorical genre, the campaign speech.[6] Artistic evaluation of genres is discussed in more detail later in this chapter.

Psychosocial Criticism

In Chapter Four we said that from a psychosocial perspective, an important function of rhetoric is to body forth through illustration, through figurative language, description, example, and the like, long-range goals so that they become as vivid and appealing as the satisfaction of immediate desires. That function corresponds to the fourth step in the motivated sequence, also discussed in Chapter Four. At this stage in the sequence, the rhetor describes vividly and memorably depicts the satisfaction—what the situation would be if the plan were adopted or the product purchased. As we said earlier, many advertisements illustrate this step. For instance, many advertisements for cosmetics such as lipstick or mascara and for hair replacement procedures include before and after photos, intended to help customers imagine a more beautiful and youthful self if they just use these cosmetics or undergo hair replacement. Ads for skin moisturizers show young, wrinkle-free, beautiful women who represent imaginatively the goal toward which customers presumably strive.

Although vivid description and depiction are intended to produce the desired response in the target audience, they are also matters of artistry because they awaken the senses or emotions of viewers and listeners. Some advertisements for fast foods—like pizza, for example—are so vivid that viewers can almost smell and taste the cheese and pepperoni. And in a completely different context, former Lieutenant Colonel Oliver North testified before the U.S. Senate committee investigating the Iran–Contra scandal while wearing his Marine uniform. The picture North presented was undoubtedly intended to stir patriotic impulses in the senators, as well as the television audience, and influence their assessment of North. Presidential candidates frequently deliver speeches in front of a backdrop composed of dozens of

---

[6]These three critiques are examples of using classical guidelines to render an aesthetic judgment of discourse. Murphy's critique appears later in this volume. See also Forbes Hill, "Conventional Wisdom—Traditional Form—The President's Message of November 3, 1969," *Quarterly Journal of Speech* 58 (1972): 373–386; and Michael C. Leff and Gerald P. Mohrmann, "Lincoln at Cooper Union: A Rhetorical Analysis of the Text," *Quarterly Journal of Speech* 60 (1974): 346–358.

U.S. flags in an effort to stir similar patriotic impulses. Thus the artistry with which psychosocial appeals are presented is clearly linked to their effectiveness.

Artistic considerations are not limited to visual images. As we also noted in Chapter Four, from a psychosocial perspective, both evidence and language can exert strong emotional influences on viewers and listeners. Poignant examples, metaphors, figurative analogies, and so forth can trigger aesthetic responses—that is, sensually awakening responses—in audiences. Like rationalistic critics, then, psychosocial critics can employ artistic standards to help account for rhetorical effectiveness.

Dramatistic Criticism

The second major criterion emphasized in dramatistic criticism arises out of the concerns just described. Applying an artistic criterion involves assessing the artistry of the rhetorical act—its strategic use of the available resources in appeal, argument, and language in order to achieve its ends. Ordinarily, basic elements of artistry (such as clear and appropriate language as opposed to jargon, ambiguity, and malapropisms), a discernible thesis, consistency in development and tone, and the like are routinely applied to all rhetoric. If these are absent, the work is probably a model of what not to do, a negative example. Considerations of artistry usually emerge when a work has unusual force and power so that critics feel a strong need to explain how and why it was able to work its wiles on audiences. In other words, analysis focused on artistic matters is likely to be appropriate when a work is particularly eloquent, effective, or unusual. For example, the form of the Declaration of Independence attracts critical interest because that form has been imitated by many other liberation or revolutionary movements. Accordingly, one asks, what is it about this form that is so powerful and so adaptable? John F. Kennedy's inaugural address is remembered by many who heard it and is often held up as a model for modern presidential inaugurals. What is it about that address that makes it so memorable and appealing?

Artistic analysis focuses on strategies that are particularly well executed, such as powerful narrative development, heightened dramatic conflict building to a climax, a wedding of language and thought, the powerful embodiment of a persona or role, or the creation of a work that seems to sum up the central ideas of a movement or to represent a value. Ordinarily, such works are highly original, even unique, meriting study as examples of the most skilled uses of symbols of which human beings are capable. Artistic analysis also enables critics to assess the poetic elements of rhetorical acts, such as the skillful use of language, the power of a metaphor, the creation of an ideal character, vivid depiction, and the like.

Further, dramatism's concern for form and genre also prompts artistic judgments. As we said in Chapter Four, dramatism recognizes that form or structure has an appeal all its own; structure adds to and intensifies content. In that sense dramatistic analysis of form results in artistic judgment. Moreover, conventional forms are genres, the forms of discourse that come to be defined socially or culturally. Genres identify situations that are culturally defined as occasions on which discourse is appropriate and specify, at least in general terms, the kinds of symbolic action that are expected to occur. Dramatistic critics can identify the characteristics of a particular genre and then use those characteristics as standards to make artistic judgments of rhetorical acts that are members of that genre. Leff and Mohrmann's critique of Lincoln's speech at Cooper Union, mentioned earlier, is illustrative. Alternatively, critics can use an exemplar of a genre as a touchstone against which to judge other discourses, or they can engage in analog criticism, comparing two members of a genre.[7] Both approaches yield artistic judgments.

The artistic criterion is especially congenial to dramatistic criticism because of its emphasis on language and because it views human symbolization in a context of conflict. Drama implies an agon or conflict in which literary or poetic elements are likely to be especially significant.

SUMMARY

The final stage completes the critical process by judging or evaluating discourse according to a clearly defined standard. Four standards or criteria are typically used: effects, truth, ethics, and artistry. Each criterion has strengths and weaknesses, and like the three broad approaches to criticism, they frequently overlap in practice. Critics must select the criterion or combination of criteria best suited to the discourse in question and the critical approach used.

---

[7]In the discussion of presidential inaugural addresses by Karlyn Kohrs Campbell and Kathleen Hall Jamieson, Abraham Lincoln's first inaugural address becomes a touchstone against which other inaugurals might be measured. See *Deeds Done in Words: Presidential Rhetoric and the Genres of Governance* (Chicago: University of Chicago Press, 1990) 14–36. For an example of analog criticism of speeches of apology or self-defense, see L. W. Rosenfield, "A Case Study in Speech Criticism: The Nixon–Truman Analog," *Communication Monographs* 35 (1968): 435–450.

CONCLUSION

This ends our discussion of the process of criticism. As we have described it, that process begins with two evidence-gathering stages: descriptive analysis in order to possess the text as fully as you can and historical–contextual analysis in order to refine your understanding of the rhetorical act by seeing it in relation to its time, place, occasion, and audience. What comes next is based on you the critic. It involves your interpretive judgment about both the approach that will best illuminate how the rhetorical act works to achieve its goals and the criteria that are most appropriate to evaluating the significance of the discourse.

Painter Critique

We have illustrated each stage of the critical process with analyses of Nell Irvin Painter's essay on affirmative action. Immediately following this chapter, you will find our finished critique of that essay. As you read it, notice that what began as separate stages of the critical process has become a seamless whole. We begin with the historical context because we believe that considerable emphasis needs to be given to the formidable obstacles the author faced in making her argument. We think you cannot appreciate her artistry without being reminded of how difficult a task she undertook. Some of that background also describes the problems involved in providing equal opportunity to minorities and women and reminds you of the credibility of the competing persuaders who make the arguments that she is refuting. We also try to indicate why her personal history is especially important on this issue. Because much of her argument is personal, the biographical data about Painter are also part of applying a truth criterion to the essay.

   The choice of a theoretical perspective begins with a generic decision about the kind of rhetorical act this is. Because the essay focuses on policy, it is deliberative. At this point a considered decision is made not to apply the standards of stock issue analysis derived from rationalistic criticism. We make that decision because to do otherwise would lead to immediate condemnation. No further criticism would be needed; however, we judge this to be a powerful act in spite of deficiencies in these areas, so we searched for an alternative perspective that would be well suited to the actual characteristics of the work itself. We found that alternative in an approach emphasizing "feminine style" that falls outside the three general critical streams we have described. The importance of ethos in this approach, however, echoes the emphasis on ethos in deliberative rhetoric by Aristotle, the founder of rationalistic criticism. The importance of identification positions feminine style at the juncture between Aristotelian rhetoric and Burke's extension of it. Recall that Burke describes his "treatment, in terms of identification," not "as a substitute for . . . but an accessory to the standard lore" (*Rhetoric of Motives* xiv). In addition, Burke's notion of using the pentad to identify philosophical commitments is introduced because this is a way to compare and contrast the views of the opposing parties.

What follows clearly reflects prior descriptive analysis, and you may find this somewhat repetitious. Most works of criticism, however, are not preceded by a complete text of the rhetorical act being analyzed, and one of the most difficult decisions a critic makes involves how much must be quoted in order to demonstrate that the claim or interpretation is supported by the text. Most critiques are written for readers who have not read the original work and who need to be convinced that the critic's conclusions are well founded. The material drawn from descriptive analysis also demonstrates that the choice of an approach based on feminine style is appropriate, as it illustrates the artistry of the essay.

When we examine the second example Painter employs, we introduce outside material that validates the truth of her characterization of John Hope Franklin. Note that Painter assumes that her readers will be familiar with him and his distinguished career. If they are not, an important element in her persuasion is lost. In effect, we betray some of our own biases by reinforcing her persuasive message with this information.

Obviously, Painter is wise to speak to disparate audiences of whites and blacks, of men and women. This is a way for her to avoid some obvious attacks. What we try to show, however, is that she does something more with those two audiences: She creates a moment of surprise, perhaps a moment of consciousness raising, by pointing out the similarities in their statements and the similarity of both to familiar racist and sexist attitudes that existed long before affirmative action policies came into existence. If Painter is successful in creating such a moment of surprised recognition, she has a good chance to prompt readers at least to rethink their positions, which is success indeed.

An ethical judgment follows that suggests that it is desirable to evaluate policies based on their effects on the real lives of individuals, which is what the feminine style attempts to do. That is reinforced by contrasting the pragmatic views of Painter with the idealistic views of the Reagan administration, a process facilitated by using Burke's pentad as an analytic tool. Finally, ethical judgments link us as critics to contemporary policy disputes, and we try to make our values explicit as we explain our position. We believe that criticism of contemporary rhetoric inevitably leads to engagement in contemporary issues. This is an important function of criticism, which can assist in making our policy decisions more enlightened by helping us as consumers to see more clearly the strengths and weaknesses of positions.

Other Critiques

The critique of Painter's essay is followed by the texts and critiques of six other rhetorical acts that we hope will help you to exercise your skills as critics and as critics of criticism. The rhetorical acts are diverse, and the critiques of them have been selected to introduce a variety of issues and perspectives. Each is preceded by a brief note indicating the critical issues addressed.

The works we have chosen are selected to display the symbolic resources available to rhetors, the significance of cultural context and knowledge in audiences and critics, the links between critical perspectives and the criteria applied for evaluation, and the overlapping character of the critical perspectives we have described in the actual practice of critics. Rhetorical criticism is challenging precisely because humans are so resourceful in their use of symbols that no simple formula can be used to interpret and evaluate their acts. We have tried to make the critical process and the alternatives available to the critic as clear as possible. These rhetorical acts and critiques should remind you that application of them demands skillful invention on the part of critics, including you.

WORKS CITED

Aristotle. *Rhetoric.* Trans. W. Rhys Roberts. New York: The Modern Library, Random House, 1954.

Black, Edwin. *Rhetorical Criticism: A Study in Method.* New York: Macmillan, 1965.

Burke, Kenneth. "The Rhetoric of Hitler's 'Battle.'" *Philosophy of Literary Form.* Baton Rouge: Louisiana State University Press, 1973. 191–220.

Burke, Kenneth. *A Rhetoric of Motives.* 1950. Berkeley: University of California Press, 1969.

Hill, Forbes. "Conventional Wisdom—Traditional Form—The President's Message of November 3, 1969." *Quarterly Journal of Speech* 58 (December 1972): 373–386.

Philipsen, Gerry. "Mayor Daley's Council Speech: A Cultural Analysis." *Quarterly Journal of Speech* 72 (1986): 247–260.

Scott, Robert L., and Donald K. Smith. "The Rhetoric of Confrontation." *Quarterly Journal of Speech* 55 (1969): 1–8.

Thonssen, Lester, and A. Craig Baird. *Speech Criticism: The Development of Standards for Rhetorical Appraisal.* New York: The Ronald Press, 1948.

Wichelns, Herbert A. "The Literary Criticism of Oratory." Reprinted in *Methods of Rhetorical Criticism.* Ed. Robert L. Scott and Bernard Brock. New York: Harper & Row, 1972. 27–60.

RECOMMENDED READINGS

Burke, Kenneth. "The Rhetoric of Hitler's Battle." *Philosophy of Literary Form.* Baton Rouge: Louisiana State University Press, 1973. 191–220. Originally published in 1941, this essay analyzes Hitler's *Mein Kampf* and argues that the ideology therein was a bastardization of Christian thought. A model of Burkean analysis, it suggests a way to approach ideology in major social movements.

Campbell, Karlyn Kohrs. "Stanton's 'The Solitude of Self': A Rationale for Feminism." *Quarterly Journal of Speech* 66 (October 1980): 304–312. This critique illustrates a distinctive approach to a unique rhetorical masterpiece produced by a movement philosopher late in a social movement, also illustrating the development of a critical framework based on characteristics of the act being analyzed.

Condit, Celeste. "The Rhetorical Limits of Polysemy." *Critical Studies in Mass Communication* 6 (June 1989): 103–122. This essay contests claims of reader-response criticism to argue that audience members respond to and recognize a common text although their differing values may cause them to evaluate it differently. Condit also identifies some of the conditions that affect whether audience members will participate in and elaborate a message.

Corbett, Edward P. J. "Analysis of the Style of John F. Kennedy's Inaugural Address." *Essays in Presidential Rhetoric,* 2d ed. Ed. Theodore Windt and Beth Ingold. Dubuque, IA: Kendall/Hunt, 1987. 95–104. This is a detailed study of the artistic qualities that made John F. Kennedy's inaugural address so memorable.

Henry, David. "The Rhetorical Dynamics of Mario Cuomo's 1984 Keynote Address: Situation, Speaker, Metaphor." *Southern Speech Communication Journal* 53 (Winter 1988): 105–120. President Reagan had used metaphors powerfully; this essay illuminates how Cuomo replaced those metaphors with others and used metaphors as argument.

Hill, Forbes. "Conventional Wisdom—Traditional Form—The President's Message of November 3, 1969." *Quarterly Journal of Speech* 58 (December 1972): 373–386. Rereading this essay will illustrate the explanatory power of psychosocial criticism as well as its limitations in addressing questions of truth or ethics.

Japp, Phyllis. "Esther or Isaiah? The Abolitionist–Feminist Rhetoric of Angelina Grimké." *Quarterly Journal of Speech* 71 (August 1985): 335–348. This critique illustrates the persuasive power of persona in public rhetoric, particularly in the rhetoric of early U.S. women speakers.

Lake, Randall A. "Enacting Red Power: The Consummatory Function in Native American Protest Rhetoric." *Quarterly Journal of Speech* 69 (May 1983): 127–142. Rhetoric is ordinarily thought of as instrumental, a means to an end; this critique suggests that some rhetoric is expressive. In addition, this essay calls into question the assumption of majority whites that the test of rhetoric is its persuasiveness for them.

———. "The Metaethical Framework of Anti-Abortion Rhetoric." *Signs: Journal of Women in Culture and Society* 11 (1986): 478–499. This essay tries to uncover differences between the ethical systems of anti-abortion and pro-choice advocates.

———. "Order and Disorder in Anti-Abortion Rhetoric: A Logological View." *Quarterly Journal of Speech* 70 (November 1984): 425–443. This dramatistic analysis of anti-abortion rhetoric emphasizes artistic and ethical considerations.

Leff, Michael, and Gerald Mohrmann. "Lincoln at Cooper Union: A Rhetorical Analysis of the Text." *Quarterly Journal of Speech* 60 (October 1974): 346–378. Mohrmann, Gerald, and Michael Leff. "Lincoln at Cooper Union: A Rationale for Neo-Classical Criticism." *Quarterly Journal of Speech* (December 1974): 459–467. The first essay is a close textual analysis of the speech; the second links close textual analysis to generic criticism to identify the special characteristics of the political campaign speech.

Leff, Michael. *Rhetorical Timing in Lincoln's "House Divided" Speech. The Van Zelst Lecture in Communication.* Evanston, IL: Northwestern University, May 1983. This lecture vividly illustrates the difference between history and rhetorical analysis. Leff shows how Lincoln managed the audience's experience of his speech through the way that it unfolded through time, illustrating the rhetorical power of structure.

Lucas, Stephen E. *Portents of Rebellion: Rhetoric and Revolution in Philadelphia, 1765–1776.* Philadelphia: Temple University Press, 1976.

167–175. This rhetorical analysis of Thomas Paine's *Common Sense* illustrates the important links between rhetorical and historical contextual analysis.

Philipsen, Gerry. "Mayor Daley's Council Speech: A Cultural Analysis." *Quarterly Journal of Speech* 72 (1986): 247–260. This is another example of analysis of a work that is not intelligible to most of the U.S. audience.

Tonn, Mari Boor, et al. "Hunting and Heritage on Trial in Maine: A Dramatistic Debate over Tragedy, Tradition, and Territory." *Quarterly Journal of Speech* 79 (May 1993): 165–181. Using the pentad, these authors show how the shooting of a woman in her backyard by a hunter was redefined by the community, which illustrates how the pentad can be used to understand talk about events.

Windt, Theodore Otto, Jr. "The Diatribe: Last Resort for Protest." *Quarterly Journal of Speech* 58 (February 1972): 1–14. Revised in *Presidents and Protestors*. Tuscaloosa: University of Alabama Press, 1990. 211–240. This analysis of the discourse of the Yippies of the 1960s compares their rhetoric to that of the Cynics of ancient Athens in order to make sense of their utterances as symbolic action—a vivid illustration of the power of genre to illuminate highly unusual rhetoric.

In the preceding chapters we have focused on criticism of more traditional rhetorical forms; however, other kinds of rhetorical acts are inviting objects of criticism. Here is a sampling of critical essays that illustrate criticism of less traditional rhetorical acts:

Bybee, Carl. "Constructing Women as Authorities: Local Journalism and the Microphysics of Power." *Critical Studies in Mass Communication* 7 (September 1990): 197–214. This analysis of a newspaper article incorporates information about the source and its history into an assessment of the rhetorical impact of its news reporting. This is also an example of a cultural studies approach to rhetorical analysis.

Cloud, Dana L. "The Limits of Interpretation: Ambivalence and the Stereotype in *Spencer for Hire.*" *Critical Studies in Mass Communication* 9 (December 1992): 311–324. This is a study of a prime-time television program from a cultural studies perspective. The author argues that the ambivalent presentation of the character Hawk becomes a way in which this series reinforces stereotypes of African Americans.

Dow, Bonnie J. "Hegemony, Feminist Criticism and *The Mary Tyler Moore Show.*" *Critical Studies in Mass Communication* 7 (September 1990): 261–274. This is a feminist and cultural studies analysis of one of the most popular television sitcoms that shows how role relationships can be used to reinforce traditional conceptions of women.

Gray, Herman. "Television, Black Americans, and the American Dream." *Critical Studies in Mass Communication* 6 (December 1989): 376–386. This is a study of the representation of African-American life in television news and prime-time programming. It treats these representations as important parts of the public discourse about U.S. race relations that have important ideological implications. This is also a cultural studies approach to rhetorical analysis.

Sandage, Scott A. "A Marble House Divided: The Lincoln Memorial, the Civil Rights Movement, and the Politics of Memory, 1939–1963." *The Journal of American History* (June 1993): 135–167. This historical study shows how the Lincoln Memorial was made into a powerful icon of the civil rights movement that strengthened and energized its rhetoric.

II

The Practice of
Rhetorical Criticism

THOMAS R. BURKHOLDER AND KARLYN KOHRS CAMPBELL

Nell Irvin Painter's "Whites Say I Must Be on Easy Street"

Few issues of public policy generate more controversy than the complex of laws, executive orders, federal mandates, and court decisions known collectively as affirmative action. Because fairness and equality are celebrated as traditional societal values, the goal of equal opportunity in education and employment is applauded by virtually everyone. Policies enacted to help achieve that goal, however, continue to provoke disagreement. Advocates of affirmative action argue vehemently that overt racism and sexism continue almost unabated. Moreover, they argue that regardless of overtly racist and sexist actions, institutionalized racism and sexism continue to thwart equal opportunity policies, making affirmative action necessary. Opponents of affirmative action argue just as vehemently that the policy creates a new form of discrimination directed at groups not protected by affirmative action. Further, they contend that the protected groups themselves are harmed by the policy. Rhetors on both sides face formidable rhetorical problems.

In this essay we examine a single rhetorical act that supports affirmative action—an essay by Nell Irvin Painter entitled "Whites Say I Must Be on Easy Street." We begin by briefly tracing the history of controversy surrounding affirmative action policies. Next we present a theoretical perspective that provides an alternative to traditional approaches for analysis of deliberative rhetoric like Painter's. Finally we evaluate Painter's discourse according to criteria consistent with that theoretical perspective. Our analysis reveals how a skilled rhetor facing a difficult rhetorical problem can tap the resources of language to adapt to a divided and skeptical (or even hostile) target audience.

THE HISTORICAL CONTEXT

Because the issues surrounding affirmative action are emotion-laden, public opinion is divided. According to Susan D. Clayton and Faye J. Crosby, "A glance at any newspaper reveals that affirmative action is currently one of the most controversial policies in the United States. The issues are complex, they stir strong feelings, and in the media everyone seems to have an opinion on the topic" (1). Despite the controversy, the issue remains unresolved. As James E. Jones, Jr., explains, "The modern debate over affirmative action has occupied us for over 20 years without achieving resolution of the underlying issues or contributing to clarification of what divides the nation" (346). The controversy is better understood in light of a brief history of the policy.

The Development of Affirmative Action

The 1964 Civil Rights Act was intended to end the brutal effects of "intentional or nonaccidental discrimination"—what most experts call "overt racism" when it is directed toward ethnic minorities. The aim was to promote equal opportunity through "race-neutral" policies (Clayton and Crosby 13). President Lyndon Johnson then augmented the Civil Rights Act with two executive orders intended to go beyond ensuring equal opportunity. In September 1965 he issued Executive Order 11246, which, according to Clayton and Crosby, "required any organization that had a contract with the federal government to take affirmative action to ensure the just treatment of employees, and potential employees, of all races, colors, religions, or national origin. . . . [T]he order was amended to prohibit sex discrimination in 1967 with Executive Order 11375" (13–14). In 1972 these executive orders were amended again to apply to educational institutions (Washington and Harvey 9).

These significant changes shifted the emphasis from promoting equal opportunity to redressing the effects of past discrimination. As Clayton and Crosby argue, "Affirmative action refers to positive measures taken to remedy the effects of past discrimination against certain groups. Whereas a policy of equal opportunity requires merely that employers and institutions not discriminate on the basis of group membership, and in fact encourages them to ignore characteristics of group membership," they conclude, "affirmative action mandates a consideration of race, ethnicity, and gender" (2–3). Proponents of affirmative action argued that because ethnic minorities and women were relegated for so long to low-wage, low-status, second-class positions in education and the workplace, racism and sexism had become institutionalized and thus could not be ameliorated through equal opportunity alone. Affirmative action was intended to combat institutionalized racism and sexism.

In higher education, the area of greatest interest for Painter, the history of both overt and institutionalized racism and sexism is similar. For decades overt racism excluded ethnic minorities from the most desirable academic positions. According to Valora Washington and William Harvey, "Before World War II, Hispanics and African Americans were virtually invisible in higher education." They go on to point out that even acquiring the necessary qualifications was no guarantee of employment in predominantly white institutions: "Even by 1936, there was a sizable group of African Americans with Ph.D.s, 80 percent of whom taught at three historically African American institutions (Atlanta, Fisk, and Howard Universities)" (iii).

The percentage of university faculty who are ethnic minorities has been consistently small for decades. Washington and Harvey explain that "by 1972 . . . African Americans represented 2.9 percent of all faculty (including those at historically African American universities). Other minority groups (including Hispanics, but not Asians) were 2.8 percent of the total faculty. There were only 1,500 faculty who could be identified as Mexican American or Chicano" (iii–iv). As in employment generally, efforts to ensure equal opportunity in academic settings were unable to overcome institutionalized racism. Traditional hiring processes, Washington and Harvey argue, "did not entail specific guidelines for posting announcements, advertising, interviewing, or extending offers. Personal connections, associations, and friendships constitute what is called the 'old boy system,' which was the mechanism through which vacant faculty positions were likely to be filled" (12). In addition, supposedly race-neutral employment policies were again subverted. For example, "an important race-neutral qualification standard in the academic marketplace is published research," Gertrude Ezorsky says. "Publication requirements, however, worked against the recruitment of black professors because the majority taught heavy course loads in predominantly black colleges, which limited their time for research and writing" (22).

Affirmative action was intended to ameliorate the effects of institutionalized racism by filling the gaps in "race-neutral," equal opportunity programs. According to Ezorsky, "The primary importance of affirmative action lies in its effectiveness as a remedy for institutional racism, by which race-neutral policies and practices can lead to the exclusion of blacks" (2). On one level the aim of affirmative action was to improve the economic conditions of ethnic minorities and women. But a larger aim was to help eliminate racism and sexism. As Clayton and Crosby explain, "On a deeper level, however, [affirmative action] also responds to a psychological and sociological condition, which is the perception that members of these groups are second-class citizens in the United States. It is hoped that affirmative action will eliminate the social barriers by eliminating the financial ones" (3–4). Virtually all people in the United States applaud that aim, but intense controversy persists over affirmative action as the best means for achieving it. That controversy and the deep divisions it produces in prospective audiences constitute the major obstacle rhetors on either side of the issue must overcome.

The Rhetorical Problem

As we indicated earlier, because of the emotion-laden issues involved, racism and sexism, because resolving those issues addresses traditional values of fairness and equality, and because affirmative action potentially affects nearly everyone in the areas of education and employment, many individuals hold strong opinions about the policy. Clayton and Crosby report the results of a recent survey: "Among white respondents, 52 percent believed that affirmative action programs had helped blacks to get better job opportunities, and only 10 percent said they had hurt; the percentages among black respondents were slightly more neutral, with only 45 percent feeling that affirmative action had helped but only 5 percent thinking it had hurt," they continued. "Thus 38 percent of whites and 50 percent of blacks felt that affirmative action had made no difference. Asked if current government efforts to help blacks get better job opportunities had gone too far, 31 percent of whites and only 13 percent of blacks answered affirmatively" (21).

As these statistics reveal, opinions on affirmative action are partly determined by ethnicity. But other factors are important as well. Clayton and Crosby argue that "demographic characteristics can predict attitudes toward affirmative action. Not surprisingly, women, nonwhites, younger people, and Democrats show more support for affirmative action" (23). Presumably, then, men, whites, older people, and non-Democrats show less support for the policy. There are, however, important exceptions to these generalizations.

Many individuals who are members of groups that theoretically benefit most from affirmative action oppose the policy. Some of those individuals are extremely influential people. In his confirmation hearings for a position on the United States Supreme Court, Clarence Thomas voiced opposition to the policy. Justice Thomas is not alone. "Thomas Sowell, Shelby Steele, and Glenn Loury are some of the more prominent black critics who have gained national attention as they have spoken and written against the policy," Clayton and Crosby point out. "Stephen Carter, the William Nelson Cromwell Professor of Law at Yale University, has also questioned the wisdom of the policy, even as he characterizes himself as an 'affirmative action baby' " (1–2). Apparently membership in one of the so-called protected classes is no guarantee of support for affirmative action, even if one has benefited personally.

Thomas Sowell, a senior fellow of the Hoover Institution at Stanford University, for example, is harshly critical of numerical requirements for hiring ethnic minorities, often called "quotas," which have sometimes been enacted because of affirmative action. "Today's grand fallacy about race and ethnicity," Sowell says, "is that the statistical 'representation' of a group—in jobs, schools, etc.—shows and measures *discrimination*. This notion is at the center of such controversial policies as affirmative action hiring, preferential admissions to college, and school busing," he continues. "But despite the fact that far-reaching judicial rulings, political crusades, and bureaucratic empires owe their existence to that belief, it remains an unexamined assumption" (417). Sowell is blunt in his attack on advocates of affirmative action based on numerical goals or requirements. " 'Representation' talk is cheap, easy, and misleading," he says. "Discrimination and opportunity are too serious to be discussed in gobbledygook" (419).

Glenn C. Loury, professor of political economy at the John F. Kennedy School of Government at Harvard University, is equally critical of affirmative action programs. Indeed, he believes that those programs can be harmful to the very groups of people they are designed to benefit. "The broad use of race preference to treat all instances of 'underrepresentation' introduces uncertainty into the process by which individuals make inferences about their own abilities," says Loury. "A frequently encountered question today from a black man or woman promoted to a position of unusual responsibility in a 'mainstream' institution is: 'Would I have been offered this position if I had not been a black?' Most people in such situations want to be reassured that their achievement has been earned, and is not based simply on the organizational requirement of racial diversity," Loury continues. "As a result, the use of racial preference tends to undermine the ability of people to confidently assert, if only to themselves, that they are as good as their achievements would seem to suggest" (447). In other words, Loury argues that affirmative action programs can hurt targeted groups by undermining their self-confidence and self-esteem, qualities essential for success in both education and employment.

In higher education, Sowell argues, the effects of affirmative action can be even more significant. Under pressure to meet numerical requirements for admissions, Sowell says, colleges and universities tend to use a double standard for screening applicants; admission requirements are lower for targeted ethnic groups than for other potential students. The result, he claims, is that "thousands of minority students who would normally qualify for good nonprestigious colleges where they could succeed, are instead enrolled in famous institutions where they fail" (422). Because Sowell and Loury are respected and potentially influential members of a group that supposedly benefits from affirmative action, their statements illustrate the rhetorical problem Painter faced with her target audience.

Clayton and Crosby also observe that "ideology, more than personal circumstances, may ultimately underlie most people's positions on affirmative action," although they quickly add that "ideology is influenced by personal circumstances" (25). The assumption is that in general, individuals with liberal political ideology tend to support the policy of affirmative action, whereas conservatives tend to oppose it. Nevertheless, there are notable exceptions to this ideological generalization as well.

Clayton and Crosby, for example, note that "the liberal Anti-Defamation League . . . has consistently filed briefs against affirmative action in court cases" (11). Apparently some liberals fear that by "highlighting category differences," affirmative action will only increase conflict and undermine efforts to achieve equality (Clayton and Crosby 11). On the other end of the ideological spectrum, many ostensibly conservative leaders of the business community wholeheartedly support affirmative action. A 1984 survey of chief executive officers of large corporations revealed that 90 percent of their companies had implemented "numerical hiring objectives," similar to those frequently required by affirmative action, and 95 percent of those who had implemented such programs indicated that they would continue regardless of government action (Clayton and Crosby 24). Such executives seem to believe "that affirmative action leads to a variety of benefits, including increased productivity, diversity of ideas, a more rational personnel policy, and improved community relations" (Clayton and Crosby 21). Thus, because of these noteworthy exceptions, conclusions about the influence of ethnicity and political ideology on attitudes toward affirmative action are far from certain. What is clear, however, is that Painter faced a deeply divided audience. Her rhetorical problem was made more difficult by the presence of powerful opponents.

A Powerful Opposition

Painter's essay was published on December 10, 1981, near the end of Ronald Reagan's first year as president. Given Reagan's strong opposition to affirmative action, his policies almost certainly prompted Painter's rhetorical act. Opponents of affirmative action found popular and influential allies in Reagan and his administration. Consistent with promises made during the 1980 presidential campaign, Reagan entered office committed to easing affirmative action requirements and perhaps even eliminating the policy outright.

According to Howard Ball and Kathanne Greene, "President Reagan's world view on civil rights is contrary to views held by his predecessors" (16). His position was apparently based on the belief that conditions that once may have justified policies such as affirmative action have changed. For Reagan, "the time has ended for extending special treatment to various groups in the larger society because an entire nation has changed its attitudes toward racial and gender discrimination," say Ball and Greene. "Wedded philosophically to an 'ability conscious' society, rather than to a society based on color consciousness, the message from the highest White House levels is that harsh remedies, e.g., busing, set-asides, quotas, etc., for naked and unrestricted discrimination based on various neutral factors are no longer appropriate" (16–17). In other words, Reagan believed that programs like affirmative action were no longer necessary because overt racism and sexism no longer existed in the United States (Ball and Greene 21).

Reagan's ideology influenced the policies of his administration. According to Janet K. Boles, "The [Reagan] Justice Department announced that it would no longer advocate affirmative action goals and timetables, even in cases where courts had found discrimination by employers. The enforcement of equal opportunity laws by both the Equal Employment Opportunity Commission (EEOC) and the Office of Federal Contract Compliance (OFCC) declined sharply under Reagan," Boles continued, "and, as a matter of announced policy, class action suits were no longer filed. Under new regulations proposed by the administration, three-quarters of all federal contractors were exempted from filing affirmative action plans; existing requirements that promoted jobs for women in construction were weakened as well" (69–70). Further, Jones explains that "under the Reagan administration the United States Department of Justice aggressively attacked affirmative action, appearing in the Supreme Court in opposition to existing programs and counseling cities and other local entities to revoke or modify their affirmative action requirements" (352). And Charles M. Lamb added that "the philosophy on school desegregation of most Reagan political appointees at DOE [the Department of Education] is that assertive enforcement is unnecessary and cooperation is absolutely essential with school systems accused of discriminating" (85). These policy changes were consistent with Reagan's political ideology.

A long-standing objection to affirmative action is that the policy reverses discrimination by favoring women and ethnic minorities at the expense of white males. The Reagan position fueled that objection. As Boles says, "The Reagan administration was much more concerned with 'reverse discrimination' against white males in the work force" than with any continuing need for affirmative action (69–70). Indeed, Ball and Greene believe that Reagan saw affirmative action programs not as the remedy, but as the cause, of racism in the 1980s: "In the president's mind, the denial of equal opportunity in the 1980s results from 'the very laws designed to secure them.' The laws that have been developed, especially the affirmative action legislation and regulations of recent decades, must be set aside because they are morally reprehensible and legally unconstitutional" (15). Clearly, in both word and deed the Reagan administration constituted the major competing persuasive influence for Painter.

That influence shaped the attitudes and opinions of potential audience members and thus contributed to Painter's rhetorical problem. For example, Clayton and Crosby comment that "white male students have complained to us about not getting into law school because of affirmative action; the implication is that the slot a student 'deserved' was reallocated to a less deserving member of a minority group" (23–24). Such resentment of affirmative action is not confined to academia. One survey indicated that "only 17 percent of whites and 7 percent of blacks felt that affirmative action programs often discriminated against whites, but 60 percent of whites and 42 percent of blacks felt that this sometimes happened" (Clayton and Crosby 21–22). These attitudes are undoubtedly due to the efforts of competing persuasive influences, and they help to reveal both the breadth and the intensity of the rhetorical problem Painter faced.

The Rhetor

In a very important sense Painter is an ideal advocate for affirmative action. Her academic credentials as a student are impressive. According to Nancy Elizabeth Fitch, Painter received her undergraduate degree in anthropology from the University of California at Berkeley in 1964, an M.A. from the University of California, Los Angeles, in 1967, and a Ph.D. in history from Harvard University in 1974. In addition, in 1962–1963 Painter studied at the University of Bordeaux in France, and she studied at the University of Ghana in 1965–1966 (379).

Her career as a professor is equally impressive. Fitch reports that Painter taught at the University of Pennsylvania from 1974 through 1980. During that time she was also a resident associate of Afro-American studies at the W. E. B. Du Bois Institute at Harvard, 1977–1978. From 1980 through 1988 Painter taught at the University of North Carolina at Chapel Hill, and in 1989 she began teaching at Princeton University. In 1991 Painter was appointed Edwards Professor of American History at Princeton, the position she currently holds (379). Moreover, Painter is a distinguished scholar who has earned numerous awards for her scholarship.[1]

Finally, Painter is a long-term advocate of civil rights and affirmative action. Her experiences as an African American woman influenced her career from the beginning. "She became interested in history," Fitch explains, "because she found inadequate treatment of race and race relations in the United States in American textbooks and wanted to correct that situation." Fitch continues to say that Painter "has been part of the recent discussion on multiculturalism on American campuses and has said that, if people remembered the past condition of college and university campuses, 'they would hesitate before assailing the attempt to forge a pedagogy appropriate for newly diversified student bodies and faculties' " (379).

For these reasons Painter is an ideal rhetor to counter the persuasive influence of the Reagan administration and especially of African American opponents of affirmative action like Carter, Sowell, and Loury. Because they are members of a group that ostensibly benefits from affirmative action, they become reluctant authorities or sources who make statements that appear to violate their own interests. They can be seen as highly credible; why would they lie only to hurt themselves? Thus their appeals are powerful. Opponents of affirmative action embrace their statements as irrefutable proof that the policy is flawed. Alternatively, other members of protected groups begin to question their own support for affirmative action. Thus the reluctant

---

[1]*Who's Who among Black Americans* reports that Painter was awarded a John Simon Guggenheim Foundation fellowship in 1982–1983. In 1988–1989 she was a fellow of the Center for Advanced Study in the Behavioral Sciences. She received a Peterson Fellowship from the American Antiquarian Society in 1991 and a fellowship from the National Endowment for the Humanities in 1992–1993. She is the author of over 30 publications and 18 reviews and review essays (1127). According to Fitch, "Her books have been critically reviewed and include *Exodusters: Black Migration to Kansas after Reconstruction* (1977), *The Narrative of Hosea Hudson: His Life as a Negro Communist in the South* (1979), *The Progressive Era* (1984), and *Standing at Armageddon* (1987)" (379). Painter was National Director of the Association of Black Women Historians, 1982–1984; she was on the executive board of the Organization of American Historians, 1984–1987; and she was a member of the National Council of the American Studies Association, 1989–1992 (*Who's Who among Black Americans* 1127).

authorities promote the very undermining of self-confidence and self-esteem for which they indict affirmative action. Painter personifies the response to such reluctant authorities. She is an articulate, intelligent, successful, African American, female professional. Even more important in this regard, she does not hesitate to credit affirmative action policies for making her professional success possible, with no loss of self-confidence or self-esteem.

THEORETICAL PERSPECTIVE

Painter's purpose is to justify her position regarding affirmative action. That becomes clear near the end of the essay. There Painter has this to say:

> Since . . . [the 1950s], the civil rights movement and the feminist movement have created a new climate that permitted affirmative action, which, in turn, opened areas previously reserved for white men. Skirts and dark skins appeared in new settings in the 1970s, but in significant numbers only after affirmative action mandated the changes and made them thinkable. (14)

The justification for her position, then, is that affirmative action is a desirable policy because it has opened employment opportunities previously denied to women and minorities. At the end of the essay Painter goes a step further to attack proposals for eliminating affirmative action: ". . . the Reagan Administration's proposed dismantling of affirmative action fuses the future and the past. If they achieve their stated goals, we will have the same old discrimination, unneedful of new clothes" (15). In short, Painter advocates one policy—affirmative action—and argues against another—the Reagan proposal to limit or eliminate affirmative action.

In a traditional sense that purpose makes Painter's essay political or deliberative rhetoric, which is characterized by audience members who function as judges of future events—that is, of proposed policies or courses of action. Before such audiences, Aristotle says, the rhetor aims "at establishing the expediency or the harmfulness of a proposed course of action: if he [sic] urges its acceptance, he does so on the ground that it will do good; if he urges its rejection, he does so on the ground that it will do harm" (1358^b20). Thus Painter's effort to gain audience support for affirmative action because it does good by helping to end racist and sexist practices in education and employment, and to promote audience opposition to the Reagan administration's effort to eliminate or weaken affirmative action because it would do harm, makes her essay deliberative rhetoric. The means of persuasion that Painter employs, however, differ greatly from those typically associated with deliberative rhetoric.

Traditionally, such rhetoric is characterized by extensive use of supporting materials and deductive structure that asserts a claim or conclusion justified through a series of arguments. According to Bonnie J. Dow and Mari Boor Tonn, traditional deliberative rhetoric "is characterized as abstract, hierarchical, dominating, and oriented toward problem solving." They note that such discourse is further characterized by "formal evidence, deductive structure, and linear modes of reasoning" (288). Painter's essay does not conform to those expectations. Rather, it is better characterized by what Dow and Tonn identify as "feminine style."

Feminine Style

In their analysis of the political rhetoric of former Texas Governor Ann Richards, Dow and Tonn explain the origin and nature of feminine style. Building on earlier work by Karlyn Kohrs Campbell (*Man Cannot Speak for Her*), the authors explain that historically, in the process of craft learning, "women developed particular capacities for concrete and contingent reasoning, for reliance on personal experience, and for participatory interaction" (287). These experiences continue to characterize the lives of contemporary women. According to Dow and Tonn, "While the historical conditions of women have changed in many ways . . . the traditionally female crafts of emotional support, nurturance, empathy, and concrete reasoning are still familiar requirements of the female role." They conclude, "Moreover, current research indicates that these skills, as well as the way they are learned, may continue to foster development of specific communicative strategies for women" (287–288). Because such experiences are so widespread, Dow and Tonn insist, those "communicative strategies" create expectations for participants. "Women are encouraged to exhibit communicative patterns that correspond to the tasks that women are expected to perform in the private sphere," they write, "just as men's communication reflects their primary roles in public life." As a result of those expectations, the authors conclude, "female communication is characterized as concrete, participatory, cooperative, and oriented toward relationship maintenance" (288).

Although these characteristics of female communication are easily discerned in private, interpersonal settings, Dow and Tonn argue that feminine style is recognizable in public, rhetorical settings as well. "In a rhetorical situation," they explain, "these attributes produce discourse that displays a personal tone, uses personal experience, anecdotes, and examples as evidence, exhibits inductive structure, emphasizes audience participation, and encourages identification between speaker and audience" (287). In sum, through acculturation into traditional social roles, women develop distinctive communication strategies that Dow and Tonn label feminine style and that are manifest in both interpersonal and rhetorical settings. Participants in those communicative settings are likewise acculturated to expect, and to respond to, those strategies. Because feminine style is highly personal and self-disclosive, it achieves persuasive influence in two ways.

Ethos   The first is ethos. At least in an ideal sense, traditional deliberative rhetoric achieves persuasive force through strength of evidence and quality of argument. The credibility or ethos of the rhetor is important but secondary. Logical or rational arguments are emphasized. Feminine style, on the other hand, emphasizes the credibility or ethos of the rhetor, manifest in personal tone and examples, self-disclosure, and the like. The persuasive influence can be powerful.

Aristotle says that ethos, or a rhetor's character, "may almost be called the most effective means of persuasion he [*sic*] possesses" (1356ª13). That is especially true in deliberative situations like Painter's. According to Aristotle, "That the orator's own character should look right is particularly important in political speaking" (1377ᵇ29). Further, ethos takes on added importance in controversial deliberations where strong arguments exist on both sides. "Persuasion is achieved by the speaker's personal character when the speech is so spoken as to make us think him [*sic*] credible," says Aristotle. "We believe good men [and women] more fully and more readily than others: this is true generally whatever the question is, and absolutely true where exact certainty is impossible and opinions are divided" (1356ª2). Given the rhetorical situation Painter faced, including the intense controversy and division of opinion about the policy of affirmative action, Aristotle's theory provides insight into her use of persona to build ethos.

Identification   The second way feminine style achieves persuasive force is through identification. Dow and Tonn argue that in the case of an individual rhetorical act, "the strategy of using concrete examples and personal experience is empowering; it encourages audiences' reliance on their own instincts and perceptions of reality, even if these dispute dominant models" (291). Thus audience members who have been similarly acculturated are invited to identify with the personal experiences of the rhetor and are empowered to make their own decisions based on that identification. The audience response is essentially inductive, moving from personal experience and identification to broader conclusions about a policy or course of action. According to Dow and Tonn, "The use of a personal tone and of personal disclosure are interrelated characteristics of feminine style. The telling of personal experience presupposes a personal attitude toward the subject and a willingness for audience identification, a goal of feminine style" (292). In other words, feminine style invites audiences to identify personally with both the rhetor and the issues or problems addressed by the rhetorical act. Persuasion is achieved through consubstantiality—that is, when members of the target audiences come to share the rhetor's view of those issues and problems.

Ethos and identification are closely related. For Aristotle ethos is created by what a rhetor says. "This kind of persuasion, like the others," he explains, "should be achieved by what the speaker says, not by what people think of this character before he [*sic*] begins to speak" (1356ª9). In this sense the persuasive force of ethos is not something a rhetor brings to a rhetorical act; rather, it is created through the rhetorical act. Campbell explains how that creation takes place. Noting that the Greek word *ethos* is closely related to the word *ethnic,* she says, "Ethos does not refer to your peculiarities as an individual but to the ways in which you reflect the characteristics and qualities that are valued by your culture or group." Those characteristics and qualities are reflected in the discourse itself. "The ethos of a rhetor refers to the relationship between the rhetor and the community as reflected in rhetorical action," she concludes (*The Rhetorical Act* 121). In other words, the persuasive power of ethos is derived from rhetorical acts that demonstrate that the rhetor possesses characteristics and qualities valued by the target audiences. That is a matter of identification, because as Kenneth Burke says, "you can persuade a man [*sic*] only insofar as you can talk his language by speech, gesture, tonality, order, image, attitude, idea, *identifying* your ways with his" (*Rhetoric of Motives* 55).

Viewed through Burke's dramatistic lens, rhetorical acts become depictions of reality that yield to pentadic analysis. Burke explains that pentadic analysis can reveal the philosophical assumptions that guide the rhetor and thus underlie the rhetorical act:

> Dramatistically, the different philosophic schools are to be distinguished by the fact that each school features a different one of the five [pentadic] terms, in developing a vocabulary designed to allow this one term full expression (as regards its resources and its temptations) with the other terms being comparatively slighted or

being placed in the perspective of the featured term. (*Grammar of Motives* 127)

Thus pentadic analysis can reveal the philosophical underpinnings of Painter's essay and suggest an approach for evaluating her rhetoric.[2]

TEXTUAL ANALYSIS

Painter's essay displays the personal tone, use of personal experience, anecdotes and examples as evidence, inductive structure, efforts to promote audience participation, and efforts to promote identification between speaker and audience that Dow and Tonn enumerate as characteristics of feminine style. Those factors function strategically to target her audiences, establish her ethos, and promote identification between rhetor and audience members.

The Target Audiences

Structurally, the introduction of the essay consists of two real, extended examples, based on Painter's own personal experiences and presented as a narrative. The detail of the narrative creates a little drama, as if it were a play with two acts. One important strategic function of the introduction is to isolate Painter's target audiences that are represented by the characters who appear in the two acts of the drama.

The setting in the first act of the narrative is a lecture hall; the scene opens with two people, Painter and "a white man of about 35," sitting side by side. The time is evening. Painter has certain props—pages of typescript and a sharpened pencil—and she is editing her work. Significantly, the man is depicted as friendly, even benevolent, certainly not overtly racist. Painter interprets his interest in her work positively, as "kindly," and answers his opening question. She writes, "He watched me intently—kindly—for several moments. 'Is that your dissertation?' I said yes, it was. 'Good luck in getting it accepted,' he said. I said that it had already been accepted, thank you" (2).[3] She perceives

---

[2]Burke describes the pentad in detail in *A Grammar of Motives*, xv–xxiii. Relationships between the terms of the pentad and the philosophic schools are discussed in depth in *A Grammar of Motives*, 127–320.

[3]Parenthetical citations are paragraph numbers. *Exodusters* (see note 1) is a revised version of her doctoral dissertation.

his good wishes for getting her dissertation accepted as "friendly": The next paragraph begins, "Still friendly" (3). She thanks him, but she is proud to tell him that she doesn't need his good wishes; it has already been accepted. The initial exchanges are cordial.

As the drama continues, the man wishes her good luck in finding a job, but, again, she does not need his good wishes; she already has employment. As in other dramas, the tension escalates when she tells him that she is a beginning assistant professor at the University of Pennsylvania, a prestigious, Ivy League school. Painter writes, " 'Aren't you lucky,' said the man, a little less generously, 'you got a job at a good university.' I agreed. Jobs in history were, still are, hard to find" (3). The man's statement suggests that luck, as accidental or undeserved good fortune, has played an important role in Painter's career. She responds to this slight shift, perceiving these words to have been said "a little less generously." However, she agrees that some luck was involved and explains, "Jobs in history were, still are, hard to find," referring to a state of affairs that she expects the audience to accept as true from their general knowledge and from her authority as a historian and a recent job-seeker.

The reason for the shift in the man's tone becomes apparent as the narrative continues: " 'I have a doctorate in history,' he resumed, 'but I couldn't get an academic job.' With regret he added that he worked in school administration. I said I was sorry he hadn't been able to find the job he wanted" (5). She responds with empathy, but he continues with a kind of attack, suggesting that, as an African American woman, she had an unfair advantage resulting from affirmative action: "He said: 'It must be great to be black and female, because of affirmative action. You count twice' " (5). In effect, he claims to have been the victim of what is usually called "reverse discrimination." "Did this man really mean to imply that I had my job at his expense?" Painter asks. (5) She is shocked, speechless, embarrassed. His words suggest that he sees himself in a competition rigged in her favor.

The movement between the first and second acts of the narrative is chronological: The first encounter happened in the past; the second occurs in the present. The setting also changes: The first encounter happened in Philadelphia; the second takes place in Chapel Hill, North Carolina. The characters in this second example are "black Carolina undergraduates," whose views of affirmative action are also negative. Painter says:

One young woman surprised me by deploring affirmative action. I wondered why. "White students and professors think we only got into the University of North Carolina because we're black," she complained, "and they don't believe we're truly qualified." She said that she knew that she was qualified and fully deserved to be at Carolina. She fulfilled all the regular admissions requirements. It was the stigma of affirmative action that bothered her; without it other students wouldn't assume she was unqualified. (7)

Another student extends that problem to nonwhite faculty, arguing that "without affirmative action, students would assume black faculty to be as good as white" (8).

The two acts of the long narrative are characterized by the elements of feminine style identified by Dow and Tonn. Painter's tone is personal; that is, the narrative is written in first person, and much of it is in dialogue form, a personal interaction. The two extended examples that make up the two acts of the narrative are Painter's personal experiences. Moreover, the two extended examples signal an inductive structure that ultimately moves from these examples, and others, to a general conclusion.

The characters that appear in the two acts of the drama represent the two groups that compose Painter's target audiences. The first targeted group, represented by the man in Philadelphia, is made up of those white males and others who Painter feels oppose affirmative action not because of rigid political ideology but because they are unfamiliar with the benefits of the legislation. Members of this target audience also oppose affirmative action because they fear that the policy creates reverse discrimination. The second targeted group, represented by the African American students in the second act, is made up of women and minorities, those affirmative action legislation was designed to help, but who have grown skeptical about the effects of the legislation. They exhibit the same frustration expressed by other African Americans, such as Sowell and Loury. Taken together, the man in Philadelphia and the young women in North Carolina exhibit the attitudes toward affirmative action that must be refuted if Painter is to achieve her purpose. She summarizes those attitudes by saying, "That's what I've been hearing from whites and blacks. . . . No one, not blacks, not whites, benefits from affirmative action, or so it would seem" (9).

Ethos

To refute those attitudes, Painter must first establish her ethos. Consistent with our earlier explanation, Painter does that by exhibiting, through rhetorical action, the characteristics and qualities valued by her target audiences. That the man in Philadelphia holds a doctorate in history, and the women in North Carolina are university students, suggests that the members of the target audiences value academic excellence and intellectual achievement. Painter exhibits those qualities through the persona she adopts. Development of that persona begins in the introductory narrative. Consistent with feminine style, Painter employs personal tone, testimony, and personal examples to establish her ethos.

For example, in the first act of the narrative, she says that she was attending a "lecture," presumably of a scholarly nature. Moreover, while waiting for the lecture to begin, she was working on her dissertation, "scratching out awkward phrases and trying out new ones" (1). Those details portray her as a conscientious scholar. She adds that she is a historian and "a beginning assistant professor at the University of Pennsylvania" (3). She provides more details. "I had worked hard as a graduate student and had written a decent dissertation," Painter says. "I knew foreign languages, had traveled widely and had taught and published" (4). That information reveals Painter to be a well-qualified professor of history. Further, she reveals that she earned her doctorate in history from Harvard (6), perhaps the most highly regarded university in the United States.

More subtle, but equally important, evidence of Painter's persona exists. She says that she was "cognizant of the job squeeze" (4), and later says that for one to admit being helped by affirmative action "is usually tantamount to admitting deficiency" (12). Her choice of the words *cognizant* and *tantamount,* not part of common usage, also helps her assume the persona of a well-educated individual. These aspects of Painter's persona reveal personal characteristics likely to be valued by her target audiences and, thus, help establish her ethos. That persona also performs important strategic functions in promoting identification.

Identification

To refute attitudes opposing affirmative action, and to gain support for the policy, Painter strategically promotes identification with the target audiences in two ways. First, members of the target audiences are invited to identify with the characters of the introductory narrative in a way that prepares them to listen to Painter's refutation. According to Burke, "Only those voices from without are effective which can speak in the language of a voice within" (*Rhetoric of Motives* 39). In the narrative, audience members hear familiar, internal voices. The man in Philadelphia expresses the doubts many well-meaning individuals hold about affirmative action, including the fear of reverse discrimination. Likewise, the North Carolina coeds express the skepticism of many women, African Americans, and other members of protected groups. To the extent that members of the target audience identify with the characters in the narrative, they are prepared for Painter's direct, personal refutation of their opinions.

Second, members of the target audience are also invited to identify with Painter herself. That identification grows from her persona and is especially important for those readers represented by the young women in North Carolina. Throughout the essay Painter acknowledges that she is African American and female. In one sense those facts alone promote identification between Painter and the North Carolina students. But they serve a larger strategic function as well: Painter enacts the role she would have the students and the members of the target audience they represent assume for themselves.

Painter first explains that opposition to affirmative action is significant, not only among whites but among African Americans as well. She says, "That's what I've been hearing from whites and blacks. . . . No one, not blacks, not whites, benefits from affirmative action, or so it would seem" (9). Then she immediately places herself outside that opposition: "Well, I have," she says (10). And later: "I am one of the few people I know who will admit to having been helped by affirmative action" (12). Because she has acknowledged that many African Americans oppose affirmative action, her unflinching support for the policy makes her distinctive, a role model who demonstrates that support for affirmative action need not be accompanied by low self-esteem or lack of self-confidence. Moreover, she reveals herself to be a courageous individual, unafraid to defend a controversial position. The young women in North Carolina and, through them, the target audience they represent are invited to follow that model. Readers who do so become the ideal audience for Painter's case for affirmative action.

The Case for Affirmative Action

Although Painter's purpose is to gain support for the policy of affirmative action and to build opposition to Reagan's plans to limit the policy, that purpose is carefully limited: She justifies the policy as a means to ensure quality education and employment for *fully qualified* individuals. She says, "To hear people talk, affirmative action exists only to employ and promote the otherwise unqualified, but I don't see it that way at all" (12). Her justification for that position consists of two compelling examples.

The first is personal. Painter begins by relating her experiences as a student prior to affirmative action: "Well, I have [been helped by affirmative action], but not in the early 1960s when I was an undergraduate in a large state university. Back then, there was no affirmative action. We applied for admission to the university like everyone else; we were accepted or rejected like everyone else," she says. "Graduate and undergraduate students together, we numbered about 200 in a student body of nearly 30,000. No preferential treatment there" (10). The statistical supporting material at the end of this example demonstrates what conditions were like for students prior to affirmative action. It is particularly well chosen to appeal to the target audience exemplified by the female, African American students at the University of North Carolina.

Later Painter again applies her experience to members of this target audience. Although these African American undergraduate and graduate students had met all regular admission requirements, she writes:

> We all knew what the rest of the university thought of us, professors especially. They thought we were stupid because we were black. Further, white women were considered frivolous students; they were only supposed to be in school to get husbands. . . . Black students, the whole atmosphere said, would not attend graduate or professional school because their grades were poor. Women had no business in postgraduate education because they would waste their training by dropping out of careers when they married or became pregnant. No one said out loud that women and minorities were simply and naturally inferior to white men, but the assumptions were as clear as day: Whites are better than blacks; men are better than women. (11)

This relatively long, extended example is a "history lesson" that draws its force from Painter's qualifications as a historian. Not only did she personally experience conditions for students prior to affirmative action, but also her standing as a historian qualifies her to describe those conditions in a general sense.

Painter then credits affirmative action for her own educational and professional success. "I'm black and female," she says, "yet I was hired by two history departments that had no black members before the late '60s, never mind females. Affirmative action cleared the way" (12). The personal example clearly links the policy to qualified individuals: "Without affirmative action, it never would have occurred to any large, white research university to consider me for professional employment, despite my degree, languages, publications, charm, grace, *despite* my qualifications" (14). That a person with Painter's obvious qualifications would not have been hired without affirmative action is strong support for her position. The personal example soundly refutes the insinuation of the man in Philadelphia that Painter was unqualified for the position she holds. Moreover, the example is strategically adapted to the target audience represented by the young women in North Carolina because, like Painter, they know that they are "truly qualified" (7).

The second example is even more compelling. Painter writes: "Thirty-five years ago, John Hope Franklin, then a star student, now a giant in the field of American history, received a doctorate in history from Harvard. He went to teach in a black college. In those days," she continues, "black men taught in black colleges. White women taught in white women's colleges. Black women taught in black women's colleges. None taught at the University of Pennsylvania or the University of North Carolina. It was the way things were" (13). This example draws its force from Franklin's character and professional accomplishments, which are considerable.

According to *Who's Who among Black Americans,* Franklin attended Fisk University, a predominantly African American institution, receiving his A.B. in 1935. He received a masters degree in 1936 and a Ph.D. in 1941, both from predominantly white Harvard University (499). From 1936 to 1937 Franklin was an instructor of history at Fisk. He was professor of history at St. Augustine's College, a predominantly African American institution, in Raleigh, North Carolina, from 1939 to 1943; professor of history at North Carolina College at Durham, a predominantly African American institution, from 1943 to 1947; and professor of history at Howard University, another predominantly African American institution in Washington, D.C., from 1947 to 1956. From 1956 through 1964 he chaired the Department of History at Brooklyn College. During that time he was also Pitt Professor of American History at Cambridge University, 1962–1963. From 1964 through 1982 he was professor of American History at the University of Chicago, and from 1982 to 1985 he was James B. Duke professor of history at Duke University. Currently he is Professor Emeritus of History, Duke University (*Who's Who among Black Americans* 499). Franklin's career as an educator was truly distinguished.

Despite the limitations placed on Franklin's career by the overt racism common in the United States at the time, he also became a renowned scholar. He was on the editorial board of *American Scholar,* 1972–1976, and he was the chair of the board of trustees of Fisk University, 1968–1974. In 1969 Franklin was president of the Southern Historical Association, and in 1979 he was president of the American Historical Association. He is a member of Phi Beta Kappa and Phi Alpha Theta (*Who's Who among Black Americans* 499). Franklin was a

Guggenheim Fellow in 1950–1951 and again in 1973–1974. He is a prolific author whose works have been recognized for excellence.[4]

Significantly, most of Franklin's career precedes affirmative action and demonstrates that without that legislation, even the most highly qualified individuals suffered employment discrimination. Thus the case of Franklin is an a fortiori example: If it was true in the case of "a star student" and "a giant in the field of American history," then it must have happened to most others as well. That is important strategically. Because Painter offers only two examples, Franklin and herself, her essay is open to the charge that these are isolated instances that do not reflect what usually takes place. Her credibility as a historian erodes that charge; she can be trusted to relate historical facts accurately without misinterpretation. And the a fortiori example refutes the charge: If this happened to the highly qualified John Hope Franklin, then without affirmative action, every qualified person who was not a white male faced such discrimination.

The conclusion of Painter's essay is also strategically adapted to her target audiences. She says, "My Philadelphia white man and my Carolina black women would be surprised to discover the convergence of their views" (15). That the views of these two divergent groups that compose her target audiences are so similar is ironic. That sense of irony grows as Painter continues: "I doubt that they know that their convictions are older than affirmative action. I wish I could take them back to the early '60s and let them see that they're reciting the same old white-male-superiority line, fixed up to fit conditions that include a policy called affirmative action," she says. "Actually, I will not have to take these people back in time at all, for the Reagan Administration's proposed dismantling of affirmative action fuses the future and the past. If they achieve their stated goals, we will have the same old discrimination, unneedful of new clothes" (15). In effect, Painter shows that what seem to be new problems created by affirmative action are simply contemporary versions of "the same old white-male-superiority line" that has always viewed women and minorities as inferior and unqualified. For both of her target audiences, that is ironic.

---

[4]Franklin is author of *From Slavery to Freedom, A History of Negro Americans*, 1987; *The Militant South*, 1956; *Reconstruction after the Civil War*, 1961; *The Emancipation Proclamation*, 1963; *A Southern Odyssey*, 1976; *Racial Equality in America*, 1976; *George Washington Williams, A Biography*, 1985; *The Color Line: Legacy for the Twenty-First Century*, 1991; and other works. His scholarly contributions in U.S. history have received the highest recognition. Franklin was awarded the Jefferson Medal in 1983; the Clarence Holte Literary Prize in 1986; the Cleanth Brooks Medal, Fellowship of Southern Writers in 1989; the John Caldwell Medal from the North Carolina Council on the Humanities in 1991; the University of North Carolina Medal in 1992; and the Encyclopedia Britannica Gold Medal Award in 1990, along with others (*Who's Who among Black Americans* 499).

For both target audiences, Painter's strategy is to make continued opposition to affirmative action as unattractive as possible. In other words, to maintain their opposition in light of Painter's own experiences and those of John Hope Franklin, members of the target audience must recognize the subtle ways in which they have been persuaded to adopt and express racist and sexist views, something that would appall them. Those who identify with the man in Philadelphia see themselves as kind and friendly, certainly not overtly racist or sexist. They must reassess their opposition to affirmative action in light of the case Painter has made. Likewise, the young women in North Carolina would recoil from affirming racist and sexist views. They too must reassess their opposition to the policy.

SUMMARY

This analysis reveals how Painter was able to tap the resources of language to adapt to divided and skeptical target audiences. The introductory narrative isolates the target audiences and acknowledges the rhetorical problem—skepticism about affirmative action on the part of both targeted audiences. The narrative invites members of the target audiences to identify personally with the issues, thus preparing them for Painter's personal justification of the policy. The narrative also establishes Painter's ethos and the grounds for identification between rhetor and target audiences.

The examples Painter uses—her own experiences and the a fortiori case of Franklin—pointedly refute the opposed claim, personified in the man from Philadelphia, that affirmative action exists only to benefit unqualified individuals. Moreover, the examples and the persona Painter develops provide a compelling response to the skepticism about affirmative action exemplified by the young women in North Carolina.

Finally, the essay leaves members of the target audiences with a clear choice between voicing and reinforcing the racist and sexist positions or reassessing their position on affirmative action. For audience members who identify with the characters in the narrative and with Painter herself, that reassessment would result in fulfillment of Painter's purpose: support for affirmative action.

EVALUATION

Painter's rhetoric deserves praise for three reasons. First, the essay is an artistically commendable example of adapting discourse to skeptical audiences. Her artistry is revealed in the triple function of the introductory narrative to isolate the target audiences, acknowledge a complex and difficult rhetorical problem, and establish her ethos. Those necessary tasks are accomplished with clarity, economy, and vividness, ensuring that members of the targeted groups are prepared for Painter's refutation of their opinions. If they read the essay through the end of the introduction, they are primed for her response.

Further, the examples Painter uses are skillfully chosen to function in different ways with each of the target audiences. On one hand they offer a compelling answer to the sort of skepticism represented by the man in Philadelphia. On the other they promote strong identification between Painter and the audience represented by the young women in North Carolina.

Finally, the convergence of the views of the target audiences in the conclusion of the essay is strategically designed to force a choice between undesirable racist and sexist characterizations of African Americans and women, respectively, and the desirability of affirmative action to ensure quality education and employment for fully qualified members of protected groups. The skill and sophistication with which Painter presents that choice is evidence of her rhetorical artistry.

Second, the essay deserves praise because it promotes constructive alternative means for making political decisions. Feminine style helps create new and distinctive criteria for rendering what Dow and Tonn call "political judgment." Noting the self-disclosive, personal nature of feminine style, they argue that "reliance on such evidence . . . creates an implicit standard for political judgment that is based on the primacy of experiential knowledge and inductive reasoning" (289). This implication of feminine style goes beyond its power to move target audiences to accept or reject a given course of action. Dow and Tonn argue, "We believe that this conclusion can be extended to include the potential for feminine style to function philosophically as well as strategically, by creating alternative grounds for testing the validity of claims for public knowledge" (291).

In other words, as opposed to the hierarchical, abstract, deductive reasoning that characterizes traditional deliberative rhetoric, feminine style approaches political decision making from a personal perspective. It acknowledges that policy decisions affect the personal lives of individual people and encourages judgments of expediency based on those personal effects. In that sense the effectiveness of Painter's essay transcends the issue of affirmative action. Readers are invited to reassess the grounds for political decision making in general in a way that promotes personal involvement and responsibility. We find that alternative means for rendering political judgment commendable, especially for judging public policies that, like affirmative action, touch the lives of almost all citizens.

Finally, Painter's essay deserves praise because it represents a philo-sophically superior assessment of issues surrounding affirmative ac-tion. As we noted earlier, Burke argues that pentadic analysis can reveal the philosophical assumptions that guide the rhetor and, thus, under-lie the rhetorical act. Pentadic analysis of Painter's essay is revealing.

Painter creates a *scene* prior to enactment of affirmative action that is dominated by virulent racism and sexism that deny qualified ethnic minorities and women access to education and desirable employ-ment. Individual *agents* within that scene—John Hope Franklin, Painter herself as an undergraduate student, and so forth—regardless of their talents and qualifications, are largely powerless to *act* in ways that overcome racism and sexism. "In those days [before affirmative action], black men taught in black colleges. White women taught in white women's colleges. Black women taught in black women's col-leges. None taught at the University of Pennsylvania or the University of North Carolina. It was the way things were," Painter says (13).

As the drama progresses, an *agency,* affirmative action, overcomes those scenic forces and makes access to quality education and employ-ment possible for qualified individuals, regardless of race or sex. "Since then, the civil rights movement and the feminist movement have created a new climate that permitted affirmative action, which, in turn, opened areas previously reserved for white men," she says. "Skirts and dark skins appeared in new settings in the 1970s, but in significant numbers only after affirmative action mandated the changes and made them thinkable" (14). In other words, Painter holds events before and after affirmative action in stark opposition. In the time before affirmative action, fully qualified, talented agents are at the mercy of the scenic forces of racism and sexism, moved against their will into poor education and less desirable jobs. After the agency appears, affirmative action overcomes those forces. *Agency* is the fea-tured term in Painter's depiction.

Conversely, opponents of affirmative action, like Reagan and his al-lies, present quite a different depiction of events. In their view scenic elements of racism and sexism may once have justified policies like affirmative action, but such an agency is no longer needed because racism and sexism have been eliminated from the scene. Thus, in the new ability-conscious society, individual agents are responsible for their own success or failure. *Agent* is the featured term in their depic-tion. The contrast between the philosophical underpinnings of *agency* and *agent* is important.

Burke enumerates the relationships between the terms of the pen-tad and the philosophical schools, saying in part, "For the featuring of *agent,* the corresponding philosophic terminology is *idealism.* For the featuring of *agency,* the corresponding terminology is *pragmatism*"

(*Grammar of Motives* 128). In effect, then, Painter's featuring of agency contrasts her own pragmatism with the idealism of opponents, who, like Reagan, argue that changes in scene have rendered affirmative action obsolete. In contrast to Painter's pragmatism, that idealism is naive at best.

Overt racism and sexism are far from dead in the United States. Ezorsky cites the following examples of overt racism, which she claims are common: increases in racial violence against African Americans; disparities in sentences imposed on murderers who kill whites compared to those who kill African Americans; housing discrimination; and lower funding and inferior education in predominantly African American schools (12–13). She concludes that "abundant evidence shows that overt racism is widespread today" (12). Moreover, even if overt racism and sexism are not as virulent as they once were, opponents of affirmative action ignore the lingering institutionalized racism and sexism that persist despite efforts to guarantee equal opportunity. Ezorsky explains that "institutional racism can occur when employees are selected through personal connections or by qualifying for certain requirements or seniority standards. These procedures are intrinsically free of race prejudice, and they exist in areas where no blacks reside. Nevertheless, these institutional procedures perpetuate the effects of overt racism" (2). Studies indicate that "communicating job information to family, friends, neighbors, and acquaintances by word of mouth is probably the most widely used recruitment method," Ezorsky says. Thus, because they lack "ties to whites as family, friends, fellow students, neighbors, or club members, blacks tend to be isolated from the networks in which connections to desirable employment—where whites predominate—are forged" (15). Because of overt racism and sexism, ethnic minorities and women were frequently excluded from training programs that would prepare them for more desirable employment. Likewise, supposedly neutral policies such as "last hired, first fired" perpetuate discrimination; because of overt racism and sexism in the past, ethnic minorities and women are often the last hired and the first fired (Ezorsky 10). In light of continuing racism and sexism, we find Painter's pragmatism to be philosophically preferable to a naive idealism that conceals "the same old white-male-superiority line, fixed up to fit conditions that include a policy called affirmative action" (Painter 15).

WORKS CITED

Aristotle. *Rhetoric*. Trans. W. Rhys Roberts. New York: The Modern Library, Random House, 1954.

Ball, Howard, and Kathanne Greene. "The Reagan Justice Department." *The Reagan Administration and Human Rights*. Ed. Tinsley E. Yarbrough. New York: Praeger, 1985. 1–28.

Boles, Janet K. "Women's Rights and the Gender Gap." *The Reagan Administration and Human Rights*. Ed. Tinsley E. Yarbrough. New York: Praeger, 1985. 55–81.

Burke, Kenneth. *A Grammar of Motives*. 1945. Berkeley: University of California Press, 1969.

———. *A Rhetoric of Motives*. 1950. Berkeley: University of California Press, 1969.

Campbell, Karlyn Kohrs. *Man Cannot Speak for Her: A Critical Study of Early Feminist Rhetoric*. Vol. I. New York: Greenwood Press, 1989.

———. *The Rhetorical Act*. Belmont, CA: Wadsworth, 1996.

Clayton, Susan D., and Faye J. Crosby. *Justice, Gender, and Affirmative Action*. Ann Arbor: University of Michigan Press, 1992.

Dow, Bonnie J., and Mari Boor Tonn. " 'Feminine Style' and Political Judgment in the Rhetoric of Ann Richards." *Quarterly Journal of Speech* 79 (1993): 286–302.

Ezorsky, Gertrude. *Racism and Justice: The Case for Affirmative Action*. Ithaca, NY: Cornell University Press, 1991.

Fitch, Nancy Elizabeth. "Nell Irvin Painter." *African American Women: A Biographical Dictionary*. Ed. Dorothy C. Salem. New York: Garland Publishing, 1993.

Jones, James E., Jr. "The Rise and Fall of Affirmative Action." *Race in America: The Struggle for Equality*. Ed. Herbert Hill and James E. Jones, Jr. Madison: University of Wisconsin Press, 1993. 345–369.

Lamb, Charles M. "Education and Housing." *The Reagan Administration and Human Rights*. Ed. Tinsley E. Yarbrough. New York: Praeger, 1985. 82–106.

Loury, Glenn C. "Beyond Civil Rights." *Racial Preference and Racial Justice: The New Affirmative Action Controversy*. Ed. Russell Nieli. Washington, DC: The Ethics and Public Policy Center, 1991. 437–451.

Painter, Nell Irvin. "Whites Say I Must Be on Easy Street." *New York Times* 10 Dec. 1981: C-2.

Phelps, Shirelle, ed. *Who's Who among Black Americans*. Detroit: Gale Research, 1994.

Sowell, Thomas. "Are Quotas Good for Blacks?" *Racial Preference and Racial Justice: The New Affirmative Action Controversy*. Ed. Russell Nieli. Washington, DC: The Ethics and Public Policy Center, 1991. 417–428.

Washington, Valora, and William Harvey. *Affirmative Rhetoric, Negative Action: African-American and Hispanic Faculty at Predominantly White Universities*. Washington, DC: School of Education and Human Development, George Washington University, 1989.

ROBERT F. KENNEDY

Address Delivered in Chicago, Illinois, February 8, 1968

On January 31, 1968, the North Vietnamese Army and Vietcong guerrillas launched a massive attack against South Vietnam. Until that time, the fighting in Vietnam had largely been confined to the jungles and outlying areas, but the "Tet offensive," so named because it coincided with Tet, the Asian celebration of the lunar new year, brought the war into major cities as well as South Vietnamese and U.S. military bases. For the people of the United States, who had been told that military victory in Vietnam was near, the attack was shocking. Criticism of continued U.S. involvement in the war mounted. Among the most vocal critics was Johnson's fellow Democrat, Robert F. Kennedy. This speech was Kennedy's strongest attack to date on Johnson's policies regarding the war in Vietnam. The text is from Robert F. Kennedy, To Seek a Newer World, *New York: Bantam Books, 1968, 221–229.*

1   The events of the last few weeks have demonstrated anew the truth of Lord Halifax's dictum that although hope "is very good company by the way . . . (it) is generally a wrong guide."

2   Our enemy, savagely striking at will across all of South Vietnam, has finally shattered the mask of official illusion with which we have concealed our true circumstances, even from ourselves. But a short time ago we were serene in our reports and predictions of progress. In April, our commanding general told us that "the South Vietnamese are fighting now better than ever before . . . their record in combat . . . reveals an exceptional performance." In August, another general told us that "the really big battles of the Vietnam War are over . . . the enemy has been so badly pummeled he'll never trouble us again." In December, we were told that we were winning "battle after battle," that "the secure proportion of the population has grown from about 45 percent to 65 percent and in the contested areas the tide continues to run with us."

3   Those dreams are gone. The Vietcong will probably withdraw from the cities, as they were forced to withdraw from the American Embassy. Thousands of them will be dead. But they will, nevertheless, have demonstrated that no part or person of South Vietnam is secure from their attacks: neither district capitals nor American bases, neither the peasant in his rice paddy nor the commanding general of our own great forces.

4   No one can predict the exact shape or outcome of the battles now in progress in Saigon or at Khesahn. Let us pray that we will succeed at the lowest possible cost to our young men. But whatever their outcome, the events of the last two weeks have taught us something. For the sake of those young Americans who are fighting today, if for no other reason, the time has come to take a new look at the war in Vietnam; not by cursing the past but by using it to illuminate the future. And the first and necessary step is to face the facts. It is to seek out the austere and painful reality of Vietnam freed from wishful thinking, false hopes and sentimental dreams. It is to rid ourselves of the "good company" of those illusions which have lured us into the deepening swamp of Vietnam. "If you would guide by the light of reason," said Holmes, "you must let your mind be bold." We will find no guide to the future in Vietnam unless we are bold enough to confront the grim anguish, the reality, of that battlefield which was once a nation called South Vietnam, stripped of deceptive illusions. It is time for the truth.

5   We must, first of all, rid ourselves of the illusion that the events of the past two weeks represent some sort of victory. That is not so.

6   It is said the Vietcong will not be able to hold the cities. This is probably true. But they have demonstrated despite all our reports of progress, of government strength and enemy weakness, that half a million American soldiers with 700,000 Vietnamese allies, with total command of the air, total command of the sea, backed by huge resources and the most modern weapons, are unable to secure even a single city from the attacks of an enemy whose total strength is about 250,000. It is as if James Madison were able to claim a great victory in 1812 because the British only burned Washington instead of annexing it to the British Empire.

7 We are told that the enemy suffered terrible losses; and there is no doubt he did. They cannot, however, be as devastating as the figures appear. The Secretary of Defense has told us that "during all of 1967 the Communists lost about 165,000 effectives," yet enemy main force strength "has been maintained at a relatively constant level of about 110,000–115,000 during the past year." Thus it would seem that no matter how many Vietcong and North Vietnamese we claim to kill, through some miraculous effort of will, enemy strength remains the same. Now our intelligence chief tells us that of 60,000 men thrown into the attacks on the cities, 20,000 have been killed. If only two men have been seriously wounded for every one dead—a very conservative estimate—the entire enemy force has been put out of action. Who, then, is doing the fighting?

8 Again it is claimed that the Communists expected a large-scale popular uprising which did not occur. How ironic it is that we should claim a victory because a people whom we have given sixteen thousand lives, billions of dollars and almost a decade to defend, did not rise in arms against us. More disillusioning and painful is the fact the population did not rise to defend its freedom against the Vietcong. Thousands of men and arms were infiltrated into populated urban areas over a period of days, if not of weeks. Yet few, if any, citizens rushed to inform their protectors of this massive infiltration. At best they simply shut their doors to concern, waiting for others to resolve the issue. Did we know the attack was coming? If so, why did we not strike first, and where were the forces needed for effective defense?

9 For years we have been told that the measure of our success and progress in Vietnam was increasing security and control for the population. Now we have seen that none of the population is secure and no area is under sure control. Four years ago when we had only about 30,000 troops in Vietnam, the Vietcong were unable to mount the assaults on cities they have now conducted against our enormous forces. At one time a suggestion that we protect enclaves was derided. Now there are no protected enclaves.

10 This has not happened because our men are not brave or effective, because they are. It is because we have misconceived the nature of the war; it is because we have sought to resolve by military might a conflict whose issue depends upon the will and conviction of the South Vietnamese people. It is like sending a lion to halt an epidemic of jungle rot.

11 This misconception rests on a second illusion—the illusion that we can win a war which the South Vietnamese cannot win for themselves.

12 Two presidents and countless officials have told us for seven years that although we can help the South Vietnamese, it is their war and they must win it; as Secretary of Defense McNamara told us last month, "We cannot provide the South Vietnamese with the will to survive as an independent nation . . . or with the ability and self-discipline a people must have to govern themselves. These qualities and attributes are essential contributions to the struggle only the South Vietnamese can supply." Yet this wise and certain counsel has gradually become an empty slogan, as mounting frustration has led us to transform the war into an American military effort.

13 The South Vietnamese Senate, with only one dissenting vote, refuses to draft 18- and 19-year-old South Vietnamese, with a member of the Assembly asking, "Why should Vietnamese boys be sent to die for Americans?"—while 19-year-old American boys fight to maintain this Senate and Assembly in Saigon. Every detached observer has testified to the enormous corruption which pervades every level of South Vietnamese official life. Hundreds of millions of dollars are stolen by private individuals and government officials while the American people are being asked to pay higher taxes to finance our assistance effort. Despite continual promises the Saigon regime refuses to act against corruption. Late last year, after all our pressure for reform, two high army officers were finally dismissed for "criminal" corruption. Last month, these same two officers were given new and powerful commands. In the meantime, incorruptible officers resign out of frustration and defeat.

14 Perhaps, we could live with corruption and inefficiency by themselves. However, the consequence is not simply the loss of money or of popular confidence; it is the loss of American lives. For government corruption is the source of the enemy's strength. It is, more than anything else, the reason why the greatest power on earth cannot defeat a tiny and primitive foe.

15 You cannot expect people to risk their lives and endure hardship unless they have a stake in their own society. They must have a clear sense of identification with their own government, a belief they are participating in a cause worth fighting for. Political and economic reform are not simply idealistic slogans or noble goals to be postponed until the fighting is over. They are the principal weapons of battle. People will not fight to line the pockets of generals or swell the bank accounts of the wealthy. They are far more likely to close their eyes and shut their doors in the face of their government—even as they did last week.

16 More than any election, more than any proud boasts, that single fact reveals the truth. We have an ally in name only. We support a government without supporters. Without the efforts of American arms that government would not last a day.

17 The third illusion is that the unswerving pursuit of military victory, whatever its cost, is in the interest of either ourselves or the people of Vietnam. For the people of Vietnam, the last three years have meant little but horror. Their tiny land has been devastated by a weight of bombs and shells greater than Nazi Germany knew in the Second World War. We have dropped twelve tons of bombs for every square mile in North and South Vietnam. Whole provinces have been substantially destroyed. More than two million South Vietnamese are now homeless refugees. Imagine the impact in our own country if an equivalent number—over 25 million Americans—were wandering homeless or interned in refugee camps, and millions more refugees were being created as New York and Chicago, Washington and Boston, were being destroyed by a war raging in their streets. Whatever the outcome of these battles, it is the people we seek to defend who are the greatest losers.

18 Nor does it serve the interests of America to fight this war as if moral standards could be subordinated to immediate necessities. Last week, a Vietcong suspect was turned over to the Chief of the Vietnamese Security Services, who executed him on the spot—a flat violation of the Geneva Convention on the Rules of War. Of course, the enemy is brutal and cruel, and has done the same thing many times. But we are not fighting the Communists in order to become more like them—we fight to preserve our differences. Moreover, such actions—like the widespread use of artillery and air power in the centers of cities—may hurt us far more in the long run than it helps us today. The photograph of the execution was on front pages all around the world—leading our best and oldest friends to ask, more in sorrow than in anger, what has happened to America?

19 The fourth illusion is that American national interest is identical with—or should be subordinated to—the selfish interest of an incompetent military regime. We are told, of course, that the battle for South Vietnam is in reality a struggle for 250 million Asians—the beginning of a Great Society for all of Asia. But this is pretension. We can and should offer reasonable assistance to Asia; but we cannot build a Great Society there if we cannot build one in our own country. We cannot speak extravagantly of a struggle for 250 million Asians, when a struggle for 15 million in one Asian country so strains our forces, that another Asian country, a fourth-rate power which we have already once defeated in battle, dares to seize an American ship and hold and humiliate her crew.

20   And we are told that the war in Vietnam will settle the future course of Asia. But that is a prayerful wish based on unsound hope, meant only to justify the enormous sacrifices we have already made. The truth is that Communism triumphed in China twenty years ago, and was extended to Tibet. It lost in Malaya and the Philippines, met disaster in Indonesia and was fought to a standstill in Korea. It has struggled against governments in Burma for twenty years without success, and it may struggle in Thailand for many more. The outcome in each country depends and will depend on the intrinsic strength of the government, the particular circumstances of the country, and the particular character of the insurgent movement. The truth is that the war in Vietnam does not promise the end of all threats to Asia and ultimately to the United States; rather, if we proceed on our present course, it promises only years and decades of further draining conflict on the mainland of Asia—conflict which, as our finest military leaders have always warned, could lead us only to national tragedy.

21   There is an American interest in South Vietnam. We have an interest in maintaining the strength of our commitments—and surely we have demonstrated that. With all the lives and resources we have poured into Vietnam, is there anyone to argue that a government with any support from its people, with any competence to rule, with any determination to defend itself, would not long ago have been victorious over any insurgent movement, however assisted from outside its borders?

22   And we have another, more immediate interest: to protect the lives of our gallant young men, and to conserve American resources. But we do not have an interest in the survival of a privileged class, growing ever more wealthy from the corruption of war, which after all our sacrifices on their behalf, can ask why Vietnamese boys should die for Americans?

23   The fifth illusion is that this war can be settled in our own way and in our own time on our own terms. Such a settlement is the privilege of the triumphant; of those who crush their enemies in battle or wear away their will to fight.

24   We have not done this, nor is there any prospect we will achieve such a victory.

25   For twenty years, first the French and then the United States have been predicting victory in Vietnam. In 1961 and in 1962, as well as 1966 and 1967, we have been told that "the tide is turning"; "there is 'light at the end of the tunnel,'" "we can soon bring home the troops—victory is near—the enemy is tiring." Once, in 1962, I participated in such predictions myself. But for twenty years we have been wrong. The history of conflict among nations does not record another such lengthy and consistent chronicle of error. It is time to discard so proven a fallacy and face the reality that a military victory is not in sight, and that it probably will never come.

26   Unable to defeat our enemy or break his will—at least without a huge, long, and ever more costly effort—we must actively seek a peaceful settlement. We can no longer harden our terms everywhere Hanoi indicates it may be prepared to negotiate; and we must be willing to foresee a settlement which will give the Vietcong a chance to participate in the political life of the country. Not because we want them to, but because that is the only way in which this struggle can be settled. No one knows if negotiations will bring a peaceful settlement, but we do know there will be no peaceful settlement without negotiations. Nor can we have these negotiations just on our own terms. We may have to make concessions and take risks, and surely we will have to negotiate directly with the NLF as well as Hanoi. Surely it is only another illusion that still denies this basic necessity. What we must not do is confuse the prestige staked on a particular policy with the interest of the United States; nor should we be unwilling to take risks for peace when we are willing to risk so many lives in war.

27   A year ago, when our adversary offered negotiations if only we would halt the bombing of the North, we replied with a demand for his virtual surrender. Officials at the highest levels of our government felt that we were on the edge of a military victory and negotiations, except on our terms, were not necessary. Now, a year too late, we have set fewer conditions for a bombing halt, conditions which clearly would have been more acceptable then. And the intervening year, for all its terrible costs, the deaths of thousands of Americans and South Vietnamese, has not improved our position in the least. When the chance for negotiations comes again, let us not postpone for another year the recognition of what is really possible and necessary to a peaceful settlement.

28   These are some of the illusions which must be discarded if the events of last week are to prove not simply a tragedy but a lesson: a lesson which carries with it some basic truths.

29   First, that a total military victory is not within sight or around the corner; that in fact, it is probably beyond our grasp; and that the effort to win such a victory will only result in the further slaughter of thousands of innocent and helpless people—a slaughter which will forever rest on our national conscience.

30   Second, that the pursuit of such a victory is not necessary to our national interest and is even damaging that interest.

31   Third, that the progress we have claimed toward increasing our control over the country and the security of the population is largely illusory.

32   Fourth, that the central battle in this war cannot be measured by body counts or bomb damage, but by the extent to which the people of South Vietnam act on a sense of common purpose and hope with those that govern them.

33   Fifth, that the current regime in Saigon is unwilling or incapable of being an effective ally in the war against the Communists.

34   Sixth, that a political compromise is not just the best path to peace, but the only path, and we must show as much willingness to risk some of our prestige for peace as to risk the lives of young men in war.

35   Seventh, that the escalation policy in Vietnam, far from strengthening and consolidating international resistance to aggression, is injuring our country through the world, reducing the faith of other peoples in our wisdom and purpose, and weakening the world's resolve to stand together for freedom and peace.

36   Eighth, that the best way to save our most precious stake in Vietnam—the lives of our soldiers—is to stop the enlargement of the war, and the best way to end casualties is to end the war.

37   Ninth, that our nation must be told the truth about this war, in all its terrible reality, both because it is right—and because only in this way can any administration rally the public confidence and unity for the shadowed days which lie ahead.

38   No war has ever demanded more bravery from our people and our government—not just bravery under fire or the bravery to make sacrifices—but the bravery to discard the comfort of illusion—to do away with false hopes and alluring promises. Reality is grim and painful. But it is only a remote echo of the anguish toward which a policy founded on illusion is surely taking us. This is a great nation and a strong people. Any who seek to comfort rather than speak plainly, reassure rather than instruct, promise satisfaction rather than reveal frustration—they deny that greatness and drain that strength. For today, as it was in the beginning, it is the truth that makes us free.

JOHN M. MURPHY

The Light of Reason:
Robert F. Kennedy on Vietnam

In this critique John M. Murphy analyzes a speech by Robert F. Kennedy that we agree cries out for rationalistic treatment. Based on what you know of rationalistic criticism and on a close reading of this speech, consider what you would expect to find in a descriptive analysis that would signal that a rationalistic approach would be appropriate or the best critical choice. In our judgment speeches of this type appear regularly, but they are not common. Murphy's analysis illustrates rationalistic criticism that is informed and modified by a Burkean sensitivity to the persuasive significance of language, which we believe adds an important dimension to that form of criticism.

Murphy's critique contains large amounts of historical background, in part because the speech was delivered more than 25 years ago and addresses issues that may not be familiar to younger contemporary readers. Ideal critics are those whose experience and knowledge equip them to function as if they were members of the target audiences of the rhetoric, and if you are not such a person, additional historical–contextual analysis will be needed to give you an understanding of the scene in which the rhetorical act occurred. That is also true when most members of the audience for your critique do not have such background.

Murphy's commentary on the history of rationalistic criticism leads him to argue for a perspective that emphasizes both truth and ethics as criteria in evaluation that is part of a situated judg-

ment on policy. The biographical information about Robert Kennedy reflects the relative importance of ethos in deliberative rhetoric. As one would expect in a speech relying on rational appeals, and as Murphy notes, the address is tightly structured and adapted to refute opposing views. The links between Kennedy's arguments and fundamental U.S. values are also emphasized, suggesting links between rationalistic appeals and the psychosocial motives that underlie the premises of arguments.

On January 31, 1968, during the Tet (the Asian lunar New Year) holiday, nearly 70,000 North Vietnamese regulars and Vietcong insurgents opened the most sweeping offensive to date against Allied forces in South Vietnam. They attacked more than a hundred cities, the massive U.S. supply base at Camranh Bay, and numerous targets within the South Vietnamese capital of Saigon, including the U.S. embassy. In a departure from their guerrilla tactics, the Communists stood and fought, precipitating particularly bloody battles at the U.S. marine outpost at Khesahn and at the South Vietnamese provincial capital of Hue. Allied firepower eventually crushed the Communists, but Americans' faith in their ultimate victory in Vietnam, and in their president, was badly shaken (Karnow 523–545).

At least three factors help to explain that shift in attitude. First, in the latter half of 1967, President Johnson orchestrated a powerful persuasive campaign aimed at increasing support for his course in Vietnam, a policy based on the belief that military pressure on the Communists would bring them to the negotiating table on U.S. terms. Committees in Washington, D.C., and in Saigon released hundreds of reports extolling Allied progress. Former Presidents Truman and Eisenhower, as well as other important public figures, endorsed the president's policy. The U.S. commander in South Vietnam, General William Westmoreland, came home to give speeches, testify in front of congressional committees, and talk with members of the media (Karnow 512–514). The public relations effort was successful; in January of 1968 Gallup reported that 50 percent of Americans believed that the United States was making progress in Vietnam, and public approval of the president's handling of the war began to creep upward (*Gallup Opinion Index* 3, 6). After these promises that the end was near, the Tet offensive came as a terrible shock.

Second, the Tet offensive stormed directly into U.S. living rooms. Prior to Tet, little combat footage appeared on television (Epstein 210–232). The difficulties inherent in taking bulky film cameras to war, combined with the hit-and-run tactics of the Communists, meant that the public saw only the aftermath of fighting. That was bad enough, but it did not compare with the film that appeared during Tet. Combat had come to the South Vietnamese cities, and it was easy to film the battles. Stanley Karnow describes the televised attack on the U.S. embassy:

> There, on color screens, dead bodies lay amid the rubble and rattle of automatic gunfire as dazed American soldiers and civilians ran back and forth trying to flush out the assailants. One man raced past the camera to a villa behind the chancery building to toss a pistol up to Colonel George Jacobson on the second floor. The senior embassy official shot the last of the enemy commandos as he crept up the stairs. (526)

Associated Press photographer Eddie Adams and Vo Suu, an NBC cameraman, encountered General Nguyen Ngoc Loan, chief of South Vietnam's national police, as he took out his pistol and blew a captive's head apart. Suu's film, edited to spare audiences the sight of the blood spurting from the prisoner's head, ran on the NBC evening news. Adams's photograph became a key image of the war (Karnow 529). Viewers, *seeing* the shock of combat, as well as a violation of the Geneva accords on prisoners of war, were horrified.

Finally, the Johnson Administration responded in, perhaps, the most inept fashion possible. U.S. officials portrayed the battle as a victory, akin to Hitler's last desperate gamble in the Battle of the Bulge. General Westmoreland argued that the enemy suffered horrific casualties. Unfortunately, the president failed to take into account the positive results of his earlier public relations effort. The public believed that the war was nearly over; the fact of the offensive widened Lyndon Johnson's "credibility gap."[1] In addition, critics of the war disputed Johnson's claims of victory. Among them was New York Senator Robert F. Kennedy in a speech given in Chicago, Illinois, on February 8, 1968.

The ostensible reason for the speech was a Book and Author's Luncheon, given to celebrate the publication of Kennedy's book, *To Seek a Newer World,* a collection of essays on political issues. He used the occasion, however, to deliver what *New York Times* writer Tom Wicker termed "the most sweeping and detailed indictment of the war and of the administration's policy yet heard from any leading figure in either

---

[1]After the war, Westmoreland and others charged that media coverage had transformed a devastating Communist defeat into a victory. The facts contradict that assessment. The Communists did, indeed, suffer heavy casualties, but they made substantial gains. Four months after the Battle of the Bulge, for instance, Hitler's Germany collapsed. Four months after Tet, the Communists launched yet another offensive ("More Important Than Words"). The Tet offensive was in no way comparable to Hitler's final attack.

party" (1). Even a cursory examination of the text reveals the truth of Wicker's assertion. Kennedy not only undermined the president's claims of victory, but he also asked the American people to make the broader judgment that Lyndon Johnson's Vietnam policy had failed; as a result, a political compromise should be pursued.

Kennedy followed the advice that he quoted from former Supreme Court Justice Oliver Wendell Holmes: "If you would guide by the light of reason, you must let your mind be bold." His attack on a sitting president of his own party was bold, and the light of reason shone powerfully in the address. His emphasis on refutation, arrangement, and evidence suggests that the speech might profitably be examined from an Aristotelian perspective. That rationalistic perspective, however, has come under criticism in recent years as scholars struggle to recast the thought of an ancient Greek philosopher in ways useful to an "MTV society." In the first section of this essay, then, I explore the elements of a classical critique as I understand them, with an emphasis on Aristotle's development of the relationships between rhetoric, political judgment, and practical wisdom. After that I review the obstacles facing Robert Kennedy as he rose to speak and the strategies he used to invoke the judgment he desired. I conclude with some thoughts on the implications of Kennedy's arguments and on the role of the classical tradition in contemporary criticism.

POLITICAL JUDGMENT AND CLASSICAL RHETORIC

For many years traditional rationalism, which came to be called "Neo-Aristotelianism," dominated the practice of rhetorical criticism in the United States. This critical approach assumed that people were reasonable beings and that the best discourse appealed to the rationality of the audience by discovering the truth in a given situation. Specific speeches were measured primarily against a checklist of strategies in Aristotle's *Rhetoric*. Good speeches met Aristotelian standards by exhibiting valid argumentative structures supported by evidence, appropriate language that put the audience in a fitting frame of mind to consider the arguments, and clear indications of the good character of the speaker; in other words, *logos, pathos,* and *ethos.* Moreover, critics thought that because people were rational and these standards were universal, good speeches would succeed. Aristotle believed that the truth would prevail if it was defended properly (Hill, *"Rhetoric* of Aristotle" 22–25). The best speeches accomplished their purpose.

Only a few speeches met these criteria. Generally, they were significant historical documents, so that their effects were known. They were delivered by educated, renowned people who could skillfully invoke the modes of proof.[2] Finally, such speeches concerned critical moral or political questions in the past (such as slavery) so we could know the truth of a speaker's position (for example, abolition).

Edwin Black's attack on Neo-Aristotelianism was the high point of a campaign that ended its dominance (*Rhetorical Criticism* 36–90). Black, among others, pointed out that circumstances can prevent the empirical success of even the best effort; that Neo-Aristotelian critics applied their precepts in a cookie-cutter fashion and failed to say much about the persuasive power of a speech; and that critics paid too much attention to historical context and too little attention to rhetorical conventions, such as the genre of a speech, that Aristotle felt were important. Other skeptics pointed out that the discovery of truth should not be the end of rhetorical studies. Rather, critics should explore the ways in which rhetors symbolically construct society and ask us to act in it (Farrell). Finally, scholars noted, the elitism of Neo-Aristotelianism eliminated from consideration artistic and successful rhetors who did not meet its specific standards (Vonnegut 29–31).

Unfortunately, the attacks on Neo-Aristotelian criticism buried not only that approach but also other perspectives based on classical rhetorical principles (Mohrmann). There were periodic efforts to resuscitate Aristotelian approaches (Hill, "Conventional Wisdom—Traditional Form"), but only recently has that program come to fruition. Exemplified by the work of Michael Leff and Gerald Mohrmann, critics have returned to the classical tradition in order to engage in the close reading of oratorical texts. What makes their work interesting is not only their skill in exploring the artistry that animates a text but also the effort to comprehend exemplary speeches as instances of situated political judgment.

The focus on judgment begins with a fresh understanding of the place of the *Rhetoric* within Aristotle's work. Scholars traditionally cited the opening of the *Rhetoric*. Aristotle said that rhetoric was the counterpart (*antistrophos* or correlative) of dialectic, the art of philosophical disputation (George Kennedy 26–28). In Aristotle's scheme of knowledge that meant rhetoric was classified as *techne:* a "means of production" that led to ethical or political action but that did not include the substance of those fields (Warnick, "Judgment" 304–308). Neo-Aristotelian scholars used this perspective to argue that rhetoric had little to do with truth or ethics. Rhetoric studied only means, and

---

[2]Consider, for example, that cultural notions of "good character" during this era virtually excluded from consideration African Americans and women. They could not possibly deploy *ethos* as a strategy and, as a result, were not considered effective rhetors by Neo-Aristotelian critics of the 20th century.

the critic should simply check a speaker's tactics against the inventory in the *Rhetoric*. As Forbes Hill concluded, "Rhetoric is the study of the use of means, not our commitments to ends" ("Reply" 456).

Contemporary scholars dispute this assumption. For instance, the most prominent student of the *Rhetoric,* George Kennedy, argues that the austere view of rhetoric announced by Aristotle in the opening contradicts the rest of the work (27–28). Although he notes that Aristotle's perspective on rhetoric shifts somewhat in the text, Kennedy believes that "its primary role is that of a 'practical' art" (13).[3] As such, rhetoric is associated with ethics and politics. According to Ronald Beiner, the student of all three arts develops the faculty of *phronesis:* the practical wisdom needed to "be a complete human being and to live a proper human life" (73). *Phronesis* is the ability to understand what principles, or virtues, are required in a specific situation and the skill to act on that analysis in order to live a virtuous life. One learns *phronesis* through experience and through the study of models. Aristotle, for instance, defines virtue as the acts of virtuous people; it is the embodiment of virtue in a person that becomes the standard to which others can aspire (Warnick, "Judgment" 306).

From this perspective ethics, politics, and rhetoric develop close connections. The study of ethics aims at a virtuous life. The living of a good life requires an ordered state. The establishment of such a state demands careful deliberation. Deliberation is the province of rhetoric. Yet rhetoric, says Beiner, is not only a means to achieve virtue and good government but also the medium through which we create meanings for virtue and good government (93–97). Beiner contends, "Rhetorical speech sets the 'target' [virtue] at which we should 'aim.' . . . Our ends are not merely pursued rhetorically, they are themselves constituted rhetorically" (95).

As a practical art, Stephen Browne and Michael Leff explain, rhetoric deals not with absolute truth but with social truths created in "diverse and changing circumstances" (198). The rhetorical strategies explained in the *Rhetoric* no longer function as a set of "static principles" against which a speech is compared (Browne and Leff 198); rather,

---

[3]George Kennedy explains Aristotle's inconsistency by noting that different parts of the treatise were probably written for different audiences. The first chapter, which emphasized rhetoric's relation to dialectic, was aimed at students of philosophy "who had completed a study of dialectic" (26). Aristotle fashioned a philosophical view of rhetoric in order to draw such students to its study. Other sections of the *Rhetoric* were written for the "general public," perhaps in lectures offered in the afternoons as a kind of extension division of the Academy and accompanied by practical exercises in speaking (5). These sections emphasized the civic function of rhetoric for a general audience. It is lovely to think of Aristotle adapting to his listeners (see also Kennedy's essay on the evolution of the *Rhetoric* on pages 299–305).

they become a flexible body of general precepts that may or may not work in specific situations. The faculty of *phronesis*, in terms of rhetoric, is the ability to know what arguments might be called for in a particular time and place and to make those choices skillfully. The speech becomes an embodied political judgment; substantive arguments and stylistic elements come together in an organic act that invites participation. The audience may reject the offer. But, ideally, the audience judges with the speaker and considers the ends and actions that might, according to Barbara Warnick, "achieve good for the citizenry and the state" ("Judgment" 305).[4]

Critics, Browne and Leff urge, should "exercise the same kind of situated judgment that argumentative performance exhibits" (199). In this view critics recognize that they comprehend speeches on at least two levels. On one hand deliberation occurs only in its concrete manifestations: in an act of judgment such as the one Robert Kennedy performed on February 8, 1968. Such acts are the focus of attention. On the other hand the argumentative principles generated by repeated case studies form a body of general knowledge (Browne and Leff 199). Such precepts cannot be applied mechanistically to every situation because they change as rhetors adapt to the particular. But they inform criticism and give critics "the space needed to judge arguments from a perspective beyond the particular" (Browne and Leff 199). Just as rhetors shape the general to meet the needs of the specific, and vice versa, so should critics.

The concern with political judgment causes "neo-classical" critics to concentrate on Aristotle's favorite genre: deliberative speech. A deliberative address concerns the policy choices that a community makes concerning its future. What programs will best ensure the establishment or the stability of a well-ordered state? The key issue, Aristotle says, is expediency: "for the deliberative speaker [the end] is the advantageous [*sympheron*]" (George Kennedy 49). Drawing on other parts of the *Rhetoric*, George Kennedy interprets the "advantageous" to mean "the enlightened, long-term advantage to the audience" (49). Argument from example, Aristotle believes, will be most useful to deliberative rhetoric because, although the future cannot be known, "future events will be like those of the past" (181). Finally, Aristotle discusses a series of topics, or places for generating arguments, that are useful to deliberative speakers (50–78) and continues that analysis in his more general examination of topics later in the *Rhetoric* (190–204). In short,

---

[4]Maurice Charland (73) has ably articulated this position, arguing that critics should view *phronesis* as an effort to grasp "the contingent good for a particular community at a particular moment." Like Charland, I tend to embrace a contemporary reinterpretation of Aristotle, rather than turning to Cicero, as Leff often does.

a deliberative speaker asks the audience to make a pragmatic judgment about the future course of the community.

Such a perspective on deliberative speech assumes that the needs and make-up of the community are self-evident. Forbes Hill notes that Aristotle speaks in and to a homogeneous culture; his value system, Aristotle assumes, "ought to apply universally" (Hill, "*Rhetoric* of Aristotle" 36). For a heterogeneous culture like the United States, this assumption is difficult to accept. If it were merely a question of updating the Greek value system, however, there would be little concern. Critics could substitute the appropriate values. That is not the whole of the problem.

Aristotelian deliberation, Beiner argues, requires community or political friendship (79–82). Aristotle defines *philia,* or friendship, as a common view of justice. For the purpose of judgment, Aristotle narrows *philia* by defining a brand of political friendship, *homonoia.* *Homonoia* is a state of harmony among community members who share an understanding of their common interest. As Beiner concludes, "To judge is to judge with, to judge-with is to be a friend. To judge well is a staple of politics" (82).

In February of 1968, Robert Kennedy could not take for granted the existence of political friendship, a common view of justice, or a shared understanding of the common interest. Rather, in the confusion created by the Tet offensive, Kennedy needed to forge both a common view of the administration's policy in Vietnam and a shared perception of the appropriate standards for judgment of that policy. That task meant that Kennedy not only asked the audience to "judge-with" him but also sought to shape the American character. He imbued listeners with the qualities necessary to make a sound judgment. Even more so than Aristotle imagined, issues of audience were critical to Robert Kennedy's success—a problem complicated by Kennedy's *ethos.*

"A GREAT NATION AND A STRONG PEOPLE"

In 1968 Kennedy was one of the more controversial figures in politics. Cartoonist Jules Feiffer aptly caught the mixed feelings about him with his drawing of the "Bobby Twins": "One is a good Bobby and one is a bad Bobby. . . . If you want one Bobby to be your president, you will have to take both. For Bobbies are widely noted for their family unity" (reproduced in Schlesinger 868).

Despite his relative youth, at 42 Kennedy had long been in the public eye. He served as a Senate counsel throughout the 1950s and became famous for his relentless pursuit of corrupt Teamsters Union president James Hoffa. He ran his brother's presidential campaign and, after that victory, became attorney general. John Kennedy was criticized for this exercise in nepotism, yet Robert Kennedy received high praise for his work. After John Kennedy's assassination, Robert Kennedy stayed in the cabinet for a short time, and then resigned to run for the Senate from New York. He won election in 1964 (Schlesinger 106–729).

This recital of facts cannot capture the contradictory feelings about the man. He was admired for his honesty and candor while being hated for his hard-nosed tactics. People saw him as effective, ruthless, compassionate, rude, intolerant, tough, loyal, and vindictive (Newfield 22). The glow of the Kennedy name also enfolded the senator. Its magic enhanced his political power; as another senator said of Robert and Edward Kennedy, "I'm a practical politician. One of these boys might be president some day and it makes you kind of cautious" ("Two Senators" 17). Skeptics, however, accused Kennedy of unfairly capitalizing on his name. As an article in the *Christian Science Monitor* explained, they felt his opposition to the war revealed only "Kennedy's unceasing and purposeful determination to seize upon every issue which he believes can bring him closer to the White House" ("Appraisal" 18).

Robert Kennedy's record on the war intensified these doubts. As his brother's adviser, he supported John Kennedy's commitment to South Vietnam; during that administration, troop strength grew from 685 advisors to 16,500 "combat support" soldiers (Kendrick 220). Presidents from John Kennedy to Richard Nixon justified this policy on three grounds (Kail 120–123). First, U.S. intervention would improve the lives of the people of South Vietnam. Second, the United States would demonstrate to the world that it kept its commitments. Finally, the critical U.S. interest in the world was the containment of Communism. Asia must be protected, and Vietnam was the place to take a stand. The first two arguments flowed out of the third. Nobody, Americans assumed, lived better under Communists than under capitalists. And of course the policy of containment depended on U.S. credibility. Attorney General Kennedy accepted this analysis and saw the Vietnam War as a "hot" byproduct of the Cold War. He visited South Vietnam in 1962 and stated, "The solution there lies in winning it. That is what the president intends to do" (quoted in Newfield 117).

Senator Kennedy came to oppose the war, but it took a long time. His public statements on the war were few and far between. He endorsed the Johnson administration's goal of protecting South Vietnam. He questioned the means to that end, however, by emphasizing the need to reform the government of South Vietnam in order to give its people a reason to fight for their nation (Murphy, "Confrontation" 16–103).

As he turned against the war, the pressure grew on him to challenge Lyndon Johnson for the Democratic party's presidential nomination. In a dreadful piece of timing, Kennedy ruled out a candidacy the day the Tet offensive began (Schlesinger 903). The February 8th speech became a way to vent his frustration with his circumstance. Adam Walinsky, a speechwriter, said that Kennedy took the toughest passages his aides offered and added some of his own (Schlesinger 905).

Emotional or not, the speech was extraordinarily well organized. Senator Kennedy developed five major points in the form of a debate; each point refuted a Johnson administration claim about the war. The body was framed by an introduction and a conclusion that echoed the same themes and language. In short, he structured the address so conventionally that it could serve as a model for public speaking students.

Such organization demands explanation; most public speeches are not so rigid. First, the speech clarified a confusing world for the audience. The text formally resolved the disarray and doubt created by the Tet offensive. The world made sense again. Second, the strategy exploited the resources of Kennedy's *ethos*. He had a reputation for brutal candor and straight talk; the organization, and the language, affirmed and used those perceptions. Finally, the dialectical nature of the speech invited participation.[5] Kennedy asked the audience to judge with him as he criticized the president's claims. They heard the administration's argument; they judged Kennedy's response. In fact, this structure played an important role in shaping several dialectic interactions that grounded the address.

The first lines revealed Kennedy's strategy. He began with an assertion: "The events of the last few weeks have demonstrated anew the truth of Lord Halifax's dictum that although hope is 'very good company by the way . . . (it) is generally a wrong guide' " (1).[6] Kennedy's view was clear; "events" demonstrated "truth." Consistent with Aristotle's admonition that policy speeches should center on expediency, he tied the evaluation of Johnson's Vietnam policy to its results. Did the policy work? The "events of the last few weeks" would tell the tale. The president's policy was to be measured against its consequences.

Yet that was not the whole standard. The reference to history opened a second dialectic. Lord Halifax served as British Foreign Secretary during the appeasement of Hitler's Germany before World War II.

---

[5]I am not arguing that Robert Kennedy engaged in philosophical disputation. Rather, I am using *dialectical* to label his strategy of asking the audience to move back and forth between his position and that of the Johnson administration in an effort to come to a good judgment.

[6]Parenthetical citations for passages from the speech are paragraph numbers. The text of the speech is drawn from the paperback edition of *To Seek a Newer World*. Kennedy added the speech to this later edition, a printing that came out for his presidential campaign.

That policy was a disaster, and, in 1968, it was still relatively fresh in audience memory. For Kennedy, the lessons of history informed good judgment and revealed right action. Throughout the speech he developed a chronological dialectic; he reached to history for forgotten ideas and experiences that could inform present judgment.

Finally, the opening line, and the rest of the introduction, invoked powerful linguistic resources that shaped audience perceptions of Johnson's policy:

> For the sake of those young Americans who are fighting today, if for no other reason, the time has come to take a new look at the war in Vietnam; not by cursing the past but by using it to illuminate the future. And the first and necessary step is to face the facts. It is to seek out the austere and painful reality of Vietnam freed from wishful thinking, false hopes and sentimental dreams. It is to rid ourselves of the "good company" of those illusions which have lured us into the deepening swamp of Vietnam. "If you would guide by the light of reason," said Holmes, "you must let your mind be bold." We will find no guide to the future in Vietnam unless we are bold enough to confront the grim anguish, the reality, of that battlefield which was once a nation called South Vietnam, stripped of deceptive illusions. It is time for the truth. (4)

For the senator, "illusions," "wishful thinking," "false hopes," and "sentimental dreams" were "good company" but "wrong guides." He contrasted these qualities to the "truth," to the "austere and painful reality of Vietnam," and to "the facts." The language indicted the president's policy and shaped the role Kennedy envisioned for the audience. They, like the senator, must be bold, must be "guide[d] by the light of reason" rather than hiding behind "the mask of official illusion" (2). Light/dark metaphors enhanced the labeling. The "light of reason" must "illuminate" the "deepening swamp of Vietnam." The audience must physically and conceptually move out of the jungle of Vietnam and into the light of home, out of the darkness of deception and into the light of reason.

From the opening lines, then, Kennedy established a key dialectic, illusion versus truth, that guided the development of his arguments and coordinated the deployment of other pairs. The illusion/truth pair was given power through other comparisons: present/past, comfort/boldness, deception/reason, and claim/evidence. These pairs dissociated (Perelman and Olbrechts-Tyteca 411–459) the president from reality and tied Robert Kennedy to reality. Johnson's policy should be rejected because it had no connection with the situation on the ground.

After the introduction Kennedy analyzed five major claims put forth by the Johnson administration. Each section built on the previous rebuttal; listeners were led from the specific—the Tet offensive was not a victory—to the general—unconditional victory in Vietnam was not possible. This approach had two advantages. First, the senator's final two claims were so controversial that the audience would likely have rejected them without the preparation provided by earlier arguments. Second, he enacted his *phronesis;* the particular event of the Tet offensive yielded a new policy. Robert Kennedy, not Lyndon Johnson, understood the appropriate relationship between the particular and the general, and he demonstrated his *phronesis* in the course of the address. He became a model for the audience to emulate as they struggled to judge the administration's position.

Nor did Kennedy deploy his pairs in a perfunctory manner. They demonstrated the distance between the president's sense and common sense. The strategy became clear in the first section: Kennedy attacked the claim "that the events of the last two weeks represent some sort of victory" (5). Four minor premises supported the major claim, and he relentlessly tore down each one. Again, the arguments developed from the specific to the general.

"It is said," Kennedy noted, that "the Vietcong will not be able to hold the cities. This is probably true" (6). Yet that victory was a hollow one. Why? Kennedy contextualized the claim in one long sentence, enumerating and amplifying the disparity between Allied forces of "half a million American soldiers" and "700,000 Vietnamese allies," who possessed "total command of the air" and "total command of the sea," and the Communists, "whose total strength is about 250,000" (6). The lengthy recitation of Allied power contrasted sharply with the brief statement of enemy strength, a construction whose form embodied Kennedy's claim.

That disparity, in turn, revealed the absurdity of assertions of victory when we "are unable to secure even a single city from the attacks" of the enemy (6). As Aristotle said, "if the lesser thing is true, the greater is also" (George Kennedy 192). The audience was unlikely to argue with Kennedy's logic: If a single city was not safe, neither was the nation of South Vietnam. A bitterly sarcastic analogy capped the argument, compared Johnson to the only other U.S. president to lose a war, and invited the audience to use a common sense of history to judge the administration's policy: "It is as if James Madison were able to claim a great victory in 1812 because the British only burned Washington instead of annexing it to the British Empire" (6).

Kennedy attacked the subsequent minor premises in the same way. He asked listeners to judge claims not only through reference to the immediate situation but also through the prism of the past. Significantly, he invoked the administration's criteria. Aristotle argues that a key way to build arguments is through the use of past decisions by the "judges themselves" (George Kennedy 197). Robert Kennedy did so.

He compared casualty figures to past body counts; relief at the lack of an uprising to previous claims of political allegiance; and the military effort as a whole to earlier U.S. goals. In each case the president's policy was found wanting, and his claims of victory were revealed as ridiculous. Sarcasm—"Who, then, is doing the fighting?" (7)—and evidence—the casualty figures—accentuated the strength of the administration's delusions. Finally, each rebuttal built on previous ones. By the end Kennedy led listeners to the conclusion that military power could not resolve this conflict, a claim vivified by a powerful figurative analogy that led nicely to the next section: "It is like sending a lion to halt an epidemic of jungle rot" (10).

The rot, Kennedy argued, infested the government of South Vietnam. By February of 1968 this claim was not difficult to sustain. Elections the previous August had resulted in South Vietnamese President Thieu arresting the runner-up (Karnow 452). The American people understood the corruption of their ally but, on the other hand, felt obligated to their ally. As Forbes Hill explained in his analysis of Richard Nixon's 1969 Vietnamization address, "Betraying allies and letting down friends is assumed to be an evil, and its opposite, loyalty to friends and allies, the virtue of a great power" ("Conventional Wisdom" 382). Senator Kennedy did not refute this feeling; rather, he dissociated the South Vietnamese leadership from the terms "allies" and "friends." The Saigon government, he argued, had not earned such consideration.

The authority of past presidents and that of the recently departed Secretary of Defense Robert McNamara set the criteria for judgment of the administration's policy.[7] A series of lurid examples revealed the "rot" in the government of South Vietnam. These examples exploited a logic that Aristotle identified as key to deliberative speech. We assume the past will resemble the future. The Saigon government had always failed to control corruption and would continue to fail. The consequences of that "rot" were clear: "It is the loss of American lives" (14). If the South Vietnamese did not "have a clear sense of identification with their own government" (15), they would quit. Their failure to act during Tet, Kennedy concluded, proved that claim. Kennedy ended with a harsh assessment of the Saigon regime: "We have an ally in name only. We support a government without supporters. Without

---

[7]McNamara had served John Kennedy and Lyndon Johnson as secretary of defense; Robert Kennedy thought very highly of him. McNamara had grown increasingly disillusioned with the war throughout 1967, and President Johnson sought to ease him out without a public dispute. In late November of 1967 Johnson nominated McNamara for the post of head of the World Bank, an international development agency. McNamara quietly accepted and left the administration (Schlesinger 883–884).

the efforts of American arms that government would not last a day" (16). The dissociation was now complete. The South Vietnamese government did not deserve the consideration accorded to allies because it did not act like an ally.

Again Kennedy invoked the authority of the past as a standard to judge the present. The legitimacy of Johnson's policy was destroyed by its failure to meet historical standards for success. The first two sections of the speech demonstrated that neither U.S. military efforts nor South Vietnamese political actions were effective. At this point, then, the speech began to broaden. Although still invoking the experience of the Tet offensive, Kennedy began to question the ideological foundation for military action in Vietnam. The third section of the speech dealt with the first of those three grounds for U.S. involvement: the claim that the war served the interest of the people of Vietnam. The argument also addressed the option of military escalation. Although he did not use that phrase, the rebuttal covered the possibility: "Unswerving pursuit of military victory" did not help anyone (17).

Senator Kennedy turned first to the interests of "the people of Vietnam" (17). Through analogy he brought the war home to Americans by tying that distant conflict to familiar markers. Vietnam had "been devastated by a weight of bombs and shells greater than Nazi Germany knew in the Second World War" (17). He made the horror of Vietnam comprehensible by painstakingly detailing "the impact in our own country" if the war raged here (17). He asked Americans to judge-with the people of Vietnam. If we suffered "as New York and Chicago, Washington and Boston, were being destroyed by a war raging in their streets," would we accede to the policy (17)? Not likely. The Vietnamese people were "the greatest losers" (17).

They were not alone. The "interests of America" were not served by fighting "this war as if moral standards could be subordinated to immediate necessities" (18). Previously Kennedy argued that "political and economic reform" by the government of South Vietnam were "the principal weapons of battle" (15). Now he extended this "right makes might" philosophy to U.S. actions. Not only did inhumanity, such as Loan's execution of "a Vietcong suspect," make us as "brutal and cruel" as the Communists, but it also "may hurt us far more in the long run than it helps us today" (18). Morality and practicality merged in Kennedy's analysis; U.S. neglect of both undermined our policy objectives.

The senator's argument demonstrates the linkage between the Aristotelian genres. The end of deliberative speech is the "advantageous," but, as Aristotle notes (George Kennedy 56–74, 85), ethical appeals are often useful in deliberation. Robert Kennedy argued that the virtuous course was the practical course. The incompetence of the Saigon government forced the United States to separate the two. The continued pursuit of a military victory, in light of this problem, damaged the moral and political standing of the United States and fatally compromised the effort to build a good government in South Vietnam.

Yet inhumanity could be justified if it saved Americans from Communism. Cold War ideology, shaken as it was by Vietnam, framed audience perceptions to a significant degree. If Vietnam were viewed in that way, Kennedy would fail. He had shown that the war did not help the people of Vietnam. Now he turned to reshaping perceptions of Vietnam and the Cold War.

"The fourth illusion," Kennedy argued, was "that the American national interest" should be the same as that of "an incompetent military regime" (19). He had documented the failures of the Saigon government, so he turned to an explanation of the national interest. As usual, the senator presented his attack as a dialogue. Several minor premises supported the fourth illusion, he questioned all of them.

In 1965, in an address at Johns Hopkins University, Lyndon Johnson argued that U.S. policy in Vietnam would, among other things, result in a vast economic development of Southeast Asia (Turner 111–133). Kennedy scoffed at such "pretension," supporting his claim with the failure of the Great Society in the United States and with the *Pueblo* incident (19).[8] Johnson's extravagance at Johns Hopkins was an easy target; it was unlikely that most Americans cared much about a Great Society in Asia anyway. The issue, however, highlighted yet another presidential misjudgment and undermined Johnson's *ethos*.

Kennedy then confronted the claim that the war in Vietnam was crucial to the survival of a free Asia. He had prepared well for this critical moment. He had established the failure of the military, the corruption of the South Vietnamese government, and the horror of the war. Conceptually, for the audience to think of this misbegotten enterprise in Vietnam as the rock upon which the tide of Communism would break seemed unlikely. Equally important, his manner of argument had shaped appropriate criteria for judgment. He consistently asked the audience to evaluate the president's policy in terms of its consequences as measured by historical standards. By this point listeners were probably judging as Kennedy judged.

Given such preparation, he wasted little time. The notion that the war would "settle the future course of Asia" was a "prayerful wish

---

[8]In January of 1968 the North Korean government seized a U.S. intelligence vessel, the *Pueblo*, and held its crew hostage. They were eventually released after undergoing a horrific experience at the hands of the North Koreans.

based on unsound hope" (20). He supported his claim with a long string of enumerated examples:

> The truth is that Communism triumphed in China twenty years ago and was extended to Tibet. It lost in Malaya and the Philippines, met disaster in Indonesia and was fought to a standstill in Korea. It has struggled against governments in Burma for twenty years without success, and it may struggle in Thailand for many more. The outcome in each country depends and will depend on the intrinsic strength of the government, the particular circumstances of the country, and the particular character of the insurgent movement. (20)

The emphasis on the "particular" was no accident; it expressed Kennedy's determination that policy makers should adapt the means of containment to each struggle throughout the world. Foreign policy, as practical wisdom, must adjust the general to the particular. The president's policy failed to meet that standard, and it promised "only years and decades of further draining conflict on the mainland of Asia" (20).

In this way Robert Kennedy reconceptualized the Cold War. The United States could no longer reflexively resort to military force every time an insurgent movement threatened an allied government. Rather, the means to prosecute the Cold War must reflect the requirements of each instance of the struggle. Kennedy developed a rationale for specific negotiations to uphold the principle of containment. Talking, not fighting, was the best strategy for Vietnam.

Even the need to demonstrate U.S. fidelity to treaty obligations did not affect his judgment. Aristotelian topical theory suggests that great powers must reveal the ability and the will to act (George Kennedy 177; Hill, "Conventional Wisdom" 379). In 1969 Richard Nixon would argue that the United States must stay in Vietnam as a demonstration of its will (Hill, "Conventional Wisdom" 379). Robert Kennedy, as he did in his discussion of South Vietnam as an ally, turned this topic to his advantage rather than attacking it directly. The United States, he stated, possessed an "interest in South Vietnam." But we had already demonstrated our will through "all the lives and resources we have poured into Vietnam" (21). No one, he concluded, could question U.S. will in light of that effort. Having disposed of all three justifications for military action, he turned to the key interest: "the lives of our gallant young men" (22). On those sacred grounds, he called for negotiations.

A fair compromise, however, implied that the United States would not win the war. As Kennedy put it, "The fifth illusion is that this war can be settled in our own way and in our own time and on our own terms" (23). This illusion was, perhaps, the most emotionally attractive of the five. For the American people to discard this "fallacy" meant giving up the cultural myth so sharply stated in the 1970 motion picture *Patton:* "Americans have never lost and will never lose a war." Kennedy, to his credit, did not mince words: "We have not done this [won the war], nor is there any prospect we will achieve such a victory" (24).

He supported this assertion by again invoking the lessons of history. He began by attacking the credibility of his opponents. Given the doubt created by the Tet offensive, this was a smart move. But the senator not only made his charges, he also reminded the audience of those haunting phrases that turned out to be so empty: " 'the tide is turning'; there is 'light at the end of the tunnel,' 'we can soon bring home the troops—victory is near—the enemy is tiring' " (25). He asked listeners, if only for a moment, to relive those words. The historical experience that Kennedy created was not reassuring. He asked listeners to confront a "consistent chronicle of error" (25).

He forced himself to do the same: "Once, in 1962, I participated in such predictions myself" (25). Rather than standing *outside* the audience, in a stance of moral and intellectual superiority, Kennedy judged with the audience. He had failed to grasp the true situation in Vietnam when he was the attorney general, but he now faced "the reality that a military victory is not in sight, and that it probably will never come" (25). Throughout the speech, Kennedy implicitly modeled the experience he wanted listeners to undergo. He stated the administration's position, compared it to historical markers, and found it wanting. He judged as he would have the audience judge. In this paragraph he made that process explicit. "Ordinary" Americans were more likely to admit their error and make changes if one of the participants in the creation of the policy did the same. Robert Kennedy provided the model.

Only after dispensing with the five illusions did the senator turn to a brief outline of his alternative. He pleaded for open negotiations, a willingness to "make concessions and take risks" (26). Given the paucity of proposals from either side, Kennedy could present only general terms. He defended his view, as Aristotle would suggest (George Kennedy 202), with arguments based on the lack of a realistic alternative. There was no other reasonable course open. In addition, he framed his alternative with language that echoed President Kennedy. Robert Kennedy argued, "No one knows if negotiations will bring a peaceful settlement, but we do know there will be no peaceful settlement without negotiations" (26). John Kennedy, when he discussed the Cold War in his inaugural, noted, "Let us never negotiate out of fear. But let us never fear to negotiate." Formally and substantively, Robert Kennedy invoked the authority of his brother—which in 1968 was an *ethos* still untrammeled by revisionism—as a warrant that supported the argument for negotiation.

The conclusion of the address developed along classical lines (George Kennedy 280–282). Senator Kennedy summarized the lessons to be learned from the Tet offensive and emphasized the qualities of judgment needed from the American people. The lengthy list of lessons, nearly twice as long as the number of illusions, hammered home his claims and accentuated the administration's miscalculations. By numbering each item, the senator dispelled the confusion afflicting the audience; the "light of reason" was clear if one chose to see it.

The final paragraph explicitly invoked the qualities Americans should bring to the task of judgment and defined the proper relationship between the leaders and the led in a democracy. Appropriately, Kennedy waited until the end of the speech to be so direct about his expectations for the public; if he had done so earlier, he might have seemed presumptuous. By the end he had enacted the qualities he demanded of his audience. He asked no more of them than he had of himself.

He began by defining the "bravery" needed "to discard the comfort of illusion" (38). Ordinary concepts of bravery would not do. They were necessary but insufficient. Rather, the nation required the intellectual and moral courage to face a "grim and painful" situation (38). The brother of a revered, martyred president assured the public that it was appropriate to question this war. They should do so not only because of the "anguish toward which a policy based on illusion is surely taking us," but also because this "is a great nation and a strong people" (38). The American character, qualities Kennedy simultaneously invoked and created, required dissent.

But the war, Kennedy said, "demanded" bravery not only from the people but also from "our government" (38). The end of the speech challenged the legitimacy of Lyndon Johnson's presidency by asserting that true leadership must reflect the bravery and strength of the American people. Asking the audience to complete the enthymeme, Kennedy said, "Any who seek to comfort rather than speak plainly, reassure rather than instruct, promise satisfaction rather than reveal frustration—they deny that greatness and drain that strength. For today, as it was in the beginning, it is the truth that makes us free" (38). The false promises of the administration and the authority of the Bible (John 8:32: "And you will know the truth and the truth will make you free.") undermined the covenant between President Johnson and the American people. He no longer believed in their judgment. Robert Kennedy spoke to their finest qualities.

CONCLUSION

This speech could be a model of political judgment for the American people. The dialectical structure induced participation, enacted the process of good judgment, and gave listeners responses to administration claims. The sarcastic language expressed the skepticism with which the audience should treat opposing arguments. Finally, Robert Kennedy provided a model to emulate, an authority figure who admitted previous errors and now sought "the only path" to peace.

Yet Kennedy's unwillingness to take the final step and challenge Lyndon Johnson for the presidency inhibited his rhetorical effectiveness. Robert Kennedy argued that Lyndon Johnson had shown fatally flawed judgment, miscalculations that resulted in dreadful consequences and promised future disasters. Kennedy, in turn, revealed his superior judgment. He also asserted the right to define the character of the American people, and he argued that Lyndon Johnson had violated his covenant with them (Murphy, "Epideictic and Deliberative"). Robert Kennedy, by so clearly contrasting his wisdom to the foolishness of the president, created for himself the obligation to remove Johnson, a duty made more compelling by his social authority. He was the brother of President Kennedy, heir to the family legacy, and leader of the liberal wing of the Democratic party. Kennedy's refusal to run contradicted his rhetoric.

The reaction to the speech reflects that assessment. The press gave Kennedy's remarks extensive coverage and recognized the speech for the "broadside" ("Broadside") that it was. *Newsweek* took the unusual step of printing excerpts from the address. Coverage in the *Washington Post* ("Kennedy Calls") and the *New York Times* (Wicker) was favorable. But the *Christian Science Monitor* vigorously attacked the speech by posing their own debate in which Johnson came out best (Davis). Columnist Joseph Alsop felt "compelled to regard Bobby Kennedy as a traitor to the United States" (quoted in Schlesinger 905).

Yet Kennedy's political situation sparked the most comment. Tom Wicker, in the *New York Times,* noted that most in Washington focused on the "political significance" of the address. The speech added to the speculation that Kennedy *had* to run for the presidency.[9] A little

---

[9]Senator Eugene McCarthy (D-MN) was running against Lyndon Johnson in the Democratic party primaries. Kennedy, however, believed that McCarthy would make a bad president. He felt he could not endorse the Minnesota senator. Kennedy himself refused to run primarily because he did not think he could defeat Lyndon Johnson. Robert Kennedy did not believe in romantic losing gestures. If he ran, he wanted to win. In late 1967 and early 1968 he did not think he could do so (Newfield 204–206, 211; Schlesinger 888–890).

over a month later, Robert Kennedy made that move. His delay, however, cost him dearly and led to a brutal primary race against fellow liberal Eugene McCarthy. Kennedy's political prospects were uncertain when he was assassinated on the evening of his victory in the California primary.

In one way, however, Robert Kennedy achieved what he set out to do on February 8, 1968. He told his speechwriters that he wanted to speak about "the meaning of Tet. . . . Johnson can't get away with saying it is really a victory for us" (quoted in Newfield 221). By reading this text as an instance of situated political judgment, Kennedy's skill at developing a "meaning for Tet" becomes readily apparent. Yet it was not only Kennedy's faculty for using argument, evidence, and disposition that leads to such an assessment. The text of the speech reveals a rhetor who understood that issues of history and audience were critical to his success.

Such concerns are not traditional fodder for Aristotelian analysis. I believe I have shown, however, that they are not foreign to a perspective that begins with judgment. Good judgment, Browne and Leff argue, requires distance. Kennedy provided that distance with his arguments from history. He invoked the historical character of the American people and evaluated Johnson's policy by the standards of history. A critique based on the concept of judgment should recognize and evaluate a rhetor's facility for coping with the ideological constraints created by a nation's collective memory. The very standards for determining the "advantageous" for a community may rest in its interpretations of its past experiences.

Judgment also inevitably concerns the character of the judges, the friendship or community feeling that binds them together. Neo-Aristotelian critics believed that audiences were inherently rational. Contemporary Aristotelian views accept the contingency of the audience's identity while arguing that an exemplary instance of situated political judgment can, temporarily at least, create the common feeling necessary for public decisions. The doubt created by the Tet offensive offered Robert Kennedy the chance to accomplish that task; his authority made him perhaps the only public figure in 1968 with the power to grasp that opportunity.[10] He deserves praise for his skilled performance on February 8, 1968.

---

[10]Contrast, for example, the political situation in February of 1968 with the conditions in November of 1969 when President Nixon spoke on Vietnam. Robert Kennedy possessed the power to challenge the president in 1968. By 1969 Robert Kennedy and Martin Luther King, Jr., were dead; former Vice President Humphrey was tainted by his association with the Johnson administration; and Edward Kennedy was politically paralyzed by the Chappaquiddick scandal. Richard Nixon's authority, unlike that of President Johnson, faced little challenge from credible opponents.

WORKS CITED

"Appraisal of Kennedy." *Christian Science Monitor* 3 March 1967: 18.

Beiner, Ronald. *Political Judgment*. Chicago: University of Chicago Press, 1983.

Black, Edwin. *Rhetorical Criticism: A Study in Method*. New York: Macmillan, 1965.

"A Broadside by Bobby." *Newsweek* 19 Feb. 1968: 23.

Browne, Stephen H. and Michael C. Leff. "Political Judgment and Rhetorical Argument: Edmund Burke's Paradigm. *Argument and Social Practice: Proceedings of the Fourth SCA/AFA Conference on Argumentation*. Ed. J. Robert Cox, Malcolm O. Sillars, and Gregg B. Walker. Annandale, VA: Speech Communication Association, 1985. 193–210.

Charland, Maurice. "Constitutive Rhetoric: The Case of the *Peuple Quebecois*." *Quarterly Journal of Speech* 73 (1987): 133–150.

Davis, Saville R. "Kennedy Sharpens Attack." *Christian Science Monitor* 10 Feb. 1968: 1.

Epstein, Edward Jay. "The Televised War." *Between Fact and Fiction: The Problem of Journalism*. New York: Vintage Books, 1975. 210–232.

Farrell, Thomas B. "Knowledge, Consensus, and Rhetorical Theory." *Quarterly Journal of Speech* 62 (1976): 1–14.

Gallup Opinion Index, Report No. 31, Jan. 1968: 3, 6.

Hill, Forbes. "Conventional Wisdom—Traditional Form: The President's Message of November 3, 1969." *Quarterly Journal of Speech* 58 (1972): 373–386.

Hill, Forbes. "Reply to Professor Campbell." *Quarterly Journal of Speech* 58 (1972): 454–460.

Hill, Forbes. "The *Rhetoric* of Aristotle." *A Synoptic History of Classical Rhetoric*. Ed. James J. Murphy. Davis, CA: Hermagoras Press, 1983.

Kail, F. M. *What Washington Said: Administration Rhetoric and the Vietnam War*. New York: Harper & Row, 1973.

Karnow, Stanley. *Vietnam: A History*. New York: Viking Press, 1983.

Kendrick, Alexander. *The Wound Within: America in the Vietnam Years 1945–1974*. Boston: Little, Brown, 1974.

"Kennedy Calls for an End to Illusion in Vietnam." *Washington Post* 9 Feb. 1968: 1, 2.

Kennedy, George. *Aristotle on Rhetoric: A Theory of Civil Discourse*. New York: Oxford University Press, 1991.

Kennedy, John F. "Let Us Begin." *Presidential Rhetoric: 1961–Present*. 5th ed. Ed. Theodore O. Windt, Jr. Dubuque, IA: Kendall/Hunt, 1994. 9–11.

Kennedy, Robert F. Address Delivered in Chicago, Illinois, February 8, 1968. *To Seek a Newer World*. New York: Bantam Books, 1968. 221–229.

Leff, Michael C., and G. P. Mohrmann. "Lincoln at Cooper Union: A Rhetorical Analysis of the Text." *Quarterly Journal of Speech* 60 (1974): 346–358.

Mohrmann, G. P. "Elegy in a Critical Graveyard." *Landmark Essays on American Public Address*. Ed. Martin J. Medhurst. Davis, CA: Hermagoras Press, 1993.

"More Important Than Words." *Newsweek* 27 May 1968: 25–30b.

Murphy, John M. "Confrontation: Robert F. Kennedy on Vietnam." Thesis. University of Kansas, 1985.

Murphy, John M. "Epideictic and Deliberative Strategies in Opposition to War: The Paradox of Honor and Expediency." *Communication Studies* 43 (1992): 65–78.

Newfield, Jack. *Robert F. Kennedy: A Memoir*. New York: Berkeley Publishing, 1978.

Perelman, Chaim, and L. Olbrechts-Tyteca. *The New Rhetoric: A Treatise on Argumentation*. Trans. John Wilkinson and Purcell Weaver. Notre Dame: University of Notre Dame Press, 1969.

Schlesinger, Arthur M. *Robert Kennedy and His Times*. New York: Random House, 1978.

Turner, Kathleen J. *Lyndon Johnson's Dual War: Vietnam and the Press*. Chicago: University of Chicago Press, 1985.

"Two Senators Named Kennedy." *Newsweek* 17 Jan. 1966: 17.

Vonnegut, Kristin M. "Listening for Women's Voices: Revisioning Courses in American Public Address." *Communication Education* 41 (1992): 26–39.

Warnick, Barbara. "Judgment, Probability, and Aristotle's *Rhetoric*." *Quarterly Journal of Speech* 75 (1989): 299–311.

Wicker, Tom. "Kennedy Asserts U.S. Cannot Win." *New York Times* 9 Feb. 1968: 1, 12.

RICHARD M. NIXON

Vietnamization: The President's Address on War

On November 3, 1969, President Richard Nixon delivered this major statement on the war in Vietnam. The speech announced Nixon's policy of "Vietnamization," wherein responsibility for actually fighting the war would shift from U.S. forces to the South Vietnamese military with continued air support and matériel provided by the United States. Despite evidence that Nixon succeeded in gaining some public support for Vietnamization, both the policy and the speech prompted sharp responses from politicians, media commentators, and rhetorical critics. The text is from Congressional Record, *Vol. 115, Part 24, pp. 32784–32786.*

1　Tonight I want to talk to you on a subject that deeply concerns every American and other people throughout the world—the war in Vietnam.

2　I believe that one of the reasons for the deep division in this nation about Vietnam is that many Americans have lost confidence in what their government has told them about our policy. The American people cannot and should not be asked to support a policy which involves the overriding issues of war and peace unless they know the truth about that policy.

3   Tonight I would like to answer some of the questions that I know are on the minds of many of you listening to me.

- How and why did America get involved in Vietnam in the first place?
- How has this administration changed the policy of the previous administration?
- What has really happened in the negotiations in Paris and on the battlefront in Vietnam?
- What choices do we have if we are to end the war?
- What are the prospects for peace?

4   Let me begin by describing the situation I found when I was inaugurated on January 20.

- The war had been going on for four years.
- 31,000 Americans had been killed in action.
- The training program for the South Vietnamese armed forces was behind schedule.
- 540,000 Americans were in Vietnam with no plans to reduce the number.
- No progress had been made at the negotiations in Paris, and the United States had not put forth a comprehensive peace proposal.
- The war was causing deep division at home and criticism from many of our friends as well as our enemies abroad.

5   In view of these circumstances there were some who urged I end the war at once by ordering the immediate withdrawal of all American forces. From a political standpoint this would have been a popular and easy course to follow. After all, we became involved in the war while my predecessor was in office. I could blame the defeat which would be the result of my action on him and come out as the peacemaker. Some put it quite bluntly: This was the only way to avoid allowing Johnson's war to become Nixon's war.

6   But I had a greater obligation than to think only of the years of my administration and the next election. I had to think of the effect of my decision on the next generation and the future of peace and freedom in America and the world.

7   Let us all understand that the question before us is not whether some Americans are for peace and some Americans against it. The great question at issue is not whether Johnson's war becomes Nixon's war. The question is: How can we win America's peace?

8   Let us now turn to the fundamental issue. Why and how did the United States become involved in Vietnam in the first place? Fifteen years ago North Vietnam, with the logistical support of Communist China and the Soviet Union, launched a campaign to impose a Communist government on South Vietnam by instigating and supporting a revolution. In response to the request of the government of South Vietnam, President Eisenhower sent economic aid and military equipment to assist the people of South Vietnam in their efforts to prevent a Communist takeover. Seven years ago, President Kennedy sent 16,000 military personnel to Vietnam as combat advisers. Four years ago, President Johnson sent American combat forces to South Vietnam.

9   Many believe that President Johnson's decision to send American combat forces to South Vietnam was wrong. Many others—I among them—have been strongly critical of the way the war has been conducted.

10   But the question facing us today is—now that we are in the war, what is the best way to end it? In January I could only conclude that the precipitate withdrawal of all American forces from Vietnam would be a disaster not only for South Vietnam but for the United States and for the cause of peace.

11   For the South Vietnamese, our precipitate withdrawal would inevitably allow the Communists to repeat the massacres which followed their takeover of the North fifteen years ago.
  • They then murdered more than fifty thousand people and hundreds of thousands more died in slave labor camps.
  • We saw a prelude of what would happen in South Vietnam when the Communists entered the city of Hue last year. During their brief rule there, there was a bloody reign of terror in which some 3,000 civilians were clubbed, shot to death and buried in mass graves.
  • With the sudden collapse of our support, these atrocities of Hue would become the nightmare of the entire nation—and particularly for the million and a half Catholic refugees who fled to South Vietnam when the Communists took over the North in 1954.

12   For the United States, this first defeat in our nation's history would result in a collapse of confidence in American leadership, not only in Asia but throughout the world.

13   Three American presidents have recognized the great stakes involved in Vietnam and understood what had to be done.

- In 1963, President Kennedy said with his characteristic eloquence and clarity, "We want to see a stable government there carrying on the struggle to maintain its national independence. We believe strongly in that. We're not going to withdraw from that effort. In my opinion for us to withdraw from that effort would mean a collapse not only of South Vietnam, but Southeast Asia, so we're going to stay there."
- President Eisenhower and President Johnson expressed the same conclusion during their terms in office.

14 For the future of peace, precipitate withdrawal would thus be a disaster of immense magnitude.

- A nation cannot remain great if it betrays its allies and lets down its friends.
- Our defeat and humiliation in South Vietnam would without question promote recklessness in the councils of those great powers who have not yet abandoned their goals of world conquest.
- This would spark violence wherever our commitments help maintain peace—in the Middle East, in Berlin, eventually even in the Western Hemisphere.

15 Ultimately, this would cost more lives. It would not bring peace. It would bring more war.

16 For these reasons, I rejected the recommendation that I should end the war by immediately withdrawing all our forces. I chose instead to change American policy on both the negotiating front and the battlefront. In order to end a war fought on many fronts, I initiated a pursuit for peace on many fronts. In a television speech on May 14, in a speech before the United Nations, and on a number of other occasions I set forth our peace proposals in great detail.

- We have offered the complete withdrawal of all outside forces within one year.
- We have proposed a ceasefire under international supervision.
- We have offered free elections under international supervision with the Communists participating in the organization and conduct of the elections as an organized political force. The Saigon government has pledged to accept the result of the elections.

17 We have not put forth our proposals on a take-it-or-leave-it basis. We have indicated that we are willing to discuss the proposals that have been put forth by the other side. We have declared that anything is negotiable except the right of the people of South Vietnam to determine their own future. At the Paris peace conference, Ambassador Lodge has demonstrated our flexibility and good faith in 40 public meetings. Hanoi has refused even to discuss our proposals. They demand our unconditional acceptance of their terms: that we withdraw all American forces immediately and unconditionally and that we overthrow the government of South Vietnam as we leave.

18   We have not limited our peace initiatives to public forums and public statements. I recognized that a long and bitter war like this usually cannot be settled in a public forum. That is why in addition to the public statements and negotiations I have explored every possible private avenue that might lead to a settlement.

19   Therefore, tonight I am taking the unprecedented step of disclosing some of our other initiatives for peace—initiatives we undertook privately and secretly because we thought that we thereby might open a door which publicly would be closed.

20   I did not wait for my inauguration to begin my quest for peace.

- Soon after my election, through an individual who is directly in contact on a personal basis with the leaders of North Vietnam, I made two private offers for a rapid, comprehensive settlement. Hanoi's replies called in effect for our surrender before negotiations.

- Since the Soviet Union furnishes most of the military equipment for North Vietnam, Secretary of State Rogers, my assistant for National Security Affairs, Dr. Kissinger, Ambassador Lodge, and I personally, have met on a number of occasions with representatives of the Soviet government to enlist their assistance in getting meaningful negotiations started.

21   In addition we have had extended discussions directed toward that same end with representatives of other governments which have diplomatic relations with North Vietnam. None of these initiatives have to date produced results.

- In mid-July, I became convinced that it was necessary to make a major move to break the deadlock in the Paris talks. I spoke directly, in this office, where I'm now sitting, with an individual who had known Ho Chi Minh on a personal basis for 25 years. Through him I sent a letter to Ho Chi Minh. I did this outside of the usual diplomatic channels with the hope that with the necessity of making statements for propaganda removed, there might be constructive progress toward bringing the war to an end. Let me read from that letter:

Dear Mr. President:

I realize that it is difficult to communicate meaningfully across the gulf of four years of war. But precisely because of this gulf, I wanted to take this opportunity to reaffirm in all solemnity my desire to work for a just peace. I deeply believe that the war in Vietnam has gone on too long and delay in bringing it to an end can benefit no one—least of all the people of Vietnam.

The time has come to move forward at the conference table toward an early resolution of this tragic war. You will find us forthcoming and open-minded in a common effort to bring the blessings of peace to the brave people of Vietnam. Let history record that at this critical juncture, both sides turned their face toward peace rather than toward conflict and war.

I received Ho Chi Minh's reply on August 30, three days before his death. It simply reiterated the public position North Vietnam had taken in the Paris talks and flatly rejected my initiative. The full text of both letters is being released to the press.

- In addition to the public meetings I have referred to, Ambassador Lodge has met with Vietnam's chief negotiator in Paris in 11 private meetings.

- We have taken other significant initiatives which must remain secret to keep open some channels of communication which may still prove to be productive.

22   The effect of all the public, private, and secret negotiations which have been undertaken since the bombing halt a year ago, and since this administration came into office on January 20, can be summed up in one sentence—no progress whatever has been made except agreement on the shape of the bargaining table.

23   Well, now, who's at fault? It has become clear that the obstacle in negotiating an end to the war is not the president of the United States. And it is not the South Vietnamese government. The obstacle is the other side's absolute refusal to show the least willingness to join us in seeking a just peace. It will not do so while it is convinced that all it has to do is to wait for our next concession, and our next concession after that one, until it gets everything it wants. There can be now no longer any doubt that progress in negotiation depends above all on Hanoi's deciding to negotiate—to negotiate seriously.

24   I realize that this report on our efforts on the diplomatic front is discouraging to the American people. But the American people are entitled to know the truth—the bad news as well as the good news where the lives of our young men are involved.

25   Let me now turn, however, to a more encouraging report on another front. At the time we launched our search for peace, I recognized that we might not succeed in bringing an end to the war through negotiation. I therefore put into effect another plan to bring peace—a plan which will bring the war to an end regardless of what happens on the negotiating front. It is in line with a major shift in U.S. foreign policy which I described in my press conference at Guam on July 25. Let me briefly explain what has been described as the Nixon Doctrine—a policy which not only will help end the war in Vietnam but which is an essential element of our program to prevent future Vietnams.

26   We Americans are a do-it-yourself people—an impatient people. Instead of teaching someone else to do a job, we like to do it ourselves. This trait has been carried over into our foreign policy. In Korea and again in Vietnam, the United States furnished most of the money, most of the arms, and most of the men to help the people of those countries defend their freedom against Communist aggression. Before any American troops were committed to Vietnam, a leader of another Asian country expressed this opinion to me when I was traveling in Asia as a private citizen. "When you are trying to assist another nation defend its freedom, U.S. policy should be to help them fight the war but not to fight the war for them."

27   Well, in accordance with this wise counsel, I laid down in Guam these three principles as guidelines for future American policy toward Asia:

1. The United States will keep all of our treaty commitments.

2. We shall provide a shield if a nuclear power threatens the freedom of a nation allied with us or of a nation whose survival we consider vital to our security.

3. In cases involving other types of aggression, we shall furnish military and economic assistance when requested in accordance with our treaty commitments. But we shall look to the nation directly threatened to assume the primary responsibility of providing the manpower for its defense.

28   After I announced this policy, I found that the leaders of the Philippines, Thailand, Vietnam, South Korea, and other nations which might be threatened by Communist aggression welcomed this new direction in American foreign policy.

29   The defense of freedom is everybody's business—not just America's business. And it is particularly the responsibility of the people whose freedom is threatened. In the previous administration we Americanized the war in Vietnam. In this administration we are Vietnamizing the search for peace. The policy of the previous administration not only resulted in our assuming the primary responsibility for fighting the war but even more significantly it did not adequately stress the goal of strengthening the South Vietnamese so that they could defend themselves when we left.

30   The Vietnamization Plan was launched following Secretary Laird's visit to Vietnam in March. Under the plan, I ordered a substantial increase in the training and equipment of South Vietnamese forces. In July, on my visit to Vietnam, I changed General Abrams' orders so that they were consistent with the objectives of our new policy. Under the new orders the primary mission of our troops is to enable the South Vietnamese forces to assume the full responsibility for the security of South Vietnam. Our air operations have been reduced by over 20 percent.

31   We have now begun to see the results of this long overdue change in American policy in Vietnam.

- After five years of Americans going into Vietnam, we are finally bringing American men home. By December 15, over 60,000 men will have been withdrawn from South Vietnam— including 20 percent of all of our combat troops.

- The South Vietnamese have continued to gain in strength. As a result they have been able to take over combat responsibilities from our American forces.

32   Two other significant developments have occurred since this administration took office in January.

- Enemy infiltration, infiltration which is essential if they are to launch an attack, over the last three months is less than 20 percent of what it was over the similar period last year.

- Most important—United States casualties have declined during the last two months to the lowest point in three years.

33   Let me turn now to our program for the future. We have adopted a plan which we have worked out in cooperation with the South Vietnamese for the complete withdrawal of all U.S. ground combat forces and their replacement by South Vietnamese forces on an orderly scheduled timetable. This withdrawal will be made from strength and not from weakness. As South Vietnamese forces become stronger, the rate of American withdrawal can become greater.

34 I have not and do not intend to announce the timetable for our program. There are obvious reasons for this decision which I am sure you will understand. As I have indicated on several occasions, the rate of withdrawal will depend on developments on three fronts:

- One is the progress which may be made at the Paris talks. An announcement of a fixed timetable for our withdrawal would completely remove any incentive for the enemy to negotiate an agreement.
- They would simply wait until our forces had withdrawn and then move in.

35 The other two factors on which we will base our withdrawal decisions are the level of enemy activity and the progress of the training program of the South Vietnamese forces. And I am glad to be able to repeat tonight progress on both these fronts has been greater than we anticipated when we started the withdrawal program in June. As a result, our timetable for withdrawal is more optimistic now than when we made our first estimates in June. This clearly demonstrates why it is not wise to be frozen in on a fixed timetable. We must retain the flexibility to base each withdrawal decision on the situation as it is at that time rather than on estimates that are no longer valid.

36 Along with this optimistic estimate, I must—in all candor— leave one note of caution. If the level of enemy activity significantly increases, we might have to adjust our timetable accordingly. However, I want the record to be completely clear on one point. At the time of the bombing halt last November, there was some confusion as to whether there was an understanding on the part of the enemy that if we stopped the bombing they would stop shelling cities of South Vietnam. I want to be sure there is no misunderstanding on the part of the enemy with regard to our withdrawal program.

37 We have noted the reduced level of infiltration and the reduction of our casualties and are basing our withdrawal decisions partially on those factors. If the level of infiltration or our casualties increase while we are trying to scale down the fighting, it will be the result of a conscious decision by the enemy. Hanoi could make no greater mistake than to assume that an increase in violence will be to its own advantage. If I conclude that increased enemy action jeopardizes our remaining forces in Vietnam, I shall not hesitate to take strong and effective measures to deal with that situation.

38 This is not a threat. This is a statement of policy which as commander-in-chief of our armed forces I am making in meeting my responsibility for the protection of American fighting men wherever they may be. I am sure that you can recognize from what I have said that we have only two choices open to us if we want to end the war.

- I can order an immediate, precipitate withdrawal of all Americans from Vietnam without regard to the effects of that action.

- Or we can persist in our search for a just peace through a negotiated settlement if possible, or through continued implementation of our plan for Vietnamization if necessary—a plan in which we will withdraw all of our forces from Vietnam on a schedule in accordance with our program, as the South Vietnamese become strong enough to defend their own freedom.

39   I have chosen the second course. It is not the easy way. It is the right way. It is a plan which will end the war and serve the cause of peace—not just in Vietnam but in the Pacific and in the world.

40   In speaking of the consequences of a precipitate withdrawal, I mentioned that our allies would lose confidence in America. Far more dangerous, we would lose confidence in ourselves. The immediate reaction would be a sense of relief as our men came home. But as we saw the consequences of what we had done, inevitable remorse and divisive recrimination would scar our spirit as a people.

41   We have faced other crises in our history and have become stronger by rejecting the easy way out and taking the right way in meeting our challenges. Our greatness as a nation has been our capacity to do what had to be done when we knew our course was right.

42   I recognize that some of my fellow citizens disagree with the plan for peace I have chosen. Honest and patriotic Americans have reached different conclusions as to how peace should be achieved. In San Francisco a few weeks ago, I saw demonstrators carrying signs reading, "Lose in Vietnam, bring the boys home."

43   One of the strengths of our free society is that any American has a right to reach that conclusion and to advocate that point of view. But as president of the United States, I would be untrue to my oath of office if I allowed the policy of this nation to be dictated by the minority who hold that view and who attempt to impose it on the nation by mounting demonstrations in the street.

44   For almost two hundred years, the policy of this nation has been made under our Constitution by those leaders in the Congress and in the White House who were elected by all the people. If a vocal minority, however fervent its cause, prevails over reason and the will of the majority, this nation has no future as a free society.

45   And now I would like to address a word, if I may, to the young people of this nation who are particularly concerned—and I understand why they are concerned—about the war.

- I respect your idealism.
- I share your concern for peace.
- I want peace as much as you do.

46   There are powerful personal reasons I want to end this war. This week I will have to sign 83 letters to mothers, fathers, wives, and loved ones of men who had given their lives for America in Vietnam. It is very little satisfaction to me that this was only one-third as many as I signed during my first week in office. There is nothing I want more than to see the day come when I no longer must write any of these letters. I want to end the war to save the lives of those brave young men in Vietnam.

- I want to end it in a way which will increase the chance that their younger brothers and their sons will not have to fight in some future Vietnam someplace in the world.
- I want to end the war so that the energy and dedication of our young people, now too often directed into bitter hatred against those they think are responsible for the war, can be turned to the great challenges of peace, a better life for all Americans and for people throughout the world.

47   I have chosen a plan for peace. I believe it will succeed. If it does not succeed, what the critics say now won't matter. Or if it does succeed, what the critics say now won't matter. If it does not succeed, anything I say then won't matter.

48   I know it may not be fashionable to speak of patriotism or national destiny these days. But I feel it is appropriate to do so on this occasion. Two hundred years ago this nation was weak and poor. But even then, America was the hope of millions in the world. Today we have become the strongest and the richest nation in the world. The wheel of destiny has turned so that any hope the world has for the survival of peace and freedom in the last third of this century will be determined by whether the American people have the moral stamina and the courage to meet the challenge of free world leadership.

49   Let historians not record that when America was the most powerful nation in the world we passed on the other side of the road and allowed the last hopes for peace and freedom of millions of people on this earth to be suffocated by the forces of totalitarianism.

50 And so tonight—to you, the great silent majority of my fellow Americans—I ask for your support.

51 I pledged in my campaign for the presidency to end the war in a way that we could win the peace. I have initiated a plan of action which will enable me to keep that pledge. The more support I can have from the American people, the sooner that pledge can be redeemed; for the more divided we are at home, the less likely the enemy is to negotiate in Paris. Let us be united for peace. Let us also be united against defeat. Because let us understand: North Vietnam cannot defeat or humiliate the United States. Only Americans can do that.

52 Fifty years ago, in this very room and at this very desk, President Woodrow Wilson wrote words which caught the imagination of a war-weary world during World War I. He said, "This is the war to end wars." His dream for peace after that war was shattered on the hard realities of great power politics, and Wilson died a broken man.

53 Tonight I do not tell you that the war in Vietnam is the war to end wars. But I do say this: I have initiated a plan which will end this war in a way that will bring us closer to that great goal of a just and lasting peace to which Woodrow Wilson and every American president in our history had been dedicated. As president I hold the responsibility for choosing the best path to that goal and then for leading our nation along it. I pledge to you tonight that I will meet this responsibility with all the strength and wisdom I can command in accordance with your hopes, mindful of our concerns, sustained by your prayers.

KARLYN KOHRS CAMPBELL

The Rhetoric of Mythical America Revisited

In this critique, Karlyn Kohrs Campbell revisits Richard M. Nixon's November 3, 1969, address. This time she attempts to explain the power of a speech that gained widespread public support despite critical commentary by credible sources that questioned many of its assumptions. As she notes, at first glance, Nixon's speech, like Kennedy's, seems to be a problem–solution policy speech that would be best treated by a rationalistic analysis. After demonstrating the inadequacies of the speech as tested by a stock issue analysis, however, the fact of the speech's persuasiveness remains. Campbell then identifies those strategies that she believes gave the speech its unusual power, strategies that invited listeners to respond to its appeals rather than to scrutinize its arguments. She labels her critique ideological because it challenges Nixon's use of appeals to patriotism as a means of silencing dissent and disempowering listeners, but her critique also acknowledges dynamics that reflect psychosocial concerns. In particular, the critique highlights the powerful impact of creating attractive roles that the audience is invited to play, and it illustrates how deep internal divisions can be transcended in the unifying figure of a leader. The controversy inherent in application of the ethical criterion is evident here—a point that should arouse lively discussion.

In 1970 I began to appear on KPFK, Pacifica Radio, as a guest commentator on the 15-minute editorial segment of their hour-long nightly newscast. On January 22, 1970, my critique of Richard Nixon's November 3, 1969, speech was broadcast. Subsequently I published an edited version of the critique in the first edition of this book, which appeared in 1972. In the December 1972 issue of the *Quarterly Journal of Speech,* Forbes Hill published an analysis of Nixon's speech that also responded to my critique, and there was a further exchange of views in the forum of that issue. Then, in 1989, 20 years after the address was delivered, a special program at the Speech Communication Association national convention reexamined the speech, with papers delivered by those who had published criticisms of it, including Robert Newman of the University of Pittsburgh, Hermann Stelzner of the University of Massachusetts, Forbes Hill of Queens College of C.U.N.Y., and me. This is an edited version of the critique that I wrote for that occasion. Obviously, familiarity with my earlier critique and the exchange between Hill and me will increase understanding of what follows.[1]

Why return to Nixon's Vietnamization Address some 25 years later? The answer is quite simple. Scholarly and journalistic critics alike have acknowledged that the speech was highly effective even in the face of escalating dissent and despite critical commentary by credible experts immediately following it. Such rhetorical power demands explanation.

In *The Symbolic Uses of Politics,* Murray Edelman examined "the conditions in which myth and symbolic reassurance become key elements in the governmental process," and concluded that "they may well be maximal in the foreign policy area" (41). Even a casual reading of Nixon's speech suggests its reliance on the cherished beliefs subsumed under the label "Americanism." As Kenneth Burke reminds us in his analysis of *Mein Kampf,* the function of criticism is to reveal just what kind of medicine powerful medicine-men concoct ("Hitler's 'Battle' " 191). I propose to argue that Nixon's speech was snake oil, a model for the rhetoric of quiescence described by Edelman, an illustration of the manipulative rhetoric of the philosopher-kings described in Plato's *Republic* (Bk. 2, 378a–378e; Bk. 3, 389b–d), a paradigm of hegemony as manifested in presidential discourse. Accordingly, what follows is an

---

[1]See Forbes I. Hill, "Conventional Wisdom—Traditional Form: The President's Message of November 3, 1969," *Quarterly Journal of Speech* 58 (1972): 373–386, and "The Forum," 451–460; Robert P. Newman, "Under the Veneer: Nixon's Vietnam Speech of November 3, 1969," *Quarterly Journal of Speech* 56 (1970): 168–178; and Hermann G. Stelzner, "The Quest Story and Nixon's November 3, 1969, Address," *Quarterly Journal of Speech* 57 (1971): 163–172.

ideological critique analyzing the way presidential discourse can dis-
empower the citizenry in a democracy.[2]

Ideologies are human constructs and, hence, as vulnerable to flaws as
their creators. Sociologist Robert Bellah argues that "religion-filled political rhetoric is perhaps the clearest and most virulent expression of
our national ideals and values, of a unique and very American consensus, of an 'American civil religion'" (Hart 1–2).[3] When ideology becomes civil religion, it becomes anagogic; that is, like a religion, it becomes a system of belief that claims to encompass all of reality, to
account for everything (Frye 119–122).[4] Once it attains such status,
members of the community find it difficult to see it as a constructed,
error-prone system of belief. It becomes instead mythology, reality re-
constructed in the shape of human desires, the world as we wish it to be.
The war in Vietnam was a special kind of crisis because the facts of the
war could not be accommodated by our civil religion. Accordingly, the
war persists as a source of conflict that, despite President George Bush's
1989 inaugural request, cannot easily be put behind us ("Text" 9A).[5]

The opening paragraphs of Nixon's speech affirmed the democratic
notion that conflict can be resolved through frank and open talk.
Nixon's purpose, however, was to increase support for his policy,
which was summed up under the title "Vietnamization." In effect,
South Vietnamese forces would take over fighting on the ground, allowing U.S. ground combat forces to be withdrawn, but U.S. air support would continue along with the provision of war matériel. Nixon's
tone shifted dramatically to characterize what he presented as the
only alternative to Vietnamization, "end[ing] the war at once by ordering the immediate withdrawal of all American forces" (5),[6] as
popular and easy, a proposal rejected in light of the higher values of

---

[2]As many theorists have recognized, ideological criticism is an ethical matter. As Burke
recognized in "Hitler's 'Battle,'" it enacts criticism as *praxis,* the point that Raymie
McKerrow emphasizes in "Critical Rhetoric: Theory and Praxis," *Communication Monographs* 56 (1989): 91–111. My earlier critique, a work of ephemeral criticism rather than
enduring criticism (see Karlyn Kohrs Campbell, "Criticism: Ephemeral and Enduring,"
Communication Education 23 (1974): 9–14), is linked to this one only by the title, "An
Exercise in the Rhetoric of Mythical America," which was published in the first edition
of this book (Belmont, CA: Wadsworth, 1972, pp. 50–57).

[3]For a fuller statement of his views, see Robert Bellah, "Civil Religion in America,"
Daedalus (Winter 1967): 1–21.

[4]This is analogous to what Burke refers to as a bastardized or caricatured version of religious thought in "Hitler's 'Battle,'" p. 199.

[5]Bush's words were, "That war cleaves us still. But, friends, that war began in earnest a
quarter of a century ago, and, surely, the Statute of Limitations has been reached. This
is a fact: The final lesson of Vietnam is that no great nation can long afford to be sun-
dered by a memory."

[6]Parenthetical citations are paragraph numbers.

"peace and freedom" (6). In this value-laden context, Nixon reduced the issue to the question "How can we win America's peace?" (7)

That bit of Orwellian doublespeak is intelligible only in terms of U.S. civil religion as shaped by Cold War ideology. Recall that Cold Warriors, Nixon among them, charged that although we won World War II on the battlefield, we lost the peace—that is, we negotiated away Eastern Europe, and we allowed China to "fall" to Communism. Immersion in the civil religion made it extremely difficult for acculturated listeners to deconstruct that question. Linguistically there were four possibilities. One could lose or win the war and lose or win the peace. Losing the war is easy to understand—it is a military matter. By analogy to the Cold War, losing the peace would mean negotiating away what had been won on the battlefield, an irrelevancy in Vietnam because the military situation remained unclear. Winning the war militarily would have divided Vietnam into two nations, with the South run by a non-Communist government sympathetic to the United States. In Nixon's speech, "winning the peace" meant just that; in other words, "winning the peace" was the same as "winning the war." As Burke remarks in his analysis of *Mein Kampf,* "It is so easy to draw a doctrine of war out of a doctrine of peace, why should the astute politician do otherwise?" ("Hitler's 'Battle' " 199).

Ideology also structured the argument. If the fundamental issue was, as Nixon told us, "Why and how did the United States become involved in Vietnam in the first place?" (8), then justifications made during the Cold War by "three American presidents [Eisenhower, Kennedy, and Johnson]" who "recognized the great stakes involved in Vietnam" (13) remained valid and salient. Thus there was no need to reexamine our intentions—we needed only to find better ways of achieving them, and this fundamental issue could be dismissed in one paragraph, followed by an even shorter paragraph in which Nixon admitted reservations only about "the way the war has been conducted" (9). He could then shift immediately to means: "Now that we are in the war, what is the best way to end it?" (10)

The debilitating effect of ideology can be illustrated by stock issue analysis of just one consideration—whether the plan proposed meets the need. Recall that Vietnamization was described in the speech as "complete withdrawal of all U.S. combat forces and their replacement by South Vietnamese forces on an orderly scheduled timetable" (33) that would "depend on developments on three fronts" (34)—progress at the Paris talks, the level of enemy activity, and the rate at which South Vietnamese troops could be trained. Nixon emphasized:

If the level of infiltration or our casualties increase while we are trying to scale down the fighting, it will be the result of a conscious decision by the enemy. . . . If I conclude that increased enemy action jeopardizes our remaining forces in Vietnam, I shall not hesitate to take strong and effective measures to deal with that situation. (37)

In other words, the success of the policy depended on the cooperation of the enemy. It would have required them to acquiesce in the division of Vietnam into two nations, which they had vowed never to do. Given their negotiating record as reported in the speech, there was no reason to expect them to agree. On its face, then, based on Nixon's own words, *the proposed policy must fail*. But if so, why wasn't that internal contradiction immediately apparent to the audience?[7] How was Nixon able to evoke assent in the face of opposition?

Throughout the speech he created the audience in the image he desired, and he did so in ways that highlight how the concepts of identification, the second *persona*, and "the people" as a rhetorical construct are interrelated. Identification, of course, is a process of symbolically calling attention to the qualities and characteristics that rhetors and audiences share and that bind audience members together (Burke, *Rhetoric of Motives* 19–23, 55–59). If the first persona is thought of as the role(s) adopted by the rhetor, then the second persona, as described by Edwin Black, is the role(s) created for the audience by the discourse ("Second Persona"). Finally, as Michael McGee argues, as a national identity, "the people" is a symbolic entity constructed and then maintained through rhetorical action ("The People").

Nixon's speech illustrates the links between these concepts very well. First, he considered just how U.S. troops came to fight in Asian wars and explained, "We Americans are a do-it-yourself people—an impatient people. Instead of teaching someone else to do a job, we like to do it ourselves. This trait has been carried over into our foreign policy" (26). Summed up in a homely, familiar phrase, U.S. know-how, frontier spirit, and entrepreneurship explained U.S. intentions and motives. Our involvement in the war became a mere peccadillo, at worst, a mistake made as a result of good intentions. Our past sins were forgiven; no atonement was necessary.

---

[7]Admitting that nothing in the speech challenged the beliefs of the target audience, one might dismiss it as pandering to the public, recalling Aristotle's comment that it is not difficult to praise Athenians to Athenians in *Rhetoric,* trans. W. Rhys Roberts (New York: Modern Library, 1954) 1367b.7; see also Plato, *Menexenus* in *The Collected Dialogues of Plato,* ed. Edith Hamilton and Huntington Cairns (Princeton, NJ: Princeton University Press, 1961) 186–199, 235d; in *Encomium of Helen,* trans. George Kennedy, in *The Older Sophists,* ed. Rosamund Sprague (Columbia: University of South Carolina Press, 1972) 50–54 at (5), Gorgias comments that "to tell the knowing what they know shows it is right but brings no delight." This speech does much more.

Second, near the end of the speech he gave the audience an identity grounded in what is probably the most familiar story of the New Testament:

> Let historians not record that when America was the most powerful nation in the world we passed on the other side of the road and allowed the last hopes for peace and freedom of millions of people on this earth to be suffocated by the forces of totalitarianism. (49)

The allusion is to the parable of the good Samaritan, which Jesus told in response to a lawyer's challenge to define just who was the neighbor he was to love as himself (Luke 10:25–36). The good Samaritan is a powerful image because the parable sums up the gospel of selfless love that Jesus preached. The story is particularly apt for foreign policy because a Samaritan helped a Jew who had been set upon by thieves. Moreover, echoing the resentment U.S. good deeds sometimes encountered abroad, Samaritans were despised by Jews, which made this charitable act even more noteworthy. Note that this identity is the essence of civil religion because it dissolves distinctions between Christianity and patriotism.

Like the first image, this identity was explanatory. It subtly reinforced Nixon's claim that the war in Indochina was begun by Communist aggression and suggested that, like the good Samaritan, Americans were good neighbors who entered the war to prevent thieves from stealing South Vietnam's right to self-determination.

These two roles addressed the past, but there was also a future role for the audience to play, a role entailing continued commitment to the war that was an essential part of the new policy. Recall that Vietnamization meant that South Vietnamese troops would take over the killing and dying on the ground, but the United States would continue to supply matériel and to fight the war in the air. Nixon's speech is famous for the phrase that presented the audience with a third image of itself, "the great silent majority of my fellow Americans" (50). That phrase linked listeners to Nixon as fellow citizens committed to democratic principles. That identity separated them from the dissenters, located them as members of a group whose will should prevail in a democracy, and projected a future role as followers who would silently accept their leader's decisions and promise him future support.

But there was more to Nixon's scheme. Identification has a dual meaning: It refers to both what a group shares and what differentiates it from others. Nixon not only created "the people" as a positive, unified identity, but he also displayed a repulsive alter ego, which he described this way: "Honest and patriotic Americans have reached different conclusions as to how peace should be achieved. In San Francisco a few weeks ago, I saw demonstrators carrying signs reading, 'Lose in Vietnam, bring the boys home' "(42). The speech reported that these honest, patriotic Americans supported a policy that would "betray" our nation's allies, risk U.S. "defeat and humiliation," and provoke "recklessness" and "violence" throughout the world (14). Through guilt by association, dissenters became druggies, hippies, and gays from that Sodom of the West Coast, San Francisco. They were also characterized as traitors, a "minority" that sought undemocratically to "impose it[s views] on the nation by mounting demonstrations in the streets" and to "prevail over reason and the will of the majority" (43, 44). They were a loathsome other, as the president explained: "Because let us understand: North Vietnam cannot defeat or humiliate the United States. Only Americans can do that" (51). To be a dissenter was to be someone who not only violated the tenets of our civil religion and the principles underlying our government but also its laws and sexual norms.

As Burke recognizes, internal division is deeply disturbing; when it exists, resentment can easily be turned against the person or group who compels acknowledgment of its existence ("Hitler's 'Battle' " 206). In Nixon's speech the source of division was a repulsive, un-American alter ego. Simultaneously Nixon emerged as one who refused to be influenced by the dissenters and who was deeply committed to his presidential oath to protect our system and its civil religion.

In that process he became the person through whom unification could be achieved. As Burke points out, uniting around the person of a leader is one means of transcending internal division, a process that takes place when the issue and the relationship between leader and followers are personalized. In other words, unity can be achieved (1) if a policy becomes indistinguishable from the leader who proposes it and (2) if the relationship between leader and followers is rendered intimate. In the speech Vietnamization became the Nixon Doctrine (25); Nixon spoke of the possibility that Johnson's war might become Nixon's war (5); his private efforts to end the war became "my quest" (20); and the policy became the fulfillment of a promise: "I pledged in my campaign for the presidency to end the war" (51). Finally, in the conclusion, he said: "As president I hold the responsibility for choosing the best path to that goal [ending the war] and then for leading our nation along it" (53). The policy and the president who proposed it became one.

Further, Nixon created a special, intimate, almost confidential relationship with his audience. In addition to a pervasive use of personal pronouns, Nixon said that he knew what was in the minds of the audience (2); he "disclosed" (19) his private efforts to achieve peace (18); he spoke directly "to the young people of this nation" whose concern he said he understood (45); and he said, "There are powerful personal reasons I want to end this war. This week I will have to sign 83 letters to mothers, fathers, wives, and loved ones of men who had given their lives for America in Vietnam" (46). These words personalized his relationship to the issue and undermined the detachment that might have enabled listeners to evaluate the policy on rational or pragmatic grounds.

Positive and negative identification, along with personalizing the policy and the speaker–audience relationship, are the trio of strategies that seem to me to best illustrate how Nixon moved rhetorically to engineer assent and to effect quiescence in the audience.[8] But it is easy to dismiss such claims as mere illustrations of manipulative, duplicitous "Tricky Dicky." The problem, as I see it, is much larger and far more serious.

In this address Nixon spoke not just as president but also as commander in chief—an office whose powers have been so enlarged through time that its limits are literally undefined. In seeking public and congressional approval for military policy, war rhetoric, under circumstances other than invasion, attempts not only to justify the use of force but also to vindicate presidential assumption of the office of commander in chief.[9] Because the powers of the commander in chief have become so vast as to be near-dictatorial, presidential war rhetoric needs to evoke virtually unanimous support because that, and that alone, can legitimize the exercise of such powers in a democracy. In the face of an invasion, such as the attack on Pearl Harbor, unanimity is easy to achieve, but under other circumstances, when events are open to varied interpretations, it is extremely difficult to evoke.[10] Presidents are empowered to act unilaterally to defend the nation, but they have often found or created a pretext that enables them to claim those powers to act without prior consultation with the Congress. Under such conditions protest becomes an attack on presidential legitimacy, not just dissent from a policy.

---

[8]As illustrated, identification is not just a matter of shared experience, values, or beliefs, and it is heightened when the positive, shared identity is a series of second personas that define "the people" through time, link them to their rhetorical–ideological past, and are social roles that entail the actions desired by the speaker.

[9]Presidential war rhetoric is defined as discourse justifying "the introduction of United States Armed Forces into hostilities, or into situations where imminent involvement in hostilities is clearly indicated by circumstances, and to the continued use of such force in hostilities or in such situations," as set forth in the War Powers Resolution of 1973.

[10]The difficulties presidents have faced and the strategic misrepresentations they have resorted to in order to marshal support are detailed in Karlyn Kohrs Campbell and Kathleen Hall Jamieson, *Deeds Done in Words: Presidential Rhetoric and the Genres of Governance* (Chicago: University of Chicago Press, 1990) 101–126.

In other words, presidential discourse justifying military policy illustrates a rather dramatic conflict between this political system and the war rhetoric of its leaders. On one hand the life-and-death decision to use force can be justified only as the product of thoughtful deliberation incorporating all available data and all points of view. Given its high costs, it should be done prudently, through a carefully planned military action aimed at achieving clearly defined goals that have been hammered out in argument that focuses on expediency and weighs the costs versus the benefits. Presidential power can tip the balance even under those circumstances.

For instance, at the end of October of 1990 President Bush made the decision to increase the size of the U.S. forces in the Persian Gulf to around 400,000 and to change their assignment from defending Saudi Arabia to taking offensive action against Iraqi forces. Bush disclosed his actions after the congressional elections on November 6. Maintaining those troops, considering the sandstorms that would come in spring and summer, created pressure to deploy them against Iraq. Bush persuaded the U.N. Security Council to authorize the use of military force if the Iraqis did not withdraw from Kuwait by January 15, intensifying the sense of urgency by imposing a deadline. In addition, he used the presidential bully pulpit to make delay seem to be the same as a U.S. defeat, which was the context in which the question of authorizing war came before Congress. That made a no vote extremely difficult to cast.

Nonetheless, the Senate debates over the Gulf War reminded Americans of the heights to which political deliberation could rise. Remarkably, the Senate vote was close—only 52 to 47 to authorize military action. At a press conference in early January, however, a "reporter asked the president whether he could order military action if Congress voted against authorizing it. Mr. Bush replied: 'I still feel that I have the constitutional authority, many attorneys having so advised me' "(cited in Lewis, A15y). That audacious comment reflects the enormous growth of presidential war powers, but no president yet has challenged the Congress under those conditions. Instead, they have used their control of information and their rhetorical resources in ways that emulate the November 3, 1969, speech of Richard Nixon.

On the other hand, as the Gulf War debates illustrate, deliberation is unlikely to produce the high level of support and intensity of commitment that would legitimize unequivocally the exercise of the extraordinary powers that have been conferred on the commander in chief.[11]

---

[11]It should be noted that Congress has connived in this process. One possible corrective is for Congress to take back some of that conferred power. In the face of congressional relinquishment of its powers, however, the Supreme Court has refused to intervene in most instances.

Hence, in war rhetoric presidents find themselves in a dilemma. They are constrained to appear deliberative—logical, calm, aware of policy options—while strategically manipulating information, language, and argument in order to preempt dissent and generate intense, widespread support.[12] Identification and personalization of the issue and of the relationship between president and citizenry are highly effective adaptations to this problem, as Nixon's speech illustrates. Sadly, Nixon was not the first president to use them, nor has he been the last. Of particular significance is that "war rhetoric also reveals that the role of commander in chief, given its extraordinary powers and the need they engender for unanimity, [is] a continuing threat to the nation's democratic principles" (Campbell and Jamieson 126).

WORKS CITED

Black, Edwin. "The Second Persona." *Quarterly Journal of Speech* 56 (1970): 109–119.

Burke, Kenneth. "The Rhetoric of Hitler's 'Battle.'" *Philosophy of Literary Form*. Baton Rouge: Louisiana State University Press, 1973. 191–220.

———. *A Rhetoric of Motives*. Berkeley: University of California Press, 1969.

Bush, George. "Text of the President's Address." *Star Tribune* [Minneapolis] 21 Jan. 1989: 9A.

Campbell, Karlyn Kohrs, and Kathleen Hall Jamieson. *Deeds Done in Words: Presidential Rhetoric and the Genres of Governance*. Chicago: University of Chicago Press, 1990.

Edelman, Murray. *The Symbolic Uses of Politics*. Urbana: University of Illinois Press, 1971.

Frye, Northrop. *Anatomy of Criticism: Four Essays*. Princeton, NJ: Princeton University Press, 1957.

Hart, Roderick P. *The Political Pulpit*. West Lafayette, IN: Purdue University Press, 1977.

Lewis, Anthony. "Presidential Power." *New York Times* 14 Jan. 1991: A15y.

---

[12]James Madison presciently recognized the potential for abuse in this area when he wrote the following:

> The management of foreign relations appears to be the most susceptible of abuse of all the trusts committed to the Government, because they can be concealed or disclosed, or disclosed in such parts and at such times as will best suit particular views; and because the body of the people are less capable of judging, and are more under the influence of prejudices, on that branch of their affairs, than of any other. (Vol. 2, 140–41)

Madison, James. *Letters and Other Writings of James Madison,* 4 vols. Philadelphia: J. Lippincott, 1865.

McGee, Michael C. "In Search of 'the People': A Rhetorical Alternative." *Quarterly Journal of Speech* 61 (1975): 235–249.

Nixon, Richard. "Vietnamization: The President's Address on War." *Congressional Record,* Vol. 115, Part 24: 32784–32786.

Plato. "Republic." Trans. Paul Shorey. *The Collected Dialogues of Plato.* Ed. Edith Hamilton and Huntington Cairns. Princeton, NJ: Princeton University Press, 1961. 575–844.

ZHAO ZIYANG

Farewell Speech at Tiananmen Square

In April 1989 an astonished world watched as nearly 200,000 Chinese students occupied Beijing's Tiananmen Square demanding democratic reforms and the end of corruption within the government of the People's Republic of China. Tension between the government and the student protesters escalated rapidly, but occupation of Tiananmen Square continued for nearly two months. On May 19, Zhao Ziyang, then General Secretary of the Communist party of China, addressed the students, urging them to end their hunger strike and return to their homes. Following Zhao's speech the hunger strike became a peaceful sit-in, but the students refused to leave the square. On May 20 the government declared martial law. On June 3 troops entered Beijing and forced their way into the square. The pro-democracy demonstration ended in the massacre at Tiananmen Square. "The Gate of Heavenly Peace," a documentary film made by Richard Gordon and Carma Hinton, shown at the 1995 New York film festival, records many of the events related to Tiananmen and includes the speech of Chai Ling, a student present at the massacre, whose views of the efficacy of protest are different from those of Zhao Ziyang.

Source: Crisis at Tiananmen: Reform and Reality in Modern China, ed. Yi Mu and Mark Thompson (San Francisco: China Books & Periodicals, 1989) 180–182. (China Books & Periodicals, Inc., 2929 24th Street, San Francisco, CA 94110, Phone: 415/282-2994, Fax: 415/282-0994.)

213

1   Students, I want to say a few words to you. We're sorry we've come too late. It is right if you should blame us, and criticize us. But I am here now not to ask for your forgiveness. I just want to say that your bodies are very weak now. You have been on a hunger strike for seven days, you must not go on like this. If you continue refusing to eat, the effects on your health could be permanent. It can endanger your lives. What is most important now is that I hope you will stop your hunger strike as soon as possible. I know that you are on a hunger strike because you want the party and government to give you satisfactory answers to your demands. But you have been on a hunger strike for seven days, do you really want to proceed to the eighth, the ninth, or the tenth day? Many problems could be solved eventually, and the channel for dialogue is still open, the door of dialogue will never be closed. But some problems need some time before they can be fully resolved. I feel that the substantive questions you have raised could eventually be solved, and we could eventually reach a consensus in solving these problems. But you should understand that in resolving any question, the situation is always complicated and more time is still needed.

2   With your hunger strike reaching the seventh day, you must not persist in the strike until satisfactory answers are given. It won't help. By that time it will be too late and you will never be able to make up for (the damage to your health). You are still young and have a long way to go. You must live on in good health, live to the day when China finally realizes the Four Modernizations. You are not like us. We are getting old and it doesn't matter what happens to us. It has not been easy for the state and your parents to raise you and send you to college. You're only eighteen, nineteen or twenty years old. Are you going to give up your lives like this? Think about it, in a more rational way. I have not come to hold a dialogue with you. I just want to urge you to think more rationally about what situation you are facing. You know that the party and government are very worried about you. The entire society is worried, people in the whole city of Beijing are talking about you. Also you know that Beijing is the capital. The situation is getting worse every day. It cannot go on like this. You comrades all mean well, you are all for the good of our country, but if this situation continues and gets out of control, the consequences could be very serious.

3   I think that is what I want to tell you. If you stop your hunger strike, the government will not thereby close the doors to further dialogue. It will definitely not do that. We will continue to study the issues you have raised. It is true that we have been slow in solving some of the problems, but our views on some questions are gradually coming closer to each other. I have come today mainly to see you students and tell you what I feel. I hope you students and the organizers of the hunger strike will think about this question [of stopping the hunger strike] very calmly and coolly. It will be very hard to think clearly about this question like this when you're not in a rational state of mind. As young people, it is understandable that you are all bursting with passion. I know that. We all used to be young. We also have taken to the streets, some of us have even lain across railroad tracks to stop trains. At that time we also never thought about what would happen afterward.

4   Students, please think about the question calmly. Many problems could be resolved gradually. I do hope that you will stop your hunger strike very soon. Thank you, comrades.

LEE LIN LEE

Zhao Ziyang's Plea to the Students in Tiananmen Square

In the spring of 1989 student protests in Beijing's Tiananmen Square electrified the world. The then-head of the Chinese Communist party, Zhao Ziyang, addressed students who were carrying out a hunger strike. His short speech was an important factor in persuading them to end it. How and why that was possible is unintelligible to most Westerners when they read Zhao's speech. The critique that follows by Lee Lin Lee, a Chinese living in Taiwan, demonstrates that in order to criticize a rhetorical act, a critic must understand, in some way be part of, the cultural context in which the rhetorical act emerges. What she attempts to do is to provide us with enough information about the cultural context, including its rhetorical conventions, and the personal history of Zhao to explain why his speech was so unusual and could have had such an impact on the student demonstrators he addressed. The Chinese use of rhetorical indirection is a special cultural adaptation of the principles underlying Aristotle's enthymeme, and the emphasis on argument grounded in character and consistency of behavior echoes Aristotle's words about the power of ethos in persuasion. In a general sense this critique underscores the importance of shared culture between rhetor and critic and should raise such questions as, What must I know and who must I be in order to be a critic of the work I am analyzing?

The Year of the Snake, 1989, was the 40th anniversary of the founding of the People's Republic of China on October 1, 1949; the 70th anniversary of the May Fourth (1919) Movement;[1] and the 10th anniversary of the imprisonment of dissident Wei Jingsheng in 1979.[2] Thus, what happened in Tiananmen Square in the spring of 1989 was neither the beginning nor the end of the democracy movement; rather, it was its climax.

The beginnings of the pro-democracy movement can be traced back to Fang Lizhi's open letter to Deng Xiaoping on January 6, 1989.[3] In an open letter to Deng, Fang requested a declaration of amnesty, and he particularly asked for the release of Wei Jingsheng. His letter was ignored by the authorities, which outraged other intellectuals and initiated their petition movement.[4] At the same time student political activities began on the campus of Beijing University, a place that activists hoped to make a center for promoting democracy. Public discourse and posters were used to transmit democratic ideas. In this period, then, the Communist party of China (C.P.C.) faced the petitions of the intellectuals as well as student demands for democracy.

The death of former C.P.C. General Secretary Hu Yaobang[5] on April 15 provided the students with an opportunity to express their

---

[1]"On May 4, 1919, about five thousand Beijing Normal University students had marched to Tiananmen Square in protest against the Versailles Treaty that followed the First World War. . . . Students demanded that the Chinese representative to the Peace Conference refuse to sign the treaty. . . . The demonstration on May 4 was an outburst of public frustration that sparked a nationalist intellectual revolution throughout the country" (Simmie and Nixon 62).

[2]Wei Jingsheng was "the most prominent dissident of the Democracy Movement of 1978–1979." An electronics worker, Wei was imprisoned for promoting democracy as a "Fifth Modernization" for China and for criticism stating that "Deng was becoming another Mao." Many Chinese were inspired by his ideas for China's democratization and economic development. "Both the older democrats and the student leaders agreed with Wei that China's economic reforms could not succeed without a concomitant democratization of the political structure" (Woei 108). Wei was reimprisoned in 1995.

[3]Fang Lizhi is an astrophysicist and "vice president of the University of Science and Technology in Hefwei. By the time Hu [Yaobang; see note 5] died on April 15, 1989, Fang was well known to the West as the man who could not come to dinner—the Chinese police prevented [him] from attending a banquet hosted by U.S. President George Bush when he [Bush] visited Beijing in February [1987]" (Simmie and Nixon 13). "Fang is the most well-known intellectual critic, and he once declared that he was the successor to Wei Jingsheng" (Woei 108). In October 1987 Zhao told NBC's Tom Brokaw "that Fang was still a respected member of the scientific community," and he appeared to be more conciliatory toward Fang's ideas about China modernization than Deng (Simmie and Nixon 14).

[4]Many older intellectuals signed petitions addressed to the National People's Congress requesting an amnesty and improvements in education, research, and the housing and financial conditions of intellectuals (Woei 111).

[5]Hu Yaobang was the general secretary of the Communist party of China until 1987, when he was dismissed for his lenient attitude toward the schools. He was an advocate of

disappointment about the government's refusal to take further steps toward democratization. Immanuel C. Y. Hsu concluded that the students "wished to honor [Hu's] memory with an elaborate commemorative service, and they also planned to use the occasion to insist on the clearing of his name and to push forward demands for freedom of speech, assembly, and the press, as well as strong anti-corruption measures" (Hsu 925). According to Michael Oksenberg, Lawrence Sullivan, and Marc Lambert, Hu's death was "the catalyst for the Beijing Spring student movement" (400). Hsu reported that in mourning of his death big posters appeared at several universities in Beijing and around Tiananmen Square, stating, " 'A good man has died, but many bad ones are still living. . . . A man of sincerity has passed away, but hypocrites are still around' " (925). Because the C.P.C. refused to clear Hu's name, thousands of students marched into Tiananmen and began a sit-in movement protesting, "Long live democracy! Long live freedom! Down with corruption!" (Hsu 925). This protest spread to 23 cities in China. On April 22, three student representatives, holding a petition over their heads, knelt in front of the People's Great Hall, waiting for Li Peng to accept their request for a dialogue with the government to discuss China's current problems. It ended when no government official appeared.[6]

On April 26 an editorial appeared in the *People's Daily* accusing the students of creating "turmoil," which provoked outrage among the students and many citizens.[7] The editorial became the basis for a whole series of demonstrations because the primary motive of the earlier student demonstrations had been a genuine patriotic striving for a more free and democratic government. In defiance of the *People's Daily* editorial, more students outside of Beijing joined the demonstration, and they called a hunger strike on May 13 at Tiananmen Square.[8]

---

cultural and educational liberalization, and he had become a symbol for liberalization in the minds of student protesters (Wasserstrom).

[6]One of the three representatives shouted, "This is how petitions were presented to the emperor. What era is this? We still have to use this method, which means we have no freedom" (quoted in Hsu 295).

[7]The editorial of April 26, 1989, in the *People's Daily* said, "In mourning the death of General Hu Yaobang, a handful of people with ulterior motives have continued to use the grief of students to poison people's minds and create national turmoil" (quoted in Chiang 26).

[8]The two major demands of the hunger strikers were (1) on an equal basis, the government should immediately conduct concrete and substantial dialogues with the delegation from Beijing institutes of higher education; and (2) the government should rename this student movement, with a fair and unbiased assessment, and should affirm that this is a patriotic and democratic student movement—that is, retract the April 26 *People's Daily* editorial. See Oksenberg, Sullivan, and Lambert 258–260; Mu and Thompson 274; Feng et al. 51.

Tiananmen Square, located in the center of Beijing, the capital of China, represents the authority of the Communist government. The People's Republic of China was established there in 1949. By occupying Tiananmen Square, student demonstrators made a direct attack on the government's legitimacy, particularly because their occupation took place during the three-day visit of Soviet leader Mikhail Gorbachev from May 15 to 17. Because of the protest, the official reception welcoming Gorbachev was shifted to the airport, and the government was forced to modify the original schedule or to cancel some events. The participating students' unyielding attitude humiliated the C.P.C., particularly Deng Xiaoping, and caused the government to lose face in front of outsiders. Accordingly, it heightened the conflict between the government and the student demonstrators. Inspired by the courageous hunger strikers, many intellectuals declared their support by signing the "May 17 Declaration" attacking Deng Xiaoping as "an emperor without title."[9]

Another tense confrontation between the government and the students occurred after an unsuccessful attempt at dialogue between the student leaders and government officials on May 18.[10] After Zhao Ziyang's speech on May 19, 1989, the hunger strike became a peaceful sit-in. On May 20, however, the government declared martial law and brought troops to Beijing to clear the 200,000 students out of Tiananmen Square. The rage of the students toward the government increased day by day, and the government lost the support of many citizens. Workers, teachers, doctors, nurses, and journalists, as well as numerous civilians, all supported this nationwide democracy movement by striking and taking part in street demonstrations. The tension reached a climax on June 3 when tens of thousands of soldiers marched to Beijing. When troops forced their way through the streets to Tiananmen Square that evening, shooting and firing at anyone in sight, the massacre began. Even today there is no complete or accurate accounting of the death toll. The bloody massacre ended the seven-week pro-democracy movement, but it has not yet shattered the Chinese people's hope for another spring to come.

---

[9]In the "May 17 Declaration," intellectuals stated, "Despite the death of the Ching Dynasty 76 years ago, there is still an emperor in China, though without such a title, a senile and fatuous autocrat" (Hsu 929).

[10]On May 18, Chinese Premier Li Peng met with five student leaders. In Chinese eyes, the government managed to look foolish and insincere during the conversation. "[I]t began with a shouting match between Mr. Li Peng and Wu'er Kaixi, the brash student leader from Beijing Normal University" (Mu and Thompson, 168). This was "highly unusual" because it was the first time that a citizen openly shouted at the leader in a televised conversation (Mu and Thompson 168; Trenholm 7).

Inevitably, any social movement produces heroes and heroines. During the "Liow-Shy"[11] democracy movement, two of the key people who emerged were a student, Chai Ling, and Zhao Ziyang, who was then general secretary of the Communist party. The former represented the student demonstrators and the latter, although a party leader, expressed his personal opinions.

ZHAO ZIYANG

Born into a wealthy landlord family in Hunan Province in 1919, Zhao Ziyang joined the Communist Youth League at age 13 and became a party comrade when he was 19. Zhao made his reputation in 1975 in Sichuan Province, a mountainous southern region and the largest and most populous province in China. Because he worked to eliminate inefficient rules and to promote a free market policy, he created an economic miracle for Sichuan Province. According to Scott Simmie and Bob Nixon, not only did he keep people from starving, but he also created "600,000 new jobs, increased 81 percent of industrial output, and boosted agricultural production by 25 percent" (60). His successful program became a model for the whole nation. According to Harrison Salisbury, the saying "If you want wheat, you go to Zhao Ziyang" (14) circulated all over China, illustrating the respect in which he was held by the Chinese people. And Nina P. Halpern concluded that in the eyes of the Chinese Zhao Ziyang is the leader who has always been strongly committed to liberal economic reform (48).

In 1984 Zhao founded the Chinese Economic System Reform Institute (CESRI), which was authorized to conduct a series of large-scale national surveys. CESRI functioned as a think tank to provide government leaders with guidance on strategic planning of economic reforms. Furthermore, according to Stanley Rosen, in October 1987 Zhao proposed the need for "public opinion" to play a role in decision making. This was the first time in Chinese history that a top party leader openly addressed and considered the importance of public opinion (65). Zhao was named general secretary of C.P.C. to replace Hu Yaobang at the Thirteenth Party Congress in November 1987. He was also the executive vice-chairman of the C.P.C. Military Commission, second only to Deng Xiaoping.

Although Zhao was the general secretary, he personally felt that the tone of the April 26 *People's Daily* editorial was biased and unfair. On

---

[11]Liow-Shy is the phonetic sound of June 4 in Chinese. It has become a rallying cry referring to the 1989 democratic movement.

May 8 he affirmed the patriotic nature of the student movement and supported their courage (Landsberger 169). For three days Zhao fought for permission to go to Tiananmen Square. Finally, early on the morning of May 19, he made an unexpected appearance there escorted by an "unsmiling, laconic" Premier Li Peng (Salisbury 165). Having failed to convince the hard-liners not to use military force to deal with the students, Zhao knew that this might be his last chance to convey his personal opinions to the protestors. When Zhao and Li approached the crowd, the students applauded and cheered them; Premier Li Peng shook a few hands, said nothing, and returned to his limousine after less than two minutes. In sharp contrast, Zhao lingered and delivered a 20-minute speech when a student hunger striker offered him a megaphone (Salisbury 164–165).

As general secretary of C.P.C. Zhao had to abide by the decisions of the top party leadership and submit to the judgments of the party elders. Therefore, when it came to making final decisions on coping with the crisis, Zhao was isolated and helpless. Yi Mu and Mark Thompson reported that despite his support for the student movement and although he was the C.P.C. general secretary, "Zhao could do nothing more than express his personal opinions and extend his sympathy to the students" (180).

THE SPEECH

Zhao's speech, delivered on May 19, 1989, on the seventh day of the hunger strike, was extemporaneous. Its purpose was to persuade the students in Tiananmen Square to abandon their hunger strike. In Zhao's words, "I hope you will stop your hunger strike as soon as possible" (1).[12] After seven unproductive days of the hunger strike, Zhao saw that the students' action was useless in terms of resolving the conflict and instead increased the tension between the government authorities and the student demonstrators.

The audience Zhao addressed was composed of young patriots to whom he referred respectfully as "comrades" and "students," unlike other party members who called them "rioters." Moreover, he argued with them in ways that showed that he believed that they could think calmly and rationally about what he urged as the best course of action. However, Zhao's speech was also likely to send a message to the whole nation that any general protest action would not prevail in contemporary China. It is possible that Zhao was trying to convince the whole

---

[12]Parenthetical citations for Zhao Ziyang's speech are paragraph numbers.

nation to end the demonstrations, strikes, and protests that had spread to all the major cities and to urge a less violent, less confrontational approach to compromise with the power of the government.

Zhao adopted two roles in this speech, that of a top party leader and that of an advocate for the democracy movement. Essentially, there were two values competing in his discourse: his devotion to his duty to the C.P.C. and his devotion to the liberalizing efforts of the students. Despite his personal identification with the students, he was obliged to represent the government and the party. Accordingly, he said:

> Many problems could be solved eventually, and the channel for dialogue is still open, the door of dialogue will never be closed. But some problems need some time before they can be fully resolved. I feel that the substantive questions you have raised could eventually be solved, and we could eventually reach a consensus in solving these problems. (1)

With those words he was trying to portray the government in a good light by emphasizing that open dialogue was still possible. The party was still attempting to make some progress to accommodate the students' demands. Although he had to defend the party, his respect for the students' courage and his sympathy for their sacrifice were evident throughout the speech. For example, he said, "*I know* that you are on a hunger strike because you want the party and government to give you satisfactory answers to your demands" (1, emphasis added). Later he asserted, "You comrades all mean well, you are all for the good of our country . . ." (2). And finally he added, "As young people, it is *understandable* that you are all bursting with passion. *I know that*" (3, emphasis added).

At each of these points, he shifted from his role as general secretary to that of a supporter of the student democracy movement. His tone became more emotional and personal when he presented himself as a peer, a comrade, of the hunger strikers. Because he was a high official in the government, Zhao might have been expected to present his views as those of an authority who could threaten the students and order them to terminate the pro-democracy action without showing any emotion. Instead, and quite atypically, he addressed the students as an ordinary Chinese citizen, and he identified himself with the students through a reference to a similar protest he had made in his youth. In addition to his personal testimony, his sincere pleas enabled him to be exceptionally persuasive.

Zhao began his speech by adapting to the student demands through some self-criticism. The apology in his introduction narrowed the distance between him and his audience. He said, "Students, I want to say a few words to you. We're sorry we've come too late. It is right if you should blame us, and criticize us. But I am here now not to ask for your forgiveness" (1). Since the beginning of the democracy movement in April, the students had been blamed for creating turmoil in the society while the government took no responsibility for the problems. Here Zhao openly admitted that the government, that is, the party leaders, deserved blame or even were responsible for the results of the hunger strike. Later he added, "It is true that we have been slow in solving some of the problems" (3), which confessed mistakes for the entire government as well as for himself. Such self-criticism rarely has been seen in the statements of any of the top leaders in contemporary China. His apology was an unexpected and personal act that connected the rhetor to the audience and successfully earned the confidence of his listeners.

After his apology, Zhao developed the rest of his speech through a problem–solution format. He first discussed the serious problem of the hunger strike by exploring its impact on students' health. Then he discussed the consequences of the hunger strike for the society in general. Besides the damage to the students' health, such concerns as those of the government, parents, the nation, and the city of Beijing were associated to amplify the emergency of the hunger strike. He said, "It has not been easy for the state and your parents to raise you and send you to college," and "You know that the party and government are very worried about you. The entire society is worried, people in the whole city of Beijing are talking about you. Also you know that Beijing is the capital. The situation is getting worse every day" (2). After setting out the problems created by the hunger strike, he proposed a solution to the crisis:

> If you stop your hunger strike, the government will not thereby close the door to further dialogue. It will definitely not do that. We will continue to study the issues you have raised. . . . I hope you students and the organizers of the hunger strike will think about this question [of stopping the hunger strike] very calmly and coolly. (3)

The solution was restated in his conclusion. He said, "Students, please think about the question calmly. Many problems could be resolved gradually. I do hope that you will stop your hunger strike very soon" (4). One possible inference can be made from his words. He implied that the problem could not be solved without the discontinuation of the hunger strike. The government apparently would not retreat; therefore, the students should not push farther or the situation would deteriorate.

Zhao relied on his own personal experience as a powerful piece of evidence to prove to the students that nonaction at that moment was the best action. He said, "We all used to be young. We also have taken to the streets, some of us have even lain across railroad tracks to stop trains. At that time we also never thought about what would happen afterward" (3). He presented himself as a powerful witness to past history in order to convince the students that action would not be beneficial in solving the problems. A similar protest had been conducted by young people in the past and no change had been made. Thus action would not necessarily achieve the desired goal.

The language Zhao employed in this speech revealed his willingness to speak with the students on an equal status. He abandoned his authoritative position to adopt the style of a peer. His language appeared to meet the demands of the students, who had been waiting for recognition from the government for their pro-democracy movement.

ANALYSIS

Zhao's speech must be interpreted in light of traditional Chinese modes of public discourse, which emphasize argument from authority, the value of harmony, figurative analogies, indirection in style, argument based on character, and cautious argument at the opportune moment.[13] Zhao's position as the general secretary of the C.P.C. made him an authority for his audience, and his position in the government automatically made his advice more credible. His message indirectly indicated that the continuation of the hunger strike would not contribute to the growth of real democracy in China at that moment. Some time would be needed before both the government and the students could compromise to reach an agreement.

His opening apology also added greatly to his credibility. It was extraordinary that someone in his position would admit the mistakes of the government in front of the students, who had been outraged by the government's resistance to their proposals for greater democracy. Unlike many Chinese public speakers, Zhao did not support his argument based on his authority. This act was primarily his personal declaration to the hunger strikers.

Zhao's May 19 speech was made to maintain social harmony, often the goal of Chinese discourse. Following the principles of Confucianism and Taoism, Zhao based his argument on the importance of social harmony. The tension in Beijing had increased day by day since the

---

[13]Traditional Chinese discourse is examined in Robert T. Oliver, *Communication and Culture in Ancient India and China* (Syracuse, NY: Syracuse University Press, 1971). See also Xing Lu and David A. Frank, "On the Study of Ancient Chinese Rhetoric/Bian," *Western Journal of Communication* 57 (Fall 1993): 445–463.

People's Daily article appeared on April 26, 1989. In spite of his support for the student demonstrators, Zhao did not entertain the possibility that greater democracy could be achieved through confrontation or through sacrifice. Instead he suggested to the students that a harmonious solution would be to have a dialogue with the government officials. As a Communist party leader, Zhao knew that the government's strong military forces were certain to overpower the students' defenses and cause unnecessary sacrifice. More action from the hunger strikers would disturb the social stability further and would not necessarily contribute to a resolution of the crisis.

Reflecting the indirect style typical of Chinese communication, part of Zhao's argument regarding the government's attitude was made implicitly and indirectly. One example of this occurred when Zhao indicated the government's attitude, saying, "You must not persist in the strike until satisfactory answers are given. It won't help" (2). In fact, he argued that no matter how persistent the hunger strikers were, the government would not act to satisfy the students' demands. The leaders had already made their decision, and they would not be influenced by the students' actions.

Another example of indirection occurred when Zhao explained the reasons for the students to stop their action. He argued, "You are still young and have a long way to go. You must live on in good health, live to the day when China finally realizes the Four Modernizations. You are not like us. We are getting *old* and it doesn't matter what happens to us" (2, emphasis added). The contrast between the young and the old suggests that youth and good health would be the better fate, which the students should cherish and make good use of. Without good health, the students would not survive to the day when the Chinese can finally enjoy true democracy. Zhao's long-term goal was the well-being of all the Chinese. With the decline of his power in the C.P.C. he would no longer be able to contribute to the development of the democracy movement from a position of power, whereas the students could still work for the dream with their lives.

Toward the end of his speech, Zhao alluded to his own past experience when he said, "We all used to be young. We also have taken to the streets, some of us have even lain across railroad tracks to stop trains. At that time we also never thought about what would happen afterward" (3). In order to make his appeal more persuasive, he used himself as vivid evidence. This personal example linked the students' protests to protests at the beginning of the revolution that brought the Communists to power, a truly astonishing bit of identification. This identification is reinforced by his final reference to students as comrades, which implied that he stood with the students fighting for China's future. His personal experience was used to defend the view that China would not be changed by the action of the hunger strike, just as protest had never changed policy in the past.

Zhao's reference to Beijing was another example of indirection. He said, "Also you know that Beijing is the capital. The situation is getting worse every day. It cannot go on like this" (2). This was a subtle warning that protest in Beijing could not be tolerated by the government or would be tolerated far less here than elsewhere.

However, in terms of his recommendations to hunger strikers, Zhao was very explicit and direct about what he hoped would occur. He said, "But I am here now not to ask for your forgiveness. I just want to say that your bodies are very weak now. You have been on a hunger strike for seven days, you must not go on like this. . . . What is most important now is that I hope you will stop your hunger strike as soon as possible" (1). He argued that more time was needed to resolve these problems. They had been on the hunger strike for seven days, and their condition was already critical. If they persisted, they would permanently injure their health before a resolution could be reached. Moreover, their protest had been successful in raising issues, and the channels for dialogue were open. Thus, it would be a useless sacrifice to continue. He first proposed the problem, then discussed the consequences of the problem and concluded with his recommendation. This part of his argument was stated clearly and directly.

What Zhao said in his farewell speech to the hunger strikers was consistent with what he had said and done earlier. This consistency was a key element in making his address successful in achieving its end: stopping the hunger strike. His support for the actions of the students had been manifested in a series of actions and statements. On May 3 he made an important speech addressing 3,000 students at the Great Hall of the People, commemorating the 70th anniversary of the May Fourth Movement. According to Simmie and Nixon, in addition to calling for political stability, he admitted that "the party had made mistakes and said that student demands to end corruption, promote democracy, and improve education were goals the government shared" (62).[14] Tony Saich explains that on May 4, when Zhao addressed the Asian Development Bank, he claimed that the "reasonable demands of the students should be met through democratic or legal means, through reforms and various other means in line with reason and order" (44).[15]

---

[14]In the *Chinese People's Movement,* Tony Saich commented, "Zhao did not include the need to 'oppose bourgeois liberalization' in his speech. The insertion of this phrase had been requested by Li Peng and various other 'comrades.' " Saich noted that this was mentioned by Li Peng in his speech of May 22, 1989 (43–44).

[15]Saich reports, "According to Li Peng, this speech had not been approved by any other member of the Standing Committee of the Politburo;" it was all Zhao's personal opinion (44).

These two speeches indicated his support for the students' aims. Then, according to Simmie and Nixon, on May 6 Zhao told his two comrades, Hu Qili and Rui Xingwen, who were in charge of propaganda and ideological work in the Central Committee, that "there was no big risk to open up a bit by reporting the demonstrations and increase the openness of news" (156). This statement supported the protest movement and encouraged an end to journalistic censorship of it. On May 8 he told the Turkish delegation that solutions to the problems raised by the students needed to be found through "democratic and lawful' means" and approvingly said that this process would promote China's democratic development (Simmie and Nixon 79). In the same statement Zhao also reaffirmed the patriotic nature of the student movement.

During a meeting of the Politburo's Standing Committee on May 13, Zhao demanded a retraction of the April 26 *People's Daily* editorial, but his proposal was outvoted 4 to 1. Again on May 16 he proposed acceptance of a number of the student demands at a meeting of the Politburo's Standing Committee, but again he was outvoted 4 to 1. Simmie and Nixon reported that during Gorbachev's visit Zhao told him, "All the comrades . . . hold that in the interests of the party we still need his [Deng's] wisdom and experience" (107), which implied that Deng was still in charge and was still being consulted on major decisions even though he had resigned from the C.P.C. at the Thirteenth National Party Congress in 1987.

On the morning of May 17 Zhao sent a message to the hunger strikers in behalf of the Politburo, acknowledging the patriotic spirit of the student movement and promising that the government would not use force against the students. On the same day, during a meeting at Deng's house, Deng proposed the implementation of martial law. Zhao was the only one who opposed this plan. Around 8:00 P.M. Zhao offered his resignation, saying that he could not continue as General Secretary because he could not support a decision with which he did not agree, yet the Politburo's Standing Committee did not accept his resignation (Landsberger 171–172). Zhao's support for the students also emerged when he visited the hospitals with Li Peng, Hu Qili, and Qiao Shi. "Li Peng seemed distinctly uncomfortable, moving stiffly about the beds and greeting students with formal reserve," Simmie and Nixon reported (117). Zhao appeared genuinely concerned about their health. In other words, prior to his farewell speech, Zhao had demonstrated his support for the democracy movement in his speeches or actions. Thus argument based on character was manifested splendidly by Zhao.

The timing of Zhao's farewell speech also was significant. It occurred three days after he had offered his resignation. After his failure to persuade his colleagues in the C.P.C., he shifted his efforts to convince the students to change their tactics in order to avoid a serious conflict with the government. In addition to expressing his concern for the nation as a whole, it was also his last chance to express his sympathy and support for the students in public. He still wanted to show his devotion to the students. After seven days of the hunger strike, the students' health posed a serious threat. According to one student leader, Wang Dan,[16] more than 2,000 students had fainted in the square. All the hospitals around Beijing had cooperated in supplying medical treatment to them. Under such circumstances, there was a great need for action to save those young lives. Zhao's speech appropriately came at a propitious moment for preserving the health of the students and for expressing his personal concern.

Since the split of China in 1949 the C.P.C. has controlled and censored public speech. The only speaking considered acceptable is at mandatory meetings and on ceremonial occasions. Mao Tse-Tung's revolutionary ideas predominated in the mandatory discussion meetings, held at least once and sometimes up to three times per week, in which all Chinese were required to participate. The Chinese people not only were required to listen to what the Communist party wanted them to hear but also were required to restate the same message in their own words. Individual thinking was prohibited and controlled by the massive, well-organized information service (Oliver, 79). In short, individuals spoke for the government but not for themselves. This mode, then, became the norm. Most political statements were decided prior to their announcement by the Politburo Committee, and they were addressed to inferiors as the rules to follow. No public deliberation or opposition was allowed; opinions contrary to the views of the government would endanger one's life. Protests usually were expressed through anonymous big posters.

On ceremonial occasions at the temple, the birthday dinner, the funeral, or the wedding ceremony, epideictic speeches often were made. These speeches either honored the ancestors or praised and remembered someone. Only on those specific occasions was it acceptable to reveal one's own feelings publicly. However, even in these settings, one's own feelings were still conveyed very subtly and indirectly, and no criticism of the government's policies was allowed. Sharing feelings with others always occurred in face-to-face circumstances; nonverbal cues supplied along with verbal cues communicated one's true feelings. The only instances of direct expression could

---

[16]Born in 1965, Wang Dan was a history major at Beijing University at the time of the Tiananmen Square protests. He was very outspoken, sincere, and calm. He was present at the hunger strikers' meeting with Li Peng. As one on the list of the 21 most wanted, unfortunately, he was arrested and is still in prison (Simmie and Nixon 54, 109, 198).

be found at the open markets or the black markets when clients bargained over prices.

Zhao Ziyang's speech adhered to some traditional norms. As has been noted, he adopted an indirect style when he mentioned the government's mistakes. Even though he disagreed with the hard-liners' decisions, he was reluctant to accuse them explicitly. It might have been self-protection; nonetheless, he responded to the government's attitude carefully and ambiguously.

He also retained his belief in the old system. He claimed that the door of dialogue would remain open and that the government's views on some questions were gradually coming closer to those of the students. This is evidence that he was not yet ready to abandon the system of which he had been a part; he wanted to go on believing that the system could and would respond to the protests of those he saw as true patriots who were seeking the good of their country. He was not deceiving the students, but he probably was deceived by the government, which is a revelation about his character. He remained a good Communist as well as a good Chinese.

Notably, Zhao's speech illustrated the force of argument based on the consistency between a speaker's words and actions. His endless devotion to the Chinese democracy movement was an example of persuasion arising out of his character as manifested in action. He tried his best to diminish the misunderstanding between the government and the public, to value the public's opinions, and to persuade his political partners. He practiced what he believed to be true, beneficial, and justifiable for his country. Accordingly, the argument he made at this moment carried the force of his past words and deeds.

Moreover, Zhao's speech came at an opportune time. The hunger strikers wanted to open a dialogue with the government and sought attention from the authorities. The students persisted because the government officials seemed to ignore their patriotic actions. Under those conditions, their health was no longer the biggest concern; their primary objective became recognition from the government. Together with his appearance at Tiananmen Square, Zhao's speech functioned to meet part of the students' demands.

In spite of his adaptation to some traditional modes of Chinese public discourse, Zhao also violated some norms. First, his speech was his own personal statement. As a Communist leader, Zhao was supposed to express the views of the government and to defend the decisions of the party. He declined that obligation to reveal his personal feelings instead.

Second, Zhao's style was both indirect and direct. His purpose in addressing the students was set forth directly. Generally the Chinese use of argument is rather like Plato's use of myths in his dialogues.

The Chinese audience actively participates in creating the message by interpreting the underlying meanings suggested through metaphors or indirect references. Zhao's speech illustrates such indirection in allusions to the students' youth and in a reference to Beijing, but his direct comments to the students violate this convention of public discourse.

Third, his egalitarian attitude toward the students does not correspond to his position of authority, nor does it reflect the traditional use of authority in discourse. Throughout the history of the People's Republic of China, the leaders have strengthened their authority by treating the entire population as inferiors, as children who need their tutelage. The leaders referred to themselves as "parental officials" (fumu guan) and to the students as "infants" (woi-woi). Zhao discarded this attitude to treat the students as equals. He did not perceive their demonstration as a cause of turmoil. He appreciated the students' good will toward the nation.

Finally, Zhao challenged the traditional idea of the role of intuition in human affairs by reasoning with his audience. The dominant Chinese philosophies instruct us to accommodate our minds to our intuitions. Passion always determines decisions. Zhao violated this convention by asking the students to rely on their reason rather than on their impulses or passions. He proclaimed that passion is conventionally associated with youth in the Chinese culture and was thus a poor guide for conduct.

As a Chinese, I personally believe that Zhao Ziyang's short speech should be praised for four reasons. First, his decision to make this speech was a courageous act. Zhao sacrificed himself in order to convince the students to stop sacrificing themselves. His confession about the government's misbehavior toward the students at Tiananmen Square was likely to be used by party leaders as evidence to deprive him of his power in the C.P.C. or to endanger his life. However, Zhao was brave enough to risk sacrificing himself to save the young lives of the hunger strikers.[17]

Second, this speech was exceptional in terms of sharing his personal emotion in public. In general, most Chinese public discourses seldom involve the rhetor's feelings. Personal feelings are conveyed through literal meanings or nonverbal cues. Zhao's speech did not

---

[17]Zhao Ziyang was dismissed from his post as head of the party, and in the words of Deng Xiaoping, " 'exposed' for 'splitting' the Chinese leadership over how to deal with thousands of pro-democracy demonstrators who occupied the center of the capital" (*New York Times,* 4 November 1993: A3). Zhao was formally arrested late in 1991 (*New York Times,* 28 January 1992: A4Y), and at last report is still being held under house arrest.

threaten the hunger strikers in an effort to compel them to stop their fasting; he relied instead on a powerful combination of argument grounded in his past experience and his knowledge of the nation's leaders and his intense feeling for the protesters. When Zhao was delivering this speech, he had tears in his eyes.

The speech played a major role in the termination of the hunger strike. That same night the students called off the hunger strike and transformed it into a sit-in demonstration. Mu and Thompson argue that "the image of Zhao's tearful response to the students may have been partially responsible for the decision to end the hunger strike that night" (58).

Third, this speech reveals Zhao's respect for the students' goals. It is rare that someone in Zhao's position would respond in ways that functioned to meet the students' demands. Unlike other party members, he treated the students as adults and believed that they were capable of finding a more rational solution to the crisis. His empathy corresponded to the demands of the students and thus influenced them to decide to end the hunger strike. The students probably ended the hunger strike less out of fear of the consequences of the hunger strike and more because they were moved by Zhao's appreciation for and understanding of their intentions.

Finally, this discourse simultaneously combines direct and indirect style. Zhao successfully incorporated different approaches toward the students and the government. He sent clear messages to the students about his intentions; therefore, the hunger strikers clearly understood his purpose. On the other hand, he criticized the party decisions very indirectly. Even though he admitted that the government deserved blame and criticism, he was very subtle in suggesting who was in control of the events. He still claimed that there was hope for the students and the government to reach some agreement.

CONCLUSION

Because of the influence of Confucianism and Taoism, the Chinese use public discourse differently than do Westerners. Traditional modes of public discourse exhibit six characteristics: argument based on authority, persuasion directed toward the ideal of social stability or social harmony, argument grounded in figurative analogy or metaphor, indirection in style, argument grounded in character, and cautious argument made at an opportune moment.

The protest and massacre at Tiananmen Square in 1989 affected the Chinese politically, economically, and rhetorically. Speeches and printed publications were used to stir the consciences of citizens. Among the most important was the farewell speech by former General Zhao Ziyang. As revealed in this analysis, Zhao spoke both as a party leader and as an individual. For someone of his high rank to express his personal views was startling; for him to continue to believe that the party eventually could respond to the student demands suggests his strong sense of duty. Reflecting his dual role, Zhao combined indirection with a clear statement of purpose. Zhao preserved his relationship to the party by expressing his criticisms indirectly and ambiguously, but he was explicit about his goal for the students. Given the importance of hierarchy and his high position, it is noteworthy that Zhao addressed the students as his peers and showed his respect by treating them as comrades. His appeal to the students was grounded in arguments drawn from his special knowledge as a government leader and from the identification he made between the protests of his youthful past when the People's Republic came into being and the protests of the students in Tiananmen Square. That identification, the consistency between his past words and deeds, and the views expressed in the speech illustrate traditional argument from character. Finally, of course, Zhao's goal was the achievement of the traditional goals of social stability or harmony and the avoidance of violence and internal conflict.

WORKS CITED

Chiang, M. Y., ed. *Fifty Days in Beijing Democracy Movement* [in Chinese]. Taipei: Shi-Pao Wen Yuan, Inc., 1989.

Feng, L. C., C. T. Lio, C. C. Chien, Y. C. Lin, C. Y. Lio, M. Y. Hsu, and C. C. Ping, eds. *Tragically Heroic Democracy Movement: The Most Peaceful Beginning and the Most Bloody Ending* [in Chinese]. Hong Kong: Ming Pao, Inc., 1989.

Halpern, Nina P. "Economic Reform, Social Mobilization, and Democratization in Post-Mao China." *Reform and Reaction in Post-Mao China: The Road to Tiananmen.* Ed. Richard Baum. New York: Routledge, Chapman and Hall, 1991. 38–59.

Hsu, Immanuel C. Y. "The Violent Crackdown at Tiananmen Square, June 3–4, 1989." *The Rise of Modern China.* 4th ed. New York: Oxford University Press, 1990. 923–938.

Landsberger, Stefan R. "Chronology of the 1989 Student Demonstrations." *The Chinese People's Movement: Perspectives on Spring, 1989.* Ed. Tony Saich. Armonk, NY: M. E. Sharpe, 1990. 164–189.

Lu, Xing, and David A. Frank. "On the Study of Ancient Chinese Rhetoric/Bian." *Western Journal of Communication* 57 (Fall 1993): 445–463.

Mu, Yi, and Mark V. Thompson. *Crisis at Tiananmen: Reform and Reality in Modern China.* San Francisco: China Books and Periodicals, 1989.

Oksenberg, Michael, Lawrence Sullivan, and Marc Lambert, eds. *Beijing Spring, 1989: Confrontation and Conflict: The Basic Documents.* New York: M. E. Sharpe, 1990.

Oliver, Robert T. *Communication and Culture in Ancient India and China.* Syracuse, NY: Syracuse University Press, 1971.

Oliver, Robert T. *Leadership in Asia: Persuasive Communication in the Making of Nations, 1850–1950.* Newark, NJ: University of Delaware Press, 1989.

Rosen, Stanley. "The Rise (and Fall) of Public Opinion in Post-Mao China." *Reform and Reaction in Post-Mao China: The Road to Tiananmen.* Ed. Richard Baum. New York: Routledge, Chapman and Hall, 1991. 60–83

Saich, Tony. "When Worlds Collide: The Beijing People's Movement of 1989." *The Chinese People's Movement: Perspectives on Spring, 1989.* Ed. Tony Saich. Armonk, NY: M. E. Sharpe, 1990. 25–49.

Salisbury, Harrison E. *Tiananmen Diary: Thirteen Days in June.* Boston: Little, Brown, 1989.

Simmie, Scott, and Bob Nixon. *Tiananmen Square.* Seattle: University of Washington Press, 1989.

Trenholm, Sarah. "Rhetoric and Response: Student Attitudes toward the Crisis at Tiananmen." Paper delivered at Midwest Conference on Asian Affairs, Bloomington, IN, November, 1990.

Wasserstrom, Jeffrey N. "Student Protests and the Chinese Tradition." *The Chinese People's Movement: Perspectives on Spring, 1989.* Ed. Tony Saich. Armonk, NY: M. E. Sharpe, 1990. 3–24.

Woei, Lien Chong. "Petitioners, Popperians, and Hunger Strikers: The Uncoordinated Efforts of the 1989 Chinese Democratic Movement." *The Chinese People's Movement: Perspectives on Spring, 1989.* Ed. Tony Saich. Armonk, NY: M. E. Sharpe, 1990. 106–126.

Zhao Ziyang. "Sorry, We Have Come Too Late" (Farewell Speech at Tiananmen). *Crisis at Tiananmen: Reform and Reality in Modern China.* Ed. Yi Mu and Mark Thompson. San Francisco: China Books and Periodicals, 1989. 180–182.

NELSON MANDELA

Address to the Joint Session of the United States Congress, June 26, 1990

No individual more vividly represents the struggle to end racist apartheid in South Africa than Nelson Mandela. Imprisoned for anti-apartheid activities for 27 years, he was freed by a declaration of South African president F. W. De Klerk in February 1990. Mandela's release from prison signaled the impending demise of apartheid.

In June 1990 Mandela visited the United States seeking continued support for the anti-apartheid movement from both the U.S. government and the people. At the time of this speech Mandela was deputy president of the African National Congress. Currently he is president of South Africa. The text is from Congressional Record—House of Representatives, *26 June 1990: H 4136–4138.*

1   Mr. Speaker; Mr. President; esteemed Members of the U.S. Congress; your excellencies, ambassadors and members of the Diplomatic Corps; distinguished guests, ladies and gentlemen:

2   It is a fact of the human condition that each shall, like a meteor, a mere passing moment in time and space, flit across the human stage and pass out of existence. Even the golden lads and lasses, as much as the chimney sweepers, come, and tomorrow are no more. After them all, they leave the people, enduring, multiplying, permanent, except to the extent that the same humanity might abuse its own genius to immolate life itself.

3   And so we have come to Washington in the District of Columbia, and into these hallowed chambers of the U.S. Congress, not as pretenders to greatness, but as a particle of a people whom we know to be noble and heroic—enduring, multiplying, permanent, rejoicing in the expectation and knowledge that their humanity will be reaffirmed and enlarged by open and unfettered communion with the nations of the world.

4   We have come here to tell you, and through you, your own people, who are equally noble and heroic, of the troubles and trials, the fond hopes and aspirations, of the people from whom we originate. We believe that we know it as a fact, that your kind and moving invitation to us to speak here derived from your own desire to convey a message to our people, and according to your humane purposes, to give them an opportunity to say what they want of you, and what they want to make of their relationship with you.

5   Our people demanded democracy. Our country, which continues to bleed and suffer pain, needs democracy. It cries out for the situation where the law will decree that the freedom to speak of freedom constitutes the very essence of legality and the very thing that makes for the legitimacy of the constitutional order.

6   It thirsts for the situation where those who are entitled by law to carry arms, as the forces of national security and law and order, will not turn their weapons against the citizens simply because the citizens assert that equality, liberty and the pursuit of happiness are fundamental human rights which are not only inalienable but must, if necessary, be defended with the weapons of war.

7   We fight for and visualize a future in which all shall, without regard to race, color, creed, or sex, have the right to vote and to be voted into all elective organs of state. We are engaged in struggle to ensure that the rights of every individual are guaranteed and protected, through a democratic constitution, the rule of law, an entrenched bill of rights, which should be enforced by an independent judiciary, as well as a multi-party political system.

8   Mr. Speaker, we are acutely conscious of the fact that we are addressing an historic institution for whose creation and integrity many men and women lost their lives in the war of independence, the civil war and the war against nazism and fascism. That very history demands that we address you with respect and candor and without any attempt to dissemble.

9   What we have said concerning the political arrangements we seek for our country is seriously meant. It is an outcome for which many of us went to prison, for which many have died in police cells, on the gallows, in our towns and villages and in the countries of Southern Africa. Indeed, we have even had our political representatives killed in countries as far away from South Africa as France.

10   Unhappily, our people continue to die to this day, victims of armed agents of the state who are still determined to turn their guns against the very idea of a nonracial democracy. But this is the perspective which we trust Congress will feel happy to support and encourage, using the enormous weight of its prestige and authority as an eminent representative of democratic practice.

11   To deny any person their human rights is to challenge their very humanity. To impose on them a wretched life of hunger and deprivation is to dehumanize them. But such has been the terrible fate of all black persons in our country under the system of apartheid. The extent of the deprivation of millions of people has to be seen to be believed. The injury is made that more intolerable by the opulence of our white compatriots and the deliberate distortion of the economy to feed that opulence.

12   The process of the reconstruction of South African society must and will also entail the transformation of its economy. We need a strong and growing economy. We require an economy that is able to address the needs of all the people of our country, that can provide food, houses, education, health services, social security and everything that makes human life human, that makes life joyful and not a protracted encounter with hopelessness and despair.

13   We believe that the fact of the apartheid structure of the South African economy and the enormous and pressing needs of the people, make it inevitable that the democratic government will intervene in this economy, acting through the elected parliament. We have put the matter to the business community of our country that the need for a public sector is one of the elements in a many-sided strategy of economic development and restructuring that has to be considered by us all, including the private sector.

14   The ANC holds no ideological positions which dictate that it must adopt a policy of nationalization. But the ANC also holds the view that there is no self-regulating mechanism within the South African economy which will, on its own, ensure growth with equity.

15   At the same time, we take it as given that the private sector is an engine of growth and development which is critical to the success of the mixed economy we hope to see in the future South Africa. We are accordingly committed to the creation of the situation in which business people, both South African and foreign, have confidence in the security of their investments, are assured of a fair rate of return on their capital and do business in conditions of stability and peace.

16   We must also make the point very firmly that the political settlement, and democracy itself, cannot survive unless the material needs of the people, the bread and butter issues, are addressed as part of the process of change and as a matter of urgency. It should never be that the anger of the poor should be the finger of accusation pointed at all of us because we failed to respond to the cries of the people for food, for shelter, for the dignity of the individual.

17   We shall need your support to achieve the postapartheid economic objectives which are an intrinsic part of the process of the restoration of the human rights of the people of South Africa. We would like to approach the issue of our economic cooperation not as a relationship between donor and recipient, between a dependent and a benefactor.

18   We would like to believe that there is a way in which we could structure this relationship so that we do indeed benefit from your enormous resources in terms of your capital, technology, all-round expertise, your enterprising spirit and your markets. This relationship should however be one from which your people should also derive benefit, so that we who are fighting to liberate the very spirit of an entire people from the bondage of the arrogance of the ideology and practice of white supremacy, do not build a relationship of subservient dependency and fawning gratitude.

19   One of the benefits that should accrue to both our peoples and to the rest of the world, should surely be that this complex South African society, which has known nothing but racism for three centuries, should be transformed into an oasis of good race relations, where the black shall to the white be sister and brother, a fellow South African, an equal human being, both citizens of the world. To destroy racism in the world, we, together, must expunge apartheid racism in South Africa. Justice and liberty must be our tool, prosperity and happiness our weapon.

20   Mr. Speaker, distinguished representatives of the American people, you know this more than we do that peace is its own reward. Our own fate, borne by a succession of generations that reach backward into centuries, has been nothing but tension, conflict, and death. In a sense we do not know the meaning of peace except in the imagination. But because we have not known true peace in its real meaning; because, for centuries, generations have had to bury the victims of state violence, we have fought for the right to experience peace.

21   On the initiative of the ANC, the process toward the conclusion of a peaceful settlement has started. According to a logic dictated by our situation, we are engaged in an effort which includes the removal of obstacles to negotiations. This will be followed by a negotiated determination of the mechanism which will draw up the new constitution.

22   This should lead to the formation of this constitution-making institution and therefore the elaboration and adoption of a democratic constitution. Elections would then be held on the basis of this constitution and, for the first time, South Africa would have a body of lawmakers which would, like yourselves, be mandated by the whole people.

23   Despite the admitted commitment of President De Klerk to walk this road with us, and despite our acceptance of his integrity and the honesty of his purposes, we would be fools to believe that the road ahead of us is without major hurdles. Too many among our white compatriots are steeped in the ideology of racism to admit easily that change must come.

24   Tragedy may yet sully the future we pray and work for if these slaves of the past take up arms in a desperate effort to resist the process which must lead to the democratic transformation of our country. For those who care to worry about violence in our country, as we do, it is at these forces that they should focus their attention, a process in which we are engaged.

25   We must contend still with the reality that South Africa is a country in the grip of the apartheid crime against humanity. The consequences of this continue to be felt not only within our borders but throughout southern Africa which continues to harvest the bitter fruits of conflict and war, especially in Mozambique and Angola. Peace will not come to our country and region until the apartheid system is ended.

26   Therefore we say we still have a struggle on our hands. Our common and noble efforts to abolish the system of white minority domination must continue. We are encouraged and strengthened by the fact of the agreement between ourselves, this Congress as well as President Bush and his administration, that sanctions should remain in place. Sanctions should remain in place because the purpose for which they were imposed has not yet been achieved.

27   We have yet to arrive at the point when we can say that South Africa is set on an irreversible course leading to its transportation into a united, democratic, and nonracial country. We plead that you cede the prerogative to the people of South Africa to determine the moment when it will be said that profound changes have occurred and an irreversible process achieved, enabling you and the rest of the international community to lift sanctions.

28   We would like to take this opportunity to thank you all for the principled struggle you waged which resulted in the adoption of the historic comprehensive Anti-Apartheid Act which made such a decisive contribution to the process of moving our country forward toward negotiations. We request that you go further and assist us with the material resources which will enable us to promote the peace process and meet other needs which arise from the changing situation you have helped to bring about.

29   The stand you took established the understanding among the millions of our people that here we have friends, here we have fighters against racism who feel hurt because we are hurt, who seek our success because they too seek the victory of democracy over tyranny. And here I speak not only about you, Members of the U.S. Congress, but also of the millions of people throughout this great land who stood up and engaged the apartheid system in struggle, the masses who have given us such strength and joy by the manner in which they have received us since we arrived in this country.

30   Mr. Speaker, Mr. President, Senators and Representatives; we went to jail because it was impossible to sit still while the obscenity of the apartheid system was being imposed on our people. It would have been immoral to keep quiet while a racist tyranny sought to reduce an entire people into a status worse than that of the beasts of the forest. It would have been an act of treason against the people and against our conscience to allow fear and the drive toward self-preservation to dominate our behavior, obliging us to absent ourselves from the struggle for democracy and human rights, not only in our country but throughout the world.

31   We could not have made an acquaintance through literature with human giants such as George Washington, Abraham Lincoln and Thomas Jefferson and not been moved to act as they were moved to act. We could not have heard of and admired John Brown,

Sojourner Truth, Frederick Douglass, W. E. B. DuBois, Marcus Garvey, Martin Luther King, Jr., and others—we could not have heard of these and not be moved to act as they were moved to act. We could not have known of your Declaration of Independence and not elected to join in the struggle to guarantee the people life, liberty and the pursuit of happiness.

32   We are grateful to you all that you persisted in your resolve to have us and other political prisoners released from jail. You have given us the gift and privilege to rejoin our people, yourselves and the rest of the international community in the common effort to transform South Africa into a united, democratic and nonracial country. You have given us the power to join hands with all people of conscience to fight for the victory of democracy and human rights throughout the world.

33   We are glad that you merged with our own people to make it possible for us to emerge from the darkness of the prison cell and join the contemporary process of the renewal of the world. We thank you most sincerely for all you have done and count on you to persist in your noble endeavors to free the rest of our political prisoners and to emancipate our people from the larger prison that is apartheid South Africa.

34   The day may not be far when we will borrow the words of Thomas Jefferson and speak of the will of the South African nation. In the exercise of that will by this united nation of black and white people, it must surely be that there will be born a country on the southern tip of Africa which you will be proud to call a friend and an ally, because of its contribution to the universal striving toward liberty, human rights, prosperity and peace among the peoples.

35   Let that day come now. Let us keep our arms locked together so that we form a solid phalanx against racism to ensure that that day comes now. By our common actions let us ensure that justice triumphs without delay. When that has come to pass, then shall we all be entitled to acknowledge the salute when others say of us, blessed are the peacemakers.

36   Thank you for your kind invitation to speak here today and thank you for your welcome and the attention you have accorded our simple message.

37   Thank you.

JANICE WATSON

In Search of a Hero:
An African American
Interpretation of
Nelson Mandela's Address
to the United States Congress

As in the critique of Zhao's speech, the issue of cultural compe-
tence is also important in the critique of Nelson Mandela's
speech to the U.S. Congress. Janice Watson recognizes that
Mandela's speech was intelligible to and moving for U.S. audi-
ences of European descent, but she argues that it was under-
stood in a different way and had a different function for audi-
ences of African descent. Her critique is premised on the
assumption that rhetorical action is collaborative, a joint cre-
ation of speaker and audience. In this case she argues that
much in the text, in prior acts, in the historical situation, and
in the cultural background of African American audiences
prompted the special collaboration that her critique details. As
Watson notes, the two-audience problem of African American
rhetors has been recognized by critics; however, her critique in-
vites us to construe that situation positively. Textual analysis
identifies the elements in Mandela's speech that invite an alter-
native reading from African Americans. Historical–contextual
analysis provides information about the speaker and the Afri-
can American audience to explain the speaker's capacity to
evoke such a reading and the auditors' experience and back-
ground, which would have enabled them to produce it. As U.S.
culture becomes increasingly diverse, occasions for ambicultural
texts also will increase. Such rhetorical acts have the potential
to contain more than one message as understood by auditors

> *who come from differing cultural backgrounds. Critics with*
> *multicultural backgrounds will be needed to interpret such mes-*
> *sages to monocultural audiences (for example, Philipsen).*

The challenge to African(-)s[1] has often been to speak or write in two tongues—one that will be clearly understood by the dominant society and another that will resonate clearly and authentically in their own communities—while at the same time seeming to communicate in only one. In most rhetorical situations they must address dual audiences: other African(-)s and non-African(-)s.

The question of multiple audiences for rhetoric has been addressed by rhetorical critics and theorists. Work has been done on the multiple audience problem faced by speakers presenting keynote addresses at U.S. political conventions (Smith, "Republican Address"; Thompson) and on the problem faced by international rhetors whose speeches must work effectively for audiences in the rhetor's homeland as well as those in the country and context in which the speeches are given (Petersen). In their analysis of Hubert Humphrey's speech to the National Association for the Advancement of Colored People (NAACP), Robert L. Scott and Wayne Brockriede speak of the " 'second' speech, addressed through the press to the national audience" (79).

African(-) rhetors face a task similar to, if not the same as, these, but with a twist of its own. Whatever their national identity, African(-) rhetors will always be perceived by many members of their audience as primarily African(-). In the United States, whether that is interpreted or evaluated as meaning that they should and/or do represent and speak *for* other African Americans or that they should and/or are speaking *to* other African Americans, they carry the additional rhetorical baggage associated with being African(-). Consequently, in addition to the "national audience" and the "second speech occasion" created by the presence of the mass media, and whatever the dominant ethnic composition of their immediate audience, they are consistently "overheard" by another audience constituted on the basis of ethnicity.[2]

---

[1]Read here African, African American, African Caribbean, and so forth. I have chosen to use the term to refer to people of African descent—that is, black people around the world. "Blacks" might be a more appropriate term, but people in the U.S. often understand "black" to mean African American and thus fail mentally to include others of African descent. I use the terms African American and European American to refer specifically to individuals who identify themselves as American by culture and citizenship.

[2]I realize the problems inherent in treating groups based on ethnicity or race as monolithic and homogeneous. I am aware that to talk of a "white," "black," "African(-)," or "African American" audience is to be overly reductionist and to ignore the widely varying attitudes, beliefs, and values of individuals within these categories. However, I believe the differences between the mainstream and subcultural norms that allow us to distinguish "African American" as depictive of a subculture in the United States also allow for this generalized usage in this context.

Scott and Brockriede note that "the rhetorician makes many inter-personal decisions. Who should address whom? Which audiences should be seen as primary? . . . Should he [*sic*] aim at identification with them or alienation? Should he try to relate to his audiences as a hero, an agent, a peer, or a suppliant?" (202). In answering these ques-tions, African(-) rhetors addressing U.S. audiences often find that their choice of primary audience determines the answer to the question of identification or alienation. For example, Brockriede and Scott argue quite persuasively that the largely negative perception of Stokely Carmichael and his rhetoric held by European Americans resulted in part from his choice to see the African American audience as primary. This choice led to stylistic and rhetorical strategies that almost inevi-tably alienated European American audiences ("Stokely Carmichael").

The choice of a non-African(-) "majority" audience as primary au-dience, with the attendant stylistic and rhetorical adaptations, often results in the alienation of the African(-) "minority" audience. Afri-can(-) rhetors attempting to succeed in this situation and not to be la-beled as an "Uncle Tom" or "unfaithful" to their roots and race must convey acceptable messages to both audiences and successfully achieve goals for both audiences while maintaining a consistency of content and commitment. This task would seem insurmountable when, as frequently occurs, the two audiences possess widely differing agendas.

For these rhetors I believe that the success of this endeavor lies in *polysemy,* or the capacity of language/discourse to mean in several ways—that is, in the intentional or unintentional creation of a text that can be, and is, read differently by members of the two audiences and that can, and will, be read similarly by members within each of the given audiences.

The critical analysis of texts that successfully achieve this polysemy or multidimensional meaning offers much to the study of rhetoric as well as to the study of interethnic and intercultural communication. An exploration of the strategies by which different groups understand and respond to the same text differently has implications not only for rhetoric but also for intercultural and interethnic communication in less formal interactions and settings.

In this analysis I look at the speech presented by Nelson Mandela to the U.S. Congress on June 26, 1990. I have chosen to look at the speech from an African American perspective, to explore its possible meanings for a "secondary audience" that overheard this speech and heard in it a voice for themselves, a rallying cry for African American nationalism, and a continuation of the U.S. civil rights movement.

I do not treat Mandela's speech primarily as intercultural rhetoric in either the traditional sense of an African communicating to a U.S. audience or in the sense of an African(-) communicating with a non-

African(-) audience, although the latter concern inevitably informs this analysis. Rather, I analyze Mandela's speech as an ambicultural (an inter-/intracultural) act—that is, an overtly intercultural act, African(-) to non-African(-)—that at the same time functions intraculturally, African(-) to African(-). I look first at the theoretical constructs that justify an exploration of alternative readings of the text and that suggest possible rhetorical strategies that render the text bisemous or polysemous. I then analyze the context and text of the speech itself and the ways in which both contribute to the alternate reading.

THE POLYSEMY OF THE AFRICAN(-) TEXT

In her work on the polysemous nature of the rhetorical text in the mass media, Celeste M. Condit lists several factors that determine the likelihood of a text being polysemous or evoking different meanings from different audiences. These include audience members' access to oppositional codes, the ratio between the work required and the pleasure produced in decoding a text, the repertoire of available texts, and the historical occasion (103). She also suggests that most texts are not polysemous; that is, most audience members interpret most texts similarly. They are, rather, "polyvalent," a term she uses "to describe the fact that audiences routinely evaluate texts differently, assigning different value to different portions of a text and hence to the text itself" (108). Thus she asserts that values are the primary determining factor for alternate readings because audience members share the denotation of the text; only their connotations differ, and those differences result from valence.

The only exception Condit allows is for the case that "requires massive cross-cultural differences and language shifts to produce such discrepant interpretations" (107). Her theory is too limited for the type of intercultural analysis attempted here because it does not allow for less severe cross-cultural differences, such as those that might exist between members of a culture and its subcultures; nor does it allow for biculturalism, which allows auditors to produce a widely discrepant interpretation even though they can also produce the "standard" interpretation.[3] In order to survive, members of subcultures and/or oppressed groups have traditionally developed and employed strategies that enable and even encourage, such polysemy.

---

[3]*Culture,* as defined by David Hoopes and Margaret D. Pusch, is "the sum total of ways of living; including values, beliefs, aesthetic standards, linguistic expression, patterns of thinking, behavioral norms, and styles of communication which a group of people has developed to assure its survival in a particular physical and human environment." A

RHETORICAL STRATEGIES FOR POLYSEMY

In his work of literary criticism, *The Signifying Monkey,* Henry Louis Gates, Jr., identifies one such strategy employed by African(-)s, which he sees as "the black trope of tropes, the figure for black rhetorical figures" (51). Gates concludes that "the black tradition is double voiced. . . . Signifyin(g) is the figure of the double-voiced, epitomized by Esu's depictions in sculpture as possessing two mouths" (xxv).[4] Roger Abrahams defines Signifyin(g) as "a language of implication," "that set of words or gestures achieving Hamlet's 'direction through indirection,'" a "technique of indirect argumentation or persuasion." Signifyin(g) shows itself in daily African American discourse in behavior such as "playing the dozens" and "woofing" (51–52, 66–67, 264; see also Kochman; Mitchell-Kernan; Smitherman).

Gates and Abrahams see Signifyin(g) as a strategy used either playfully, seriously, or in "serious play" whereby the speaker "says" one thing, verbally or nonverbally, while "meaning" another. Signifyin(g) differs from simple implication in its function of revising the received sign. For example, Gates's study demonstrates the way in which Signifyin(g) appears outside the realm of conversational discourse. He asserts that African(-) literary texts Signify on each other—that is, they participate in "repetition and revision, or repetition with a signal difference" (xxiv). They also Signify on Western texts, revising the received sign and thereby managing to "critique the nature of (white) meaning itself, to challenge through a literal critique of the sign the meaning of meaning" (47).

The tradition of Signifyin(g) most often occurs within the African(-) community as an in-house joke or a display of verbal dexterity, although it is sometimes used among the young to "signify on someone"—to humiliate an adversary. On the other hand, "Inversion," another strategy that contributes to polysemy, has functioned as a protective device against individuals outside of the community, a "linguistic survival process." As Grace Sims Holt explains:

> The traditional process of inversion was based in the concept that you can't disguise black skin but you can disguise speech which

---

subculture is "a group of people within a larger sociopolitical structure who share cultural (and often linguistic or dialectical) characteristics which distinguish it from others within the society" (3). Thus the effect of culture on the interpretation of a text involves more than a difference in values, although a difference in values definitely forms part of the rationale for the difference in interpretation.

[4]Esu is not said to possess two *faces* with its connotation of duplicity or even to "speak on two sides of his mouth"; rather, he possesses two mouths, therefore two tongues, an image more connotative of bilingualism or bidialectism than of duplicity.

permits you to verbally 'turn the tables' on an unknowledgeable opponent. . . . Whites, denied access to the semantic extensions of duality, connotations and denotations that developed within black usage, could only interpret the same material according to its original singular meaning. White interpretation of the communication event was quite different from that made by the other person in the interaction. (154)

African American rhetors, preachers, and revolutionaries have used Signifyin(g), in its formal sense of implicature and connotation, and also in its sense as ridicule. They have also commonly used inversion. The Negro spirituals used to guide slaves to freedom functioned as an effective means of communication largely due to the Signification of terms like "the promised land." Through this process slave owners and African American slaves hungry for liberty decoded totally different messages.

During the 1960s the inversion of the denotation of terms like "bad" and of the connotations of the term "black" added rhetorical power to the speeches of rhetors like Stokely Carmichael and Malcolm X as they exhorted African American audiences to take pride in black power. For example, Malcolm X's inversion of the term "black" transformed it from an insult into a badge of pride. Their intended audiences not only revised the received sign by adopting an alternate denotation but received great pleasure from a process that in enhancing group solidarity through in-group language usage critiqued, perhaps even ridiculed, the nature of European American meaning.

More detailed discussion and examples of Signifyin(g) and Inversion can be found in the works of Smitherman, Kochman, and Mitchell-Kernan. Mitchell-Kernan applies it to a variety of specific speech acts emphasizing that "the indirection, then, depends for its decoding upon shared knowledge of the participants . . . the recognition that signifying is occurring. . . . Secondly, this shared knowledge must be employed in the reinterpretation of the utterance" (325). She also notes that in Signifyin(g), and as Smitherman suggests, in most African(-) verbal art, great emphasis is placed on the audience member or hearer's ability to correctly decode a text and its alternate, often primary, meanings.

Much of the examination of Signifyin(g) and other methods of rendering African(-) texts polysemous has restricted itself to conversation and verbal games (Kochman; Mitchell-Kernan; Abrahams) or to rhetoric used in African(-) settings—that is, African(-) rhetors speaking to African(-) audiences about African(-) topics, such as sermons in African American churches (Smitherman). Formal speeches of African American rhetors rendered in public, culturally mixed contexts have largely been read as straight, monosemous texts. Yet most African American auditors would be primed to understand more. They would bring to their understanding of the texts their cultural norms and influences for both presentation and interpretation.

Studies in the ethnography of communication by writers such as Gerry Philipsen and Randall Lake demonstrate the importance of culture in the analysis of rhetoric. For Philipsen culture "serves as the interpretive background" for rhetoric. When the "background" changes, so does the auditor's interpretation of the speech ("Mayor Daley"). Lake demonstrates the importance of culture and a shared history to the audience's interpretation of the text and its effectiveness ("Enacting Red Power").

African American auditors would also bring to the text their highly developed skill at discovering and decoding the underlying text. For these auditors "straight" speeches might conceivably Signify upon themselves—speak with a double voice, giving the overt meaning a second meaning with a signal difference, "a blackness of voice."

A less uniquely African(-) or subcultural strategy for the construction of alternative meaning resides in the rhetor's choice of *ideographs,* words that function as "one-term sums of an orientation" and that are often used to "symbolize a line of argument." Ideographs have much more rhetorical power than their denotations suggest (McGee). Using the rhetoric of Martin Luther King and Malcolm X as examples, John Louis Lucaites and Celeste Michelle Condit demonstrate the rhetorical power of ideographs ("Reconstructing Equality"). Because ideographs, like language, are anchored in a particular culture and society, and one ideograph may carry distinctly different baggage in two different cultures (McGee), a skillful intercultural or ambicultural rhetor could create a polysemous text through careful use of ideographs common to both audiences but differing in their meaning and/or usage within the cultures or subcultures those audiences represent.

An analysis of Condit's factors for polysemy in the case of the African American auditor of Nelson Mandela's speech leads to the conclusion that members of the subculture possess the factors necessary to produce oppositional or alternate readings of the text. From the history of the civil rights and black power movements in this country, African American auditors would possess access to, and probably mastery of, ideological and rhetorical oppositional codes, having available a larger repertoire of texts than most of their European American contemporaries. From a history of exposure to rhetoric that often said much by implication while saying something completely different on the surface, African American audiences have become adept at reading between the lines and/or decoding two messages from one piece of rhetoric. Thus the work required to decode the text in an oppositional manner would be minimal. On the other hand, the pleasure derived from a nonstandard reading of Mandela's speech would be enough to justify even a difficult decoding. With little work required and much pleasure produced, the ratio definitely suggests the likelihood of an alternate reading. In addition, the historical occasion reflected in the auditor's reading of the meaning of Mandela's visit to the United States, as well as of his invitation to speak to Congress, would contribute to an alternate reading of the text.

RETURN OF THE NATIVE SON: THE CONTEXT OF NELSON MANDELA'S SPEECH

Mandela's impact on the audience was evident even before he appeared and began to speak. According to John Kiener:

> The galleries overhead were jammed, as was the standing room at the back of the House. An overflow crowd sat in 250 seats in the Statuary Hall. . . . The House chamber is rarely filled for joint meetings receiving visitors, but today was an exception, with even jaded lawmakers reacting as fans in the presence of a celebrity. (A11)

At 11:09 A.M., June 26, 1990, the doorkeeper of the U.S. House of Representatives announced the deputy president of the African National Congress (ANC) to the record crowd assembled. The audience greeted Mandela with a standing ovation lasting three-and-one-half minutes (*Congressional Record,* H 4136). His 45-minute speech was interrupted 16 times for bursts of applause, three of which turned into standing ovations (A11).

That a private citizen from a foreign country had been invited to speak before a joint session of Congress marked the occasion as unusual. That he would not have been allowed to speak before a governmental body in his own country, that he had a criminal record, that Congress had declared his organization a "terrorist organization" (Kopkind 76; "Guess Who's Coming to Dinner"), and that he was not the head of the organization that he represented, made the event even more noteworthy. Perhaps most noteworthy was that the man about to address the U.S. Congress was also black.

The acclaim with which he was received by Congress was and had been Signified, duplicated with a significant difference, in the African American community. As European America hailed him as a hero, African America claimed him as *their* hero. When Mandela arrived in New York City on June 20, 1990, to begin an eight-day tour of the

United States, the discourse surrounding his visit within the African American community displayed an emotional intensity unprecedented in recent years. According to Isabel Wilkerson, "All across the country, blacks who wept and cheered as Mr. Mandela walked free four months ago are anticipating the arrival this week of a man who they say has taken on greater symbolism for them than any civil rights leader since Dr. King" (8). The words of a man waiting to hear Mandela speak describe perhaps even more accurately the hope of the African American for his tour: "I came to witness the redemption of nationalism by Nelson Mandela" (Aneckwe 37).

The reception accorded him paid tribute to the history of the man as much as to the movement that he stood for. At the time of the address Mandela was 71 years old, and his life could be embodied in three words that seemed to encapsulate the fight for civil rights around the world: struggle, imprisonment, and liberation. Twenty years of his life had been spent actively engaged in the struggle for the liberation of black Africans living in South Africa. For 27 years he had conducted his part of the struggle from jail cells in South Africa, where he was subjected to great physical and emotional hardship.[5] In February 1990 a presidential declaration freed him.

Mandela's personal history of suffering and his active participation in the South African struggle provided the raison d'être for his invitation to speak to Congress and determined to a large extent the direction and style of his subsequent rhetoric. In his 1990 rhetoric Mandela drew heavily on the Freedom Charter of the African National Congress, which he had helped to shape, and on previous works with which audiences might have been familiar. Perhaps the work best known to African(-) and revolutionary audiences would have been selections from his four-hour (Harwood 110) statement presented from the dock at the Rivonia trial, which ends with his last spoken words to the public until his release from prison in February 1990:

> I have cherished the ideal of a democratic and free society in which all persons live together in harmony and with equal opportunities. It is an ideal which I hope to live for and to achieve. But if needs be, it is an ideal for which I am prepared to die. (Mandela, *The Struggle* 181)

In his first public address after his release, Mandela said, "In conclusion, I wish to go to my own words during my trial in 1964. They are as true today as they were then" ("Apartheid Has No Future" 297). Thus he tied his present persona to that of the man who had gone to jail 27 years earlier and ensured that any future rhetoric would be

---

[5]For further information on Mandela's life, see Winnie Mandela 1984 and Meer 1988.

viewed as a continuation and expansion of his pre-imprisonment body of work.

Mandela's pre-imprisonment rhetoric was characterized by a clarity and argumentative structure that evidences his training as a lawyer, and by an ability to make clear, emotional appeals to people's shared history. The rhetoric that emerged following his release showed clear continuity with his former style and ideology. He continued to identify himself as a loyal member of the ANC and as a part of the people. He continued to assert that he acted as a voice for the people and to represent himself as totally supporting a multiracial society. At the same time he continued to call for pressure on the South African government.

The world to which he addressed that rhetoric had changed dramatically, however, and with his release, Mandela's rhetoric also had changed in some ways. He evidently believed that negotiations between blacks and the South African government were not only possible but inevitable, and that the major contemporary task in the struggle was to prepare for and conduct these negotiations. Other strategies, such as the armed struggle and economic sanctions, functioned to facilitate the accomplishment of this goal.

In January and February of 1990 F. W. de Klerk, the newly elected South African president, changed the picture of South African race relations for many European Americans by rescinding the Separate Amenities Act, lifting the 30-year ban on black political demonstrations, releasing several prominent political prisoners, and promising the release of Nelson Mandela.

It was against this backdrop of ostensibly improving South African relations, the plea from de Klerk for negotiations and an end to violence, and the softening of the attitude of the international community toward the South African government that Mandela undertook his six-week, 14-nation tour during which he spoke to the U.S. Congress. Bruce W. Nelan notes that the tour had several purposes. Mandela hoped to raise funds to help support the newly repatriated ANC. He also intended to thank the peoples and governments around the world who had supported the ANC's struggle and given such intense and continued support to him personally. His most essential task, however, involved consolidating the political credibility of the ANC and gaining support for its positions, thus strengthening its clout at the bargaining table with the South African government. In order to ensure bargaining clout with the South African government, he needed assurance from heads of state in Europe and the United States that they would not lift the economic sanctions (Nelan, "Burden of Being a Superstar"). His European visits enjoyed great success. On the day following Mandela's speech to Congress, Kiener reported that the European

Community had done exactly what Mandela had urged and "decided today not to lift sanctions against South Africa, despite pressure from Prime Minister Margaret Thatcher of Britain to release them" (A11).

Mandela hoped to persuade the U.S. government to follow suit. He needed to convince the people of this country, particularly the lawmakers and influential and affluent European Americans who had campaigned for his release, that he was not a Communist, that the ANC was not primarily Communist, that the ANC was willing to use negotiation rather than violence, and that if and when majority rule came to South Africa, whites would not suffer undue harm and/or discrimination. He addressed all these issues in his speech to Congress.

If Mandela's rhetorical task with European Americans was primarily persuasive, allaying fears for the future and convincing them that the struggle still continued, his task with African Americans was primarily exhortative and epideictic. He needed to thank and praise those African Americans who had spearheaded and supported the movements for sanctions in this country, to reinforce unity and identification of African(-)s with the struggle in South Africa, and to encourage and consolidate their continued support. Perhaps his goals for African(-) audiences were fulfilled partly by his physical presence—his enactment of liberation—and his rhetoric performed a secondary function for most African(-)s around the world.

Mandela's speech must be considered not only in light of his personal history, events taking place around the world and in South Africa, and the purposes of his "world" tour, but also, and perhaps primarily for purposes of this analysis, in light of events happening in race relations in the United States. The African American community in the United States viewed itself in early 1990 as being in a state of peril.

Many African(-)s here saw the 1980s as a catastrophic decade. They, like the rest of the country, were feeling the early pangs of what would later be termed an economic depression. Ronald Reagan's policies, economic and otherwise, had produced what many saw as a return to near pre-civil rights conditions. The Supreme Court seemed finally to tilt in the direction of anti-civil rights lobbyists. President Bush had promised to veto the 1990 Civil Rights Act, and there was little optimism about its eventual passage.

Comparisons of the conditions of African(-)s in the United States and in South Africa occurred in many different forums. Louis Martin noted that "in one way or another, we are all in the same boat" ("Mandela Speaks" 24). The rhetoric of the 1960s referring to African Americans as colonized persons resurfaced, and individuals extended the label of "apartheid" to apply to the domestic situation, as did Benjamin Chavis, Jr.: "Racist apartheid should not be tolerated in South Africa nor in Alabama" (15).

Such comparisons were validated to some extent by the media. Television coverage of riots and police brutality in South Africa were shockingly reminiscent of similar scenes from the 1960s in Selma, Alabama, and other parts of the United States. Movies such as *Mandela* and *Biko*, and musicals like *Sarafina*, contributed to a view of South African liberation leaders as heroes and as leaders in a common movement.

At the same time the movements for civil rights and racial equality in the United States seemed to have lost their impetus. There was disagreement over strategies and methods of accomplishing their goals. The movement also lacked credible leadership. Writing in *Newsweek*, Mark Whitaker lamented that no African American had Mandela's stature: "The last one who did was Martin Luther King, Jr., by virtue not only of the gospel of justice he preached but the principled means he used to fight for it" (20).

African American communities remained riddled by ever-increasing poverty, declining public education, drug addiction, and violence (*Ebony*). The current issues of discrimination and equality did not lend themselves to dramatic physical acts and rhetoric as had the issues of the 1950s and 1960s. African Americans needed not a new issue to rally around, because the issues seemed relatively clear, but a visible, easily invoked issue that would allow public expression. Apartheid provided such an issue. According to Richard Lacayo, "It offered a focal point for the inchoate resentments felt of the greed and selfishness spawned during the Reagan years" (18). Anti-apartheid supporters in the United States lobbied and protested. Lacayo estimated that in the five years from TransAfrica's first act of civil disobedience at a South African consulate in 1984, 4,000 protesters went to jail, and "another 5,000 were arrested at South African consulates around the country" (18–19).

When Congress passed a law in 1986 that effectively imposed economic sanctions on South Africa (Walsh), and de Klerk's actions seemed to signal a change in direction, African(-)s around the country claimed the victory as theirs. Randall Robinson, executive director of TransAfrica, the Washington lobbying group representing the views of African Americans on Caribbean and African issues, was quoted in *Ebony* as saying, "So it is important to document here that the movement that helped bring about the sanctions was initiated, organized and thought through by Black Americans" (182). Andrew Kopkind noted,

In one sense, the struggle for majority power in South Africa did for African Americans what the struggle to establish a homeland in Israel did for American Jews after World War II. It provided a context for nationalist aspirations that became an integral part of a people's identity—even for people who had no intention of changing their passports. (77)

Mandela's presence in the United States signified to African Americans both a victory over oppression and a hope for the future. In an ironic reversal, people here hoped his visit would revitalize their domestic struggle as the words and actions of civil rights activists in this country had inspired liberation struggles all over the world. "We've forgotten how to do it. We don't have anybody who can get the adrenalin going like he does. I hope this will bring black Americans together. . . . His cause is our cause," said a Mrs. Clements, owner of a ribs shack in Atlanta (quoted in Wilkerson 8).

Mandela fulfilled many of their expectations. He looked as a hero should: tall, stately, and well dressed. He and his wife, Winnie, identified themselves with African Americans and with the struggles for equality in this country. At Yankee stadium Mandela declared himself a Yankee (Lacayo 16). In Harlem Winnie Mandela drew an even closer link between blacks in South Africa and the United States: "I greet you here in the Soweto of America, the capital of the Revolution throughout the world, Harlem" (Browne 45).

The people had found a hero who acknowledged that he was a part of them. Thus it followed clearly that they, the African(-)s, were his people too. Several other incidents that occurred during Mandela's New York visit fed African American perception of him as a championing hero. He showed himself to be undaunted in the face of white opposition and unintimidated by symbols of white power. When asked to address the issue of his continuing praise for leaders such as Yasir Arafat, Mu'ammar Khadafy, and Fidel Castro, which was infuriating members of the powerful U.S. Jewish community and the Cuban American community, he refused to back down, asserting that they had "supported our struggle to the hilt" (Martz et al. 19).

In an interview on the television news program *Nightline*, Mandela chided Ted Koppel, known for his persistent, even aggressive interviewing, and who could easily be taken as representative of the power of the European American–oriented U.S. news media, for inconsistency. *Newsweek* reported that he reduced Koppel to "stammering silence" and then remarked, "I don't know if I have paralyzed you" (Martz et al. 19). African(-)s would have recognized the one-upmanship in the verbal encounter in which, if your adversary has no retort, you win; and you draw attention to that victory by remarking on his or her silence. Mandela had symbolically and effectively triumphed over the European American establishment.

From this look at Mandela's personal history prior to his appearance before Congress, there emerges a picture of a skilled rhetor, whose training and personality combine to make his rhetoric highly persuasive, whose life experience embodies the principles he espouses, and who serves as an enactment of his ideology and for many of his listeners of the struggle itself. A speaker equally comfortable speaking with the poorly educated in Africa and elsewhere or with his professional colleagues around the world, Mandela not only represents the struggle for civil rights; for many African(-)s, he *is* the struggle and thus is eminently qualified to speak both for the struggle and for them.

Within this context, one can examine the significance to the African American community of Mandela's invitation to speak before Congress. No African American non-member of Congress had ever made an address to a joint session of Congress. No other African(-) non-head of state had ever been invited to speak before Congress. Not even such heroes of the civil rights movement as Dr. Martin Luther King, Jr., had addressed Congress. African(-)s were aware of the distinctive nature of the honor. In an editorial entitled "Mandela Speaks for All of Us" that appeared in *The Chicago Defender,* an African American newspaper, Martin noted that "to speak before a joint session of Congress is a tribute only a few persons have ever enjoyed. Tributes are given Mandela, not for his mission alone, but because of his nobility of character" (24).

When Mandela rose to speak to the U.S. Congress, he faced the fears of many European Americans outside of Congress who needed reassurance about his plans for a future South Africa. He also faced the hopes of African Americans inside and outside of Congress who depended on him to represent them appropriately in front of the European American establishment. As an editorial in the *New York Amsterdam News*, a prominent African American newspaper, put it:

> We have longed for a Black leader of epic proportions, and we have found him embodied in what Nelson Mandela means to us: the quiet strength, the nobility of bearing, the sincerity of purpose, and the courage of conviction that will deliver Black people everywhere in the world up from the slavery and oppression that has been so much a part of our history of oppression. Mr. Mandela has become the symbol that we will rally around until the last vestige of racism is driven out of South Africa as well as out of New York City.
>
> For Mr. Mandela, it is a burden to carry . . . having almost a billion persons of color throughout the Black Diaspora looking to him to lead us to a land that is not promised, but one that must be taken by our wit and by our will. South Africa's champion has accepted . . . the mantle of leadership with grace and resolve. We have willingly placed it upon [his] shoulders, for we understand, as Black Americans

subjected to the same kind of inhumanity that they have experienced in South Africa. . . . [W]e understand the implications of that with which we have charged him, and we stand ready to support his efforts with our money, our lives and our sacred honor. Welcome to New York Mr. Nelson Mandela. ("Welcome Mr. Mandela" 14)

Mandela's task was to receive a positive response to his requests for aid from the predominantly European American legislators while at the same time making it clear to his "constituency" in the United States as well as in South Africa that he was still the Black Pimpernel, unafraid and a little defiant of European Americans and their bureaucracy. That he fulfilled the expectations of both groups attests to his skill as a rhetor and to the excellence of the discourse that he presented.

TEXTUAL ANALYSIS

Mandela's speech surprised very few political analysts. As anticipated, he thanked the United States for its support, requested economic aid for the ANC, and made a plea to maintain economic sanctions against South Africa. I shall not explore the mainstream interpretation of Mandela's speech, although such an approach would undoubtedly yield interesting insights into his strategy and effectiveness for European(-) audiences.[6] Because this analysis concentrates on the alternative reading of this text, however, a brief overview of the traditional reading of the text and a summary of mainstream reaction to it will suffice for purposes of comparison.

Mandela presented himself to the audience as a representative of the people of South Africa come to present his case to a people who have a history of fighting for independence and against threats to civil liberty (8)[7] just as his people are currently fighting (7). His persona was that of a well-read intellectual presenting a well-reasoned and tightly constructed argument.

His audience was flattered by his characterization of them: Congress "desired" to convey a message, to listen to what it is Mandela's people want (4). Congress was "happy to support and encourage" the cause "as an eminent representative of democratic practice" (10).

---

[6]For an example of using dramatism as a contrast to more traditional argumentative analysis of African American rhetoric, see Karlyn Kohrs Campbell "The Rhetoric of Radical Black Nationalism: A Case in Self-Conscious Criticism," *Central States Speech Journal* 22 (Fall 1971): 151–160.

[7]Parenthetical citations are paragraph numbers.

Throughout, he carefully constructed a second persona[8] that was fair, humanitarian, on the side of justice, and willing to act.

He created identification through appeals to U.S. ideals and traditions; and he tied them to his appeal for democracy for his people. Most accounts of his speech clearly isolated his goals and highlighted his acknowledgment of debt to U.S. heroes. His "Americanness" as exemplified in the speech, combined with carefully worded direct statements in the speech such as "The ANC holds no ideological positions which dictate that it must adopt a policy of nationalization" (14), allayed the fears of his audience regarding the militancy and alleged Communism of the ANC and the future of a post-apartheid South Africa. Mandela was careful to balance his appeal for sanctions with an acknowledgment of "the admitted commitment of President de Klerk" (23), thus contributing to an image of himself, and by extension the ANC, as pro–United States, reasonable, and willing to negotiate.

The mainstream press touted Mandela's speech as a major success (Shea; Kiener). It accomplished most of his goals for his majority audience in both the long and the short run. First, Congress did not yield to pressure from de Klerk and from Bush to relax sanctions on South Africa. In fact, according to Carrol J. Doherty, "Mandela proved that the U.S. government, especially Congress, is still in his corner, at least on sanctions." Congress adopted a waiting strategy, placing the burden on the de Klerk government of proving that the movement to democracy was, to use Mandela's term, "irreversible." Mandela seemed also to have won the "bidding war for international public opinion" between him and de Klerk and thus to have garnered moral support for the ANC as it approached the bargaining table. This was evidenced at least partially in the lukewarm reception given de Klerk by Congress on his visit to Washington in September 1990 (3143).

Mandela's speech was least successful in its bid for financial support for the ANC. President Bush failed to commit himself to earmarking for the ANC any of the $10 million in aid to once-banned political organizations in South Africa. Immediately following Mandela's visit to Congress, however, there was a shift in position. The State Department backed away from its initial denial of the ANC's eligibility for such funds and instead noted that they would have to consult their lawyers in order to determine their eligibility. At the same time Mandela's tour successfully raised much of the needed funds from private contributions.[9]

---

[8]For an explanation of the "second persona," see Edwin Black, "The Second Persona," *Quarterly Journal of Speech* 56 (1970): 109–119.

[9]Congressional reaction to the issues raised in Mandela's speech is discussed in Michael P. Shea, "Capitol Hill Reaffirms Support for Mandela and Sanctions," *Congressional Quarterly Weekly Report* 48 (30 June 1990): 2082–2084.

To explain the significance of the speech for African American audiences that, for the most part, already shared Mandela's views on sanctions, aid to the ANC, and the future of South Africa, the text must be reexamined for instances of polysemy, areas in which it might, in some sense, "Signify" on itself—that is, say or implicate something other than what it seemed to be saying to the predominantly European American audience.

AFRICAN AMERICAN ANALYSIS

Mandela began his speech with the customary acknowledgments of dignitaries present. Having completed the formalities, his opening paragraphs set the tone for the rest of his speech and firmly establish the possibility for a dual interpretation. He began with the "meteor"-like transience of each individual on the "human stage": "Even the golden lads and lasses as much as the chimney sweepers" are here only briefly (2). The Shakespearean allusion might conceivably be lost to most African Americans on the street, and perhaps even the image of a chimney sweep would seem distant; however, the contrasting color imagery—blonde versus black—would not. Thus, both European and African Americans pass swiftly off the human stage. What remains then? "After them all, they leave the people" (2). The phrase "the people," which occurred repeatedly, and the image it invokes would resonate with African American audiences particularly as the people are characterized by Mandela: "enduring, multiplying, permanent" (2).

Mandela then presented the first aspect of the persona that he established for himself, "not as pretenders to greatness, but as a particle of a people . . . noble and heroic . . . enduring, multiplying, permanent" (3). It was very easy to make a step from a particle of the South African people to a particle of all African(-) peoples, because it is under that rubric more than any other that African(-) peoples see themselves as enduring and permanent. This leap was facilitated because it was not until the ninth paragraph of his address that Mandela specifically referred to South Africa by name, and then it was a reference to a geographical locality only. He most frequently used "South Africa" in its adjectival form as a descriptor of the economy or society, thus distancing his plea from the South African state, which also made his constituency more easily generalizable. Because he never referred to South Africa, the first 11 paragraphs of the address could quite easily be taken out of context to refer to the plight of many black peoples on the African continent and in the Diaspora.

Mandela's persona developed further in his statement of purpose: "We have come here to tell you, and through you, your own people, . . . of the troubles and trials, the fond hopes and aspirations, of the people from whom we originate" (4). Clearly, he established himself as a representative of a people.

Throughout his address, he chose to use the pronoun "we" in referring to himself, e.g., "we have come to Washington," thus emphasizing and strengthening his persona as representative of "the people."[10] In his use of the royal "we" and the clear parallelism between his people and the people represented by the Congress or the president, he also conveyed a sense of himself as a symbolic head of state, an impression that was bolstered by his appearance before the Congress.

The vagueness of his definition of his constituency as "the people from whom we originate" and his position as the first African(-) non-head of state to address the predominantly European American Congress with its European American head of state lend further credence to a reading of his persona as representative of a constituency that includes African Americans. His purpose then, as interpreted from the alternate perspective, was to inform Congress and the president of the troubles, trials, hopes, and aspirations of his people, the African(-)s.

He created a persona for his audience partially through comparison with his constituency and through the tone of the discourse. His constituency was "noble and heroic," and his auditors' constituency was "equally" so (4). In addition, by stating the nature of his constituency first and comparing that of his auditors to it, he gave primacy to "the people" and reversed the usual method of cross-racial comparison. As noted earlier, he characterized his audience as supportive of his people and of the struggle.

The rhetor's tone conveyed great respect for this constructed audience. Their "history demands . . . respect and candor" and prohibits dissembling (8). The language and the grammatical constructions used gave the speech a formal and weighty nature appropriate to the occasion and to the demonstrations of respect for the audience and the occasion. Sentences tended to be long and to be separated into phrases, which required that the speech be read aloud at a dignified stately pace. In addition to respect, Mandela's persona displayed grati-

---

[10]This could be considered a reference to his wife, Winnie, who accompanied him on his tour, although there is no mention of her presence in any of the accounts of the speech to Congress. A review of his writings and speeches surrounding his release reveals a very careful consistent use of "we" as opposed to "I" when he speaks for the ANC or for the South African people. For examples of rhetoric in which he uses both, see Nelson Mandela, "A Document to Create a Climate of Understanding" and "Address to Rally in Cape Town 11 February 1990," *The Struggle Is My Life,* 208–213 and 214–217.

tude for the part that this audience has played in supporting the "victory of democracy over tyranny" (29).

The African American auditor heard this characterization of the audience as ironic, if not satirical, given the civil rights record of the Reagan and Bush administrations and the difficulties entailed in persuading the United States to take a firm stand on the issue of sanctions for South Africa (Walsh). Mandela used terms that in common usage might be seen as hyperbolic: "your kind and moving invitation" (4), "people whom we know to be noble and heroic" (3), "your humane purposes" (4), and so forth. Such usage by an African American might denote sarcastic overkill, drawing attention through exaggeration to the absence or minimal presence of praiseworthy action or sentiment.[11]

The supporting material used by Mandela in this speech drew heavily on two sources: the experience of the people and U.S. history. He referred specifically to the American Revolution and the civil rights movement. Notably, he listed the great men of the historical movements as moving him to act as they acted. Thus he shared a little of their glory and placed himself squarely within a tradition respected by African Americans. The African American leaders he mentioned have widespread support and, with perhaps the exception of Marcus Garvey, create little dissension in the African American community as to their heroic status. Several times in the discourse he referred to people's right to "life, liberty and the pursuit of happiness," thus invoking the Declaration of Independence (31).

Much of the polysemy of the speech rested on Mandela's invocation of U.S. *culturetypes,* or words and images "sacred" to U.S. society. The ideals these terms embody strongly influenced the positive mainstream reaction to the speech. Phrases such as "equality, liberty and the pursuit of happiness" (6) and "fundamental human rights" (6) conjure up, for many European Americans, pride in a nation that has achieved these goals while nations such as South Africa have not. These phrases are more likely to remind African(-)s living in the United States of what has yet to be achieved, of Martin Luther King, Jr.'s metaphor of the Declaration of Independence as a "promissory note" on which the nation had "defaulted" (217).

Mandela's use of ideographs such as "justice" (19, 35), "liberty" (6, 19, 31, 34), and "democracy" (5, 10, 16, 29, 30, 32), and phrases such as "nonracial democracy" (10) and "citizens of the world" (19), whose

---

[11]I hesitate to attribute it to the discourse given the cultural and rhetorical background of the rhetor. I note it rather as significant to an African American perspective. See, however, Mitchell-Kernan and Smitherman for discussion of the use of exaggeration or counterfactual information in Signifyin(g).

definitions are imprecise, allowed members of his audience to hear in sections of his rhetoric what they wanted to hear or what they were conditioned by their culture to hear.

Perhaps most significant to an alternate reading of the text were the allusions and images familiar to veterans of the civil rights movement and their students. His descriptions and enumerations of the people's suffering and trials formed a moving means of support by example with which most veterans of the civil rights movement could identify. Certain phrases, which seemed to echo those of Martin Luther King, Jr., and others, would have particular poignancy for African Americans, although they would resonate positively for all audience members who recognized them. As an example, consider these passages from Dr. King's most quoted speech:

> I am not unmindful that some of you have come here out of excessive trials and tribulations. Some of you have come fresh from narrow jail cells. Some of you have come from areas where your quest for freedom left you battered by the storms of persecution and staggered by the winds of police brutality. . . .
>
> This note was a promise that all men, yes, black men as well as white men, would be granted the unalienable rights of life, liberty and the pursuit of happiness . . . I have a dream that one day . . . a state sweltering with the heat of injustice . . . will be transformed into an oasis of freedom and justice. (219)

Many of these images appear in Mandela's address. He came to talk of the "troubles and trials" (4) of his people, echoing the alliteration of King's "trials and tribulations." Three times during the speech he invoked the image of those jailed or having been in jail (9, 30, 33), using it to build the metaphor of "the larger prison that is apartheid South Africa." He stated, "It is an outcome for which many of us went to prison, for which many have died in police cells, on the gallows, in our towns and villages and in the countries of Southern Africa" (9). Although in this instance he made a direct reference to the countries of Southern Africa, the reference is preceded by a list of effects familiar to an audience that had experienced similar incidents in the United States either personally or vicariously through the media, and who believed that in this country, too, people endured these atrocities in pursuit of a similar outcome.

The image of police or state brutality occurred throughout the speech. For example, he noted that his people, his country,

> [thirst] for a situation where those who are entitled by law to carry arms, as the forces of national security and law and order, will not turn their weapons against the citizens simply because the citizens

assert that equality, liberty and the pursuit of happiness are fundamental human rights which are not only inalienable but must, if
necessary, be defended with weapons of war. (6)

He invoked an oasis image, calling for the transformation of South African society "into an oasis of good race relations, where the black
shall to the white be sister and brother" (19). The power of these images lies not only in their historical resonance but also in their significance for the current view of civil rights in this country. The situation
that he finds intolerable and that he requested Congress to help
change, although specifically located in South Africa, would sound to
his African American audience as also describing their situation in the
United States. This was demonstrated graphically as he talked in New
York City, where his descriptions of the economic and educational
situation in South Africa were met with shouts of "Same here, same
here!" (Lacayo 14).

The apparent similarities between the two situations weakens the
strongest objection to the alternate reading of the text, the view that
the specific references to South Africa do not translate into the African
American experience. If seen as a literal analogy for the situation of
African Americans in the United States, Mandela's statements on the
need for an economic solution "able to address the needs of all the
people of our country, that can provide food, houses, education,
health services, social security and everything that makes human life
human, that makes life joyful and not a protracted encounter with
hopelessness and despair" (12), can be accepted as a statement representing the voice of the people. His request for help that does not
leave the helped in a "relationship of subservient dependency and
fawning gratitude" (18), his assertion that "we still have a struggle on
our hands" (26), and his claim that "We have yet to arrive at the point
where we can say that South Africa is set on an irreversible course
leading to its transportation into a united, democratic, and nonracial
country" (27), achieve greater force and meaning when seen in a context wider than South Africa.

Mandela's conclusion strongly reinforces this sense as it brings together with specifics related to the South African situation a citation
from Thomas Jefferson, an image of a "united nation of black and
white people"(34), and probably the most famous image of the civil
rights movement, a mixed mass of protesters who "keep our arms
locked together so that we form a solid phalanx against racism to ensure that the day comes now" (35).

Thus, at the points at which the discourse seems most strongly
South African and therefore less African(-), its imagery invokes a
tradition based in the U.S. civil rights movement and embraced by Af-
rican(-) revolutionary struggles around the world. This sense of

interconnectedness allowed the sections of the speech that are specific to the South African situation to be seen as analogic or metaphorical representations of the U.S. situation.

CONCLUSION

This analysis of Nelson Mandela's speech to the U.S. Congress shows the ways in which the text lends itself to interpretation as a representative voice for African Americans in front of "the white man." Through its formal tone, its persona of official representative of the people, its tendency to use general terms in describing the constituency for whom he speaks, its invocation and echoing of language and images familiar to Americans as part of the civil rights movement, and its mirroring of negative conditions facing current African American auditors, it becomes a rallying cry for African American nationalism and a continuation of the U.S. civil rights movement. Even overt references to South Africa and its situation lend themselves to such a reading if these are understood as analogies to a parallel situation in the United States. The text has surprising consistency and uniformity when viewed as a powerful new discourse in the continuing rhetoric of the U.S. civil rights struggle and as an example of the polysemous nature of intercultural and ambicultural rhetoric.

No attempt has been made to assert Mandela's intent to present an ambicultural text. Rather, I choose to emphasize his ability to do so. It is often problematic for critics to assert intent, especially when addressing issues of polysemy and other ambicultural characteristics. Because these characteristics are largely functions of audience interpretation, it is not necessary to assert intent in order for a text to possess them. Thus it would be presumptuous of me to claim that Mandela "intended" his speech to signify on itself and perhaps also on the United States Congress.

At the same time, however, given the prevalence of variations of Signifyin(g) throughout the African(-) experience (see Gates and Abrahams for examples in African and Caribbean context), Mandela's knowledge of the African American situation, his skill as a rhetor, and his proven abilities in intercultural rhetoric, I find it difficult to believe that Mandela was unaware of the potential and likelihood of his text being interpreted in the manner given here. Accordingly, it would not be unreasonable to suggest that his creation of such a text could be intentional.

In addition, this essay in no way suggests that all African Americans would choose to interpret Mandela's speech to the U.S. Congress in this way. Rather, this essay asserts first that both Nelson Mandela and his African American audience were capable of, and stood to gain by, viewing this speech as an ambicultural text and decoding it accordingly; and second, a critical reading of the text from this perspective supports a view of the speech as an example of ambicultural rhetoric.

This analysis of the text highlights a need for further research into the nature of ambicultural texts and also for systematic examination of audiences' ability to decode texts in ambicultural ways, and of the frequency with which they choose to do so.

WORKS CITED

Abrahams, Roger. *Deep Down in the Jungle . . . Negro Narrative Folklore from the Streets of Philadelphia.* Chicago: Aldine, 1970.

Aneckwe, Simon. "Harlem Rocks with Mandela." *New York Amsterdam News* 30 June 1990: 1, 37, 45.

Black, Edwin. "The Second Persona." *Quarterly Journal of Speech* 56 (1970): 109–119.

Brockriede, Wayne, and Robert L. Scott. "Stokely Carmichael: Two Speeches on Black Power." *Central States Speech Journal* 19 (1968): 3–13.

Browne, J. Zamgba. "Young, Old Greet Mandela at Harlem's Africa Square." *New Amsterdam News* 30 June 1990: 3, 45.

Campbell, Karlyn Kohrs. "The Rhetoric of Radical Black Nationalism: A Case in Self-Conscious Criticism." *Central States Speech Journal* 22 (1971): 151–160.

Chavis, Benjamin, Jr. "Let's Fight America's Apartheid in Alabama." *New York Amsterdam News* 9 June 1990: 15.

Condit, Celeste M. "The Rhetorical Limits of Polysemy." *Critical Studies in Mass Communication* 6 (1989): 103–122.

Congressional Record—House of Representatives. Tuesday 26 June 1990: H4137–4138.

Doherty, Carrol J. "De Klerk, Cristiani Receive Wary Welcome on the Hill." *Congressional Quarterly Weekly Report* 48 (29 Sept. 1990): 3143.

Ebony. 45th Anniversary Issue 46 (November 1990).

Gates, Henry Louis, Jr. *The Signifying Monkey: A Theory of African American Literary Criticism.* New York: Oxford University Press, 1988.

"Guess Who's Coming to Dinner." *Nation* 251 (16/23 July 1990): 76.

Harwood, Ronald. *Mandela.* New York: New American Library, 1987.

Holt, Grace Sims. " 'Inversion' in Black Communication." *Rappin' and Stylin' Out: Communication in Urban Black America.* Ed. Thomas Kochman. Chicago: University of Illinois Press, 1972. 152–159.

Hoopes, David, and Margaret D. Pusch. "Definition of Terms." *Multicultural Education: A Cross-Cultural Training Approach.* Ed. Margaret D. Pusch. Yarmouth, ME: Intercultural Press, 1979. 2–8.

"How African Americans Helped Free Nelson Mandela." *Ebony* 45 (May 1990): 182.

Kiener, John. "Mandela Invokes Struggles of U.S., Rousing Congress." *New York Times* 27 June 1991: A11.

King, Martin Luther, Jr. "I Have a Dream." *Testament of Hope*. Ed. James M. Washington. San Francisco: Harper, 1986. 217–220.

Kochman, Thomas. *Black and White Styles in Conflict*. Chicago: University of Chicago Press, 1981.

———, ed. *Rappin' and Stylin' Out: Communication in Urban Black America*. Chicago: University of Illinois Press, 1972.

Kopkind, Andrew. "Out of Africa." *Nation* 251 (16/23 July 1990): 76–77.

Lacayo, Richard. "A Hero's Welcome." *Time* 2 July 1990: 14–20.

Lake, Randall. "Enacting Red Power: The Consummatory Function in Native American Protest Rhetoric." *Quarterly Journal of Speech* 69 (1983): 127–142.

Lucaites, John Louis, and Celeste Michelle Condit. "Reconstructing Equality: Culturetypal and Counter-Cultural Rhetorics in the Martyred Black Vision." *Communication Monographs* 57 (March 1990): 5–24.

Mandela, Nelson. "Address to Congress." *Congressional Record—House of Representatives*. Tuesday 26 June 1990: H4136–4138.

———. "Apartheid Has No Future: Africa Is Ours." *Vital Speeches of the Day* 56 (1 March 1990): 295–297.

———. "Enough Is Enough." Address to the United Nations. *The City Sun* 27 June–3 July 1990: 33–34.

———. *I Am Prepared to Die*. London: International Defence and Aid Fund for Southern Africa, 1979.

———. *The Struggle Is My Life*. London: International Defence and Aid Fund for Southern Africa, 1986.

Mandela, Winnie. *Part of My Soul Went with Him*. London: W. W. Norton, 1984.

Martin, Louis. "Mandela Speaks for All of Us." *Chicago Defender* 23 June 1990: 24.

Martz, Larry, et al. "Mandela." *Newsweek* 2 July 1990: 19.

McCartan, Greg, ed. *Nelson Mandela's Speeches 1990: "Intensify the Struggle to Abolish Apartheid."* New York: Pathfinder Press, 1990.

McGee, Michael Calvin. "The 'Ideograph': A Link Between Rhetoric and Ideology." *Quarterly Journal of Speech* 66 (Feb. 1980): 1–16.

Meer, Fatima. *Higher Than Hope: A Biography of Nelson Mandela*. London: Hamish Hamilton, 1988.

Mitchell-Kernan, Claudia. "Signifying as a Form of Verbal Art." *Mother Wit from the Laughing Barrel*. Ed. Alan Dundes. Englewood Cliffs, NJ: Prentice Hall, 1973. 318–319.

Nelan, Bruce W. "The Burden of Being a Superstar." *Time* 25 June 1990: 20–21.

Petersen, Debra L. "President Corazón Aquiño's Official Working Visit to the United States, September 15–23, 1986: A Case Study in Intercultural Rhetoric." Diss. University of Minnesota, 1991.

Philipsen, Gerry. "Mayor Daley's Council Speech: A Cultural Analysis." *Quarterly Journal of Speech* 72 (1986): 247–260.

Robinson, Randall. "De Klerk Is No Hero to Me." *New York Times* 25 Sept. 1990: A27.

Scott, Robert L., and Wayne Brockriede. *The Rhetoric of Black Power.* New York: Harper and Row, 1969.

Shea, Michael P. "Capitol Hill Reaffirms Support for Mandela and Sanctions." *Congressional Quarterly Weekly Report* 48 (30 June 1990): 2082–2084.

Smith, Arthur L. *Rhetoric of Black Revolution.* Boston: Allyn & Bacon, 1969.

Smith, Craig R. "The Republican Keynote Address of 1968: Adaptive Rhetoric for Multiple Audiences." *Western Speech* 39 (Winter 1975): 32–39.

Smitherman, Geneva. *Talkin' and Testifyin'.* Detroit: Wayne State University Press, 1986.

Thompson, Wayne N. "Barbara Jordan's Keynote Address: Fulfilling Dual and Conflicting Purposes." *Central States Speech Journal* 30 (Fall 1979): 271–277.

Walsh, Edward. "Sanctions Imposed on S. Africa as Senate Overrides Veto, 78–21." *Washington Post* 3 Oct. 1986: A1–2.

"Welcome Mr. Mandela." Editorial. *New York Amsterdam News* 23 June 1990: 14–22.

Whitaker, Mark. "Hailing a Hero—and Looking for Our Own." *Newsweek* 2 July 1990: 20.

Wilkerson, Isabel. "After Weeping for Mandela, Many Prepare to Savor Visit." *New York Times* 17 June 1990: 8.

RONALD REAGAN

Address to the 1988 Republican National Convention

Near the end of his second term as president, Ronald Reagan addressed the Republican National Convention in New Orleans. He used the occasion to enumerate the successes of his administration and the Republican party and to rally support for the party's 1988 presidential nominee, George Bush. The text is from The New York Times, *16 August 1988, p. A20.*

1   Madam Chairman, delegates to the convention and fellow citizens, thank you for that warm and generous welcome. Nancy and I have been enjoying the finest of Southern hospitality since we arrived here yesterday—and, believe me, after that reception, I don't think the "Big Easy" has ever been bigger than it is tonight. And with all due respect to Cajun cuisine—cooking—and New Orleans jazz, nothing could be hotter than the spirit of the delegates in this hall— except maybe a victory celebration on November 8th.

2   In that spirit, in that spirit, I think we can be forgiven if we give ourselves a little pat on the back for having made "Republican" a proud word once again and America a proud nation again. Nancy and I are so honored to be your guests tonight, to share a little of your special time. And we thank you.

3   Now, I want to invoke executive privilege to talk for a moment about a very special lady who has been selfless, not just for our party, but for the entire nation. She is a strong, courageous, and compassionate woman. And wherever she's gone, here in the U.S. as well as abroad—whether with young or old, whether comforting the grieving or supporting the youngsters who are fighting the scourge of drugs—she makes us proud.

4   I've been proud of her for a long time, but never more so than in these last eight years. With your tribute to Nancy today, you warmed my heart as well as hers. And believe me, she deserved your tribute, and I am deeply grateful to you for what you have done.

5   When people tell me that I became president on January 20th, 1981, I feel I have to correct them. You don't become president of the United States. You are given temporary custody of an institution called the presidency, which belongs to our people.

6   Having temporary custody of this office has been for me a sacred trust and an honor beyond words or measure. That trust began with many of you in this room many conventions ago.

7   Many's the time that I've said a prayer of thanks to all Americans who placed this trust in my hands, and tonight, please accept again our heartfelt gratitude, Nancy's and mine, for this special time that you've given in our lives.

8   Just a moment ago, you multiplied the honor with a moving tribute. Being only human, there's a part of me that would like to take credit for what we've achieved.

9   But tonight, before we do anything else, let us remember, that tribute really belongs to the 245 million citizens who make up the greatest and the first three words in our Constitution: We the people.

10   It is the American people who endured the great challenge of lifting us from the depths of national calamity, renewing our mighty economic strength and leading the way to restoring our respect in the world. They are an extraordinary breed we call Americans.

11   So if there's any salute deserved tonight—it's to the heroes everywhere in this land who make up the doers, the dreamers, and the life-builders without which our glorious experiment in democracy would have failed.

12   So, this convention brings back so many memories to a fellow like me. I can still remember my first Republican convention. Abraham Lincoln giving a speech that sent tingles down my spine. No, I have to confess, I wasn't actually there. The truth is, way back then I belonged to the other party.

13   But surely we can remember another convention. Eight years ago, we gathered in Detroit in a troubled time for our beloved country.

14   And we gathered solemnly to share our dreams. And when I look back, I wonder if we dared be so bold to take on those burdens. But in that same city of Detroit, when the 20th century was only in its second year, another great Republican, Teddy Roosevelt, told Americans not to hold back from dangers ahead but to rejoice. "Our hearts lifted with the faith that to us and to our children, it shall be given to make this Republic the mightiest among the peoples of mankind," Teddy said those years ago.

15   In 1980, we needed every bit of that kind of faith.

16   That year, it was our dream that together we could rescue America and make a new beginning—to create anew that shining city on a hill.

17   The dream we shared was to reclaim our government, to transform it from one that was consuming our prosperity into one that would get out of the way of those who created prosperity.

18   It was a dream of again making our nation strong enough to preserve world peace and freedom and to recapture our national destiny.

19   We made a determination that our dream would not be built on a foundation of sand—something called "Trust Me Government"—but we would trust instead, the American spirit.

20   And, yes, we were unashamed in believing that this dream was driven by a community of shared values of family, work, neighborhood, peace and freedom.

21   And on the night of July 17th, 1980, we left with a mutual pledge to conduct a national crusade to make America great again. We had faith, because the heroes in our midst had never failed us before.

22   Tom Paine knew what these Americans with character of steel could do when he wrote, "The harder the conflict, the more glorious the triumph."

23   And my fellow citizens, while our triumph is not yet complete, the road has been glorious, indeed.

24   Eight years ago, we met at a time when America was in economic chaos, and today we meet in a time of economic promise. We met then in international distress and today with global hope.

25 Now, I think we can be forgiven if we engage in a little review of that history tonight. As the saying goes, "Just a friendly reminder."

26 I've been doing a little remembering of my own because of all the inflated rhetoric by our friends in Atlanta last month. But then, inflation is their specialty.

27 Before we came to Washington, Americans had just suffered the two worst back-to-back years of inflation in 60 years. Those are the facts. And as John Adams said, "Facts are stubborn things."

28 Interest rates had jumped to over 21 percent—the highest in 120 years—more than doubling the average monthly mortgage payments for working families, our families. When they sat around the kitchen table, it was not to plan summer vacations, it was to plan economic survival.

29 Facts are stubborn things.

30 Industrial production was down, and productivity was down for two consecutive years.

31 The average weekly wage plunged 9 percent. The median family income fell $5\frac{1}{2}$ percent.

32 Facts are stubborn things.

33 Our friends on the other side had actually passed the single highest tax bill in the 200-year history of the United States. Auto loans, because of their policies, went up to 17 percent—so our great factories began shutting down. Fuel costs jumped through the atmosphere, more than doubling. Then people waited in gas lines as well as unemployment lines.

34 Facts are stupid things—stubborn things, I should say.

35 And then there was the misery index. That was an election year gimmick they designed for the 1976 campaign: They added the unemployment and inflation rates. And it came to 13.4 percent in 1976, and they declared that our candidate, Jerry Ford, had no right to seek reelection with that kind of misery index. But four years later, in the 1980 campaign, they didn't mention the misery index. Do you suppose it was because it was no longer 13.4 percent? In those four years it had become almost 21 percent.

36 And last month, in Atlanta at their convention, there was again no mention of the misery index. Why? Because right now, it's less than 9.2 percent.

37 Facts—facts are stubborn things.

38   When we met in Detroit in that summer of 1980, it was a summer of discontent for America around the world. Our national defense had been so weakened, the Soviet Union had begun to engage in reckless aggression, including the invasion and occupation of Afghanistan. The U.S. response to that was to forbid our athletes to participate in the 1980 Olympics and to try to pull the rug out from under our farmers with a grain and soybean embargo.

39   And in those years, on any given day, we had military aircraft that couldn't fly for lack of spare parts, and ships that couldn't leave port for the same reason or for lack of a crew. Our embassy in Pakistan was burned to the ground, and the one in Iran was stormed and occupied with all Americans taken as hostages. The world began to question the constancy and resolve of the United States. Our leaders answered, not that there was something wrong with our government, but that our people were at fault because of some malaise.

40   Well, facts are stubborn things.

41   When our friends last month talked of unemployment, despair, hopelessness, economic weakness, I wondered why on Earth they were talking about 1978 instead of 1988.

42   And now, now we hear talk that it's time for a change. Well, ladies and gentlemen, another friendly reminder: We are the change.

43   We rolled up our sleeves and went to work in January of 1981. We focused on hope, not despair. We challenged the failed policies of the past, because we believed that a society is great, not because of promises made by its government, but only because of progress made by its people. And that was our change.

44   We said something shocking. Taxes ought to be reduced, not raised. We cut the tax rates for the working folks of America. We indexed taxes and that stopped the bracket creep which kicked average wage-earners into higher tax brackets when they had only received a cost-of-living pay raise. And we initiated reform of the unfairness in our tax system.

45   And what do you know—the top 5 percent of earners are paying a higher percentage of the total tax revenue at the lower rates than they ever had before, and millions of earners at the bottom of the scale have been freed from paying any income tax at all.

46   That was our change.

47   So together we pulled out of a tailspin and created $17\frac{1}{2}$ million good jobs. That's more than a quarter of a million jobs a month, every month, for 68 consecutive months. America is working again.

And just since our 1984 convention, we have created over 11 million of those new jobs. Now, just why would our friends on the other side want to change that? Why do they think putting you out of work is better than putting you to work?

48   New homes are being built. New car sales reached record levels. Exports are starting to climb again. Factory capacity is approaching maximum use. You know, I've noticed they don't call it "Reaganomics" any more.

49   As for inflation—well, that, too, has changed. We changed it from the time it hit 18 percent in 1980, down to between $3\frac{1}{2}$ and 4 percent. Interest rates are less than half of what they were. In fact, in fact, nearly half of all mortgages taken out on family homes in 1986 and more than a third of those in 1987 were actually old loans being refinanced at the new lower rates. Young families have finally been able to get some relief.

50   These, too, were our changes:

51   We rebuilt our armed forces. We liberated Grenada from the Communists and helped return that island to democracy. We struck a firm blow against Libyan terrorism. We've seen the growth of democracy in 90 percent of Latin America. The Soviets have begun to pull out of Afghanistan. The bloody Iran–Iraq war is coming to an end. And for the first time in eight years, we—we have the prospects of peace in Southwest Africa and the removal of Cuban and other foreign forces from that region. And in the 2,765 days of our administration, not one inch of ground has fallen to the Communists.

52   Today—today—thank you—today—today we have the first treaty in world history to eliminate an entire class of U.S. and Soviet nuclear missiles. We are working on the Strategic Defense Initiative to defend ourselves and our allies against nuclear terror, and American and Soviet relations are the best they've been since World War II.

53   And virtually all this change occurred, and continues to occur, in spite of the resistance of those liberal elites who loudly proclaim that it's time for a change. They resisted our defense buildup, they resisted our tax cuts, they resisted cutting the fat out of government and they resisted our appointments of judges committed to the law and the Constitution.

54   And it's time for some more straight talk. This time it's about the budget deficit. Yes, it's much too high. But the president doesn't vote for the budget, and the president can't spend a dime. Only the Congress can do that. They blame, they blame the defense increases for the deficit, yet defense spending today, in real dollars, is almost exactly what it was six years ago. In a six-year period, Congress cut defense spending authority by over $125 billion. And for every one-dollar reduction in defense outlays, they added two dollars to domestic spending. Now if they had passed my first budget, my first spending plan, in 1982, the cumulative outlays in deficits would have been $207 billion lower by 1986.

55   Every—every single year I've been in office, I have supported and called for a balanced budget amendment to the Constitution, and the liberals have said no every year. I called for the line-item veto, which 43 governors have, to cut fat in the budget, and the liberals have said no. Every year, I've attempted to limit their wild spending sprees, and they've said no.

56   They would have us believe that runaway budget deficits began in 1981, when we took office. Well, let me tell you something. The fact is, when they began their war on poverty in the middle '60s, from 1965 through 1980—in just those 15 years—the budgets increased to five times what they had been, and the deficits went up to 52 times what they had been before their war on poverty. Now, now don't we know that, if they were elected—they're elected, their answer will be the one they have relied on in the past—and that is higher taxes?

57   The other party has controlled—the other party has controlled the House of Representatives for 52 out of the last 56 years. They've controlled the Senate also for 46 of those years. Where we really need a change is to elect Republican majorities in both houses. Then—and then George Bush can have a team that will protect your tax cuts, keep America strong, hold down inflation and interest rates, appoint judges to preserve your rights, and, yes, reduce the budget deficit.

58   Early in the first term, we set out to reduce federal regulations that had been imposed on the people, on business, and on local and state governments. Today, I'm proud to say, that we have eliminated so many unnecessary regulations that government-required paperwork imposed on citizens, businesses, and other levels of government has been reduced by an estimated 600 million man-hours a year.

59   And George was there. No—no. You haven't heard it all yet. George Bush headed up that task force that eliminated those regulations.

60   In 1980 and before, it took seven weeks to get a Social Security card. Now it takes 10 days. It only takes 10 days to get a passport; it used to take 43 days. It took 75 days to get an export license; now it's only 17 days, and for some countries, only 5. It took over 100 days to process a claim for a Department of Housing and Urban Development Title I loan—100 days. It now takes less than one-fourth of that—22 days.

61   I think these specifics suggest there is a new level of competent management in the departments of our government. George played a major role in everything that we have accomplished in these eight years.

62   Now, early on, we had a foreign policy problem. Our NATO allies were under the threat of Soviet intermediate-range missiles, and NATO had no equivalent deterrent. Our effort to provide a deterrent—Pershing and ground-launched cruise missiles on the NATO line—resulted in political problems for our NATO allies. There was objection on the part of many of their people to the deployment of our missiles. George represented us in Brussels with the heads of the NATO countries, and they agreed, when he finished, to take the missiles. This subsequently persuaded the Soviets to sign the I.N.F. Treaty and begin removing their SS-20's.

63   None of our achievements happened by accident, but only because we overcame liberal opposition to put our programs in place. And without George Bush to build on those policies, everything we've achieved will be at risk. All the work, sacrifice, and effort of the American people could end in the very same disaster that we inherited in 1981.

64   Because I feel so strongly about the work that must continue and the need to protect our gains for the American family and for national security, I want to share with you the qualities we should seek in the next President.

65   We need someone who's big enough and experienced enough to handle tough and demanding negotiations with Mr. Gorbachev— because this is no time to gamble with on-the-job training. We need someone who's prepared to be president and who has the commitment to stand up for you against massive new taxes and who will keep alive the hope and promise that keeps our economy strong.

66   It'll take someone who has seen this office from the inside, who senses the danger points, will be cool under fire and knows the range of answers when the tough questions come.

67   Well, that's the George Bush that I've seen up close when the staff and cabinet members have closed the door and when the two of us are alone. Someone who's not afraid to speak his mind and who can cut to the core of an issue. Someone who never runs away from a fight, never backs away from his beliefs and never makes excuses.

68   This office is not mine to give—only you, the people, can do that. But I love America too much and care too much about where we will be in the next few years. I care that we give custody of this office to someone who will build on our changes, not retreat to the past. Someone who will continue the change all of us fought for. To preserve what we have and not risk losing it all—America needs George Bush—and Barbara Bush as first lady.

69   With George Bush I'll know, as we approach the new millennium, our children will have a future secure with a nation at peace and protected against aggression; we'll have a prosperity that spreads the blessings of our abundance and opportunity across all America; we'll have safe and active neighborhoods; drug-free schools that send our children soaring in the atmosphere of great ideas and deep values; and a nation confidently willing to take its leadership into the uncharted reaches of a new age.

70   So, George, I'm in your corner. I'm ready to volunteer a—I'm ready to volunteer a little advice now and then, and offer a pointer or two on strategy, if asked. I'll help keep the facts straight or just stand back and cheer. But George, just one personal request: Go out there and win one for the Gipper.

71   As you can imagine—as you can imagine, I'm sorely tempted to spend the rest of this evening telling the truth about our friends who met in Atlanta—but, then, why should I have all the fun.

72   So, for the next few moments, let's talk about the future.

73   This is the last Republican convention I will address as president. Maybe you'll see your way to inviting me back sometime.

74   But like so many of us, as I said earlier, I started out in the other party. But 40 years ago, I cast my last vote as a Democrat. It was a—it was a party in which Franklin Delano Roosevelt promised the return of power to the states. It was a party where Harry Truman committed a strong and resolute America to preserving freedom. F.D.R. had run on a platform of eliminating useless boards and commissions and returning autonomy and authority to local governments and to the states.

75   That party changed—and it will never be the same. They left me; I didn't leave them.

76   So, it was our Republican party that gave me a political home. When I signed up for the duty, I didn't have to check my principles at the door. And I soon found out that the desire for victory did not overcome our devotion to ideals.

77   And what ideals those have been.

78   Our party speaks for human freedom—for the sweep of liberties that are at the core of our existence. We do not shirk from our duties to preserve freedom so it can unfold across the world for yearning millions.

79   We believe that lasting peace comes only through strength and not through the goodwill of our adversaries.

80   We have a healthy skepticism of government—checking its excesses at the same time we're willing to harness its energy when it helps improve the lives of our citizens.

81   We have pretty strong notions that higher tax receipts are no inherent right of the federal government. We don't think that inflation and high interest rates show compassion for the poor, the young, and the elderly.

82   We respect the values that bind us together as families and as a nation.

83   For our children—we don't think it's wrong to have them committed to pledging each day to the "one nation, under God, indivisible, with liberty and justice for all."

84   And—and we have so many requirements in their classrooms, why can't we at least have one thing that is voluntary—and that is allow our kids to repair quietly to their faith to say a prayer to start the day as Congress does.

85   And for the unborn—quite simply—shouldn't they be able to live to become children in those classrooms?

86   Those—those are some of our principles. You in this room, and millions like you watching and listening tonight, are selfless and dedicated to a better world based on these principles.

87   You aren't quitters. You walk not just precincts, but for a cause. You stand for something—the finest warriors for free government that I have known. Nancy and I thank you for letting us be a part of your tireless determination to leave a better world for our children.

88   And that's why we're here, isn't it? A better world.

89   I know I've said this before, but I believe that God put this land between the two great oceans to be found by special people of the— from every corner of the world who had that extra love of freedom that prompted them to leave their homeland and come to this land to make it a brilliant light beam of freedom to the world.

90   It's our gift to have visions, and I want to share that of a young boy who wrote to me shortly after I took office. In his letter he said, "I love America because you can join Cub Scouts if you want to. You have a right to worship as you please. If you have the ability, you can try to be anything you want to be. I also like America because we have about 200 flavors of ice cream."

91   That's America. Everyone with his or her vision of the American promise. That's why we're a magnet for the world—for those who dodged bullets and gave their lives coming over the Berlin Wall and others, only a few of whom avoided death, coming in tiny boats on turbulent oceans.

92   This land, its people, the dreams that unfold here and the freedom to bring it all together—well, those are what make America soar—up where you can see hope billowing in those freedom winds.

93   When our children turn the pages of our lives, I hope they'll see that we had a vision to pass forward a nation as nearly perfect as we could. Where there's decency, tolerance, generosity, honesty, courage, common sense, fairness and piety.

94   This is my vision, and I'm grateful to God for blessing me with a good life and a long one. But when I pack up my bags in Washington, don't expect me to be happy to hear all this talk about the twilight of my life.

95   Twilight? Twilight? Not in America.

96   Here, it's a sunrise every day. Fresh new opportunities. Dreams to build.

97   Twilight? That's not possible, because I confess there are times when I feel like I'm still little Dutch Reagan racing my brother down the hill to the swimming hole under the railroad bridge over the Rock River.

98   You see, there's a sweet—there's no sweeter day than each new one because here in our country, it means something wonderful can happen to you.

99   And something wonderful happened to me.

100   We lit a prairie fire a few years back. Those flames were fed by passionate ideas and convictions, and we were determined to make them run all—burn, I should say, all across America. And what times we've had!

101 Together we've fought for causes we love. But we can never let the fire go out or quit the fight, because the battle is never over. Our freedom must be defended over and over again. And then again.

102 There's still a lot of brush to clear out at the ranch, fences that need repair and horses to ride.

103 But I want you to know that if the fires ever dim, I'll leave my phone number and address behind just in case you need a foot soldier. Just let me know. I'll be there—as long as words don't leave me and as long as this sweet country strives to be special during its shining moment on earth.

104 Twilight, you say?

105 Listen to H. G. Wells. H. G. Wells says, "The past is but the beginning of a beginning, and all that is and has been is but the twilight of the dawn."

106 Well, that's a new day—our sunlit new day—to keep alive the fire so that when we look back at the time of choosing, we can say that we did all that could be done. Never less.

107 Thank you, good night. God bless you and God bless America.

ANN CHISHOLM

Conventional Narrative as Rhetorical Strategy: Ronald Reagan's "Address to the 1988 Republican National Convention"

Perhaps no recent political leader has exploited the resources of narrative more than Ronald Reagan. Ann Chisholm's critique explores the power of narrative in a speech delivered at the end of his two terms as president at the 1988 Republican National Convention. Moreover, the critique alerts readers to the many resources of narrative that include the narrator's persona, the roles created for the audience, and the enthymemic power of narrative to link anecdotes to cultural myths. This critique is powerful support for viewing humans as storytellers and for raising questions about the relative power of traditionally structured arguments when compared with the skillful use of narrative. Note the links between the capacities of narrative as she identifies them and psychosocial appeals to cultural motives and values.

Walter R. Fisher argues that all forms of human communication can be understood as stories. Transcending traditional perspectives that equate the notion of reasoning with argumentation and formal logic, Fisher asserts that all stories are persuasive because they are "moral inducements grounded in good reasons" ("Public Moral Argument" 3). A narrative text, then, comprises good reasons. In this context Fisher defines *good reasons* as "elements that give warrants for believing or acting in accord with the message fostered by that text" ("Narrative

Paradigm" 357).[1] Good reasons, he notes, are expressed by many forms: " 'argument,' metaphor, myth, gesture and so on" ("Narrative Paradigm" 357). Because they manifest good reasons, appeal to human values, and entail informal assessments of consistency and fidelity, these individuated forms constitute the persuasive potential of all discursive texts. In this essay I use the term *conventional narrative* to denote factual or fictional stories or successions of events that make up plots enunciated by narrators (Genette 26–32). Relying on this definition, I contend that some conventional narratives manifest persuasive characteristics that incorporate and exceed expressions of good reasons.

To support this claim, I examine the persuasive attributes of a particular type of conventional narrative: first-person narratives that appeal to the national identities of their audiences. Extending Fisher's conception of the storyteller and developing his assertion that narratives foster identification rather than deliberation, I explain how such first-person conventional narratives can gain persuasive force over and above their expression of good reasons. The subsequent analysis of Ronald Reagan's "Address to the 1988 Republican National Convention" illustrates my explanation.

FIRST-PERSON CONVENTIONAL NARRATIVES

The persuasive potential of many first-person conventional narratives depends on the relations established between storytellers, their narratives, and their audiences. In particular, a first-person narrative can gain persuasive force by reinforcing links among the narrator's public persona, the narrative personae he or she adopts, and the overall content of the narrative. Moreover, by constructing roles for their audiences and by endowing those roles with mythic and legendary significance, some first-person conventional narratives can appeal to the national identities of their audiences.

The credibility of a narrator's account often hinges on the extent to which it unifies its narrator's public and narrative personae. In this vein, John Louis Lucaites and Celeste Michelle Condit argue that rhetorical narratives must promote agreement between the narrators' public persona as "speaker" and their other narrative persona as "narrator"

---

[1]In his path-breaking essay, "Toward a Logic of Good Reasons," Fisher defines *good reasons*, in a similar manner, as "those elements that provide warrants for accepting or adhering to the advice fostered by any form of communication that can be considered rhetorical" (378).

(101–102). Moreover, William F. Lewis maintains that if storytellers act in ways that become distinct from their other role as characters in the story, the story becomes vulnerable to objection (286–287).

Both views are pertinent to the case at hand. The first-person narrator is both the narrator of and a character within the story (Genette 244–245; Martin 135). As narrator and character, the first-person narrator adopts two narrative roles. In order to be credible, a first-person narrator must maintain consistency between his or her public persona and the narrative personae of narrator and character. Likewise, the overall narrative must be consistent with the narrator's manifold personae. If a narrator's account is to be believed, if it is to present a feasible guide for action, the story must contain a narrator whose personae are harmonious with the choices within, and with the trajectory of, the story in its entirety (Booth 158; Chatman 149; Martin 142).

Generally, a given type of narrator accompanies a corresponding type of narratee (Chatman 255; Genette 259–260). First-person narrators who function as bystanders invite audiences to see themselves as bystanders (Chatman 150–151; Genette 260). To the extent that they construct and mark implied audiences, first-person narratives may encourage and enhance audience identification and participation.

Consequently, Seymour Chatman writes, "In general, a given type of narrator tends to evoke a parallel type of narratee: overt narrators evoke overt narratees, and so on" (255). Therefore, while creating personae for himself or herself both as the narrator and as a character within a story, the narrator may also constitute the narratee, the implied audience of the story, by constructing and marking a role within the story for the audience to assume (Chatman 149–151; Genette 260). To the extent that this occurs, first-person narratives may encourage and enhance audience identification and participation. First-person narratives may also augment the persuasive power of the roles they construct for their audiences by making those roles recognizable in some way. For example, by imbuing the role it constructs for its audience with mythic, historic, and legendary precedent, a first-person narrative may appeal to the national identity and patriotism of its audience.

Bronislaw Malinowski defines *myth* as a narrative construct, enmeshed in culture, that encompasses and determines belief and ritual (*Sex, Culture and Myth*). Subsuming Malinowski's definition within his own explanation of the formal and functional attributes of myth, Robert C. Rowland asserts that myth functions to provide " 'true' answers to crucial social and personal problems" that cannot be resolved by discursive forms ("On Mythic Criticism" 103). Therefore, in Rowland's view, myth functions to define particular societies and the lives of individuals within those societies ("On Mythic Criticism").[2] Further, Rowland proposes that mythic forms have five characteristics: They are stories; they are heroic; they transcend or transform historical time; they transcend or transform geographic space; and they rely on archetypal language ("On Mythic Criticism"). More important for this essay, Rowland grants that "the invocation of one mythic characteristic may call into mind the entire myth" and that "myth may function enthymematically" ("Rejoinder" 154).

Providing a model of the "good society," myth promotes and perpetuates transcendental values (Rowland, "On Mythic Criticism" 102; Fisher, "Narrative Paradigm"). Myth also functions as a "statement of reality" and as "a reality lived" (Osborn 122; Rowland, "On Mythic Criticism" 103–105). Myth therefore exists "outside of historical time" and, at the same time, provides solutions to "problems of value" in the present (Rowland, "On Mythic Criticism" 103–105). Audiences accept myths, commit to them, identify with them, and use them as a frame of reference for understanding and participating in social life. Accordingly, when a first-person conventional narrative infuses an audience's role with mythic significance, it gains rhetorical power because it conjures up related, culturally familiar stories relevant to group identity that rehearse accepted values and articulate prevailing conceptions of the "good society."

Overall, a first-person conventional narrative that appeals to the national identity of its audience can incorporate and exceed expressions of good reasons. Such conventional narratives can confirm or enhance credibility by negotiating their narrator's public persona, their narrator's narrative personae, and the narratives themselves. Further, a conventional narrative of this kind may encourage audience identification and participation by constructing a role for its audience and by endowing that role with mythic, historic, and legendary significance.

REAGAN'S ADDRESS

An analysis of Ronald Reagan's "Address to the 1988 Republican National Convention" illustrates and clarifies the persuasive attributes of first-person conventional narratives that appeal to the national

---

[2]Although other scholars (Brummett, Osborn, Rushing, and Solomon) have advanced compelling arguments regarding their reluctance to delimit their views of myth in this way, Rowland's functional perspective provides a useful starting point for my investigation.

identities of their audiences. Concurrently, this analysis demonstrates that such narratives may gain persuasive force over and above their expression of good reasons. Reagan's address to the convention offers a useful example of the persuasive narrative attributes discussed thus far not only because Reagan's presidential rhetoric is distinguished by his use of narrative but also because these persuasive attributes constitute the key strategies at work in this speech. As Paul Erickson remarks, "The constant transformation of political material into stories, is, in fact, the chief distinction of Reagan's rhetoric" (25). Lewis extends that claim, asserting that "it is the predominance of the narrative form in Reagan's rhetoric that has established the climate of interpretation within which he is seen and judged" (281).

In his speech to the 1988 Republican convention Reagan employed a first-person conventional narrative that encompassed and managed his persuasive message. Through his speech Reagan sought to transfer Republican party leadership to George Bush and to anoint Bush as the heir apparent to the presidency.

To achieve this goal Reagan had to overcome formidable rhetorical obstacles. There was the likelihood that the popular president would obscure the less popular nominee, making it more difficult for Republicans to succeed in electing the next president (Barret 22). In fact, the Republican candidate's "negatives" were higher than those of any other presidential candidate in election history (Kramer, "Dukakis" 27). Negative public perceptions of Bush were intensified by the "wimp factor" and by suspicions about his possible involvement in the Iran–Contra affair (Borger 18).[3]

Moreover, the Democrats, including their nominee Michael Dukakis, had seized this moment to attack Bush as well as the Reagan administration. The most notable attack on Bush's credibility was initiated by Ted Kennedy, who, several weeks earlier at the Democratic National Convention, had referred to the Iran–Contra scandal. "Where was George?" Kennedy asked the U.S. public (Dionne A22). At the time of the convention the Bush campaign was faltering; Bush had been unable to defend himself, much less to entice support from Reagan Democrats, who were vital to his success in November.[4]

Analysis of Reagan's address reveals that he managed the problems of the immediate situation and those of the Bush campaign through a strategic use of conventional narrative. Toward this end Reagan nar-

---

[3]The Gallup Poll of July 1988 revealed that Bush had not overcome the stigma of the Iran–Contra affair (Kramer, "What Does Bush Stand For?" 16).

[4]Dukakis consistently led Bush in opinion polls during the months prior to the Republican convention (Barret 20). More important, Reagan Democrats favored Dukakis over Bush by 59 to 34 percent (Barnes 20).

rated his version of an ongoing American Revolution, recounting the nation's battle to secure its values and to achieve its manifest destiny. While relating that story Reagan linked the persona he adopted as narrator, the mythic role he constructed for his audience, and the narrative's central claim—that the audience should support George Bush.

REAGAN'S NARRATIVE PERSONA

Although Reagan's narrative was a powerful strategy in and of itself, it was made more so by the persona Reagan assumed as narrator. Throughout his speech Reagan presented himself as the nation's citizen-president, as an average American with temporary custody of the presidency. By associating aspects of Reagan's narrative persona with aspects of his public persona, Reagan's narrative confirmed his credibility and invited the participation and adherence of his audience. Concomitantly, Reagan asked his audience to secure the presidency for George Bush.

As narrator Reagan did not distance himself by relying on his official position as president. Instead Reagan emphasized his role as citizen. He referred to the audience as "fellow citizens" (1, 23)[5] and described himself in terms of the common American who does not hold political office. His assertion of similarity disassociated him from his elevated status as the head of government and implied that he was one of the people while minimizing the likelihood that he would overshadow Bush. Like the heroes of the American Revolution and members of the audience, Reagan was a "foot soldier" (103) fighting for American beliefs and values.

Although Reagan had been one of America's more private presidents, Kathleen Hall Jamieson has suggested that Reagan, more than any other president, cultivated a "personal public style" (184). In this address Reagan's role as narrator both personalized and mythologized him. Using mythic referents, Reagan associated his personal public persona with his narrative persona as citizen, creating the illusion that an intimate relationship existed between him and the American people.

At one point Reagan offered his audience a vignette of "little Dutch Reagan racing [his] brother down the hill to the swimming hole under the railroad bridge over the Rock River" (97). This childhood episode

---

[5]The text of Reagan's speech appeared in *The New York Times*, 16 August 1988, p. A20. Parenthetical citations are paragraph numbers.

was familiar Americana; it could have described Huck Finn or Andy Hardy; it was the childhood of a mythical American boy. Reagan's personal history was retold in terms that merged it into U.S. cultural history. As citizen, Reagan became an American of myth as he simultaneously heightened the intimate tone of his address.

Reagan's narrative portrayed him not only as a president who had a close personal relationship with the American people but also as a president who understood and championed the people. Professing the sentiments of true Americanism, Reagan said that he "loves America" (68), and he imparted his vision of "this land, its people," and "the dreams that unfold here" (92). Thus his love for America and its people was the implied motivation for his address.

Although Reagan did not emphasize his official status as president, he exploited his position within the narrative in order to enhance his ethos and to assume an emphatically partisan stance while appearing to be unbiased. At the beginning of the speech, Reagan redefined his presidential status for the audience: "You don't become president of the United States," he said, "you are given temporary custody of an institution called the presidency" (5). The American people, Reagan continued, "placed this trust in my hands" (7).

As an elected custodian, Reagan did not have to establish his trustworthiness as narrator; it had been granted already. Because he was the caretaker of our national and international well-being, his version of national and international affairs was assumed to reflect his privileged access to information. Repeatedly reminding the audience of his special access to "the facts" (27), Reagan gave his audience a history lesson and justified his version of the past from his special sources of knowledge. "I've been doing a little remembering," (26) said Reagan as he launched into his 12-year retrospective of national and international politics. His memory was the authority for the accuracy of his account and a sufficient basis for national decision making.

The authority that Reagan assumed from his role as an elected custodian of the presidency became apparent as Reagan enlarged his persona to adopt the role of omniscient narrator. His presidential office, his "sacred trust" (6), was enhanced by divine associations. Reagan was blessed: "I'm grateful to God for blessing me with a good life" (94). As high priest of our civil religion, he was able to invoke God's blessings: "God bless you, and God bless America" (107). As high priest he also was able to interpret God's intentions: "I believe that God put this land between the two great oceans to be found by special people" (89).

Reagan's divine surrogacy underscored the trustworthiness of his message. God had blessed him and the nation, and if the audience followed the course Reagan recommended, the nation's manifest destiny would be assured and American values would be upheld: "With

George Bush, I'll know, as we approach the new millennium, our children will have a future secure with a nation at peace . . . we'll have a prosperity that spreads the blessings of our abundance and opportunity across all America" (69). Adopting an omniscient role, Reagan assured Americans that they would "recapture our national destiny" (18) if they voted for Bush and transferred the sacred trust of the presidency to him.

Each aspect of Reagan's narrative persona created a distinct dimension of ethos and furthered his cause. In order to identify with his diverse television audience, Reagan featured that aspect of his narrative persona that emphasized his role as ordinary citizen. Merging this aspect of his narrative persona with personal recollections and mythic referents, he invested his narrative with a sense of personal honor and integrity nurtured both by the common bond of shared American values and by the illusion of a relationship between himself and all Americans.

As citizen-president Reagan subtly qualified the intimate association he had cultivated with his audience, shifting from his role as a citizen to his role as the custodian of the presidency. The links Reagan forged between his official public persona and his narrative persona as presidential custodian allowed him to become an omniscient narrator. That omniscience, in turn, allowed him to control the content of his narrative, which was his version of the nation's battle to achieve its manifest destiny.

Further, the mythic dimensions of Reagan's address unified aspects of his public persona, his narrative persona as citizen-president, and the story that was his message. This convergence of role with narrative magnified the persuasive impact of the strategies Reagan employed toward a partisan end and minimized his role as chief Republican and preeminent Republican party leader.

Reagan's address, then, has illustrated my first claim: Reagan's first-person conventional narrative promoted a correspondence among his public persona, his narrative persona, and his narrative. This correspondence invited the audience to find both Reagan and his narrative credible.

CONSTRUCTING A ROLE FOR THE AUDIENCE

The ethos Reagan derived from his role as narrator enhanced the narrative as a strategic means to constitute a role for his audience. The narrative persona that Reagan assumed promoted a relationship with his audience that, in turn, implied an appropriate role for them.

Reagan addressed the audience as "Americans" (7, 10, 14, 22, 27, 39) and encouraged the audience in the convention hall and watching on television to identify with the American heritage and American values. He recited "the greatest and the first three words in our Constitution: We the people" (9); he referred to "the shining city on the hill" (16) and to our Puritan origins; and he discussed the values of "family, work, neighborhood, peace and freedom" (20) that are the foundations for "our dream" (16).

Having defined his audience as Americans, Reagan transformed American values into Republican values. To facilitate this merger of American and Republican values, he minimized Republican partisanship: He treated the convention delegates and Republicans generally as part of a larger whole, Americans. Introducing his narrative, for example, Reagan remarked, "I think we can be forgiven if we give ourselves a little pat on the back for having made 'Republican' a proud word again and America a proud nation again" (2). Expanding the locus of identification from himself and his wife, "we arrived here yesterday" (1), to the party, "we can be forgiven if we give ourselves a little pat on the back" (2), and to the nation, "We the People"(9), Reagan subsumed references to the convention and to the Republican party under references to the nation as a whole.

Reagan also consolidated American and Republican values by associating Republican goals with great Americans, regardless of their party affiliation. He characterized Franklin D. Roosevelt and Harry Truman as Democrats who supported Republican values and ideals (74). Roosevelt's platform paralleled the Republican platform because it was, according to Reagan, "a platform of eliminating useless boards and commissions and returning autonomy and authority to local government and to the states" (74). Reagan failed to note that Roosevelt's actions as president contradicted his campaign platform because this fact would have qualified the asserted correspondence between American values and the Republican party.

The commonality of American and Republican values was also in evidence as Reagan reviewed several planks of the 1988 Republican party platform. Because "our principles" (86), that is, American principles, were the principles of Republicans, the Republican party became "our party"—that is, the party that upholds American values. Consequently, Reagan maintained that "our party speaks for human freedom—for the sweep of liberties that are at the core of our existence" (78). "We respect the values that bind us together as families and as a nation" (82), he continued, encouraging the audience to support school prayer and to adopt a pro-life, rather than a pro-choice, stance regarding abortion. Here again, his implied audience was defined by its commitment to what Reagan identified as American values. By extension, the audience he addressed was invited to support the values and policies of the Republican party.

As he defined his implied audience as Americans/Republicans, he empowered them. He declared that Americans had restored their national pride and prestige, and he presented their achievements as Republican victories. The audience Reagan created won the American Revolution, rescued America in 1980, revitalized the American Dream, and actively pursued and achieved goals predicated on American/Republican values.

In this vein Reagan repeatedly preempted the Democrats' slogan, "It's time for a change," with the affirmation "We are the change" (42). The "we" who had made these changes ambiguously referred to his Republican administration, to the Republican party, and to the U.S. public. Reagan asked the audience to vote for George Bush because, as a Republican, of necessity, Bush would maintain, support, and promote American values. Accordingly, his narrative also suggested that Bush was the best candidate for the entire U.S. audience, including the Reagan Democrats.

Reagan's portrayal of his audience facilitated a second strategy characteristic of first-person conventional narratives that also appeal to the national identities of their audiences. Reagan's narrative depicted his audience as Americans, associated that depiction with the Republican party, and urged his audience to further the American/Republican cause with their votes.

ENDOWING THE AUDIENCE'S ROLE WITH MYTHIC SIGNIFICANCE

Reagan's allusions to American/Republican values were linked to a battle motif that permeated his address. According to Reagan, the outcome of the battle to which he alluded would determine the nation's manifest destiny. Thus Reagan's narrative endowed the role it constituted for his audience with mythic, historic, and legendary significance. Concomitantly, Reagan sought to move members of his audience toward commitment to the narrative's resolution.

Reagan developed a conflict in his narrative, and through it, the values of the Democrats were depicted as antagonistic to the American/Republican values that defined his narrative personae, his audience, and his party. This conflict created grounds not only for identification of Republican and American values but also for division between Democratic and American values.

Specifically, Democrats were described as supporting big government and opposed to the interests of the American people. Republicans, on the other hand, were portrayed as standing for American values. The Democratic party was composed of "liberal elites" (53), not citizen-politicians like Reagan. The "other party" (74) was characterized by "inflated rhetoric" (26), as opposed to Reagan's straight talk and facts. Building on these oppositions, Reagan charged that the Democrats, the "other side" (33), had "check[ed their] principles at the door" (76). The disparity between Republican truths and Democratic disloyalty and dishonesty not only put the Democrats on the defensive but also sidestepped issues of credibility that had been raised about Bush and other individuals in Reagan's administration.[6]

Reagan illustrated the Democratic threat to American/Republican values with an account that contrasted the national and international scene during the Carter administration and the achievements of his administration. Reagan described Americans as helplessly eking out a living during the late 1970s. Americans "suffered" as they struggled "to plan [their] economic survival" (27–28). During that time, he asserted, Americans were helpless in international matters. "All Americans taken as hostages" (39), he said, recalling the Iranian hostage crisis and the Soviet invasion of Afghanistan. In contrast to this negative picture of the 1970s, Reagan painted a rosy picture of the 1980s, thereby portraying his administration as a corrective force. Inspired by "a community of shared values" (20), the Republicans righted the wrongs of the Democrats. Under the guidance of the Republican party and the American people, the misery index fell,[7] jobs were created, inflation decreased, the United States became an international power once again, and American values were revitalized. By juxtaposing the negative results of Democratic leadership with the implementation of American values under Republicans, Reagan portrayed the Democrats as ineffective and as dangerous to American/Republican values.

Reagan's 12-year retrospective, however, was highly selective. His history reached back only as far as the Carter administration, excluding references to the policies of Ford and Nixon that may have precipitated the inflation of the late 1970s.[8] His retrospective also omit-

---

[6]Several weeks before the convention, former attorney general and presidential counselor Ed Meese's financial dealings were investigated; Meese subsequently resigned. The Democrats used that opportunity to point out that over 100 Reagan appointees were indicted during Reagan's two terms (Duffy 10).

[7]Carter devised the "misery index" during his 1976 presidential campaign against Gerald Ford. The "misery index," according to Carter, was the sum of the inflation and unemployment rates. Between 1976 and 1980 the index rose 7.5 percent. Reagan often cited this fact during his 1980 campaign against Carter (White 55).

[8]At the close of the Nixon administration, the high cost of living was, for the first time in 20 years, the primary concern of the nation. Unemployment accompanied the high cost of living as a primary concern in March of 1975, during Gerald Ford's presidency (The Gallup Report #177, 24.)

ted Watergate, which would have lessened the Republican claim to be the special guardians of the American heritage. Further, he ignored his own initiatives that had had negative effects.[9] Because his narrative represented Republican values as radically opposed to those of the Democrats, all achievements naturally were associated with the Republican party; all failures were attributed to the Democrats.

Casting the current election as an extension of the 1980 presidential election, Reagan characterized both elections as recurrences (reruns?) of the Revolutionary War. Thomas Paine, for example, was depicted as fighting for Republican causes. After summarizing how the Republican party motivated the American people to fight for American values in 1980, Reagan commented, "Paine knew what these Americans with characters of steel could do. . . . While our triumph is not yet complete, the road has been glorious, indeed" (22–23). He continued, arguing that the goals and triumphs of the Republican party in 1988 were synonymous with those of the American Revolution.

Through Reagan's narrative, the Republican party emerged at the vanguard of American values. Reagan's administration, his party, and the American people had "challenged the failed policies" (43) of the Democratic party in the name of American values; F.D.R., Paine, and "the American spirit" (19) were enlisted as soldiers in the ongoing battle for American/Republican values, as were members of his American/Republican audience.

Reagan's mythic battle sustained the central agon of his narrative and the division that he was seeking to establish. Grounding his arguments in references to the American Revolution, Reagan presented the battle for American values as a "national crusade" (21) whose end would be "a glorious . . . triumph" (22). As a "foot soldier" (103), he and the implied audience, American/Republican "warriors for free government" (87), were participants in that battle. But "the battle is never over," Reagan reminded the audience, because "our freedom must be defended over and over again" (101). In view of the ongoing battle, there was only one logical course of action for Americans to take. They had to elect an American/Republican president to lead them. Bush was the right choice because he was another soldier in the battle against liberalism and big government. Reagan remarked that Bush "is cool under fire" (66) and "never runs away from a fight" (67). As head of a "task force" (59) to eliminate government regulations, Bush had proven himself by fighting big government. He also distinguished

---

[9]For example, Reagan omitted mention of the 1982 recession, the worst recession since the 1930s (Nathan 63). He did not refer to his 1982 budget, which called for a $40 billion cut in domestic programs, nor did he mention the tax increases initiated during his presidency.

himself by defending U.S. interests, by persuading the NATO allies to deploy Pershing missiles, and by paving the way for the INF Treaty (62). Bush, Reagan argued, was someone who would "keep America strong" (57).

In other words, Reagan's narrative showed that "George was there" (59). Bush had supported the people as they "overcame liberal opposition" (63) and as they quelled the threat of Communism. In this way Reagan's narrative answered the Democrats' recent attack on Bush and minimized the "wimp factor."

As Reagan restaged the American Revolution, he advanced a third strategy, a strategy characteristic of first-person conventional narratives that appeal to the national identities of their audiences. Encouraging audience members to assume the role constructed for them by his narrative, he endowed that role with mythic, historic, and legendary significance: American/Republican voters supporting Bush, Reagan asserted, were the defenders of freedom and the American way.

CONCLUSION

This analysis of Reagan's address has shown that a first-person conventional narrative can manifest persuasive attributes that incorporate and exceed the expression of good reasons. Linking his public and narrative personae with narrative content, Reagan's speech enhanced his credibility and encouraged his audience to accept his story as a reliable guide for action. Reagan's narrative also gained persuasive force by constructing a role for his audience and by infusing that role with mythic authority. In these ways Reagan's address invited his listeners to participate in and to affirm the resolution of his narrative.

Reagan's first-person conventional narrative, moreover, ultimately addressed the rhetorical problems of the moment by rendering comparisons between Bush and Reagan irrelevant. They were superseded by comparisons between Republicans and Democrats. Reagan's narrative proved that the Republican party was the American party; by extension, the Democratic party became un-American. His narrative facilitated this division by omitting significant details and by simplifying complex perspectives on governance into two conflicting alternatives, mythical American/Republican values versus those of the Democratic party. Both Reagan and the American heritage proclaimed the Republican party and its candidate to be the only fitting choice for voters committed to American values. Championing those values, Reagan achieved his goals at the cost of excluding Democrats from America's heritage and dividing the nation.

WORKS CITED

Barnes, Fred. "Bentsen and Hedges." *New Republic* 1 Aug. 1988: 18–20.

Barret, Laurence I. "Shifting Mist." *Time* 12 Sept. 1988: 20–21.

Booth, Wayne. *The Rhetoric of Fiction.* Chicago: University of Chicago Press, 1961.

Borger, Gloria. "Why Everybody Is Saying Such Terrible Things about George." *U.S. News and World Report* 1 Aug. 1988: 19.

Brummett, Barry. "How to Propose a Discourse—Reply to Rowland." *Communication Studies* 41 (1990): 128–135.

Chatman, Seymour. *Story and Discourse: Narrative Structure in Fiction and Film.* Ithaca, NY: Cornell University Press, 1978.

Dionne, E. J. "Reagan Offers Republicans a Sentimental Valedictory and Full Support for Bush." *New York Times* 16 Aug. 1988: A22.

Duffy, Brian, et al. "Can Bush Battle Back?" *U.S. News and World Report* 1 Aug. 1988: 18–19.

Erickson, Paul. *Reagan Speaks: The Making of an American Myth.* New York: New York University Press, 1985.

Fisher, Walter R. "Toward a Logic of Good Reasons." *Quarterly Journal of Speech* 64 (1978): 376–384.

———. "Narration as a Human Communication Paradigm: The Case of Public Moral Argument." *Communication Monographs* 51 (1984): 1–22.

———. "The Narrative Paradigm: An Elaboration." *Communication Monographs* 52 (1985): 347–364.

———. (1989). "Clarifying the Narrative Paradigm." *Communication Monographs* 56 (1989): 55–58.

The Gallup Report. *Report No. 177.* Princeton, NJ: Gallup Poll, 1980.

Genette, Gerard. *Narrative Discourse: An Essay in Method.* 1972. Trans. J. E. Lewin. Ithaca, NY: Cornell University Press, 1980.

Jamieson, Kathleen Hall. *Eloquence in an Electronic Age: The Transformation of Political Speechmaking.* New York: Oxford University Press, 1988.

Kramer, Michael. "What Does Bush Stand For?" *U.S. News and World Report* 22 Aug. 1988: 12–22.

———. "Dukakis Is Ready to Play . . . Is Bush? *U.S. News and World Report* 4 July 1988: 27.

Lewis, William F. "Telling America's Story: Narrative Form and the Reagan Presidency." *Quarterly Journal of Speech* 73 (1987): 280–302.

Lucaites, John L., and Celeste M. Condit. "Reconstructing Narrative Theory: A Functional Perspective." *Journal of Communication* 35 (1985): 90–108.

Malinowski, Bronislaw. *Sex, Culture and Myth.* New York: Harcourt, Brace and World, 1961.

Martin, Wallace. *Recent Theories of Narrative*. Ithaca, NY: Cornell University Press, 1986.

Nathan, Richard P. *The Administrative Presidency*. New York: Wiley, 1983.

Osborn, Michael. "In Defense of Broad Mythic Criticism—A Reply to Rowland." *Communication Studies* 41 (1990): 121–127.

Reagan, Ronald. "Address to the 1988 Republican National Convention." *New York Times* 16 Aug. 1988: A20.

Rowland, Robert C. "On Mythic Criticism." *Communication Studies* 41 (1990): 101–116.

———. "On a Limited Approach to Mythic Criticism—Rowland's Rejoinder." *Communication Studies* 41 (1990): 150–160.

Rushing, Janice Hocker. "On Saving Mythic Criticism—A Reply to Rowland." *Communication Studies* 41 (1990): 136–149.

Solomon, Martha. "In Defense of Mythic Criticism—A Reply to Rowland." *Communication Studies* 41 (1990): 117–120.

White, John Kenneth. *The New Politics of Old Values*. Hanover, NH: University Press of New England, 1988.

MILES W. LORD

Plea for Corporate Conscience

This speech is extraordinary because it so completely violated audience expectations. Presiding over the negotiated, pretrial settlement of a civil suit brought against the A. H. Robins Company, manufacturer of a contraceptive device known as the Dalkon Shield, Judge Miles W. Lord delivered this "plea" to a packed courtroom in Minneapolis, Minnesota, on February 29, 1984. In the audience were top officials of the Robins Company. Stepping outside the expected role for a judge in such a proceeding, Lord urged the Robins officials to accept moral as well as legal responsibility for injuries suffered by plaintiffs due to use of the Dalkon Shield. The text is from Transcript, Further Pretrial Proceedings, February 29, 1984. *Gardiner & Michalek v. Robins. D. Minn.,* Civ. 3–83–1025, 3–83–106.

1   Mr. Robins, Mr. Forrest, and Dr. Lunsford, after months of reflection, study and cogitation and no small amount of prayer I have concluded it perfectly appropriate to make to you this statement, which will constitute my plea to you to seek new horizons in corporate consciousness and a new sense of personal responsibility for the activities of those who work under you in the name of A. H. Robins Company.

2   It is not enough to say, "I did not know," "It was not me," "Look elsewhere."

3   Time and time again each of you have [*sic*] used this kind of argument in refusing to acknowledge your responsibility and pretending to the world that the chief officers and directors of your gigantic multinational corporation have no responsibility for the company's acts and omissions.

4   In a speech I made several years ago—the document which I have just asked you to read—I suggested to hundreds of ministers of the Gospel, who constitute the Minnesota Council of Churches, that the accumulation of corporate wrongs is in my mind a manifestation of individual sin.

5   You, Mr. Robins, Jr., have been heard to boast many times that the growth and prosperity of this company is a direct result of its having been in the Robins family for three generations, the stamp of the Robins family is upon it, the corporation is built in the image of the Robins mentality.

6   You, Dr. Lunsford, as director of the company's most sensitive and important subdivision, the medical division, have violated every ethical precept to which every doctor under your supervision must pledge as he gives the oath of Hippocrates and assumes the mantle of one who would cure and nurture unto the physical needs of the populace.

7   You, Mr. Forrest, are a lawyer who, upon finding his client in trouble, should counsel and guide him along a course which will comport with the legal and moral and ethical principles which must bind us all.

8   You have not brought honor to your profession, Mr. Forrest.

9   Gentlemen, the result of these activities and attitudes on your part have been catastrophic.

10   Today, as you sit here, attempting once more to extricate yourselves from the legal consequences of your acts, none of you have faced up to the fact that more than 9,000 women have made claims that they gave a part of their womanhood so that your company might prosper. It is alleged that others gave their lives so you might prosper. And there stand behind legions more who have been injured but who have not sought relief in the courts of this land.

11   I dread to think what would have been the consequences if your victims had been men rather than women, women who seem through some strange quirk of our society's mores to be expected to suffer pain, suffering, and humiliation.

12   If one poor young man were by some act of his, without authority or consent, to inflict such damage upon one woman, he would be jailed for a good portion of the rest of his life.

13   And yet your company, without warning to women, invaded their bodies by the millions and caused them injuries by the thousands.

14   And when the time came for these women to make their claims against your company, you attacked their characters, you inquired into their sexual practices and into the identity of their sex partners.

15   You exposed these women and ruined families and reputations and careers in order to intimidate those who would raise their voices against you.

16   You introduced issues that had no relationship whatsoever to the fact that you planted in the bodies of these women instruments of death, of mutilation, and of disease.

17   I wish to make it absolutely clear that I am specifically directing and limiting my remarks to that which I have learned and observed in these consolidated cases before me.

18   If an incident arises involving another product made by A. H. Robins Company, an independent judgment would have to be made as to the conduct of your company concerning that product.

19   Likewise, a product made by any other company must of course be adjudged upon the individual facts of that case.

20   Gentlemen, you state that your company has suffered enough, that the infliction of further punishment in a form of punitive damages will cause harm to your ongoing business, will punish innocent shareholders and, conceivably, depress your profits to the point where you would not survive as a competitor in this industry.

21   Well, when the poor and downtrodden in this country commit crimes, they too plead that these are crimes of survival, and that they should be excused for illegal acts which helped them escape desperate economic straits.

22   On a few occasions when these excuses are made and [a] contrite and remorseful defendant promises to mend his ways, courts will give heed to such a plea.

23   But no court would heed this plea when the individual denies the wrongful nature of his deed and gives no indication that he will mend his ways.

24   Your company in the face of overwhelming evidence denies its guilt and continues its monstrous mischief.

25   Mr. Forrest, you have told me that you are working with members of the Congress of the United States to ask them to find a way of forgiving you for punitive damages which might otherwise be imposed.

26   Yet the profits of your company continue to mount. Your last financial report boasts of new records for sales and earnings with a profit of more than fifty-eight million in 1983.

27   And all the while, insofar as this court is able to determine, you three men and your company still engage in the same course of wrongdoing on which you originally commenced.

28   Until such time as your company indicates that it is willing to cease and desist this deception and seek out and advise victims, your remonstrances to Congress and to the courts of this country are indeed hollow and cynical.

29   The company has not suffered, nor have you men personally.

30   You are collectively being enriched by millions of dollars each year.

31   There is as yet no evidence that your company has suffered any penalty whatsoever from these litigations. In fact the evidence is to the contrary.

32   The case law indicates that the purpose of punitive damages is to make an award which will punish a defendant for his wrongdoing.

33   Punishment traditionally involves the principles of revenge, rehabilitation, and deterrence.

34   There is no evidence I have been able to find, in my review of these cases, to indicate that any one of these factors has been accomplished.

35   Mr. Robins, Mr. Forrest, Dr. Lunsford, you have not been rehabilitated by the punitive damage awards that have been made so far. In fact, I don't think one of them has ever been paid yet, up until this settlement.

36   Under your direction your company has in fact continued to allow women, tens of thousands of them, to wear this device, a deadly depth charge in their wombs, ready to explode at any time.

37   Your attorney, Mr. Alexander Slaughter, denies that tens of thousands of these devices are still in the bodies of women.

38   But I submit to you that Mr. Slaughter has no more basis for his denial than the plaintiffs for stating it as a truth—because we simply do not know how many women are still wearing these devices; and your company, run by you three men, is not willing to find out.

39   The only conceivable reasons you have not recalled this product are that it would hurt your balance sheet and alert women, who already have been harmed, that you may be liable for their injuries.

40   As I said before, and out of context, you have taken the bottom line as your guiding beacon and the low road as your route.

41   This is corporate irresponsibility at its meanest.

42   Rehabilitation involves an admission of guilt, a certain contrition, an acknowledgment of wrongdoing, and a resolution to take a new course toward a better life.

43   I find none of this in the instance of you and your corporation.

44   Confession is good for the soul, Gentlemen.

45   Face up to your misdeeds. Acknowledge the responsibility that you have for the activities of those who work under you. Rectify this evil situation. Warn the potential future victim and recompense those who have already been harmed.

46   Mr. Robins, Mr. Forrest, Dr. Lunsford, I see little in the history of this case that would deter others from partaking of like acts.

47   The policy of delay and obfuscation practiced by your lawyers in courts throughout this country has made it possible for your insurance company and you, the Aetna Casualty and Assurance Company and the A. H. Robins Corporation, to delay the payment of these claims for such a long period that the interest you earn in the interim covers the costs of these cases.

48   You, in essence, assuming you owe something at the time the harm came, pay nothing out of your pocket to settle these cases.

49   What other corporate officials anywhere could possibly learn a lesson from this?

50   The only lesson could be that it pays to delay compensating victims, and to intimidate, harass, and shame your victims, the injured parties.

51   Mr. Forrest, Mr. Robins and Dr. Lunsford, you gentlemen have consistently denied any knowledge of the deeds of the company you control.

52   You, Mr. Robins, Jr., I read your deposition.

53   Many times you state that your management style was such as to delegate work and responsibility to other employees in matters involving the most important aspects of this nation's health.

54   Judge Frank Theis (phonetic), who presided over the discovery of these cases during the Multi-District Litigation proceedings, noted this phenomenon in a recent opinion. He wrote, I quote:

55   "The project manager for Dalkon Shield explains that a particular question should have gone to the medical department."

56   "The medical department representative explains that the question was really the bailiwick of the quality control department."

57   "The quality control department representative explains that the project manager was the one with the authority to make a decision on that question."

58   Under these circumstances, Judge Theis noted, it is not at all unusual for the hard questions posed in Dalkon Shield cases to be unanswerable by anyone from Robins.

59   Your company seeks and has sought to segment and fragment litigation of these cases nationwide.

60   The courts of this country are now burdened with more than 3,000 Dalkon Shield cases.

61   The sheer number of claims and the dilatory tactics used by your company's attorneys clog court calendars and consume vast amounts of judicial and jury time.

62   Your company settles those cases in which it finds itself in an uncomfortable position, a handy device for avoiding any proceeding which would give continuity or cohesiveness to this nationwide problem.

63   The decision as to which cases to try rests almost solely at the whim and discretion of the A. H. Robins Company.

64   In order that no plaintiff or group of plaintiffs might assert a sustained assault upon your system, evasion, and avoidance, you have time after time demanded that able lawyers who have knowledge of the facts must, as a price of settling their cases, agree to never again take a Dalkon Shield case nor to help any less experienced lawyers with their cases against your company.

65   Minnesota lawyers have filed cases in this jurisdiction for women from throughout the United States.

66   The cases of these women have waited on the calendar of this court for as many as three years.

67   Until such time as this settlement came about, the evidence that the women were to present was simply their own testimony and/or that of their doctor, usually taken by deposition, and then the generic evidence concerning the company's actions—which is as easy to produce in Minnesota as anywhere else.

68   Yet your company's attorneys were persisting in asking that these cases be transferred to other jurisdictions and to other judges unfamiliar with the cases, there to wait at the bottom of the calendar for additional months and years before they could have their day in court.

69   Another of your callous legal tactics is to force women of little means to withstand the onslaught of your well-financed nationwide team of attorneys, and to default if they cannot keep up with the pace.

70   Your target, your worst tactics were reserved for the meek and the poor.

71   Now again I point out that Faegre & Benson and the local law firms do not come under any of the strictures of that which I have said.

72   As far as I have been able to know and has been reported to me, they have acted honorably with the evidence that was available to them.

73   Despite your company's protestations, it is evident that these thousands of cases cannot be viewed in isolation, and that is one of the main reasons why I feel free to make this statement here today.

74   If every judge is terminated as soon as he catches on to what's going on, if you settle the case and flee the jurisdiction, that leaves no one to follow up to make any cohesiveness to this.

75   The multi-district litigation panel of the Federal District Court found these cases to have sufficient similarity on issues of law and fact to warrant their reference to a single judge who, for varying periods of time, conducted discovery depositions and proceedings designed to devise an efficient method of handling these cases.

76   Yet I find, as I previously indicated, from the report of the Masters—as late as this morning—that the Multi-District Litigation Unit was only given about a third of the documents, and the most relevant documents are in the hands of the lawyers for the defendant.

77   So that is 12 years of delay.

78   In each of the thousands of cases, the focal point of the inquiry is the same, the conduct of your company, through its acts and omissions.

79   Indeed as I speak here of when judge, judges being spun off from time to time, Judge Gerald Heaney of the Court of Appeals, I believe he said it, with the Eighth Circuit, recently urged judges in Minnesota to work together to devise a coordinated system for dealing with all of their Dalkon Shield cases.

80   These litigations must be viewed as a whole.

81   If a judge were to wait until all the cases were over before he spoke out on the evils he sees inherent in the system and in the trial tactics, then no one would ever speak out.

82   There is a time when measures must be taken, when steps must be taken to see that fair play and ethical standards apply to the disposition of all the cases that are come to [*sic*] the future, regardless of what might have happened in the past.

83   These litigations must be viewed as a whole.

84   Were these women to be gathered together with their injuries in one location, this matter would be denominated a disaster of the highest magnitude.

85   The mere fact that these women are separated by geography blurs the total picture.

86   Here we have thousands of victims, present and potential, whose injuries arise from the same series of operative facts.

87   You three gentlemen have made no effort whatsoever to locate them and bring them together to seek a common solution to their plight.

88   If this were a case in equity, I would order that your company make an effort to locate each and every woman who still wears this device, and to recall your product.

89   I would order you now to take to the Food and Drug Administration a correct and proper report on what's happened with these devices.

90   If I did that, they would order you to recall.

91   So while the governmental agencies are set up to protect the public, there is evidence here that you didn't tell the truth to the governmental agencies.

92 I believe that evidence, I've made it—I've made a judgment on it. These matters of which I speak are not matters about which I speculate. They are matters contained in the evidence that has gone before me in the briefs of counsel, in the admissions and in the documents—some of which I have seen and no lawyer has seen—but I haven't disclosed anything about them except my conclusion about the matters about which I here spoke.

93 I do not have the power to order you to do this.

94 I must therefore resort to moral persuasion and a personal appeal to each of you.

95 Would you believe it, Gentlemen, I am not angry with you. I don't dislike you personally.

96 I am not happy with some of the things you have done.

97 I would really like to try to talk you into doing this.

98 It's just awful, and you can't get hung up in that corporate thing, you can't worry about whether or not the stocks are going to drop.

99 You've got lives out there, people, women, wives, moms, and some who will never be moms.

100 Can't you move in on this thing now?

101 You are the people with the power to recall. You are the corporate conscience.

102 Please, in the name of humanity, lift your eyes above the bottom line.

103 You, the men in charge, must surely—I know you have hearts and souls and consciences—and I am not a great "Bible pounder," but this almost takes you into a Biblical reference, you can only explain it in that way.

104 If the thought of facing up to your transgressions is so unbearable to you—and I think it will be difficult for you—you might do as Roger Tuttle did and confess to your Maker and beg forgiveness and mend your ways.

105 The options are few.

106 Either you go along stonewalling it, like you are going, or you face up to what you have done, and then you have to start thinking about how you might make amends for that.

107 Please, Gentlemen, give consideration to tracing down the victims and sparing them the agony that will surely be theirs.

108 And I just want to say I love you. I am not mad at you.

VERNA C. CORGAN

Miles W. Lord's "Plea for Corporate Conscience"

*Court TV and coverage of celebrity trials have given greater pub-
lic prominence to legal rhetoric. The controversial Judge Miles
Lord, however, made a deliberate effort to transcend the courtroom in order to reach the public in his final statement to the
corporate leadership of the A. H. Robins Company. Robins had
made and sold the Dalkon Shield, a contraceptive device with
devastating effects on many women's health. Verna Corgan uses
a dramatistic approach to reveal the processes by which Lord
made his unconventional appeal forceful and effective. Throughout her analysis she recognizes the powerful argumentative structure buttressed with evidence underlying what is, at base, an instance of forensic rhetoric that accuses the corporate leadership
of the A. H. Robins Company of sins as well as crimes. Her focus, however, is on Lord's decision to violate the conventions of
the courtroom and of Lord's role as judge in order to achieve his
purpose. Although a rationalistic approach would tell us more
about Lord's use of argument and evidence, dramatism allows
Corgan to explain the strategies by which he transcended the
venue of the courtroom to make a statement that reverberated
throughout the mass media to reach a substantial portion of the
U.S. citizenry. Again, note the links between dramatistic perspectives and the application of artistic and ethical criteria to a rhetorical act.*

In 1984 U.S. District Court Judge Miles W. Lord approved a negotiated settlement of a legal dispute. The agreement was between persons who claimed they had been injured by a contraceptive device, the Dalkon Shield, and the maker of the device, A. H. Robins Co. It directly affected the outcome of only a small portion of the thousands of similar claims being made throughout the United States. In order to reach a settlement, defendant Robins had acquiesced to the plaintiffs' insistence that its "top management" confirm the agreement in the presence of the judge (Engelmayer and Wagman 225–226). Robins's president E. Claiborne Robins, Jr., senior vice president for research and development Carl D. Lunsford, and vice president and general counsel William A. Forrest, Jr., were called to the courtroom along with the company's local attorneys, the plaintiffs, and the plaintiffs' attorneys.

Once the principals had assembled, along with spectators who included other Dalkon Shield plaintiffs, lawyers, and reporters, the courtroom became the scene of an extraordinary legal event. In the course of sanctioning the settlement agreement, Judge Lord delivered a speech. Ostensibly addressed to the Robins executives, the speech characterized the executives' behavior and the company's development, manufacture, marketing, and legal defense of their contraceptive device; described the action Lord wished he could take to mitigate harm; and ended with what Lord termed a "plea" for change in the conduct of the company's business.

As a plea to Robins officials, the speech failed dismally. In response to it, A. H. Robins Co. charged Lord with grossly abusing his judicial authority, and the Court of Appeals expunged the speech from the record as having "crossed the line separating permissible judicial comments from impermissible public accusations" (AP, "Panel Dismisses Action" A14; *Gardiner v. Robins*, 474 F.2d 1180, 1984, at 1192). However, the speech did appeal to others. It was excerpted in newspapers and national magazines (Marcotty, "Attention" 1B; Oberdorfer, "Court Panel" 13A); newspaper columnists and readers praised it (Carr 5; Kaszaba 4B; McCarthy 10A; "Miles Lord's Speech" 22A); and a former Robins attorney cited it as his inspiration in defying threats of disbarment to testify that Robins had burned "legally damning" documents after its first trial loss 10 years previously (Carr 4; Walsh and Schwadel 13). Given such varied responses, the rhetorical significance of Lord's speech cannot be understood simply through a noting of its effects.

Instead this critique suggests that Lord's "Plea for Corporate Conscience" is significant as an illustration of how a rhetor can use the rhetorical resources of a recognized authority to transcend the limits of that authority. Such a rhetorical transcendence attempts to alter perceptions of the source and purpose of authority, reconstituting its substance, transmuting its form, and thereby changing the meaning of acts performed in its name. In his speech Lord seeks to achieve transcendence by rhetorically reordering an accepted hierarchy of judicial values that places law at the apex as the source of public good. In Lord's reordered hierarchy, justice is the transcendent value. Law is demoted, becoming only one means to obtain justice. Such a reordering has been suggested by Milner S. Ball, who observed that "above the entrance to the United States Supreme Court there is chiseled the motto: 'Equal Justice Under Law.' . . . At least since the days of the prophet Amos, others have thought justice has priority over law and that equal law under justice is a more fit order" (23). If Lord's rhetorical reordering is persuasive, it enables him, in the name of justice, to transcend the limits of his *legal* authority to address an urgent need beyond its ordinary scope, and to do so as a defender of the U.S. judicial tradition rather than as an offender against it.

BACKGROUND

Knowledge of events that preceded Lord's rhetorical reordering may help us to better understand it. By February 29, 1984, when Lord addressed the A. H. Robins executives, U.S. courts had been hearing product liability cases against the A. H. Robins Company for over a decade. The preceding 12 years had witnessed 36 trials, of which Robins lost 17, and 6,900 settlements in which Robins agreed to pay approximately $200 million (Zack, "Ex-Robins Attorney" 1A). Four thousand cases were still pending in courts nationwide. In addition, the courts could anticipate legal actions regarding cases already resolved. As plaintiffs attempted to enforce their settlement contracts, Robins argued that they were not binding. Claiming that its management was not aware of settlement terms agreed to by attorneys, the company had paid only two awards (Engelmayer and Wagman 219).

All of these product liability actions focused on one intrauterine contraceptive device, the Dalkon Shield. Thousands of women in whom the device was inserted, among them women who became pregnant with the Shield in place, developed pelvic inflammatory disease—a sudden, painful, acute infection of the fallopian tubes and ovaries that may spread to other organs (Engelmayer and Wagman 20). For stricken Dalkon Shield users, consequences of the disease included abscesses in the reproductive organs that could be treated with antibiotics and surgical draining, more serious abscesses that led to sterility or hysterectomies, spontaneous septic abortions caused by the spread of infection to fetuses, and/or death (Walsh 1).

The question before the courts was whether Dalkon Shield users' pelvic inflammatory disease resulted from a known defect in the device—a string attached to the device that drew bacteria from the vagina into the normally sterile uterus (Carr 4)—or from the sexual practices and hygiene habits of the women in whom Dalkon Shields were inserted, such as active sex lives, more than one sex partner, oral or anal sex during the period of contraceptive use, and/or back-to-front cleaning of the genital area (Engelmayer and Wagman 87–93).

On February 29, 1984, Miles W. Lord, Chief Judge for the District of Minnesota, was to approve the settlement of the last of the Dalkon Shield cases assigned to him. Lord had consolidated the cases over Robins's objections, and he had disqualified himself from hearing other cases after Robins hired his son-in-law's firm as defense counsel. The settlement came at a time when the U.S. Senate was considering the Uniform Product Liability Act. This bill would provide retroactively that only the first person whose complaint against a product was resolved in court could recover punitive damages, even if a manufacturer consciously chose not to modify or recall a defective product (Zack, "Ex-Robins Attorney" 1A). It came at a time when the federal courts were attempting to consolidate the remaining Dalkon Shield cases.

The settlement came after 3 months, 17 pretrial hearings, 7 motions for delay, 65 pleadings, and many judicial orders in the cases before Lord (Engelmayer and Wagman 146–147). It came after Lord had attended depositions of Robins officials in Richmond, Virginia, flying there to avoid delay in ruling on the numerous defense objections that previously had interfered with the completion of discovery (Engelmayer and Wagman 163–193). It came after a Lord-instituted court search of Robins's files uncovered 120,000 relevant documents previously withheld from a Kansas court (Transcript, *Gardiner & Michalik v. Robins*, p. 16; hereafter Transcript).[1] It came after Robins had transferred documents to its insurer, thus removing them from the scope of court discovery orders. It came one day after a court of appeals upheld the file search and refused to delay the trial (Engelmayer and Wagman 209), and after Lord issued a nondestruct order covering the newly discovered documents. It came one day after attorneys told Lord they could not reach a settlement, and he expressed regret that he would not have the opportunity to deliver remarks he had prepared in anticipation of settlement (Engelmayer and Wagman 224).

---

[1]In the 1970s the Kansas court had been assigned the task of completing discovery. It had accepted Robins's claim that its submission of 60,000 documents revealed its entire record of the contraceptive device. Courts in other jurisdictions later rejected plaintiffs' motions for additional discovery on the grounds that all existing documents had been submitted to the Kansas court.

The settlement came when Lord felt he was racing against time. Contrary to Robins's assertions, Lord believed the Dalkon Shield issues were simple and the same in all cases. Agreeing with other judges who had called Robins's conduct "fraudulent and dangerous to its customers" and its sale of the Dalkon Shield "a conscious decision . . . to market an inadequately tested, dangerous product by unethical and improper means using false and misleading advertising" (Oslund 1A), Lord wanted answers to essential questions. Did Robins lie to the government about the device in order to avoid the Food and Drug Administration's rigorous testing requirements? Did Robins conduct tests as it claimed? Did the tests produce the results Robins claimed? Did Robins officials know of the problems encountered by Dalkon Shield users? When? What did they do about it?

Lord knew the contents of some of the 120,000 newly discovered documents, and he believed that undeniable, inculpatory answers to his questions were contained in them. He believed that they would prove Robins's responsibility for its customers' injuries. He also believed that Robins's legal strategy would frustrate public revelation of this information and involve the courts in the perpetuation of injury. So Lord decided to do "exactly the right thing" (Oslund 4A). He would try to convince Robins officials to abandon a strategy of delay and tactical settlement in favor of repentance and atonement. On February 24, 1984, Judge Miles W. Lord meant to change things.

THE RHETORICAL PROBLEM

"To change things" is not an unusual rhetorical purpose, and in many ways Lord's speech was conventional. It responded to rhetorical problems in an environment of widely shared rhetorical expectations, and the choices Lord had to make are familiar to speakers, audiences, and critics in that culture. Because his thesis indicted them, Lord could expect that his immediate audience would be hostile to his conclusions. Therefore his arguments had to be clear, his evidence had to be strong, and his language had to be well chosen to elicit interest, assist understanding, and evoke sympathy. With these conventional characteristics, stemming from conventional needs, the speech is accessible to traditional criticism.

However, Lord also faced a less common problem: By giving his speech he would violate the conventions of a special rhetorical context, the U.S. court of law. Lord had been asked to witness the signing of a pretrial settlement agreement. Although it is not unusual for judges to approve such agreements, it is unusual for them to give more than formal approval. A judge may be expected to ensure that an agreement is not notoriously unfair to any litigant. However, because approval is granted before there has been an arbitrated hearing on the facts and law in controversy, he or she is not expected to form, let alone to declare, a judgment on the merits of the case. Because Judge Lord intended to do just that, he needed to reinvent the courtroom context in a way that would transcend conventional understandings of that context. He needed to provide an alternative to a perspective that might view him as acting outside the law. Lord faced the challenge of rhetorically inventing a new judicial order.

THEORETICAL PERSPECTIVE

Lord's rhetoric is, then, a blend of the unconventional and the conventional. How may a critic approach it? One way is through dramatistic criticism, which has been used to analyze both kinds of speech. For example, in criticizing the rhetoric of radical Black Nationalism, Karlyn Kohrs Campbell ("Black Nationalism") has demonstrated how dramatistic criticism can illuminate rhetorical acts that violate convention. The dramatistic approach also has been applied to rhetoric that seems neither extreme nor alien to most critics. Among other works, Kenneth Burke's analysis of Adolf Hitler's propaganda ("Hitler's Battle"), David Ling's criticism of Edward Kennedy's Chappaquiddick speech ("Pentadic Analysis"), and Ernest G. Bormann's criticism of Puritan rhetoric ("Fetching Good") all demonstrate the potential of dramatistic criticism to explain the persuasive power of more conventional rhetorical acts.

Transcendence

Burke's dramatistic concept of transcendence provides a link between the conventional and unconventional aspects of Lord's rhetorical act. In his *Rhetoric of Motives* (183–197), Burke suggests that in a competition between different interests, the translation of interests into a language of principles can change the meaning of the contest; it can render inappropriate compromises that would be acceptable in a resolution of differences based on "horse trading" (187). The language of principles accomplishes this redefinition by creating a hierarchy of terms. Such hierarchies "organize one's attitude toward the struggles" (188) involved in competition; they transform compromises into violations of principle, and they order inviolable principles into a series of progressive steps toward a "principle of principles."

A "principle of principles" forms the "head" or "spirit" of a body of supporting principles or motivational terms (188–189). Burke notes that the "principle of principles," or ultimate order, both fulfills and transcends underlying principles, terms, and ideas (189), much as the mind or spirit of a person is thought to give purpose and meaning to her or his physical existence. Further, Burke points out that the ultimate order "invariably aims to encompass conflicting orders of motivation, not by outlawing any order . . . but by finding a place for it in a developmental series" (189). Thus "inferior" principles become "a *way into* 'spirit' " (189), as a person's body and physical sensations inform her or his mind and spirit.

Lord's rhetorical situation demanded that his rhetorical act establish the primacy of a principle that would transcend the "orders of motivation" created by conventional understandings of the court and the law and would "find a place" for them in the service of the ultimate principle. This was necessary because the U.S. courtroom is a "reality" steeped in tradition and ritual that are sources of security for legal practitioners who know the rules of the legal contest. They may seek to exploit those rules to win advantage, but they depend upon a judge to limit severely the extent of any deviation and thus to preserve the fairness of the contest.

However, in delivering his "Plea for Corporate Conscience," it was Lord who deviated, and a judge's violation of shared expectations within the legal context presents a threefold danger. First, a litigant who depends on the legal system for the fair adjudication of her or his complaint may be unduly burdened by an abrupt change in the rules. Second, the fitness of the individual judge who violates the rules is likely to be questioned, thus casting doubt on all of the decisions she or he has made. Third, the efficacy of the institution that made possible such a violation may be challenged, thereby undermining the authority of the courts. In responding to the exigencies of his rhetorical situation, Lord confronted rhetorical problems that went beyond the immediate case in more than one way.

Lord clearly perceived an urgent need to address an injustice. Yet he was sensitive to the apparently conflicting requirements of norms, rules, laws, and justice. He also was aware that his status in the rhetorical situation depended on both his individual *ethos* and the respect accorded the court he represented. Impugning any of these sources of rhetorical power would result not only in a failed speech but also, potentially, in more long-term damage to his and the court's ability to arbitrate matters of law with the consent of citizens. Lord easily could anticipate negative responses to the means he chose to gain his end, even from those who found those ends laudable. There seemed to be tension between the principle of justice and the integrity of the courts, a tension that had to generate invention to argue the transcendency of justice.

Lord's strategy for achieving transcendence evokes the strategy of abolitionists who sought to displace the Constitution as the embodiment of United States justice. So long as the Constitution was interpreted as condoning slavery and protecting the property rights of slaveholders, as a statement of the law of the land it was seen as "an agreement with hell" (William Lloyd Garrison, in Garraty 438). For abolitionists the more "fundamental" symbol of United States justice was the Declaration of Independence. The Declaration's prior pronouncement of equality voided the Constitution's later sufferance of slavery. The Declaration of Independence became the principle of principles. The "place" for the Constitution was subordinate to the Declaration. It was an instrument *through which* the Declaration's principles should be made concrete; it should serve as citizens' *way into* the spirit of the Declaration.

Unlike those historical rhetors, Lord did not quarrel with the legitimacy of the written law; it was not corrupt law but corrupt individuals who bore the burden for unjust outcomes. But he did seek to transfer his audience's first allegiance from the written law to its reason for being, the pursuit of justice. Prior principles of universal humanity, the dignity of the individual, and the ideal of equality provided the materials from which Lord built his alternative framework. Calling upon the source of law, justice, as the principle of principles, as well as the law itself, he provided himself with a broader base on which to rest the propriety of his judgments. If he was successful in his attempt at transcendence, he would strengthen rather than weaken adherence to the legal system that empowered him, and he would be open to attack only to the extent that his audience believed that the purpose of that system was not to ensure that justice is done.

To forestall anticipated negative responses, Lord was constrained to do more than deliver a good speech. He needed to effect dramatic alterations in perception. That is, to maintain the sources of his legitimacy as a speaker, Lord needed to create an order of principles that would transcend the understood constraints created by law. To accomplish this transcendent rhetorical task he also needed to construct a rhetorical situation that his audience would accept as a compelling alternative to their previous mental image of a normal and appropriate courtroom situation.

Dramatistic Pentad

The construction could be no halfway measure; alternative interpretations of several elements present in the rhetorical situation had to be established firmly in the face of strong competition. These elements mirror the five key terms of Burke's dramatistic pentad: Act, what was done; Scene, when or where an act was performed; Agent, who performed the act; Agency, how the agent performed the act; and Purpose, why the act was performed (*Grammar of Motives* xv). According to Burke, "all statements that assign motives can be shown to arise out of [these five terms] and to terminate in them" (*Grammar of Motives* xvi). The continuing drama of human relations can be explained by the interaction of these elements.

In transcending his immediate rhetorical situation, Lord had to address these five elements of symbolic action to establish the ascendancy of his motivating order. His act had to be perceived as necessary to fulfill the principle of principles rather than as wanton disregard of judicial restraint. The scene had to be viewed as the entire field of U.S. justice rather than the legalistic confines of a pretrial court appearance. Lord, as the agent, had to appear to be a responsible judge rather than a renegade opportunist, to be operating from judicial reasoning rather than personal animus. Lord's speech, the agency through which he acted, had to be perceived to be judicial deliberation rather than illicit talk. Finally, the purpose had to be perceived as the rendering of a reasoned judgment in the service of justice rather than indulgence in partisan vilification. Only if all five elements interacted rhetorically to present Lord's motivation as just, necessary, and right would the rhetorical situation become one in which transcendence might be possible.

Miles W. Lord's "Plea for Corporate Conscience" resembles abolitionist rhetoric in that it seeks to replace one cultural consciousness with another and violates rhetorical conventions within a rhetorical "field." It resembles more traditional rhetoric in that it seeks to use widely shared cultural assumptions to construct a new social reality. Like those other rhetorical acts, it seeks to transcend. Thus Lord's plea may be illuminated by dramatistic criticism.

LORD'S RHETORICAL ACT

The Rhetor

Lord's attempt to transcend the judicial setting was not without risk; doing the "exactly right thing" could be costly to him. He was aware that an unsuccessful plea to the men in his courtroom could result in a judicial reprimand. But these were the men who could effect immediate change. At enormous cost to their profits and reputations, the Robins officials could concede their product's defects, trace its millions of users, accept responsibility for the damage it had caused, attempt to compensate for that damage, and set a new example of corporate conduct for U.S. businesses. In asking this audience to accept the high cost of change, Lord had to provide the model: He had to transcend fear of substantial personal risk to do the right thing.

This was not the first time Lord had done the "exactly right thing," putting himself at the center of controversy. In 1972 his judgment, made during a drug price-fixing case involving Johnson & Johnson, that the U.S. Patent Office was "the sickest institution our government has ever created" earned him a judicial reprimand (Walsh 1). In 1974 he ordered a taconite plant closed after finding that the tailings it dumped into Lake Superior were carcinogenic (*Reserve Mining Company v. United States of America*). He was removed from this environmental case when the Court of Appeals decided that he had "shed the robe of the judge and assumed the mantle of the advocate" (*Reserve Mining Company v. Lord* at 185), even though the judge who replaced him reached the same conclusion (Oslund 1A). In 1980 *The American Lawyer,* a lawyers' magazine, named him the Eighth Circuit's worst judge ("Best and Worst" 27); in 1981 the Association of Trial Lawyers of America named him one of the nation's best judges (Walsh 1A). His decrees that high schools must afford the same opportunities for participation to female and male athletes (*Brenden v. Independent School District 742*) and that poor and affluent school districts must offer the same educational opportunities were overturned (Engelmayer and Wagman 122). And in 1983 an appeals court overturned five drug convictions because he had "improperly coached the prosecutor" (Walsh 1A). Judge Lord's courtroom rhetoric was preceded by his reputation for judicial activism, an activism that was variously deplored and admired.

A. H. Robins was aware of Lord's reputation as the "warrior judge" and of his thirst for "facts." Two weeks before the settlement Robins's attorneys had asked him to remove himself from the cases on the ground of bias (Oberdorfer, "Maker of Dalkon Shield" 1A). When Lord summoned Robins officials and their attorneys to his courtroom, questioned them about the settlement, declared his power to approve it, and insisted that they read a transcript of his speech to the State Council of Churches and his "powerful" and "profound" personal plea to them, they objected vigorously, accusing Lord of exceeding his authority and abusing his discretion (Transcript 11–22). In response to Robins's rejection of his plea, their request that the proceedings be terminated, and their stated intention to appeal his rulings, Lord changed his rhetorical strategy. He offered his message to another audience.

The Audience

Inside the courtroom were others who were potential and actual agents of change. There were attorneys who had spent months investigating cases, designing legal strategies, and arguing in court. Sacrificing privacy, risking payment, and investing time, these attorneys and their clients had refused settlements that would deny other plaintiffs access to crucial information (Engelmayer and Wagman 218–225). There were reporters who, together with their employers and at the expense of other news stories, could focus media attention on the Dalkon Shield cases and their relationship to political, medical, and moral issues. Through them Lord could reach yet another audience, the public. Company officials would "never again [be able to] testify in any court that they knew nothing about the dangers inherent in the Dalkon Shield" (Transcript 23), and their public denials would be met with disbelief. So now all would hear what Lord had written. Knowing that his words would be read by other courts, he stated for the record that "Judge Lord has concluded that these cases in effect are all one" and began to read aloud his plea (Transcript 23).

When Lord intoned "Mr. Robins, Jr., Mr. Forrest and Dr. Lunsford," whispered courtroom conversations ceased. As he read from his text, from time to time departing from his prepared remarks to speak directly to the defendants, the Robins officials and attorneys remained "stony-faced and motionless." Plaintiffs wept. Their attorneys were overcome with admiration and gratitude. The speech ended. Lord wrote "So ordered" on the settlement, transforming it from a private contract to a judicial decree. Thus violation of its terms would constitute contempt of court. Robins's attorneys announced that they would add to their other appeals a charge of personal misconduct against Lord (Engelmayer and Wagman 254–257). What was the message that elicited such responses?

The Speech

The central idea of Lord's "Plea for Corporate Conscience" is clear: There is no such thing as corporate guilt or innocence. Corporations are artificial legal constructs that mask human beings. Guilt, innocence, and justice are concepts that define human beings. All human acts are those of individuals, and justice is served only when individuals are made to account for the morality as well as the legality of their acts. Lord clearly stated his thesis, saying that "the accumulation of corporate wrongs is . . . a manifestation of individual sin" (4).[2] He applied his standard of individual responsibility to himself in explaining his motive for speaking:

---

[2]Parenthetical citations are paragraph numbers. It should be noted that Lord's speech was 10 minutes long. The typed transcript contains many one-sentence paragraphs, and numbering them may leave the impression that the speech is substantially longer.

Despite your company's protestations, it is evident that these thousands of cases cannot be viewed in isolation, and that is one of the main reasons why I feel free to make this statement here today.

If every judge is terminated as soon as he catches on to what's going on, if you settle the case and flee the jurisdiction, that leaves no one to follow up to make any cohesiveness to this. (73–74)

And later Lord said,

If a judge were to wait until all the cases were over before he spoke out on the evils he sees inherent in the system and in the trial tactics, then no one would ever speak out.

There is a time when measures must be taken, when steps must be taken to see that fair play and ethical standards apply to the disposition of all the cases that are come to the future, regardless of what might have happened in the past. (81–82)

In an important sense these passages constitute a statement of Lord's transcendent purpose. If justice is the ultimate principle, each individual must act to attain it regardless of organizational norms and rules that might discourage or even forbid action. This is the basis on which Lord condemned the acts of the A. H. Robins executives. In laying this foundation Lord also supplied the rationale for his own transformation of judicial authority. He, like the executives, was an individual within a "system" who had power to influence both the aims and the acts of the system. And like the executives, when he recognized a wrong within the system, he was required to act to right it, to pursue justice regardless of personal or corporate consequences.

Brushed aside were considerations of only what the law allows. Lord was exasperated with the legal allowances that enabled the executives to escape the consequences of their acts: "Time and time again each of you ha[s] . . . refus[ed] to acknowledge your responsibility and pretend[ed] to the world that the chief officers and directors of your gigantic multinational corporation have no responsibility for the company's acts and omissions" (3). He was outraged that as a result of their strategic use of legal rules, the executives maintained the fiction that they were ignorant of the issues involved in a decade of litigation:

Gentlemen, the result of these activities and attitudes on your part have been catastrophic.

Today, as you sit here, attempting once more to extricate yourselves from the legal consequences of your acts, none of you have faced up to the fact that more than 9,000 women have made claims that they gave a part of their womanhood so that your company might prosper. (9–10)

Lord believed judges no longer could permit Robins's exploitation of rules to further a "policy of delay and obfuscation practiced by your lawyers in courts [that] has made it possible for your insurance company and you . . . to delay the payment of these claims for such a long period" (47). Specifically, rule-governed permissiveness toward delay and obfuscation had resulted in Robins, not the courts, controlling the legal process. Lord said,

> Your company seeks and has sought to segment and fragment the litigation of these cases nationwide.
>
> The courts of this country are now burdened with more than 3,000 Dalkon Shield cases.
>
> The sheer number of claims and the dilatory tactics used by your company's attorneys clog court calendars and consume vast amounts of judicial and jury time.
>
> Your company settles those cases in which it finds itself in an uncomfortable position, a handy device for avoiding any proceeding which would give continuity or cohesiveness to this nationwide problem.
>
> The decision as to which cases to try rests almost solely at the whim and discretion of the A. H. Robins company. (59–63)

Further, according to Lord, Robins's "system [of legal] evasion and avoidance" (64) and "callous legal tactics" (69) resulted in justice delayed and denied: "The cases of these women have waited on the calendar of this court for as many as three years. . . . Yet [you want them] to wait at the bottom of the calendar for additional months and years before they could have their day in court" (66–68).

This was the courtroom scene Lord painted with his rhetoric. It was a scene in which the letter of the law and legal procedures had been permitted to eclipse the spirit of justice that had given birth to them, and one in which a powerful litigant had been allowed to undermine both the authority of judges and the rights of other litigants. The time had come to transcend this scene, to broaden the scope of the courts' authority and focus on justice rather than on legal artificialities. Lord spoke of good and evil, not about complex legal concepts.

The whole of Lord's speech was informed by his rhetorical persona. As agent in this rhetorical drama, he was the quintessential judge acting in an expanded judicial arena. In moral as well as legal matters he was sanctioned by the highest authorities; right action would lead to justice. He indicted, he determined facts, he rendered judgment, and he prescribed penalties. But as a judge in the moral sphere, he could not enforce the law he pronounced or absolve the transgressors. His opinions were true, but his audience's duty to be persuaded by them was as great as his duty to persuade, and it was another's prerogative to forgive. Viewed from this perspective, Lord's harsh tone can be reconciled with an intention to seek agreement and change through his speech.

Although he claimed not to be a "Bible pounder," Lord turned to that book for words to explain his plea. Telling the Robins executives that their situation "almost takes you into a Biblical reference, you can only explain it that way," Lord counseled them, "If the thought of facing up to your transgressions is so unbearable to you—and I think it will be difficult for you—you might do as Roger Tuttle[3] did and confess to your Maker and beg forgiveness and mend your ways" (103).

Biblical appeals emphasized Lord's transcendent purpose and the rightness of his, the agent's, acting in an expanded field of justice. And Lord had prepared the way for these appeals by developing a God-sanctioned persona. In his first sentence he announced that he had sought divine guidance for the step he was taking, acting only "after months of reflection, study and cogitation—and no small amount of prayer" (1). Further, he suggested that such guidance was no novelty: "Several years ago . . . I suggested to the hundreds of ministers of the Gospel, who constitute the Minnesota Council of Churches, that the accumulation of corporate wrongs is in my mind a manifestation of individual sin" (4). He followed his announcement with a speech replete with the language of religion: for example, injured women "raise their voices" (15); "the poor and downtrodden" plead for clemency (21); the Robins executives negotiate with Congress for ways of "forgiving you from punitive damages" (25); Robins's device threatens women's "wombs" (36); "Rehabilitation involves an admission of guilt, a certain contrition, an acknowledgment of wrongdoing, and a resolution to take a new course" (42); A. H. Robins targets as victims "the meek and the poor" (70); the company's "acts and omissions" are the focus of all of the Dalkon Shield cases (78); and the Robins executives are "the corporate conscience" (101).

Nevertheless, Lord was no savior. Although he asserted that "confession is good for the soul" (44), nowhere in his speech did he hold out the promise of salvation. For salvation the executives must turn to an even higher power; they must "confess to your Maker and beg forgiveness" (104). Neither was Lord a prophet: He dwelt almost entirely on past occurrences and the present situation. Lord was judge, and the certainty of his judge persona contrasts dramatically to the doubtful character of those he indicted. In protesting that "you, the men in charge, must surely . . . have hearts and souls and consciences" (103), Lord emphasized that, partly through the grace of God, he was superior to his immediate audience.

---

[3]Roger Tuttle is the former Robins attorney who testified to burning documents.

But grace was not enough, even for Lord. There must be human works. As he served an "ultimate order," Lord "encompassed" rather than "outlawed" subordinate orders. He remained an interpreter of human law, a legal judge, and he characterized the agency of his speech as the court's deliberation. Referring to himself as "this court" (27), he became the embodiment of the legal system. As the system's embodiment, he sought to demonstrate appropriate legal restraint in the areas of delimitation of issues, reliance on precedent, consistency with other judges' conclusions, and examination of evidence.

Lord maintained that he was "specifically directing and limiting my remarks to that which I have learned and observed in these consolidated cases before me. If an incident arises involving another product made by A. H. Robins Company, an independent judgment would have to be made as to the conduct of your company concerning that product" (17–18). His careful isolation of relevant issues was echoed in his careful exclusion of the blameless from his judgment (19, 71–72).

In discussing appropriate punishments, Lord turned to what "the case law indicates" (32) as precedent for his judgments. His respect for precedent was reinforced by the consistency of his decisions with those of other judges. According to Lord, his rejection of the executives' claim to have suffered merely confirmed universal standards of judgment: "No court would heed this plea when the individual denies the wrongful nature of his deed and gives no indication that he will mend his ways" (23). In addition, his identification of Robins's obfuscation was supported by other judicial authorities:

> Judge Frank Theis, who presided over the discovery of these cases, [and recently wrote that] "The project manager . . . explains that a particular question should have gone to the medical department. The medical department . . . explains that the question was really the bailiwick of the quality control department. The quality control department . . . explains that the project manager was the one with the authority . . . on that question." Under these circumstances, Judge Theis noted, it is not at all unusual for the hard questions . . . to be unanswerable by anyone from Robins. (54–58)

Moreover, Lord's conclusion that all of the Dalkon Shield cases "must be viewed as a whole" (80) was consistent with the findings of a multidistrict litigation panel (75) and of "Judge Gerald Heaney of the Court of Appeals . . . [who] recently urged judges in Minnesota to work together to devise a coordinated system for dealing with all of their Dalkon Shield cases" (79).

The strategies of delimiting issues, citing precedent, and showing consistency with other judges assisted Lord in presenting himself as an impartial translator of the legal code, a principled agent. Perhaps even more persuasive arguments of impartiality were Lord's references to facts. Lord insisted that "these matters of which I speak are not matters about which I speculate. They are matters contained in the evidence that has gone before me in the briefs of counsel, in the admissions, and in the documents" (92; see also 17, 34, 76, 91). With this combination of conventional appeals to judicial restraint, Lord underscored the propriety of his legal persona. The propriety of his legal persona constituted a rhetorical resource for claiming the sanction of higher authority, a "way into" the spirit of justice. The integration of legal and moral sanctions created a transcendent persona, an agent of justice entitled to speak on behalf of society, not just on behalf of the courts. "In the name of humanity" (102), Lord could direct the accused to right conduct.

Having established his claim to his judge persona on moral as well as legal grounds, Lord indicted the transgressors. Lord's first words, "Mr. Robins, Mr. Forrest and Dr. Lunsford," were repeated throughout the text of the speech (5–8, 25, 35, 46, 51–52), and mention was made of the "Robins family" and the "Robins mentality" (5). Lord addressed "you three men" (27, 38), "you men personally" (29), "you gentlemen" (51), "you three gentlemen" (87), "gentlemen" (9, 20, 44, 95, 107), and "you, the men in charge" (103). He used the plural "you" 64 times, the plural "your" 48 times, "yourselves" once, the singular "you" eight times, and the singular "your" six times in contexts that admitted no doubt as to his meaning.

Neither is there doubt about the nature of the indictment. Lord concluded his one-sentence opening paragraph with a "plea to you to seek . . . a new sense of personal responsibility," thus setting out the encompassing charge of personal irresponsibility. A review of each man's area of special responsibility followed:

> You, Mr. Robins, Jr., have been heard to boast many times that the growth and prosperity of this company is a direct result of its having been in the Robins family for three generations, the stamp of the Robins family is upon it, the corporation is built in the image of the Robins mentality.
>
> You, Dr. Lunsford, as director of the company's most sensitive and important subdivision, the medical division, have violated every ethical precept to which every doctor under your supervision must pledge as he gives the oath of Hippocrates and assumes the mantle of one who would cure and nurture unto the physical needs of the populace.
>
> You, Mr. Forrest, are a lawyer who, upon finding his client in trouble, should counsel and guide him along a course which will

comport with the legal and moral and ethical principles which must
bind us all.

You have not brought honor to your profession, Mr. Forrest. (5–8)

Lord supported these broad accusations with a bill of particulars.
For example, individually and together the executives had "invaded
[women's] bodies . . . , caused them injuries . . . , attacked their characters . . . , ruined families and reputations and careers . . . [and]
planted in [their] bodies instruments of death, of mutilation, of disease" (13–16); refused to recall "this product [because] it would hurt
your balance sheet and alert women, who already have been harmed"
(39); and "force[d] women of little means to withstand the onslaught
of your well-financed nationwide team of attorneys" (69). Nor did
Lord neglect lack of repentance: "Your company in the face of overwhelming evidence denies its guilt and continues its monstrous mischief" (24); "[I]nsofar as this court is able to determine, you three men
and your company still engage in the same course of wrongdoing on
which you originally commenced. Until your company indicates that
it is willing to cease and desist this deception and seek out and advise
victims, your remonstrances to Congress and to the courts of this
country are indeed hollow and cynical" (27–28); "you have taken the
bottom line as your guiding beacon and the low road as your route.
This is corporate responsibility at its meanest" (40); and "You three
gentlemen have made no effort whatsoever to locate [the women] and
bring them together to seek a common solution to their plight" (87).
Lord had prepared his brief.

With regard to punishment, Lord was equally specific. By enumerating the ways in which the sinners had not suffered, he suggested the
ways in which they should have: "Yet the profits of your company
continue to mount. Your last financial report boasts of new records for
sales and earnings with a profit of more than fifty-eight million in
1983" (26); "The company has not suffered, nor have you men personally. You are collectively being enriched by millions of dollars each
year. There is as yet no evidence that your company has suffered any
penalty whatsoever from these litigations. In fact the evidence is to
the contrary" (29–31; see also 47–50). Lord's "dread" of "the consequences if your victims had been men rather than women, women
who seem through some strange quirk of our society's mores to be expected to suffer pain, suffering and humiliation" (11); and his obser-
vation that "if one poor young man were by some act of his, without
authority or consent, to inflict such damage upon one woman, he
would be jailed for a good portion of the rest of his life" (12), were
suggestions of just penalties that also exposed the law's inability to
deal effectively with corporate misconduct. As a judge who respected

the source of his sanctions, Lord acknowledged his limitations: "I do not have the power to order you" (93). He ended his speech with a plea to repent and sin no more: "Please, Gentlemen, give consideration to tracing down the victims and sparing them the agony that will surely be theirs" (107). What would be the reward for repentance? Not forgiveness, not absolution, but reclamation of hearts, souls, and consciences. The rest was up to the sanctioners; the persona of the judge was complete.

In the light of his persona, Lord's purposes became clear. He was targeting multiple audiences. With regard to the immediate audience, Lord's failure to search for common ground was a function of persona, not an indication that they were not part of the rhetorical act. The speech is a forensic form of religious and secular sermon. The immediate audience had relinquished any claim to common ground. Lord's purpose was to instruct them as to their sins and to point the way back to the higher ground. As in Puritan sermons and the confiscation speeches of Radical Republicans, the transgressors had to repent and work their ways back to higher ground before discourse could occur on a more even level. The individuals were their own agents of change, and Lord's speech was his effort to change the scene of the controversy to one that corresponded to his view of a transcendent reality.

Although he extended to the Robins executives the option of reading his speech privately, Lord may have expected their negative response. Thus he seems to have anticipated a wider audience. His concern for the perceived propriety of his speech (1) and his testimony regarding his judicial fitness suggest awareness that others better qualified than his immediate audience would evaluate it. Lord's plain speaking approach informed those audiences that, regardless of legal niceties, to condemn his words would be to reject what is right and to condone and cooperate in the degradation of justice, in the sacrifice of the most defenseless of human victims (11), and in criminals' notorious enjoyment of the fruits of their moral crimes. To reject the words of the judge would be to join the ranks of the judged. To embrace them would be to acknowledge individual responsibility and to grant the court a role as agent of change, to broaden its power to do justice.

As suggested above, Lord used language appropriate to his persona and the new reality he attempted to create. Words and phrases common to religious speech linked his address with a major, culturally accepted, moral agency, thus extending the sanction for the speech. The consistent use of "victims" to refer to real and potential plaintiffs served multiple purposes. It reinforced the characterization of the defendants, because if there are victims there must be perpetrators of crime. It underscored the helplessness of plaintiffs, particularly in conjunction with such words as "catastrophic" and "disaster." And it called to mind culturally recognized power differences between individuals and corporations, an evocation that tended to eliminate the potential leveling influence of "middlepersons," such as lawyers, and to contribute to the importance of the court's agency. Lord portrayed the enormity of the evil lurking behind a civilized veneer partly through reliance on words that conveyed magnitude without specificity—for example, "your gigantic multinational corporation" (3), "there stand behind legions more" (10), "invaded their bodies by the millions and caused them injuries by the thousands" (13), "monstrous mischief" (24), "boasts of new records for sales and earnings" (26), "tens of thousands of them" (36), "the sheer number of claims" (61), "this nationwide problem" (62), "thousands of cases" (73), "a disaster of the highest magnitude" (84), and "thousands of victims" (86). And finally, Lord's avoidance of technical language enabled him to state his case in the moral as well as the legal sphere and to paint his picture in vivid contrasts. This judicial pronouncement used legal references only to illustrate Lord's interpretation of moral choices or to establish the propriety of his remarks. Even then the terms *punitive damages, litigation,* and *plaintiffs* were likely to be familiar to most laypersons. Lord's natural language was a powerful device for accentuating the fundamental accessibility of the issues he addressed.

Lord used a strategy of contrasts throughout his speech, beginning with his efficient, climactic first paragraph. He began by addressing individuals by name, a tactic with which he started to construct a new frame within which to consider the issues at hand. Referring to the thought preceding and the sanction for his speech, he made an ethical claim and, at the same time, built suspense because only an unconventional address would be preceded by careful consideration of its propriety rather than its legal correctness. Then Lord described his plea, his description reinforcing the changed frame of reference and setting out in general terms the response he sought.

Lord proceeded with his reconstruction of the context for argument by rejecting the perception of reality contained in the individuals' protestations of innocence. Even more important, he rejected their sincerity in advancing it (3). Bolstering his refutation with another ethical claim, he contrasted their pretense to his own reality—that is, the reality of individual sin (4). Lord addressed each of the named individuals separately, outlining the bases for their personal responsibility and their voluntary assumption of that responsibility: The owner made his company prosperous in his image, suggesting godlike control over its doings; the doctor-director adopted leadership responsibility and the medical profession's oath to heal, cure, and nurture; the lawyer designed his client's legal strategy and bound himself to the same legal, moral, and ethical principles by which Lord was bound (5–8). Having portrayed the executives as independent agents with individual responsibility, Lord continued his introduction with a series of contrasts: between the significant import of the individuals' commercial activities (a catastrophe) and the trivial import of their legal efforts (extrication); between legal reality (extrication) and moral reality (legions of women had been injured and were not relieved); between society's valuation of women and men; between the punishment of a "legal" person and that faced by the defendants; and between the "real" issue and the issues raised by the defendants. After ending his long introduction with a statement limiting the scope of his remarks, a statement that also reinforced his judicial *ethos,* Lord continued with his strategy of contrasts, topically ordered, throughout his speech. He contrasted the defendants' purported suffering to that of sincere pleaders, to that of their victims, and to their actual financial prosperity. He contrasted their activities to those that would earn mercy. He contrasted their claims on justice to their legal strategies of selectively settling cases, silencing attorneys, and dividing plaintiffs. And he contrasted their separation of cases to the consistency of their actions, the uniformity of the legal issues, and the collectivity of victims.

Lord's conclusion introduced a final contrast between what he, as legal judge, would have liked to do—order them to take remedial action—and what he, as a moral judge, had to do—plead with them to take remedial action. This final contrast gave added coherence to the drama presented in the preceding series of contrasts. The fundamental contrasts were between what the accused said and what was real, between what they did and what they should do. The implied contrast was between what the court was permitted to do by law and what it should do to work justice. Lord ended his speech with the statement that only the individuals he addressed could rectify the wrong; that to be human, in contrast to legal, beings they must right it; and that in not righting it they must accept responsibility for the further agony of their victims. The speech's conclusion evoked its beginning: Sins were being committed, and these three individuals were committing them.

Lord's *ethos* was a major source of evidence. He offered analogies and illustrations that were based on his experience and interpretation of the case before him; one had to believe in his conscientiousness and impartiality, as well as in individual responsibility for corporate acts, in order to accept his version of the facts. The few statistics he used, e.g., "9,000 women" (10), "a profit of more than fifty-eight million" (26), "3,000 Dalkon Shield cases" (60), "three years" (66), and "12 years of delay"(77), gave form to his more general, and dramatic, narrative of the problem's magnitude and suggested his grasp of the underlying facts. Specific examples—an attorney (37–38) and an insurance company (47)—made more concrete his impeachment of defendants' testimony and his depiction of their corrupting influence. His endorsement of a law firm, Faegre & Benson (71–72), served to highlight his fairness, as did his disavowals of personal animosity (95, 108). His appeal to the authority of judicial colleagues (54, 79) suggested that he conformed to the trend in judicial findings and the principles of judicial conduct at the same time that he sought to make them work in the "real" world.

But details were not what could make the speech effective. In the end, Lord's persona was what proved or disproved the truth of what he said. If he succeeded in persuading his auditors that the scene of argument was the field of justice rather than an isolated court of law, and that as an agent he was "The Judge" fit to judge in the expanded scene, they would believe in his reality: that the causes he identified created the effects he enumerated, and that the solution he advanced was the only one that would rectify the problem he had described. If his persona did not persuade, there had been no transcendence.

CONCLUSION

Miles W. Lord encountered a complex rhetorical problem in delivering his "Plea for Corporate Conscience." Violating judicial convention in a court of law would threaten his authority as an individual judge and the authority of the judiciary he represented at a time when both sources of authority were essential for him to maintain his *ethos* as a fit speaker. Dramatistic criticism enables us to recognize rhetorical strategies that afforded Lord an opportunity to overcome the obstacles in his situation in addressing an issue beyond the scope of his strictly legal authority.

First, dramatistic criticism draws our attention to the language of principles, both judicial and religious, that enabled Lord to create a symbolic context in which he could not compromise without destroying his reason for being. The principle of justice, particularly when it is associated with the notion of a just God, is not a medium of exchange; it cannot be bartered without being extinguished. Second, by focusing on the principle of justice as the reason for law and, therefore, as the reason for courts, Lord was able to portray himself as a principled actor or agent even when he acted outside the constraints of legal authority. In his speech he depicted the A. H. Robins executives having bested the law; they exerted power *over* the courts through the rules *of* the courts. The executives, in effect, owned the instruments of justice, and a court that is powerless to act as the agency through which justice is done has lost its meaning. To regain meaning, the courts must wrest control from the usurpers. Having been shown that the law is not equal to the battle, they can do that only by reclaiming the original source of their authority—the principle of justice that is prior to, transcendent of, and operative in a sphere broader than that of the law.

Finally, dramatistic criticism enables us to identify the interaction of symbolic elements in Lord's speech that contribute to its persuasiveness. Viewing Lord's rhetorical recreation of a legal controversy as drama highlights the alternative scripts offered in the speech. An audience member is called upon to identify with one or the other polarized act-scene-agent-agency-purpose sets. One set will result in the audience symbolically becoming Lord-like, sharing in his reality, in his persona, and in his action. The other will place the audience against Lord, his reality, and his action. In an important sense it also will result in the audience symbolically becoming like the Robins executives and sharing in the quality of their acts. Because Lord's drama depicts law as unable to ensure a just outcome, the alternative script also will place the audience at odds with the principle of justice.

EPILOGUE

After Lord delivered his speech, Robins and its officials appealed his rulings to the Eighth Circuit Court of Appeals and asked for a special judicial council to review his conduct. The Court of Appeals expunged Lord's speech from the record and confirmed that the settlement was not a court order (AP, "Panel Dismisses Action" A14). But this was not the last act in the drama.

Lord was granted his unusual request that the special court inquiry into his conduct be open to the media; thus, the Dalkon Shield issues remained in public view (George 1A). Articles about the speech and the resulting controversy appeared in newspapers and magazines across the nation (Oberdorfer, "Court Panel" 13A). Television's "60 Minutes" re-aired its 1981 Dalkon Shield story along with the story of Lord's speech (Carr 4). The Uniform Products Liability Act lost support ("Boschwitz Backs Off"). In May a California doctor wrote personally to one of the Robins officials to report that his patient had died because of the Dalkon Shield (Engelmayer and Wagman 267–268). Robins began a $4 million effort to have Dalkon Shields removed from U.S. women, but not from the estimated 1.7 million users in 79 foreign countries (Tai 7A). By April over 4,400 Dalkon Shields had been removed, and doctors continued to remove over 100 of them each week (Engelmayer and Wagman 299).

A former Robins attorney, saying Lord had inspired him to reclaim his integrity (Carr 4), testified that Robins had burned "legally damning" documents after its first trial loss 10 years earlier (Walsh and Schwadel 13). The first trial in which his testimony was admitted ended in a $4.5 million jury verdict against the company (Walsh 1). Across the nation judges began to grant plaintiffs' requests for documents and to sanction Robins's failures to produce them (AP, "Panel Dismisses Action" A14). They followed Lord's example in barring Robins's routine questioning about women's sex lives in the absence of proof of its relevance (Walsh 1).

In November 1984 Robins settled 198 Minnesota cases for approximately $40 million, increasing the average settlement sixfold over those reached before the additional Robins documents became available. The lawyers in the Minnesota cases offered to other attorneys the information they had garnered in a $1.5 million research effort. They also would advise lawyers regarding the potential settlement value of individual cases (Peterson 1A). In June the Colorado Supreme Court upheld a $6.2 million punitive damage verdict against Robins. The number of injury claims grew to over 11,000. Seven hundred additional cases were settled, and 16 cases went to trial; Robins won five of them (Peterson 1A). The courts proceeded in their consolidation efforts. Momentum gathered, lives may have been saved, and the Dalkon Shield cases moved toward resolution. At least for a time, public attention was focused on business and legal ethics.

The Dalkon Shield claimed at least 30 lives. A. H. Robins's Chapter 11 protection rendered the payment of claims—14,000 filed, 9,000 settled, and 5,000 pending—uncertain (Schwadel 3). The resurgence of attempts to cap recovery of punitive damages has not been accompanied by a resurrection of attempts to mandate criminal penalties for manufacturers who knowingly sell defective products. On the other hand, the conduct of Robins executives was investigated by a federal grand jury (AP, "Federal Jury" 10Y), and for a time they faced the prospect of criminal charges that faintly resembled those Lord suggested.

As for Miles Lord, he continues to be controversial. He has reaffirmed his belief that justice is grounded in a reality broader than the courts of law (Engelmayer and Wagman 119). A Robins executive called him "a World War II mine loose in the channel"; an executive from another company thought of him as a "friendly buoy to keep corporations from going up on more dangerous shores" (Oslund 1A). In 1984 the ATLA gave him its Presidential Award of Merit "in recognition of his judicial independence, courage and integrity of purpose"

(Engelmayer and Wagman 300). On December 26, 1984, the special judicial council dismissed the misconduct charge against him (UPI 46), and on January 24, 1985, it found him not guilty of judicial misconduct (Engelmayer and Wagman 286). In July of 1985 Lord retired from the judiciary (Engelmayer and Wagman 300). He now practices law in Minneapolis, Minnesota. His telephone book advertisement reads, "Miles Lord will help you or he will find the lawyer who can" (Northwestern Bell).

WORKS CITED

Associated Press. "Federal Jury Studying Maker of Contraceptive." *New York Times* 21 Nov. 1986: 10Y.

——. "Panel Dismisses Action against Federal Judge." *New York Times* 27 Dec. 1984: A14.

Ball, Milner S. *Lying Down Together: Law, Metaphor, and Theology.* Madison: University of Wisconsin Press, 1985.

"Best and Worst Federal Judges." *The American Lawyer* (July 1980): 16–30.

Bormann, Ernest G. "Fetching Good Out of Evil: A Rhetorical Use of Calamity." *Quarterly Journal of Speech* 63 (1977): 130–139.

"Boschwitz Backs Off on Product Liability Bill." *St. Paul Dispatch* 16 Aug. 1984: 1A, 4A.

Brenden v. Independent School District 742, 342 F.Supp. 1221 (1972).

Burke, Kenneth. *A Rhetoric of Motives.* Berkeley: University of California Press, 1969.

——. *A Grammar of Motives.* Berkeley: University of California Press, 1969.

——. "The Rhetoric of Hitler's Battle." *Philosophy of Literary Form: Studies in Symbolic Action.* New York: Vintage Books, 1957. 164–189.

Campbell, Karlyn Kohrs. "The Rhetoric of Radical Black Nationalism: A Case Study in Self-Conscious Criticism." *Central States Speech Journal* 22 (1971): 81–86.

Carr, David. "Dalkon Shield: Robins Races Burning Issue." *Twin Cities Reader* 8–14 Aug. 1984: 4, 5.

Corgan, Verna Corrine. *Stories of Justice: Controversial Judicial Opinions and the Community.* Diss. University of Minnesota, 1992. Ann Arbor: UMI, 1993. 9239112.

Corgan, Verna C. *Controversy, Courts, and Community: The Rhetoric of Judge Miles Welton Lord.* New York: Greenwood Press, 1995.

Engelmayer, Sheldon, and Robert Wagman. *Lord's Justice.* Garden City, NY: Anchor Press, 1985.

Gardiner v. Robins, 474 F.2d 1180 (1984).

Gardiner & Michalek v. Robins, D. Minn., Civ. 3–83–1025, 3–83–106. Transcript, Further Pretrial Proceedings, February 29, 1984.

Garraty, John A. *The American Nation: A History of the United States to 1877*. New York: Harper & Row, 1971.

George, Jim. "Dalkon Firm Says Lord Abused Office." *St. Paul Dispatch* 15 May 1984: 1A, 4A.

Kaszaba, Mike. "Lawyers Criticize Probe of Miles Lord." *Star Tribune* [Minneapolis] 4 July 1984: 4B.

Ling, David. "A Pentadic Analysis of Senator Edward Kennedy's Address to the People of Massachusetts, July 25, 1969." *Central States Speech Journal*. 21 (1970): 81–86.

Lord, Miles W. "Plea for Corporate Conscience." Transcript, Further Pretrial Proceedings, February 29, 1984. *Gardiner & Michalek v. Robins*, D. Minn., Civ. 3–83–1025, 3–83–106.

Marcotty, Josephine. "Attention Focuses on Review of Lord." *Star Tribune* [Minneapolis] 9 July 1984: 1B.

McCarthy, Coleman. "Judge Lord's Beautiful Anger Penetrates the Corporate Shield" Editorial. *Star Tribune* [Minneapolis] 3 April 1984: 10A.

"Miles Lord's Speech in the Cause of Justice." Editorial. *Star Tribune* [Minneapolis] 18 May 1984: 22A.

Northwestern Bell. *1986 Minneapolis Consumer Directory*. U.S. West Direct, 1985–1986.

Oberdorfer, Dan. "Court Panel Hears Testimony on Firm's Complaint against Lord." *Star Tribune* [Minneapolis] 15 Sept. 1984: 13A.

———. "Maker of Dalkon Shield Lodges Complaints against Judge Lord." *Star Tribune* [Minneapolis] 15 May 1984: 1A, 8A.

Oslund, John J. "Is Lord Antibusiness?" *Star Tribune* [Minneapolis] 25 Nov. 1984: 1A, 4A, 6A.

Peterson, David. "A. H. Robins to Pay Nearly $40 Million in Dalkon Shield Case." *Star Tribune* [Minneapolis] 15 Nov. 1984: 1A, 7A.

Reserve Mining Company v. Lord, 529 F.2d 181 (1976).

Reserve Mining Company v. United States of America, 498 F.2d 1073 (1974).

Schwadel, Francine. "Robins Files for Protection of Chapter 11." *The Wall Street Journal* 22 Aug. 1985: 3.

Tai, Wendy S. "IUD Firm Spending $4 Million on Ad Effort." *Star Tribune* [Minneapolis] 15 Nov. 1984: 7A.

United Press International. "Judge Rebuked over Remark." *New York Times* 3 Nov. 1984: 46.

Walsh, Mary Williams. "Jurist's Tactics Hasten the Pace of Litigation in Dalkon Shield Cases." *The Wall Street Journal* 14 Sept. 1984: 1, 20

Walsh, Mary Williams, and Francine Schwadel. "Bizarre Twist in Lawsuits on Contraceptive Is Provided by Ex-A. H. Robins Attorney." *The Wall Street Journal* 3 Aug. 1984: 13.

Zack, Margaret. "Ex-Robins Attorney Suggests Firm Lied." *Star Tribune* [Minneapolis] 3 Aug. 1984: 1B, 4B.

INDEX

THE AUTHORS

Karlyn Kohrs Campbell teaches in and is chair of the Department of Speech Communication of the University of Minnesota. She is the co-author of *Interplay of Influence: News, Advertising, Politics and the Mass Media* and *Deeds Done in Words: Presidential Rhetoric and the Genres of Governance* and author of *Man Cannot Speak for Her* and *The Rhetorical Act*. Her work has appeared in *Philosophy and Rhetoric* and the *Quarterly Journal of Speech*, among others. She is editor of a two-volume reference work, *Women Public Speakers in the United States*. She received the Woolbert Award for scholarship of exceptional originality and influence (1987), the Winans–Wichelns Book Award (1990), and the Ehninger Award for outstanding scholarship in rhetoric (1991), and she was recognized as a Distinguished Scholar by the Speech Communication Association (1992). She has served on the editorial boards of *Communication Monographs, Quarterly Journal of Speech, Philosophy and Rhetoric, Communication Education, Communication Quarterly, Communication Studies,* and *Critical Studies in Mass Communication*.

Thomas R. Burkholder teaches in the Department of Speech Communication, Southwest Texas State University, San Marcos. He received an M.A. (1974) from Emporia State University and a Ph.D. (1988) from the University of Kansas. His work has appeared in *Communication Studies* and the *Southern Communication Journal*, among others.

THE CONTRIBUTORS

Ann Chisholm earned a Ph.D. at the University of Minnesota (1993). She now teaches in the Annenberg School for Communication of the University of Southern California. Her current research examines relationships between rhetoric, film, and the body.

Verna C. Corgan earned a Ph.D. at the University of Minnesota (1992). She now teaches in the Theatre and Communication Arts Department of Hamline University, St. Paul, Minnesota. She is the author of *Controversy, Courts, and Community: The Rhetoric of Judge Miles Welton Lord* (New York: Greenwood Press, 1995). She is currently working on a study of the judicial rhetoric of Supreme Court Justice John Marshall Harlan.

Lee Lin Lee earned a B.A. degree from the University of Wisconsin, Eau Claire (1990), and an M.A. from the University of Minnesota (1992). She now teaches in the English Department of Wen Tzao Ursuline Junior College of Foreign Languages, Kaohsiung, Taiwan, Republic of China. She developed her interest in Asian rhetoric while studying at the University of Minnesota and hopes to continue her research in this area.

John M. Murphy teaches in the Communication Department of North Dakota State University, Fargo. He received his M.A. (1985) and Ph.D. (1986) at the University of Kansas. His work has appeared in the *Quarterly Journal of Speech*, *Communication Monographs*, and *Argumentation and Advocacy*, among others.

Janice Watson teaches in the Communications Department of Andrews University in Berrien Springs, Michigan. Her area of expertise is intercultural communication, and she is writing a dissertation on mediation and culture.